The Junior Encyclopedia
of Israel

THE JUNIOR ENCYCLOPEDIA OF ISRAEL

by
Harriet Sirof

With Photographs
by Neil Tepper

jD | JONATHAN DAVID PUBLISHERS, INC.
MIDDLE VILLAGE, NY 11379

THE JUNIOR
ENCYCLOPEDIA OF ISRAEL

Copyright © 1980
by
Harriet Sirof

JONATHAN DAVID PUBLISHERS, INC.
68-22 Eliot Avenue
Middle Village, NY 11379

Library of Congress Cataloging in Publication Data

Sirof, Harriet.
    The junior encyclopedia of Israel.

    SUMMARY: An encyclopedia of subjects, including persons, places, events, institutions, foods, and holidays, related to life in Israel—past and present.
    1. Israel—Dictionaries and encyclopedias—Juvenile literature.   [1. Israel—Dictionaries and encyclopedias] I. Title.
DS126.5.S55   956.94'003   77-29246
ISBN 0-8246-0228-5

Printed in the United States of America

Acknowledgements

My sincere thanks to Rabbi Alfred J. Kolatch who suggested that I write this book and gave me the benefit of his knowledge and experience; to my husband, Sidney Sirof, for his patience and encouragement and for his careful reading of the manuscript; and to Lorraine Bennett, who remained a true friend through endless telephone calls. I would like to express my appreciation for the wealth of material supplied by the Consulate General of Israel, the Government of Israel Trade Center, the Israel Government Tourist Office, State of Israel Bonds, the United States Committee for Sports in Israel, Women's American ORT, Women's League for Israel, Hadassah, and the Pioneer Women. And a very special thank you to the librarians of the Brooklyn Public Library telephone reference service, who found or verified facts on a moment's notice.

Introduction

Israel is a young nation. It was born on May 14, 1948. In the few decades since its birth, the state of Israel has absorbed almost two million immigrants and has reclaimed hundreds of thousands of acres of land that had been neglected for centuries. Swamps that were filled with malaria-carrying mosquitoes have been drained and turned into rich farmland producing an abundance of fruits, vegetables, and grain. Green forests have replaced the stony hillsides and water is being piped to the desert. Modern cities now stand where there were only sand dunes not long ago.

The land on which the young nation has risen is an ancient one, filled with history and drama. It has known great kings and inspired prophets. It has also known great suffering. The land has been ravaged by war again and again, over thousands of years. It has trembled under Assyrian war chariots and the tramp of Roman legions. It has been conquered by the Babylonians, Persians, Greeks, Romans, Byzantines, Arabs, Crusaders, Mamelukes, Turks, and British. But Israel is also the land that spread the word of God to the world through three great religions. Here, Moses received the Ten Commandments on Mount Sinai; Jesus Christ was born in a manger in Bethlehem; Mohammud rose to heaven from a rock in Jerusalem.

The Junior Encyclopedia of Israel is designed to give young people a picture of the young-old land of Israel. It covers the history, geography, culture, and institutions of Israel—its poets and prophets and politicians, its religious and ethnic groups, its agriculture and industry, its cities and kibbutzim, its schools and holidays, and the everyday life of its citizens.

Since this encyclopedia was written specifically for young people, the emphasis is on material that is most likely to be interesting and meaningful to them. The entries have purposely been kept simple and concise. The aim is to give youngsters a basic understanding of the subject rather than to confront them with a mass of details that may be difficult to assimilate. It is hoped that boys and girls reading this book will gain a greater knowledge, understanding, and appreciation of the land of Israel.

Author's Note

The Junior Encyclopedia of Israel is simple enough for a fifth or sixth grader to use without help in writing a social studies report, yet is thorough enough to answer any question a junior high school student might have about Israel. Each entry is complete in itself. Essential background information is included in parentheses in the entry, as are definitions of Hebrew or unusual words. Most entries are followed by a *See also* list, which directs the reader to related subjects. There are a number of entries, such as GOVERNMENT or SPORTS, that present an overview of an entire subject. For these, the *See also* list divides the subject into its component parts. This system is designed to present information in manageable units for the reader to use according to his or her age or needs. Younger readers may find all they need to know about a subject contained in a single entry. Older students consulting all the references listed after an entry will come away with full understanding of complex subjects.

The inclusion of numerous cross-references should make it easier for young readers to locate desired information. For example, youngsters looking under CHURCH OF THE HOLY SEPULCHRE will find a reference directing them to HOLY SEPULCHRE. A reader looking for the Hebrew OT HASPORT is directed to the English PHYSICAL FITNESS BADGE. Names with two dissimilar spellings, like JAFFA and YAFO, are also cross-referenced.

The rendering of Hebrew names and words into English presents problems. Hebrew words are commonly written without vowels and Hebrew and English consonants do not always correspond. I have chosen to head entries with the form of Hebrew words young people are most likely to encounter in American books and newspapers and to give common alternate spellings in parentheses. In general: *v* is favored over *b* in names such as Akiva; *t* is favored over *th* in names such as *Bet Shean*; *h* is omitted after a final vowel in names such as *Netanya,* unless American usage is strongly to the contrary. Depending on common usage, either *h* or *ch* is used to represent the guttural Hebrew consonant found in such words as *Hanukkah* and *chutzpa.* Where a plural does not follow the usual rule of adding an *s,* it is listed after the entry heading in parentheses.

Many men and women changed or Hebraized their names when they emigrated to Israel. Such people are listed under their new name with the original in parentheses.

ISRAEL

Dotted areas indicate territories acquired during the Six-Day War (1967). Broken lines along borders indicate the armistice lines established in 1949.

ISRAEL AND HER NEIGHBORS
The Middle East

A

AARONSON, AARON (1876-1919)   Rumanian-born land and soil expert who was brought to Palestine by his Zionist father at the age of six. Aaronson discovered a new type of wheat, called Wild Emmer Wheat, and founded a station for experiments in agriculture at Athlit 10 miles south of Haifa. He wrote many articles about agriculture and plants. During World War I he was a founder and leader of NILI, an underground group working to free Palestine from Turkish rule. After the war he went to the 1919 Paris Peace Conference to work for Zionist interests in Palestine. Upon his return he was killed in a plane crash. (See also AGRICULTURE; NILI; TURKEY; ZIONISM.)

AARONSON, SARAH (1890-1917)   Palestinian heroine born and raised at Zikhron Yaakov, an early settlement in northern Israel. In 1915 she joined her brother Aaron Aaronson in NILI (an organization working against the Turkish rule of Palestine). She passed intelligence information to the British (who were then fighting the Turks in World War I) and smuggled gold to help the Jewish community in Palestine. She was only 27 years old when the Turks arrested her and tortured her for four days. She shot herself rather than reveal any of NILI's secrets. Her bravery is remembered each year at her grave at Zikhron Yaakov. (See also AARONSON, AARON; NILI; TURKEY; ZIKHRON YAAKOV.)

ABBA SIKRA (also called SAKKARA)   First century C.E. Zealot leader who fought against Roman rule in Jerusalem during the first century revolt. He was a nephew of Rabbi Johanan ben Zakkai. (See also HISTORY; JOHANAN BEN ZAKKAI; ROME; ZEALOTS.)

ABDULLAH IBN HUSSEIN (1882-1951)   Ruler of Transjordan who in 1946 became king of Jordan. His attitude toward Zionism was more moderate than that of most Arab leaders. In 1922 he met with the Zionist leader Chaim Weizmann. Although Abdullah invaded Israel with the rest of the Arab countries in the 1948 War of Independence, he later tried to find a way of living in peace with the Jewish State. He was assassinated in the El Aqsa mosque in Jerusalem in 1951. Many people believe that the extreme anti-Zionist Mufti Hajj Amin el-Husseini ordered the assassination because of Abdullah's friendly policy toward Israel. (See also EL AQSA MOSQUE; HUSSEINI, HAJJ AMIN; JORDAN; WAR OF INDEPENDENCE; WEIZMANN, CHAIM; ZIONISM.)

ABEYAH The outer garment of Arab clothing worn by the Bedouin of the Negev Desert. The abeyah is open in front and hangs loosely from the shoulders. It serves as a coat and a raincoat, and can be pulled over the head for extra protection. It can also be used as a blanket when sleeping outdoors in the desert at night. (See also BEDOUIN; KEFIYAH; NEGEV.)

ABIATHER BEN HA-COHEN (about 1040-1109) The last Gaon (chief scholar) in Palestine. He left Palestine at the time of the First Crusade (invasion of European Christian knights) and settled in Syria.

ABIJAH (also spelled ABIJAM) Second king of Judah, who ruled about 917-915 B.C.E. He was constantly at war with his fellow Jews in the neighboring kingdom of Israel. (See also ISRAEL, KINGDOM OF; JUDAH, KINGDOM OF.)

ABIMELECH A son of Gideon, one of Israel's Judges, who tried to become king of Israel in the twelfth century B.C.E. The second Book of Samuel (9:21) tells how Abimelech killed his 70 brothers, ruled for three years, and then was killed himself.

ABRAHAM (name changed from ABRAM) The name Abraham means "father of many." Abraham, the first of the three biblical patriarchs, is considered the father of the Jewish people and, through his son Ishmael, the ancestor of some Arab tribes.

The Book of Genesis (Chapters 12-26) describes how Abraham left his home in Ur of the Chaldees, followed the Euphrates River into what is now Turkey, and settled in Haran among the Philistines. God then told him to move south into the land of Canaan where the land from the Nile to the Euphrates rivers would be given to him and his descendants. Much of the land promised by God to Abraham is now a part of modern Israel, and God's promise is the original claim of the Jewish people to that land.

Abraham traveled south through the Negev and into Egypt before returning to live the rest of his days in Hebron. He and his wife Sarah are said to be buried in the Cave of Machpelah in Hebron. Today, thousands of tourists visit the cave every year.

Abraham was the son of Terah and the father of Isaac and Ishmael. The Bible tells of God testing Abraham's loyalty by commanding him to sacrifice his beloved son Isaac on Mount Moriah and then stopping him at the last moment. Abraham is often thought of as the founder of monotheism (the worship of one God).

Abraham's Well, in Beersheba

The circumcision of Jewish boys on the seventh day after birth is called the Covenant of Abraham. Some biblical scholars say that Abraham was a real person who actually lived about 1800 B.C.E., while others feel that he is a symbol for a number of Jewish leaders living over a period of several hundred years. (See also CANAAN; COVENANT; EUPHRATES RIVER; HEBRON; HISTORY; ISHMAEL; MACHPELAH, CAVE OF; MOUNT MORIAH; PATRIARCHS; PHILISTINES.)

ABSALOM (tenth century B.C.E.)   King David's third son, who lead a revolt against his father. Absalom's army was defeated, and he was killed when his long hair became entangled in a tree. Absalom's Tomb, sometimes called Absalom's Pillar, in the Kidron Valley near Jerusalem, was really built about 1,000 years after his death. (See also DAVID; JERUSALEM.)

ABU GOSH   A colorful Arab village about five miles from Jerusalem. It is located on the biblical site of Kiryat Yearim where the Ark of the Covenant remained for 20 years until King David brought it to Jerusalem. The Abu Gosh Music Festival is held in the Monastery of the Ark every May. A church built by the Crusaders stands in the village and is still used. (See also ARK OF THE COVENANT; CRUSADES; DAVID; KIRYAT YEARIM.)

ABU RUDEIS (also spelled ABU RODEIS)   Town on the Gulf of Suez in the Sinai peninsula. Abu Rudeis is surrounded by oil fields. Israel captured these oil fields from Egypt in the 1967 Six-Day War and returned them under the terms of the 1979 Israel-Egypt Peace Treaty. (See also ISRAEL-EGYPT PEACE TREATY; OIL; SINAI; SIX-DAY WAR.)

ACADEMIC SPORTS ASSOCIATION   Founded in 1953, it represents Israel at international university sports events and chess contests. In 1978 the A.S.A. had 5,000 members from Israel's nine universities. (See also PHYSICAL EDUCATION; SPORTS.)

ACCO   see ACRE

ACRA   Fortress built by the Greeks in Jerusalem in the second century B.C.E. Judah the Maccabee tried and failed to capture Acra when he took the rest of Jerusalem in the 165 B.C.E. revolt against Syrian rule of Palestine. Judah's brother, Simon the Hasmonean, finally captured Acra in 142 B.C.E. (See also HISTORY; JUDAH THE MACCABEE; SIMON THE HASMONEAN; SYRIA.)

ACRE (also called AKKO and ACCO)   City on Haifa Bay with a long and bloody history. About 3,500 years ago Acre was an important Phoenician port. Glass, manufactured from white sand, and purple dye made from the snails in the bay, were traded to the rest

Tomb of Absalom

of the civilized world. In the twelfth century B.C.E., Acre was a Canaanite city; the Israelites tried to conquer it and failed. By the time of Alexander the Great (fourth century B.C.E.) Acre had become a Hellenistic, or Greek, city. In about 104 B.C.E. Alexander Jannaeus, the Hasmonean king, attacked the city and was beaten off.

Palestine was under Roman rule in the first century C.E. During the Jewish revolt against Rome in 66 C.E., 2,000 Jews were put to death in Acre. The Moslems conquered the city in 638. In 1191 the Crusaders captured Acre and made it the capital of Palestine. The Turks, who occupied the city in 1517, built the Mosque of El Jazzar, the largest in Galilee, which still serves as a center of the Islamic religion. In 1918 the British took the city from the Turks and held it under the Mandate until Israel became a state in 1948. Acre's Citadel was a prison for Jewish liberation leaders who fought the British Mandate. (See also ACRE PRISON; ALEXANDER JANNAEUS; CANAAN; CRUSADES; HISTORY; MANDATE; PHOENICIANS; ROME; TURKEY.)

ACRE PRISON (also called CITADEL)   Medieval fortress in Acre that was used as Palestine's main prison under the British Mandate. Hundreds of members of the three Jewish underground organizations (Haganah, Irgun, and the Stern Group) were imprisoned there in the 1930s and 1940s, and seven Irgun members were hanged there in 1947. The Irgun stormed the Citadel in 1947 and freed many of the prisoners. Today part of the prison, including the death cell, is a national shrine called the Museum of Courage. (See also ACRE; HAGANAH; IRGUN; MANDATE; STERN GROUP.)

ADLER, SAUL (1895-1966)   Doctor and scientist who studied tropical diseases caused by parasites. He did research in the Near East and taught at the Hebrew University of Jerusalem. (See also HEBREW UNIVERSITY.)

ADMINISTERED AREAS (also called OCCUPIED AREAS)   Land occupied by Israel in the 1967 Six-Day War. The four administered areas were: the West Bank (also called Judea and Samaria), the Gaza Strip, the Sinai, and the Golan Heights. These areas have been governed by Israel since 1967. The Israeli government provides health and social services, education, and agricultural help to the people living there. Although the administered areas were not made part of Israel, a number of Jewish settlements have been established on the land.

In the 1979 Israel-Egypt Peace Treaty, Israel agreed to remove all its troops and settlements from the Sinai within three years. It also agreed to give self-rule to the Palestinian Arabs in the West Bank and the Gaza Strip. The treaty left the fate of the Jewish settlements in Gaza and the West Bank to be worked out in the future. (See also GAZA STRIP; GOLAN HEIGHTS; ISRAEL-EGYPT PEACE TREATY; PALESTINIANS; SINAI; SIX-DAY WAR; WEST BANK.)

ADMON, YEDIDYAH (name changed from GOROCHOV)

(1896-   ) Israeli composer. His songs and stage music have an oriental flavor.

AELIA CAPITOLINA   The new name the Roman emperor Hadrian gave to Jerusalem when he rebuilt the city after putting down the 135 C.E. Jewish revolt against Roman rule. As one punishment for the revolt, Jews were forbidden to enter the city. (See also BAR KOKHBA, SIMEON; HADRIAN; HISTORY; JERUSALEM; ROME.)

AFFORESTATION   see REFORESTATION

AFULA   Settlement founded in 1925 by the American Zion Commonwealth on swamp land in the Jezreel Valley. After the 1948 War of Independence, temporary villages for new immigrants *(maabarot)* were built at Afula. Today it is a city of 18,000 people in the middle of one of the most fertile areas of Israel. (See also AMERICAN ZION COMMONWEALTH; IMMIGRANT CAMPS; JEZREEL VALLEY; MAABARAH; WAR OF INDEPENDENCE.)

AGNON, SHEMUEL YOSEPH (name changed from CZACZKES) (1888-1970) Winner of the Nobel Prize for Literature in 1966. Israel's most honored writer. Teddy Kollek, Mayor of Jerusalem, once had a sign put up near Agnon's house that read, "Quiet! Agnon is writing!"

Agnon was born in Galicia, Poland. He began writing at a very

Shemuel Yoseph Agnon

A street in Afula, capital of the Jezreel Valley, in the northern part
of Israel.

young age and had poems published in newspapers when he was only 15. He went to Palestine in 1909, but returned to Europe and lived in Germany from 1912 to 1923. He then returned to Palestine where he spent the rest of his long life.

The inspiration for his stories and novels comes from the Bible, from folk tales, and from his early life in Galicia. His novel *The Bridal Canopy* has been translated from the Hebrew into English. It tells of Reb Yudel, a poor Hasid (religious Jew) in Europe who has three daughters to marry off. Reb Yudel and his friend wander the country searching for money for the girls' dowries, meet many different kinds of people, and swap stories about life. Some of Agnon's other books are: *A Guest for the Night, The Book of Tales,* and *Shirah.* Besides the Nobel Prize, Agnon twice won the Bialik Prize, the highest award Israel can give a writer, as well as the Israel Prize. (See also BIALIK PRIZE; ISRAEL PRIZE; LITERATURE.)

AGORA (the plural is AGOROT) Coin of Israel. There are 100 agorot to one Israeli pound. Agorot come in coins of 1, 5, 10, and 25. (See also ISRAELI POUND.)

AGRANAT, SHIMON (1906-) Supreme Court judge who was born and educated in the United States and settled in Israel in 1930. Agranat practiced law in Israel, became a judge, and served as president of the District Court of Haifa before being appointed president of the Supreme Court in 1965. He was awarded the Israel Prize for law in 1968. (See also COURTS; ISRAEL PRIZE; JUDGES; SUPREME COURT.)

AGRICULTURE Corn, barley, wheat, grapes, figs, almonds, dates, and olives were grown in Palestine in biblical times, and poultry and cattle were raised. Today all these crops are still grown in Israel along with citrus fruits, vegetables, cotton, and sugar beets. Although agricultural products make up only about 7% of all goods produced in Israel, enough fruit, vegetables, eggs, and dairy products are produced to feed the country's people. Wheat production is increasing, but half of Israel's wheat used to make bread must still be imported. Citrus fruits, tropical fruits, and flowers are mainly grown for export to other countries, particularly Europe.

Israel's warm climate provides a long growing season and much of the land would be fertile if there were enough water. Water is the big problem for agriculture. Almost half the land now being farmed is under irrigation. Since most of the water for irrigation is in the north of the country and the land needing irrigation is in the south, a huge National Water Carrier was built to carry water from the Jordan River south. Experiments

The Dagon Company, in Haifa, where grain is stored before it is loaded onto transoceanic ships.

Kibbutz workers harvest hay in a field near Tiberias.

are being carried out to find inexpensive ways to take the salt out of sea water so the water can be used for agriculture.

When the new settlers began to come to Palestine in the late 1800s, their dream was to work the land. They established many agricultural settlements or villages. Most farming in Israel today is still done on these agricultural settlements, called kibbutzim or moshavim, on land leased from the government. (See also CITRUS FRUIT; CLIMATE; FLOWERS; IRRIGATION; KIBBUTZ; LAND OWNERSHIP; MOSHAV; NATIONAL WATER CARRIER; WATER; WINE.)

AGRICULTURAL RESEARCH   Since Israel is a small country with little water, the Israelis are trying to improve their irrigation methods and to find ways of growing more and better crops. The first agricultural experimental station was set up by Aaron Aaronson at Athlit in 1911, but it was shut down when World War I started in 1914. After the war, Yitzhak Elazari-Volcani helped start experimental farms at Degania and other agricultural settlements. Today research in farming methods and new kinds of crops is carried out by the Volcani Institute for Agricultural Research. (See also AARONSON, AARON; DEGANIA; ELAZARI-VOLCANI, YITZHAK: IRRIGATION; VOLCANI INSTITUTE FOR AGRICULTURAL RESEARCH.)

AGRICULTURAL SCHOOLS   The first school to teach farming methods in Palestine was Mikveh Israel, founded in 1870. In the 1920s and 1930s several new agricultural schools were established along with a number of training farms for women *(meshek poalot)* which later became coeducational schools. By the late 1970s there were 29 schools in Israel teaching farming to over 7,000 students. Agricultural school graduates usually settle in farming communities, become village instructors, or go on for university degrees in agriculture at the Hebrew University, in Rehovot, or the Technion, in Haifa. (See also EDUCATION; HEBREW UNIVERSITY; MESHEK POALOT; MIKVEH ISRAEL; TECHNION.)

AGRON, GERSHON (name changed from AGRONSKY) (1894-1959) Newspaperman and politician. Born in Russia, Agron went to Palestine with the Jewish Legion during World War I. In 1932 he founded the *Jerusalem Post,* Israel's leading English language newspaper. He was head of the Israel Government Information Office and later became Mayor of Jerusalem. (See also JERUSALEM POST.)

AGUDAT ISRAEL   The name means Union of Israel and stands for a world organization of Orthodox Jews founded in 1912. It is also an Orthodox religious right-wing political party of Israel. It stands for strict observance of the Halakha (Jewish religious law). Until 1948 Agudat Israel was opposed to Zionism and would have nothing to do with the Jewish Agency. However, when Israel became a state in 1948, the party worked with the Provisional Government and held three seats in the first Knesset. In 1973 Agudat Israel joined with Poale Agudat Israel to form the Torah Religious Front. The new party has elected five to six of the Knesset's 120 members in elections since 1973. It publishes a daily newspaper in Jerusalem called *Ha-Modia.*

Agudat Israel runs a system of yeshivot (religious schools) throughout Israel. About 6% of Israeli elementary school children attend Agudat Israel schools. (See also KNESSET; POLITICAL PARTIES; YESHIVA.)

AHAB   King of Israel who ruled about 876-853 B.C.E. His wife Jezebel believed in and worshipped Baal. This aroused the anger of the prophet Elijah. Ahab fought wars both against the Syrians and the Assyrians, and succeeded in gaining some land for Israel. Later he was killed in battle. Archaeologists have dug up the remains of his magnificent palace in Samaria. (See also ASSYRIA; BAAL; ELIJAH; ISRAEL, KINGDOM OF; JEZEBEL; SAMARIA; SYRIA.)

AHAD HAAM (pen name of ASHER HIRSH GINZBERG) (1856-1927) Russian writer who was a leader of Hibbat Zion (a Russian Zionist organization) in Odessa. Ahad Haam founded *Hashiloah* (a magazine of Hebrew literature) and was its editor for eight years. After a visit to Palestine, he wrote *At the Crossroads,* a book of essays criticizing the Jewish settlements. He believed in a spiritual Zionism that would use education to bring about a new growth of Jewish values. Only after a long period of education would it be time for a Jewish State in Palestine to serve as a spiritual center for Jews scattered throughout the world. He therefore opposed Theodor Herzl's political Zionism which called for the immediate establishment of a Jewish State. Although most Zionists favored Herzl's ideas, they were also influenced by Ahad Haam's call for spiritual and cultural values. Ahad Haam settled in Palestine in 1920. (See also HASHILOAH; HERZL, THEODOR; HIBBAT ZION; ZIONISM.)

AHARONI, ISRAEL (name changed from AHARONOWITZ) (1877-1946) Lithuanian-born lecturer in zoology at the Hebrew University of Jerusalem who wrote scientific articles about the animals and insects of Palestine. (See also HEBREW UNIVERSITY.)

AHARONOWITZ, JOSEPH (1877-1937) Zionist and labor leader who left Eastern Europe for Palestine in 1906. He was one of the founders of Hapoel Hatzair, a Zionist labor party. He was married to the writer Devorah Baron. (See also BARON, DEVORAH; HAPOEL HATZAIR; ZIONISM.)

AHAZ King of Judah about 735-720 B.C.E. When he asked Assyria to help him in his war against Israel and Syria, Assyria agreed. As a result Judah became subject to Assyrian rule and Jews were forced to worship Assyrian gods. (See also ASSYRIA; ISRAEL, KINGDOM OF; JUDAH, KINGDOM OF; SYRIA.)

AHDUT HA-AVODA Israel Socialist Party. A left-wing political party that grew out of the National Organization of Kibbutzim and that takes many of its policies from the ideals of kibbutz life. David Ben-Gurion and Yitzhak Ben-Zvi were the party's founders, and Yigal Allon is one of its present leaders. Because the party is small, over the years it has joined forces with other parties. In 1968 Ahdut Ha-avoda joined with Mapai and Rafi to form the Israel Labor Party. (See also ALLON, YIGAL; BEN-GURION, DAVID; BEN-ZVI, YITZHAK; ISRAEL LABOR PARTY; MAPAI; POLITICAL PARTIES; RAFI.)

AKIVA BEN JOSEPH (also spelled AKIBA) (about 50-135 C.E.) The greatest scholar of his time. Rabbi Akiva has influenced Jewish scholarship and philosophy throughout the centuries. It is said that he had no education until he was 40 years old. Then, with his wife Rachel's encouragement and help, he devoted his life to studying the Torah (the Bible and its interpretations). He developed a method of interpreting every word and letter in the Bible. He took on and completed the enormous task of arranging the whole Oral Law according to subject.

Akiva taught thousands of students in his school at Bene Berak near modern Tel Aviv and also traveled to Jewish communities outside of Palestine to teach.

Since Rome ruled Palestine at that time, Akiva went to Rome to argue against anti-Jewish laws that Rome had passed. When Simeon Bar Kokhba led the revolt against Rome in 132, Akiva called him the Messiah. Rome issued a decree against the study of Jewish Law, but Akiva refused to obey. He continued to teach his students and as a result was jailed. He remained in prison until his execution at Caesarea. (See also BAR KOKHBA, SIMEON; BENE BERAK; BIBLE; CAESAREA; ORAL LAW; MESSIAH; ROME; TALMUD.)

AKKO see ACRE

AKSA see EL AKSA MOSQUE

ALBECK, SHALOM (1931-) German-born lawyer who settled in Israel in 1935 and became professor of law and Talmud at Bar-Ilan University. Albeck has written articles and books on Jewish law and its history. (See also BAR-ILAN UNIVERSITY; TALMUD.)

ALBRIGHT, WILLIAM FOXWELL (1889-1971) American archaeologist who pioneered new methods of archaeology in Palestine. He was the director of the American School of Oriental Research in Jerusalem, and wrote several books on the archaeology and religion of Palestine. (See also ARCHAEOLOGY.)

ALDOUBY, ZVI YEHUDA (1904-) Sculptor who was born in Eastern Europe and settled in Israel in 1924. Aldouby has designed monuments that stand in several Israeli cities. His smaller sculptures have been shown in museums in Israel and have been bought by collectors in Europe and Canada.

ALEXANDER JANNAEUS (also called ALEXANDER YANNAI) Hasmonean king and high priest of Judea who ruled over Palestine from 103 to 76 B.C.E. Alexander Jannaeus was a tyrant who hired foreign soldiers to enforce his rule. He conquered the Greek cities along the coast of Palestine and added the coastal land to Judea. The Pharisees, a powerful religious group, tried to overthrow him, but they were defeated. (See also HASMONEANS; JUDAH, KINGDOM OF; PHARISEES.)

AL FATAH In Arabic its full name means Movement for the Liberation of Palestine. Al Fatah is a Palestinian commando group whose aim is to destroy Israel. It ambushes Israeli patrols and raids Israeli settlements and blows up buildings, schools, and buses. Al Fatah is supported by some Arab countries but is not controlled by them. Its leader is Yasir Arafat, who is also the leader of the Palestine Liberation Organization. (See also ARAFAT, YASIR; FEDAYEEN; PALESTINE LIBERATION ORGANIZATION.)

AL HAMISHMAR (English, ON GUARD)   Israeli daily newspaper founded in Tel Aviv in 1943. *Al Hamishmar* is the newspaper of the Mapam political party. Its literary supplement prints stories by young Israeli writers, particularly those writing about life in the kibbutzim (cooperative farming villages). (See also KIBBUTZ; MAPAM.)

ALI BABA see OPERATION ALI BABA

ALIYAH   The Hebrew word for "ascent" or "going up" that has come to mean the large-scale immigration of Jews to Israel.

By 1880 there were between 20,000 and 30,000 Jews living under Turkish rule in Palestine. They were mostly Hasidim and other Orthodox Jews living in the cities of Jerusalem, Safed, and Tiberias, but a few small agricultural settlements had been started outside of the cities. Petah Tikva, founded in 1878, was the first of these new villages.

The growth of the Zionist idea in Europe in the late 1800s sparked the beginning of new immigration to Palestine. The first wave of immigrants, called the First Aliyah, were Eastern European Jews eager to build up the land of Palestine. From 1882 to 1903 about 25,000 Jews came to try to farm the harsh land. Many died from malaria or were forced to return to Europe because of the terrible living conditions.

The Second Aliyah (1904-1914) brought 50,000 more European Jews to Palestine. Some were fleeing the bloody pogroms (killing of Jews) in Russia, but many of the immigrants were Socialist Zionists who wanted to establish a new kind of society in the land of Palestine. They moved into the existing villages or founded new ones. They set up the first kibbutzim, which were Socialist cooperatives where everyone shared the work and profits. They began building the city of Tel Aviv on the sand dunes outside of Jaffa, and adopted Hebrew as their language.

Although some of these immigrants, like many who arrived earlier, could not take the hard life and returned to Europe, by the beginning of World War I there were about 85,000 Jews living in Palestine.

The Third Aliyah (1919-1923) was encouraged by the Balfour Declaration in which Great Britain (then governing Palestine under the Mandate) came out for a Jewish national home in Palestine. The Third Aliyah was made up of many members of Hehalutz, the pioneer youth movement, who went to Palestine to build new agricultural villages and to farm and defend the land.

They came from different parts of Europe to work the land of Palestine. The halutz—the pioneer with the plow and the gun—is still the ideal of Israel.

The Fourth Aliyah (1924-1931) consisted mainly of middle-class Polish Jews who went to Palestine to live in the cities rather than on farms.

European Jews fleeing Nazi persecution made up the Fifth Aliyah (1932-1940). Many Jews who had been proud to call themselves Germans now looked to Palestine as the place where they could live in peace and be proud of being Jews. The 1930s was also the period of the Youth Aliyah, which rescued children and young people from Hitler's Germany and settled them in youth villages in Palestine.

As many as 50,000 Jews a year were streaming into Palestine when Great Britain issued the White Paper in 1939 restricting Jewish immigration to 15,000 people a year. Almost half of the immigrants of the Sixth Aliyah (1941-1947) were smuggled into the country by the Haganah and other Jewish defense groups. Those immigrants caught by the British while trying to enter the country were put into camps on Cyprus.

When Israel became a state in 1948, any Jew from any part of the world was made welcome. Jews who had survived the Nazi concentration camps came, as did Jews from behind the Iron Curtain, as well as Jews from Arab countries such as Yemen and Iraq. From 1948 to 1978 over a million and a half Jews emigrated to Israel and immediately became citizens of their new country. (See also BILU; BALFOUR DECLARATION; CYPRUS; GREAT BRITAIN; HAGANAH; HALUTZ; HEBREW; HOLOCAUST; IMMIGRANTS; IMMIGRANTS, ILLEGAL; KIBBUTZ; MANDATE; NAZIS; OLIM; OPERATION ALI BABA; OPERATION MAGIC CARPET; PETAH TIKVA; WHITE PAPER; YISHUV; YOUTH ALIYAH; YORDIM; ZIONISM.)

ALLENBY BRIDGE   Bridge over the Jordan River on the road that runs from Jerusalem to Amman, Jordan. Until 1948, people traveling between Palestine and Jordan went through customs inspection at the Allenby Bridge. It was named for Edmund Allenby, the British general who captured Palestine from the Turks in 1918. (See also ALLENBY, EDMOND HENRY HYNMAN; JORDAN; JORDAN RIVER.)

ALLENBY, EDMUND HENRY HYNMAN (1861-1936)   British field marshal. In 1917, during World War I, he fought in France and later was given command of the British forces in Palestine and Egypt. His armies attacked the Turks in Gaza, captured Jerusalem, and surrounded the Turkish army near Meggido. After the defeat of the Turks, Allenby was made the head of the

British Military Administration of Palestine, a job he held until 1919 when he was made High Commissioner of Egypt. While he was stationed in Palestine, Allenby did not favor the Zionist aim of a Jewish State, although his attitude softened somewhat in later years. (See also GREAT BRITAIN.)

ALLON, YIGAL (1918-   )   Native Israeli soldier and politician. As a boy, Allon worked on the family farm before and after school. The farm was in a settlement which was often raided by Arabs. A story about his early bravery tells how at age 13 he stood guard against the raiders with a pistol his father had given him as a Bar Mitzvah present.

At age 16 he joined the Haganah, the Jewish self-defense army. By the time he was in his early 20s he was an officer in the Palmah, the striking force of the Haganah, and became known for his bravery and daring. The Haganah helped the British in Syria during World War II, and Allon fought with them. In 1945, after he became commander of the Palmah, he succeeded in smuggling thousands of "illegal" immigrants through the British blockade and into Palestine. He commanded Israeli forces in Galilee in the north of Israel during the 1948 War of Independence and participated in the capture of the Negev in the south. After the war he went back to being a farmer on the Gennosar kibbutz, a settlement he had helped establish and build. He also studied economics in England.

In 1954 he entered politics, became a leader of the Ahdut Ha-avoda party, and was elected to the Israeli Knesset (legislature).

Allon is known as a farmer-politician because he works at his kibbutz whenever he can take time off from politics. He has served as Minister of Labor, Minister of Finance, Deputy Prime Minister, and Foreign Minister. His autobiography, *My Father's House,* was published in 1976. (See also AHDUT HA-AVODA; GENNOSAR; HAGANAH; IMMIGRANTS, ILLEGAL; KIBBUTZ; KNESSET; PALMAH; WAR OF INDEPENDENCE.)

ALMOG, SHMUEL (1926-   )   Journalist and radio broadcaster who was brought to Israel from Germany as a young child. Almog has been a correspondent, announcer, and broadcaster for Kol Israel (Israel's radio network). He has also written articles for Israeli and foreign magazines and newspapers. (See also KOL ISRAEL.)

ALMOGI, YOSEPH AHARON (1910-   )   Polish-born Israeli labor leader. He has served in the government as Minister of Labor and Minister of Housing, and was Mayor of Haifa. (See also HISTADRUT; KNESSET.)

ALONI, NISSIM (1926-   )   Playwright born in Tel Aviv. After serving in the 1948 War of Independence, he founded the Theater of the Seasons. Aloni uses masks, films, tape recorders, and other unusual devices in staging his plays. His first play, *Cruel is the King,* is about Rehoboam, king of Judah in the tenth century B.C.E. Aloni has also written several short stories about children. (See also REHOBOAM; WAR OF INDEPENDENCE.)

ALONI, SHULAMIT   Native Israeli writer and politician. She was a member of the Israeli Knesset (legislature) and served as Minister Without Portfolio. Shulamit Aloni has written several books on the rights of women and children. (See also KNESSET.)

ALTALENA   Ship named for Vladimir Jabotinsky, the militant Zionist leader and writer whose pen name was "Altalena." The *Altalena* was used by the Irgun (a Jewish fighting group) to ship guns and ammunition into Israel during a cease-fire between the Jewish and Arab armies in the 1948 War of Independence. The Israeli government did not want to break the cease-fire and forbade the *Altalena* to unload the arms. When the Irgun refused to obey the government order, the ship was blown up and several members of the Irgun were killed in the explosion. (See also IRGUN; WAR OF INDEPENDENCE; JABOTINSKY, VLADIMIR.)

ALTERMAN, NATAN (1910-1970)   A leading Hebrew poet. He was born in Poland and moved to Palestine in 1925. Alterman wrote in modern Hebrew rather than in the biblical Hebrew of the earlier poets. Many of his poems are comments on current events. His best known book of poetry is *Seventh Column.* Besides writing poetry, Alterman translated Shakespeare into Hebrew. (See also HEBREW; LITERATURE.)

AM OVED   Publishing house run by Histadrut, Israel's Labor Federation. Am Oved was founded in 1941, and in its first 35 years has published more than 1,500 different titles in Hebrew. (See also HISTADRUT.)

AMAZIAH   King of Judah about 796-780 B.C.E. He defeated Edom in a war and was, in turn, defeated by Samaria. Amaziah was killed during a palace revolt. (See also EDOM; JUDAH, KINGDOM OF; SAMARIA.)

AMERICAN JEWISH CONGRESS   Organization founded in the United States in 1922. Its aims are to fight religious prejudice, to work for the survival of the Jewish people, and to help Israel grow in peace. In the 1930s and 1940s, the American Jewish Congress led the protest against the Nazi persecution of Jews in Europe while it fought anti-Semitism in the United States. The organization is a member of the World Jewish Congress. (See also HOLOCAUST; NAZIS; WORLD JEWISH CONGRESS.)

AMERICAN JEWISH JOINT DISTRIBUTION COMMITTEE see JDC

AMERICAN ZION COMMONWEALTH   An agency that bought land for Jewish settlement in Palestine from 1914 to 1931.

AMIR, ANDA   see PINKERFELD, ANDA

AMORA (the plural is AMORAIM)   Jewish scholars who lived and taught in Palestine and Babylonia from the 200s through the 500s C.E. An Amora was both a scholar who studied the Law and a judge who interpreted the Law for the common people. Amoraim explained how the Mishnah (which is the first part of the Talmud) applied to the everyday lives and activities of Jews. The interpretations and teachings of the Amoraim is called the Gemara, and is the second part of the Talmud. (See also MISHNA; TALMUD; TANNA.)

AMOS (8th century B.C.E.)   Biblical prophet. He was born in Judah where he tended animals before he went to the neighboring kingdom of Israel to prophesy. Israel was prosperous under the rule of King Jeroboam II, but the ordinary people suffered from many injustices. The wealthy landowners lived off the labor of the poor serfs and slaves. The judges were dishonest and corrupt. Amos spoke out against these sins and prophesied that God would punish the country for its greed and oppression. His prophesies are contained in the Bible in the Book of Amos. (See also JEROBOAM II.)

ANAKIM   The word for "giants" in Hebrew. The Anakim were a tribe of tall people living in Canaan before the Israelites conquered the country. (See also CANAAN.)

ANAN BEN DAVID (about 730-780 C.E.)   Babylonian founder of the Karaites, a Jewish sect that had about 10,000 members in Israel in 1978. Anan taught that the Bible is the only law of the Jews and that it must be obeyed to the letter. He rejected the Talmud and all rabbinical authority. He and his followers fasted often, did not eat meat or drink wine, and refused to leave their homes on Saturday. (See also BIBLE; KARAITES; TALMUD.)

ANATHOTH   Biblical town near Jerusalem where the Prophet Jeremiah was born. Today it is an Arab village. (See also JEREMIAH.)

ANILEWICZ, MORDECAI (1919-1943)   Young Polish Zionist who was arrested in 1939 for helping Soviet Jews leave for

Palestine. He was a leader of the Warsaw Ghetto revolt against the Nazis in 1943 and was killed in the fighting. A statue of Anilewicz stands at Yad Mordecai, an Israeli kibbutz named in his honor. (See also HOLOCAUST; KIBBUTZ; NAZIS; YAD MORDECAI.)

ANIMALS   Most of the wild animals mentioned in the Bible as having lived in ancient Palestine can only be found in Jerusalem's Biblical Zoo today. The most common wild animals still living in modern Israel are porcupines, hedgehogs, badgers, and foxes. Jackels and hyenas find their food in garbage dumps and their wailing can often be heard near villages and even near large cities. Leopards and cheetahs are fairly rare, but wolves occasionally attack flocks of sheep in winter. (See also BIBLICAL ZOO; BIRDS; INSECTS; REPTILES.)

ANNUNCIATION, FEAST OF   Holiday celebrated in Christian churches throughout Israel on March 25th. A special celebration is held in the Church of the Annunciation in Nazareth. (See also CHRISTIANS; HOLIDAYS; NAZARETH.)

ANTIGONUS (also called MATTATHIAS)   Last Hasmonean king of Judea who ruled 40-47 B.C.E. He was taken to Rome as a hostage when Roman forces helped his uncle Hyrcanus defeat his father, Aristobulus II, in a civil war. In 40 B.C.E. Antigonus captured Jerusalem, maimed Hyrcanus so he could no longer be high priest, and ruled as both king and high priest. Herod the Great, with Roman help, took Jerusalem in 47 B.C.E. and killed Antigonus. (See also ARISTOBULUS II; HASMONEANS; HEROD I; HYRCANUS II; JUDEA; ROME.)

ANTIPAS, HEROD (20 B.C.E.-39 C.E.)   Ruler of Galilee, the northern area of Palestine. Son of Herod the Great. When Antipas married his sister-in-law, John the Baptist spoke out against the marriage. Antipas then had John killed. The marriage also led to war with Aretas, the Nabatean king— a war that ended badly for Antipas. During his rule, Antipas built a new capital city for Galilee and named it Tiberias for the Roman emperor Tiberius. (See also GALILEE; HEROD I; JOHN THE BAPTIST; NABATEANS; TIBERIAS; TIBERIUS.)

ANTIPATER   Ruler of Judea 63-43 B.C.E. Father of Herod the Great. Antipater sent Jewish troops to join Julius Caesar's Roman army. In return, Caesar gave him control of the government of Judea. (See also HEROD I; JUDEA; ROME.)

ANTIPATRIS   City in Judea built by Herod the Great in the first century B.C.E. Herod named the city for his father, Antipater. (See also ANTIPATER; HEROD I.)

ANTONIA   Fortress built in Jerusalem by Simon the Hasmonean, ruler of Judea, in the second century B.C.E. Antonia was enlarged later by Herod the Great. (See also HEROD I; JERUSALEM; SIMON THE HASMONEAN.)

APHIKIM   Kibbutz just south of Lake Kinneret (Sea of Galilee). It was founded by Russian Jews in 1932. Aphikim has grown into one of the largest and most successful agricultural settlements in Israel. (See also KIBBUTZ.)

APOLLONIA   City on the coast of Palestine, north of modern Tel Aviv. Built by the Greeks in the third and fourth centuries B.C.E. Throughout its history Apollonia was held in turn by the Jews, Romans, Arabs, Crusaders, and Mamelukes, and was also known as Rishpon and Arshaf. It was here that the Crusader king, Richard the Lionhearted, defeated the sultan Saladin in 1191. Only ruins remain today. (See also RICHARD I; SALADIN.)

APPELFELD, AHARON   (1932-   ) Rumanian-born writer who was in a concentration camp during World War II. Appelfeld settled in Israel in 1947 and wrote short stories about the Holocaust. *In The Wilderness* is an English translation of a collection of his stories. (See also HOLOCAUST.)

AQABA, GULF OF   see EILAT, GULF OF

AQSA MOSQUE   see EL AQSA MOSQUE

ARAB HIGHER COMMITTEE   Arab group whose purpose it was to fight Zionism and drive the Jews out of Palestine. It was organized in 1936 and was responsible for Arab attacks against Jews in that year and again in 1947 and 1948. The Arab Higher Committee was part of the Arab National Movement in Palestine and was led by Hajj Amin Husseini, the Mufti of Jerusalem. The group was outlawed in 1948 by Abdullah, king of Jordan. (See also ABDULLAH IBN HUSSEIN; HUSSEINI, HAJJ AMIN; ZIONISM.)

ARAB LEAGUE   A political alliance of Egypt, Jordan, Syria, Iraq, and Lebanon established in 1945 and joined by Libya in 1953. The countries of the Arab League do not have to support the League's policies or decisions. The main agreement between the member countries has been their hatred of Israel. The League was at its strongest under the leadership of President Nasser of Egypt, and has become less important since his death in 1970. (See also EGYPT; JORDAN; LEBANON; NASSER, GAMAL ABDUL; SYRIA.)

ARAB RIOTS   Although many Palestinian Arabs objected to the settlement of Jews in Palestine in the late 1800s, they limited themselves to occasional small raids on Jewish villages. By the early 1900s the attacks became more organized and the Hashomer ("watchmen") was founded to combat them. In the 1920s the first Arab riots broke out in Jerusalem while attacks were made on Jewish settlements in other parts of the country. Because the British (who ruled Palestine under the Mandate) did little to stop the raids, Jews formed a defense organization called Haganah. The Haganah grew in strength and did much to check the 1929 Jerusalem riots.

An Arab Revolt took place in 1936-1939. First, an Arab general strike that lasted for six months was called. Then, an Arab High Command united the different terrorist bands to attack both the Jews and the British. Before the Arab High Command was outlawed and the trouble was ended, 91 Jews and a British district commissioner were killed. (See also GREAT BRITAIN; HASHOMER; HAGANAH; MANDATE.)

ARABA (also spelled ARABAH and ARAVA)   A deep valley that runs for about a hundred miles from the Dead Sea through the Negev to the Gulf of Eilat. Once only scorched desert, Araba now has a number of new farming settlements growing vegetables and dates. (See also NEGEV.)

ARABIA   A peninsula (body of land surrounded on three sides by water) in Southwest Asia. The Red Sea is on its west, the Persian Gulf on the east, and the Indian Ocean on the south. The main countries of the Arabian peninsula are Saudi Arabia, Yemen, and Oman. Nearby Syria, Iraq, and Jordan are not considered part of Arabia even though they are Arab countries.

There have been Jewish communities in Arabia for the past 2,000 years. At some times in history, particularly in the 600s and 700s C.E., Jews were accepted and permitted to live in peace in Arabia. At other times they were taxed, persecuted, thrown out of their homes and countries, or killed. During this century, Arab hatred of Zionism made the lives of Jews in Arabia very difficult. Almost all Arabian Jews emigrated to Israel soon after the Jewish State was established in 1948. (See also OPERATION ALI BABA; OPERATION MAGIC CARPET.)

ARABIC   A Semitic language. One of the two official languages of Israel. It is used along with Hebrew on road signs, money, and stamps. Arabic is the native language of about a quarter of Israel's people. It is spoken by Jews who emigrated to Israel from Arab lands as well as by Arabs living in Israel.

The children of Arabic-speaking Jews learn to speak Hebrew in school and all their classes are taught in Hebrew. Arab children are taught in Arabic, although beginning in third grade they learn Hebrew as a second language.

There are four daily newspapers published in Arabic in Israel; and Network D, one of Israel's radio stations, broadcasts its programs in Arabic. Government offices and courts use Arabic in dealing with Arabs. Arab members of the Israeli Knesset (legislature) may make speeches in Arabic and are given earphones through which translated Hebrew speeches are transmitted to them. (See also BROADCASTING; EDUCATION; GOVERNMENT; SEMITIC LANGUAGES.)

ARABS, ISRAELI   In 1980 there were over 475,000 Arabs living in Israel and about another million living in the areas governed by Israel since the 1967 Six-Day War. These Arabs are part of a Semitic people who trace their ancestors back to Ishmael, son of Abraham. They have lived in the Arabian peninsula throughout known history. In the 700s C.E. the Arabs built an empire that stretched from Spain to India, included Palestine, and lasted for 200 years.

Today, a little more than half of Israeli Arabs live in small villages where they farm the land. Most Arab villages are in the Galilee in the north of Israel. Nazareth is mainly an Arab city, and many Arabs live in or near Haifa. About 20,000 Bedouin Arabs roam the Negev Desert, living in much the same way as their ancestors did thousands of years ago.

All Israeli citizens—Jews, Arabs, Christians, or other ethnic groups—are equal under the law. Their right to practice their own religion is protected by law. About three-quarters of Israeli Arabs are Moslem. The rest are Christian or Druze. Each re-

Arab women leaving the Dome of the Rock.

An Arab funeral procession leaves the Dome of the Rock.

An Arab small businessman and his son getting ready for a day's
work.

ligious community has its own religious courts. Each has the legal right to celebrate its own Sabbath and religious holidays.

Arabs vote with other Israeli citizens for the Knesset (legislature) and members of local councils. Three of the 120 seats in the first Knesset were held by Arabs. Since then there have been seven or eight Arabs elected to each Knesset. In 1975 there were 46 local councils whose members were mostly Arabs.

The health, education, and earning power of the Arab population has improved greatly since Israel became a state. In 1948, 19 out of 20 Arabs living in Israel could not read or write; and by 1973, almost all could. In 1948, few Arab homes had electricity. But, 25 years later, about three-quarters had electric lights. Irrigation and new farming methods have improved the quality of Arab crops and have helped farmers earn more money.

About two-thirds of Arab workers belong to the Histadrut, the labor federation that protects the interests of Israeli workers. Arabs are also entitled to all health services. As a result the average Arab can now expect to live to 72 years of age, while in 1948 his average life span was only 52.

Although some Israeli Arabs feel that their position in the country could still be improved, in general they are loyal citizens. This is not true of the Arabs in the administered areas. They think of themselves as Palestinians and demand a separate Arab Palestinian state. (See also ADMINISTERED AREAS; AGRICULTURE; ARABIA; ARABIC; BEDOUINS; CHRISTIANS; COURTS, RELIGIOUS; DRUZE; EDUCATION; GOVERNMENT; HEALTH; HISTADRUT; HOLIDAYS; ISHMAEL; KNESSET; LOCAL GOVERNMENT; MOSLEMS; NAZARETH; NEGEV; PALESTINIANS; RELIGION.)

ARAD In biblical times Arad was an important town in the eastern Negev. Archaeologists have uncovered the ruins of a Bronze Age city built nearly 5,000 years ago. They have also found the remains of an Israelite city from the eleventh century B.C.E. which contains a temple that resembles the Temple of Solomon in Jerusalem. The modern town of Arad stands near the ancient ruins. (See also ARCHAEOLOGY; BRONZE AGE; NEGEV; TEMPLE.)

ARAFAT, YASIR (1929-) Palestinian commando leader. Arafat was trained in the use of explosives at the Egyptian military academy and served in the Egyptian army. In the late 1950s he joined Al Fatah, a Palestinian terrorist group, and later became its leader. When Al Fatah gained control of the Palestine Liberation Organization, Arafat was named its Executive Chairman. (See also AL FATAH; EGYPT; PALESTINE LIBERATION ORGANIZATION.)

ARAMAIC A Semitic language. Aramaic was a popular language from the sixth century B.C.E. until well into the Common

Era. It was spoken when people from different countries speaking different languages needed to communicate—much as English is today. It was also the everyday language of the people of Palestine. The Palestinian Talmud was written in Aramaic, as was much literature and poetry. A small number of people in the Near East still speak the language today. (See also SEMITIC LANGUAGES; TALMUD.)

ARAMEANS A Semitic people who lived in Aram (an ancient Middle Eastern country in what is now Syria) from about the fifteenth century to the eighth century B.C.E. Their language was Aramaic. The kingdoms of Israel and Aram had common ancestors and Israelites sometimes married Arameans. (See also ARAMAIC; SYRIA.)

ARANNE, ZALMAN (name changed from AHARONOWITZ) (1899-1970) Labor leader and politician. Aranne left Russia for Palestine in 1926. As a construction worker, he became active in Histadrut, the Israeli labor federation. He served as a Mapai Party member of the Knesset and was also Minister of Education and Culture. (See also HISTADRUT; KNESSET; MAPAI.)

ARCHAEOLOGY A science that gathers information about the people and cultures of the past by excavating into ancient sites, and studying their buildings, pottery, and other remains.

Israel is a rich field for archaeologists. The million-year-old bones of early man have been found in the Jordan Valley and Galilee. Traces of Canaanite villages of 5,000 years ago have been dug up in Hazor, Megiddo, and other sites. Almost the entire 3,000 year history of the Jews in Palestine can be traced through archaeological remains. Buildings from the kingdoms of Israel and Judah give information about the way Jews lived in biblical times. Splendid remains from the time of the Second Temple (455 B.C.E.-70 C.E.) have been unearthed in places like Jerusalem and Bet Shean. The desert fortress at Masada makes the history of the Jewish revolt against the Romans come alive. In addition to Jewish remains, archaeologists have studied the buildings left by the Moslems, Crusaders, and Turks in Israel.

The Israeli government Department of Antiquities makes archaeological surveys, protects ancient sites, and helps both Israeli and foreign archaeologists with their excavations. Most Israelis are very interested in archaeology, and discoveries are reported in newspapers and on radio and television. (See also ARAD; ASHKELON; BET SHEAN; BRONZE AGE; CAESAREA; CANAAN; CRUSADES; GEZER; HAZOR; HISTORY; IRON AGE; ISRAEL, KINGDOM OF; JERICHO; JERUSALEM; JUDAH, KINGDOM OF; MASADA; MEGIDDO; QUMRAN; RAMAT RAHEL; ROME; SAMARIA; TEMPLE; TURKEY.)

A millstone for grinding grain found during the archaeological explorations in the vicinity of Capernaum, on the northern shore of the Sea of Galilee.

ARCHELAUS   Tyrant who ruled Judea from 4 B.C.E. to 6 C.E. until he was removed by the Roman emperor Augustus. (See also JUDEA; ROME.)

ARCHITECTURE   Remains of ancient buildings dug up by archaeologists show that there was no special Jewish architecture. Palaces, temples, and other buildings were in the same general architectural styles as those built in neighboring countries during the same period of time. For example, when Herod the Great built palaces and theaters in the first century B.C.E., they were built in the Roman style.

Architecture in Israel today is similar to American or European architecture, but it takes into account the hot climate. Homes are often built of concrete with thick walls to keep out the heat, and may be painted white to reflect the strong sun. Public buildings designed by Israeli architects are usually modern in style. The Knesset (legislature) building and the Hebrew University buildings in Jerusalem show new developments in Israeli architecture. (See also ARCHAEOLOGY; HEBREW UNIVERSITY; HEROD I; KNESSET.)

ARCHIVES   A collection of public records or historical documents. Important archives in Israel are the Central Zionist Archives, the General Jewish Historical Archives, the records of the Rescue Committee of the Jewish Agency, and the archives at Yad Vashem. All four are in Jerusalem. (See also JEWISH AGENCY; YAD VASHEM.)

The architecture of Jerusalem is unique. Rock is plentiful and most buildings are built from stone. Above is the main building of Ohr Someyech Institutions. Below is the Ort school in Jerusalem.

The IBM building in Tel Aviv is one of the unique architectural
structures in Israel.

ARDON, MORDEKHAI (name changed from BRONSTEIN) (1896-   ) German-born Israeli painter who was also director of the Bezalel School of Arts and Crafts in Jerusalem. (See also BEZALEL SCHOOL OF ARTS AND CRAFTS.)

ARI   See LURIA, ISAAC BEN SOLOMON.

ARISTOBULUS I   King of Judah who ruled 104-103 B.C.E. Aristobulus was appointed high priest of Judah by his father, John Hyrcanus. He murdered his mother and brothers in order to become king of Judah. (See also HYRCANUS, JOHN; JUDAH, KINGDOM OF.)

ARISTOBULUS II   King of Judea 67-63 B.C.E. Son of Alexander Jannaeus. Aristobulus fought his brother Hyrcanus for the throne in a civil war. When Pompey, the Roman general, sided with Hyrcanus and captured Jerusalem in 63 B.C.E., Aristobulus was taken to Rome as a prisoner. From then on Judea was no longer an independent nation, but was subject to Rome. Aristobulus escaped from Rome and tried to regain control of his country, but he failed. (See also HISTORY; HYRCANUS II; JUDEA; POMPEY; ROME.)

ARISTOBULUS III (died 35 B.C.E.)   Last Hasmonean high priest of Judea. Herod the Great was jealous of Aristobulus' popularity with the people and had him drowned. (See also HASMONEANS; HEROD I; JUDEA.)

ARK OF THE COVENANT   The chest that held the two stone tablets engraved with the Ten Commandments that Moses brought down from Mount Sinai. The Ark was made of inlaid wood and gold and was covered with a golden cover. It was carried by the Children of Israel on their journey through the Sinai Desert until they reached the Promised Land. Later, it was placed in the Holy of Holies (inner shrine) of Solomon's Temple. It remained in the Temple until the Temple was destroyed by the Romans in 70 C.E. (See also COVENANT; JABEL MUSA; MOSES; PROMISED LAND; TEMPLE.)

ARLOSOROFF, CHAIM (1899-1933)   Zionist and writer. Born in Russia and brought up in Germany where he became an active Zionist, Arlosoroff went to Palestine in 1924. He wrote about Zionism and about Jews in Palestine, and was on the executive board of the Jewish Agency. When Hitler came to power in Germany in 1933, Arlosoroff worked to help German Jews immigrate to Palestine. He was murdered on a beach near Tel Aviv. His murderers were never caught. (See also JEWISH AGENCY; ZIONISM.)

ARMENIAN MOSAIC (also called MOSAIC OF THE BIRDS) The oldest unknown soldier monument in the world. This memorial to the Armenian soldiers who died defending their Christian faith in 451 C.E. was unearthed by archaeologists in Jerusalem in 1894. (See also ARCHAEOLOGY; JERUSALEM; MOSAICS.)

ARMENIAN QUARTER Section of the Old City of Jerusalem where many Armenians live. (Armenia was an ancient kingdom in what is now part of Iran, Turkey, and Russia. It was the first nation to become Christian.) The Armenian quarter is almost like a city in itself, with schools, a museum, a library, and the beautiful St. James Cathedral. (See also CHRISTIANS, ISRAELI; JERUSALEM.)

ART There were only a few artists in Jerusalem in 1906 when Boris Schatz founded the Bezalel School of Arts and Crafts to try to create a national Jewish art form in Palestine. In the 1930s, many Jewish artists left Europe for Palestine where they continued to paint and sculpt. Not much art was produced in Palestine in the 1940s during World War II and while the struggle for Israeli independence was in progress. But by the 1950s and 1960s older artists like Reuben Rubin, Yoseph Zaritsky, and Anna Ticho were being joined by a new group of young painters and sculptors.

Israeli artists have been more interested in realistic painting than in abstract art. Landscapes and Jewish scenes have been popular subjects for paintings. However, starting in the 1960s, younger artists began to experiment with abstract colors and shapes.

Public interest in art is growing rapidly in Israel. Large museums, like the Israel Museum and the Tel Aviv Museum, have exhibits of foreign artists next to displays of Israeli paintings. Most cities have art galleries or museums and there are artists' colonies in several towns. Public buildings like the Knesset are decorated with works of art. Although Israel has not yet produced a great artist, it has a number of good painters whose work has been shown and admired in other countries. (See also ARTISTS' COLONY; BEZALEL SCHOOL OF ARTS AND CRAFTS; ISRAEL MUSEUM; RUBIN, REUBEN; TEL AVIV MUSEUM; TICHO, ANNA; ZARITSKY, YOSEPH.)

ARTISTS' COLONY Section of a town or city where a number of painters, sculptors, and craftsmen live and work. The colony also has galleries and shops to show and sell the artists' work. The four most important artists' colonies in Israel are in Safed, Ein Hod, Jaffa, and Jerusalem. (See also ART; EIN HOD; JAFFA; JERUSALEM; SAFED.)

ASA King of Judah who ruled 915-875 B.C.E. Asa forbade the worship of heathen idols in his country, and like his father Abijah, was often at war with the neighboring Jewish kingdom of Israel. Asa built fortresses along the border between Judah and Israel. (See also ABIJAH; ISRAEL, KINGDOM OF; JUDAH, KINGDOM OF.)

ASEFAT HANIVHARIM (English, ELECTED ASSEMBLY) Body elected by the Jews of Palestine to represent them in internal matters and in their dealings with the ruling British government during the period of the British Mandate over Palestine (1920-1948). The Asefat Hanivharim did not meet often, and even then only for a few days at a time. Most of its work was done by the Vaad Leumi (National Council), a smaller group elected by the Assembly. (See also MANDATE; VAAD LEUMI.)

ASHDOD A city on the Mediterranean Sea about 20 miles south of Tel Aviv. Archaeologists have uncovered the remains of the Philistine city of Ashdod that stood about three miles inland from the modern city. The Philistines built ancient Ashdod before the eleventh century B.C.E. and it became one of their five city-states. The city was held by the Assyrians in the eighth century B.C.E. and later was occupied by the Jews. It was an important Jewish center in Roman times.

Ashdod has no natural harbor, but in 1961 a huge dyke was built out into the Mediterranean Sea to make an artificial harbor.

Docked in Ashdod, the second largest port in Israel, *The Ashdod* was the first ship to pass through the Suez Canal after the 1979 Peace Treaty between Israel and Egypt was signed.

Today Ashdod is one of Israel's three major ports (the other two are Haifa and Eilat) with ships carrying cargo to all parts of the world. The port can handle two and a half million tons of cargo a year. (See also ARCHAEOLOGY; ASSYRIA; HISTORY; MEDITERRANEAN SEA; PHILISTINES; PORTS; ROME; SHIPPING.)

ASHDOT YAAKOV Two kibbutzim that split off from a single kibbutz that had been founded in the Jordan Valley in 1922. Ashdot Yaakov was a frequent target for Arab raiders after the Six-Day War. (See also FEDAYEEN; KIBBUTZ; JORDAN VALLEY; SIX-DAY WAR.)

ASHER One of the Twelve Tribes of ancient Israel. The tribe of Asher settled the fertile land between Galilee and Carmel when the Israelites occupied Canaan in the thirteenth century B.C.E. Its ancestor was Asher, the eighth son of Jacob. (See also CANAAN; GALILEE; JACOB; TWELVE TRIBES.)

ASHKELON (also spelled ASCALON) One of the five ancient Philistine city-states. The city was captured by the Philistines in the thirteenth century B.C.E., was held by the Assyrians in the eighth century B.C.E., and was a center of Greek culture in the second to fourth centuries B.C.E. It was a Roman town and later was held by the Crusaders. Today ancient ruins can be seen in a national park, as can the Greek and Roman statues that archaeologists unearthed in the ruins. The modern city of Ashkelon is a beach resort. (See also ARCHAEOLOGY; ASSYRIA; CRUSADES; HISTORY; PHILISTINES; ROME.)

New housing being built in the vicinity of Ashkelon. The supply of apartments has not kept pace with the increase in population.

ASHKENAZIM   Originally Ashkenazim referred to the Jews who lived in Germany and used a High German dialect which eventually became Yiddish. When many of the German Jews moved to Poland and Russia in the 1400s and 1500s, they continued to be called Ashkenazim. Today the word is loosely used in Israel to refer to those Jews who came to Israel from Europe or America.

Before six million European Jews were murdered by the Nazis during World War II, nine out of ten Jews in the world were Ashkenazim. Today it is nearer nine out of eleven; 9,500,000 of the total world Jewish population of 11,500,000 are Ashkenazim.

In Israel today slightly less than half the population are Ashkenazim or their Israeli-born children. The other half are Sephardim or Oriental Jews who have come from Arabia and Africa. This has caused a number of social problems because the Ashkenazim are generally better educated, have more job skills, and therefore earn more money than the Orientals. The Israeli government has been trying to close the gap with education and social programs. (See also EDUCATION; HOLOCAUST; JEWS; NAZIS; ORIENTAL JEWS; SEPHARDIM.)

ASSAF, SIMHA (1889-1953)   Scholar, teacher, and judge. In 1925 Assaf went to Palestine from Russia, where he had been the head of the Odessa Yeshiva. He taught at the Hebrew University in Jerusalem and wrote many books on Jewish history, particularly about the Gaonic Period. In 1948 he was appointed as a Justice of the Israeli Supreme Court. (See also GAON; HEBREW UNIVERSITY; SUPREME COURT.)

ASSUMPTION DAY   Holiday celebrated on August 15th in Christian churches throughout Israel, with special services at the Dormition Monastery in Jerusalem. The holiday marks the death of the Virgin Mary and her Assumption into heaven. (See also CHRISTIANS; DORMITION MONASTERY; HOLIDAYS.)

ASSYRIA   An ancient Semitic kingdom established in the twentieth century B.C.E. on the fertile plain between the Tigris and Euphrates rivers in Western Asia. The history of Assyria is closely related to the history of Babylon, another important kingdom in the area. Assyrians and Babylonians ruled large parts of Western Asia for over 1,000 years.

The Assyrians were a warlike people. They learned about iron from the Hittites, and then in the ninth century B.C.E. used iron weapons to break the power of the Hittite Empire. They also overran Syria and conquered the Phoenician cities of Western Asia. They established an empire that stretched throughout the fertile crescent, taking in most of what is now modern Israel,

Jordan, Syria, Iraq, and part of Turkey. The Assyrian Empire lasted for about 150 years, until its capital city, Nineveh, fell to Babylon in 612 B.C.E.

During the growth of the Assyrian Empire, the kingdoms of Israel and Judah were frequently involved in wars between Assyria and Syria. The Jewish kingdoms remained generally independent, although at different times they were forced to pay tribute to one side or the other. However, in 722 B.C.E. Israel was conquered and destroyed by the Assyrians and part of the Jewish population was sent into exile. Judah suffered a similar fate at the hands of the Babylonians in 586 B.C.E. (See also BABYLON; EUPHRATES RIVER; FERTILE CRESCENT; HISTORY; IRON AGE; ISRAEL, KINGDOM OF; JUDAH, KINGDOM OF; SYRIA; TIGRIS RIVER.)

ASTARTE (also called ASHTORETH)   Goddess worshipped by the ancient Canaanites who believed that she had the power to make the land fertile. Archaeologists have found the remains of Canaanite temples to Astarte at Ashkelon and Bet Shean in Israel. (See also ARCHAEOLOGY; ASHKELON; BET SHEAN; CANAAN.)

ATHALIAH   Queen of Judah who ruled 842-836 B.C.E. She was the daughter of Jezebel and Ahab. When her son Ahaziah died, Athaliah seized the throne and murdered all the other members of the royal family. Only her grandson Joash escaped. Six years later there was a successful revolution in Joash's favor and Athaliah was executed. (See also AHAB; JEZEBEL; JOASH; JUDAH, KINGDOM OF.)

ATHLIT (also spelled ATLIT)   Village about nine miles south of Haifa. Walls of a Crusader castle with two 98-foot-high towers still stand at Athlit, which was a harbor for European knights arriving to fight for possession of the Holy Land in the 1100s and 1200s. During World War I, Athlit was a center for the activities of NILI, the Palestinian underground Jewish organization fighting against Turkish rule. Later, during the British Mandate, it was a camp for Jewish refugees who were caught trying to enter Palestine illegally. Today there is an Israeli naval station at Athlit. A moshav (farming village) is nearby, and so is a plant for taking salt out of sea water. (See also CRUSADES; DESALINIZATION; GREAT BRITAIN; HISTORY; IMMIGRANTS, ILLEGAL; MANDATE; MOSHAV; NILI; TURKEY.)

ATLAS, DALIA (1935-   )   Native Israeli pianist and conductor. Dalia Atlas has given concerts in Israel, England, and the United States. She has also brought music to border settlements, youth institutes, and schools for handicapped children throughout Israel.

ATONEMENT, DAY OF see YOM KIPPUR

ATZMON A mountain in Galilee where the Jews fought a battle against Roman troops in 66 C.E. (See also GALILEE; ROME.)

AUGUSTA VICTORIA HOSPITAL Hospital in northeastern Jerusalem run by the Lutheran World Federation. The hospital building was originally used by the British government (which then ruled Palestine under the Mandate) as a Government House and the home of the British High Commissioner. (See also GREAT BRITAIN; HEALTH; JERUSALEM.)

AUGUSTUS (63 B.C.E.-14 C.E.) The name given by the Roman Senate to Gaius Julius Caesar Octavianus, Roman emperor from 31 B.C.E. to 14 C.E. Augustus confirmed Herod the Great as king of Judea and gave him great power within the country. However, Judea's foreign policy was still controlled from Rome. Augustus returned the city of Straton's Tower to Judea, and Herod changed its name to Caesarea to honor the emperor. After Herod's death, Augustus had Judea ruled by a Roman governor who lived in Caesarea. (See also CAESAREA; HEROD I; HISTORY; JUDEA; ROME.)

AV, NINTH OF see TISHA B'AV

AVDAT (also spelled AVEDAT) Ancient city in the Negev about 40 miles south of Beersheba. It was founded in the third century B.C.E. by the Nabateans (an Arab people) as a road station for their trade caravans crossing the desert. The ruins of the city, which was at the height of its power in the first century B.C.E., have been uncovered by archaeologists and partially rebuilt. Remains of the irrigation system the Nabateans built to grow crops in the desert can be seen today, as can a Roman fort built about 150 C.E. and Byzantine churches from the 500s C.E. (See also ARCHAEOLOGY; BYZANTIUM; IRRIGATION; NABATEANS; NEGEV; ROME.)

AVENUE OF THE JUST Path lined with carob trees at Jerusalem's Yad Vashem memorial to the six million Jews who died under Nazi oppression during World War II. The Avenue of the Just honors the Christians who risked their own lives to hide and save Jews. (See also CAROB; HOLOCAUST; NAZIS; YAD VASHEM.)

AVIDAN, DAVID (1934-) Native Israeli writer who has published 14 books of Hebrew and English poetry. Avidan has also made several experimental films.

AVIDOM, MENAHEM (name changed from MAHLER-KALKSTEIN) (1908-) Composer. Born in Galicia in Europe, he went to Tel Aviv in 1935. Avidom has written many songs, symphonies, and operas, including the symphony *David* and the opera *Alexandra, the Hasmonean.*

AVIHAYIL Israeli moshav (farming village) about 35 miles south of Haifa. It was founded in 1932 by Jews who fought in the Jewish Legion in World War I to free Palestine from Turkish rule. There is a museum of Legion mementos in the village. (See also JEWISH LEGION; MOSHAV.)

AVINOAM, REUBEN (name changed from GROSSMAN) (1905-1974) Poet and author. Born in Chicago, Avinoam went to Palestine in 1929. Besides writing books of Hebrew poetry and and a novel, he translated English books into Hebrew and published the writings of Israeli soldiers who died in the 1947-1949 War of Independence. (See also WAR OF INDEPENDENCE.)

AVNER, GERSHOM (1919-) German-born diplomat who served as Israel's ambassador to Norway and to Canada. In 1977 Avner became president of Haifa University. (See also HAIFA UNIVERSITY.)

AVNI, ZVI (1927-) Composer who was brought to Israel from Germany as a child. Avni has written music for piano, string instruments, and full orchestras, as well as ballet and electronic music.

AYALON VALLEY One of the main passes through the Judean Hills between Tel Aviv and Jerusalem. The Bible says that this was the battlefield where Joshua commanded the sun to stand still (Joshua 10:12). The Ayalon Valley was again the scene of battles when Judah the Maccabee fought the Syrians in the second century B.C.E., when the Crusader king, Richard the Lionhearted, fought Saladin in the 1100s, and when Israeli forces battled their way through the Arab Legion in their successful attempt to liberate Jerusalem during the Six-Day War in 1967. (See also CRUSADES; HISTORY; JOSHUA; JUDAH THE MACCABEE; JUDE-AN HILLS; SIX-DAY WAR.)

AYELET HA-SHAHAR Israeli kibbutz in Galilee that houses a museum of archaeological finds from the ruins of the ancient city of Hazor. (See also ARCHAEOLOGY; GALILEE; HAZOR; KIBBUTZ.)

AZARIAH see UZZIAH

B

BAAL A God worshipped by the ancient Canaanites. One tribe might worship a Baal in the shape of a bull, another tribe's idol might be a man, but each Baal was believed to have the power to make the land fertile. Women without children also would pray to Baal for a baby. When the Israelites entered the land of Canaan, many of them began to worship Baals. The Book of Kings in the Bible tells of the conflicts between Jewish monotheism (worship of one God) and the worship of heathen idols like Baal. (See also CANAAN.)

BAASHA King of Israel who ruled 908-885 B.C.E. He entered into a war against Asa, king of the neighboring Jewish kingdom of Judah. Baasha was defeated and forced to give up some land to Judah. (See also ASA; ISRAEL, KINGDOM OF; JUDAH, KINGDOM OF.)

BABYLON (also called BABYLONIA) An ancient Semitic kingdom in Western Asia. The Bible also calls Babylon the land of Shinar and the land of the Chaldees, and Genesis says that man began in this land. Abraham was born in Ur of the Chaldees.

In about 1900 B.C.E. the Babylonians came out of the Arabian desert to invade the fertile plain between the Tigris and Euphrates rivers. By 1750 B.C.E. under Hammurabi, they had established an empire that took in all of Mesopotamia (which means the land between the rivers). Hammurabi's Code of Laws, which was enforced throughout the empire, is the earliest legal system known.

The Babylonian Empire crumbled in a series of wars. By the ninth century B.C.E. the Assyrian Empire ruled Mesopotamia. Then, in 612 B.C.E., the Babylonians defeated the Assyrians, took their capital city, and were once again the power in the area.

Under Nebuchadnezzar, the Babylonians conquered Judah in 586 B.C.E. and exiled the Jews to Babylon, where they found other Jews who had been exiled when the Assyrians conquered Israel. In 538 B.C.E. Persia defeated Babylon, and King Cyrus permitted the Jews to return to Palestine. Although some Jews chose to remain in Babylon, they stayed in touch with those who returned. (See also ARABIA; ASSYRIA; BABYLONIAN EXILE; CYRUS I;

EUPHRATES RIVER; HISTORY; ISRAEL, KINGDOM OF ; JUDAH, KINGDOM OF; MESOPOTAMIA; NEBUCHADNEZZAR; PERSIA.)

BABYLONIAN EXILE The years of the sixth century B.C.E. during which the Jews were forced to live in Babylon. The Babylonian Exile began with the destruction of the Jewish kingdom of Judah by Nebuchadnezzar in 586 B.C.E. and ended when the Persian ruler Cyrus the Great allowed the Jews to return to Palestine. Inspired by the prophesies of Ezekiel, the Jews were able to maintain their religion throughout the years of exile. (See also BABYLON; CYRUS I; EZEKIEL; JUDAH, KINGDOM OF; NEBUCHADNEZZAR.)

BAER, YITZHAK (1888-) German-born historian who taught at the Hebrew University in Jerusalem and wrote books and articles about the history of the Jews in the Middle Ages. He was also editor of the journal of the Israel Historical Society. (See also HEBREW UNIVERSITY.)

BAHAI An Islamic religion that uses the Old and New Testaments as well as the Koran and teaches that God's will is shown from time to time through new prophets. The religion was founded by Mirza Ali Mohammed in Persia in 1844. Although only a few hundred of the several million members of the Bahai religion live in Israel, the main religious shrines are at Acre and Haifa. (See also ACRE; BAHAI SHRINE; HAIFA; RELIGION.)

BAHAI SHRINE White marble building topped with a gold dome and set in Persian gardens on Mount Carmel in Haifa. It is the burial place of Mizra Ali Mohammed, founder of the Bahai religion. (See also BAHAI; HAIFA; MOUNT CARMEL.)

BAKLAVA A very sweet pastry made with thin layers of flaky dough, honey, and nuts. It is popular in Israel as well as in the surrounding Middle Eastern countries.

BALDWIN I (1058-1118 C.E.) First Crusader king of Jerusalem. He joined the First Crusade of European knights fighting to take the Holy Land from the Moslems. Jerusalem was already in Christian hands when Baldwin arrived, but was being governed by the church. Baldwin won the struggle between church and state, ruled as king of Jerusalem 1100-1118 C.E., and greatly strengthened the kingdom. (See also CRUSADES; HISTORY; JERUSALEM.)

BALDWIN II (died 1131 C.E.) Crusader king of Jerusalem from 1118 to 1131 C.E. He was a fierce warrior who fought the Moslems throughout his life. The Crusader state of Jerusalem was at its strongest under his rule. (See also CRUSADES; HISTORY; JERUSALEM.)

Bahai Shrine (foreground)

BALDWIN III ((1130-1162 C.E.)   Crusader king of Jerusalem who ruled 1143-1162 C.E. He was the first Crusader king to be born in the Holy Land. He tried to take Damascus from the Moslems during the Second Crusade, but failed. (See also CRUSADES; HISTORY; JERUSALEM.)

BALFOUR, ARTHUR JAMES (1848-1930)   British politician. Balfour was a Conservative Party member of the British Parliament, a leader in the House of Commons. He held the posts of Lord of the Treasury and later Foreign Secretary (similar to the American Secretary of State). In 1917, as Foreign Secretary, Balfour issued a statement in which the British government favored a Jewish national home in Palestine. This historic statement is known as the Balfour Declaration. When Balfour visited Palestine in 1925 to open the Hebrew University in Jerusalem, he was greeted as a friend of the Jews. He then continued on to Syria where the reaction of the people was so hostile that he had to leave the country. (See also BALFOUR DECLARATION; GREAT BRITAIN; HEBREW UNIVERSITY; SYRIA.)

BALFOUR DECLARATION   A statement by the British government supporting Zionist aims in Palestine. It was issued after long discussions between Lord Balfour and the Zionist leader Chaim Weizmann, and was supported by President Woodrow Wilson in the United States. On November 2, 1917, British Foreign Secretary Balfour sent a letter to Baron Rothschild, who represented the Zionist Federation, saying that Britain favored "the establishment in Palestine of a national home for the Jewish people" and that Britain would work toward such a national home. A month later the British drove the Turks out of Jerusalem, and in 1920 Britain was given the Mandate by the League of Nations to govern Palestine; but no Jewish state was established. However, the Balfour Declaration gave legal backing to the following 30 years of struggle for a Jewish homeland in Palestine. (See also BALFOUR, ARTHUR JAMES; GREAT BRITAIN; HISTORY; TURKEY; WEIZMANN, CHAIM; ZIONISM.)

BALFOUR FOREST   A forest of a half-million pine trees in the hills near Nazareth planted by British Jews in honor of Lord Balfour. (See also BALFOUR, ARTHUR JAMES; REFORESTATION.)

BALFOURIYA   Agricultural settlement founded in 1922 in the Jezreel Valley and named in honor of Lord Balfour. (See also BALFOUR, ARTHUR JAMES; JEZREEL VALLEY.)

BANETH, DAVID (1893-1973)   Polish-born specialist in Arabic language and literature who went to Palestine in 1924 and taught at the Hebrew University in Jerusalem. (See also HEBREW UNIVERSITY.)

BANIAS (also spelled BANYAS)   A spring and waterfall in the extreme north of Israel; one of the sources of the Jordan River. The Greeks called the spot Paneas, and the remains of a Greek shrine to the god Pan can still be seen there. Herod the Great built a temple at Banias and his son Philip chose it as the place to build the city he named Caesarea Philippi. (See also HELLENISM; HEROD I; JORDAN RIVER; PHILIP.)

BANK LEUMI LE-ISRAEL   Israel's leading commercial bank. It was established in 1903 as the Anglo-Palestine Company to serve the banking needs of the Jewish community in Palestine. From 1948, when the State of Israel was founded, until 1954, when the Bank of Israel was established, Bank Leumi was the national bank of the Israeli government. (See also BANK OF ISRAEL.)

BANK OF ISRAEL   The central national bank of Israel. It was established in 1954 with a loan of 20 million Israeli pounds (about six million dollars) from the government and was given the sole right to print money. The Bank of Israel is responsible for regulating the money, credit, and banking system of the country. Its governor is appointed by the President of Israel for a five-year term and has as much power as a Cabinet Minister. He acts as an advisor to the government. (See also GOVERNMENT.)

BAR   Aramaic word meaning "son" or "son of" often used in names. For example, the name Yisrael Bar-Yehuda means "Yisrael the son of Yehuda." "Ben" is the Hebrew equivalent. (See also ARAMAIC; BEN.)

BAR-DAVID, MOLLY (1910-   )   Canadian-born writer who settled in Israel in 1936. Molly Bar-David has written columns for the *Jerusalem Post* and other newspapers. She is also the author of several popular cookbooks. (See also JERUSALEM POST.)

BAR GIORA   A Palestinian defense organization named after Simon Bar Giora. It was founded by pioneers of the Second Aliyah (wave of immigration) in 1907 and later became part of Hashomer (the Jewish "watchmen" organization). (See also ALIYAH; HASHOMER.)

BAR GIORA, SIMON (first century C.E.)   Jewish leader in the revolt against Rome in 66-70 C.E. He believed in the equality of all men and in freeing the slaves. Bar Giora helped defeat the army of the Syrian governor and then led his band of Zealots through southern Judea, attacking settlements that were not loyal to the revolt. He quarreled with the heads of the temporary Jewish government and fought with them in Jerusalem. The Jews united when the Roman general (later emperor) Titus attacked Jerusalem. Bar Giora was a leader of the defense of the city and was executed soon after Titus conquered Jerusalem. (See also HISTORY; JERUSALEM; ROME; TITUS; ZEALOTS.)

BAR-HAIM, SHAUL (1924-   )   Diplomat who was born in Iraq and settled in Israel in 1944. Bar-Haim served as Israel's representative to Turkey and later as ambassador to Cyprus. In 1975 he became the director of Arabic broadcasting for Kol Israel (Israel's radio network). (See also KOL ISRAEL.)

BAR-ILAN, MEIR (name changed from BERLIN) (1880-1949) Orthodox Zionist leader. His father, Naphtali Berlin, was one of the first rabbis to support Zionism and Bar-Ilan became a Zionist as a very young man. He went to New York in 1914 and was elected president of the Mizrahi (a religious Zionist organization) in the United States. In 1926 he settled in Jerusalem and continued as a leader of Mizrahi in Palestine. There, he founded *Hatzofe,* the daily newspaper published by Mizrahi. Rabbi Bar-Ilan was also the editor of the *Talmudic Encyclopedia.* Bar-Ilan University is named in his honor. (See also BAR-ILAN UNIVERSITY; HATZOFE; MIZRAHI; ZIONISM.)

BAR-ILAN UNIVERSITY   University named in honor of Rabbi Meir Bar-Ilan. It was founded at Ramat Gan near Tel Aviv in 1955 with the support of the United States Mizrahi organization. The motto of the university is "Torah with general knowledge," and its aim is to teach Judaism along with the arts and sciences. Bar-Ilan university has departments of Jewish Studies, Humanities, Science, Social Science, Mathematics, Law, as well as Schools of Social Work and Education. In 1978 there were about 7,000 students and 850 teachers. About 500 of the students came from other countries to study in Israel. Research in science, computers, and mathematics is carried on at the university. (See also BAR-ILAN, MEIR; MIZRAHI; TORAH.)

BAR KOKHBA, SIMEON (name changed from BEN KOSIBA) (died 135 C.E.)   Leader of the Second Revolt against Rome. The name Bar Kokhba means "son of the star" and was probably given to him by Rabbi Akiva, who saw Bar Kokhba as the Messiah who had come to deliver the Jews.

When the Roman emperor Hadrian ordered Jerusalem rebuilt as a pagan city and its name changed to Aelia Capitolina, it sparked a Jewish revolt against Rome. The revolt lasted from 132 to 135 C.E. and Jews came from all over the country to fight under Bar Kokhba.

In 132 C.E. Bar Kokhba's army captured Jerusalem and held it for more than two years. A Roman army sent by Hadrian finally recaptured the city. Bar Kokhba and his men retreated to the fortress of Betar, where they made a brave stand. Betar fell in 135 C.E., and Bar Kokhba was killed in the fighting.

As punishment for the revolt, many thousands of Jews were killed and their villages destroyed. The remaining Jews were forbidden to practice their religion or to enter Jerusalem.

Letters written by Bar Kokhba and the bones of some of his followers have been found by archaeologists in a cave near the Dead Sea. (See also AKIVA BEN JOSEPH; BETAR; CAVE OF LETTERS; HADRIAN; HISTORY; JERUSALEM; MESSIAH; ROME.)

BAR-LEV, HAYIM (1924-   )   Soldier who was born in Yugoslavia and went to Palestine in 1939. He fought with the Haganah (the Jewish defense organization). When the Haganah became the Israeli army in 1948, Bar-Lev continued to serve and finally rose to Chief-of-Staff of the army. In 1972 he was elected a member of the Israeli Knesset (legislature) and served as Minister of Commerce and Industry. (See also DEFENSE FORCES; HAGANAH; KNESSET.)

Hayim Bar-Lev

BAR MITZVAH   Hebrew for "son of the law." When a Jewish boy reaches the age of thirteen, he becomes a Bar Mitzvah. This means that he is now responsible for observing all Jewish religious commandments. The words "Bar Mitzvah" are also used to describe the ceremony and celebration that marks the boy's coming of age. The young man is called up to read the Torah in the synagogue. After the religious service, a celebration for family and friends is usually held.

Since Jerusalem was reunited in 1967, thousands of boys have

Bar Mitzvahs are popular at the Western Wall. Above, a Sephardi
Bar Mitzvah is celebrated. Below, an Ashkenazi Bar Mitzvah boy
carries the Torah from the subterranean passageway north of the
Wall. Torahs are kept there in arks when not being used.

come to Israel from all over the world to celebrate their Bar Mitzvahs at the Western Wall. Others have chosen to have the ceremony in the synagogue in the ancient fortress of Masada in the Judean Desert. (See also BAT MITZVAH; JERUSALEM; MASADA; TORAH; WESTERN WALL.)

At the Western Wall, a boy kisses his *tefilin* after putting them on for the Monday morning service at which time he will be Bar Mitzvah.

BAR-YEHUDA, YISRAEL (name changed from IDELSON) (1895-1965) Russian-born politician. He went to Palestine in 1926 and became active in the Socialist movement. He was a member of the Israeli Knesset and served as Minister of the Interior and as Minister of Communications. (See also KNESSET; SOCIALISM.)

BARAK BEN ABINOAM (twelfth century B.C.E.) Israelite commander called by the prophetess Deborah to lead the Israelites in battle against the Canaanites. The biblical story of their battles is told in the Book of Judges, Chapter 4. (See also CANAAN; DEBORAH.)

BARAM Israeli kibbutz founded in 1949 near the border with Lebanon. The ruins of a synagogue from the 200s C.E. stand nearby, and legends say that Queen Esther was buried at Baram. (See also ESTHER; KIBBUTZ; LEBANON.)

BARASH, ASHER (1889-1952) Writer born in Galicia in Central Europe. Barash went to Palestine in 1914. He has written short stories and novels about life in Galicia in the early 1900s as well as books about pioneers in Palestine.

BARATZ, JOSEPH (1890-1968) Russian-born Palestinian pioneer. He was one of the founders of Kibbutz Degania (Palestine's first cooperative farming village) and wrote a history of Degania called *A Village by the Jordan.* (See also DEGANIA; KIBBUTZ.)

BARKAI Israeli kibbutz founded in 1949 in the Iron Hills of northwest Samaria. Many of the settlers came from the United States and Canada. (See also KIBBUTZ; SAMARIA.)

BARON, DEVORAH (1887-1956) Russian-born writer who went to Palestine in 1911. Her short stories and novels were written in Hebrew and were usually about Jewish life in the small towns of Russia. In 1934 Devorah Baron was the first winner of the Bialik Prize for literature, the highest award Israel can give a writer. She was married to the Zionist leader Joseph Aharonowitz. (See also AHARONOWITZ, JOSEPH; BIALIK PRIZE; LITERATURE.)

BARTH, AARON (1980-1957) German-born banker who settled in Palestine in 1931 and became the director of Bank Leumi. (See also BANK LEUMI LE-ISRAEL.)

BARTOV, HANOKH (1926-) Native Israeli writer of stories, novels, and plays. Bartov served in the Jewish Brigade in World War II, fought in the 1948 War of Independence, and he used these experiences in his writing. *The Brigade* is about soldiers in the Jewish Brigade; *The Reckoning and the Soul* tells of men returning to civilian life after the War of Independence. Bartov has won the Ussishkin Prize and the Shlonsky Prize. (See also JEWISH BRIGADE; PRIZES; LITERATURE; WAR OF INDEPENDENCE.)

BARZILLA, ISRAEL (name changed from EISENBERG) (1913-1970) Polish-born politician and labor leader who went to Palestine in 1934. He was a member of the Israeli Knesset (legislature) and served as Minister of Health and as Deputy Speaker. (See also KNESSET.)

BASIC LAWS When Israel became a state, the Knesset (legislature) decided against adopting a Constitution immediately. Instead, it planned to pass Basic Laws as needed and to have these Laws eventually become chapters of a Constitution. The first Basic Law, passed in 1958, defined the working of the Knesset. Other Basic Laws are the Israel Land Regime (1960) and Laws dealing with the role of the President (1964) and the working of the Government (1968). (See also GOVERNMENT; KNESSET; LAND OWNERSHIP; PRESIDENT.)

BASKETBALL   The second most popular sport in Israel. (Soccer, which the Israelis call football, is the most popular.) The Israel Basketball Union includes 300 different teams. It has a National League, two First Leagues, and two Second Leagues, as well as Women's Leagues and Youth Leagues. (See also SPORTS.)

BASLE PROGRAM   Program adopted at the First Zionist Congress which was held at Basle (now spelled Basel) in Switzerland in 1897. The program stated that the aim of Zionism is "to create for the Jewish people a home in Palestine secured by public law" and went on to describe ways of achieving that aim. (See also WORLD ZIONIST ORGANIZATION; ZIONISM.)

BAT DOR DANCE COMPANY   Dance group founded in 1968. Bat Dor performs both modern and classical dances. It is very popular in Israel and has appeared at the Israel Festival. The company has also danced in Europe, Asia, Africa, and South America. (See also DANCE; ISRAEL FESTIVAL.)

BAT MITZVAH (also spelled BAS MITZVAH)   Hebrew for "daughter of the law." When a Jewish girl is twelve years of age, she becomes a Bat Mitzvah and takes on the religious responsibilities of a Jewish woman. After the synagogue service, a celebration is held which marks the happy occasion. In some congregations the Bat Mitzvah is held when a girl is thirteen or even older.

Many girls go to Israel to celebrate their Bat Mitzvahs at the Western Wall in Jerusalem or in the synagogue of the ancient fortress of Masada in the Judean Desert. Since services at the Western Wall follow Orthodox law, a Bat Mitzvah cannot read from the Torah, although her father may do so in her honor. (See also BAR MITZVAH; MASADA; TORAH; WESTERN WALL.)

BAT YAM   Resort town south of Tel Aviv with an excellent beach. A number of artists and writers live in the town. Bat Yam's city hall is a good example of modern Israeli architecture. (See also ARCHITECTURE.)

BATHSHEBA   Wife of King David who had her husband, Uriah, killed in battle so David could marry her. Bathsheba saw to it that her son Solomon ruled Israel after David's death. (See also DAVID; SOLOMON.)

BATZAL YAROK (English, GREEN ONIONS)   A group of entertainers in the Israeli army. Led by actor Chaim Topol, Batzal Yarok toured army units and built troop morale with their special brand of humor. The group stayed together after their discharge from the army and became as popular with Israeli civilians as they had been with the soldiers. (See also DEFENSE FORCES; THEATER; TOPOL, CHAIM.)

BAUER, YEHUDA (1936-   )   Scholar who was born in Czechoslovakia and settled in Israel in 1939. Bauer is the head of the Department of Holocaust Studies at the Hebrew University in Jerusalem, as well as a consultant to Yad Vashem, the memorial to the Jewish martyrs of the Holocaust. (See also HEBREW UNIVERSITY; HOLOCAUST; YAD VASHEM.)

B.C.E.   Abbbreviation used after dates to stand for Before Common Era. It is the same as B.C., which stands for Before Christ.

BECKER, ISRAEL (1917-   )   Actor and director who appeared in many theaters in his native Poland before settling in Israel and acting with the Habimah Theater. Becker has also produced several films. (See also HABIMAH.)

BEDOUIN (also spelled BEDUIN)   Tribes of Arab nomads who roam the desert of the Negev and Sinai with their flocks. Some of the more than 20,000 Bedouin in Israel still live as their ancestors did in biblical times. They pitch their tents near water holes, stay until their sheep and camels have eaten all the grass near the water, and then move on. Today more and more Bedouin are settling in villages and growing grain on the land given to them by a government land settlement plan. The Israeli government has piped water to some Bedouin settlements for the crops and flocks, and has set up schools and health clinics. The government also sends trucks with doctors and medicine to treat the tribes that still roam the desert. (See also ARABS; EDUCATION; HEALTH; NEGEV; SINAI.)

BEER TUVYAH   Israeli moshav (farming village) founded in 1887 about 20 miles south of Tel Aviv with the help of Baron Edmond de Rothschild. The village was destroyed in the Arab riots of 1929 but was rebuilt in 1930. (See also ARAB RIOTS; MOSHAV; ROTHSCHILD, EDMOND DE.)

BEERI   Israeli kibbutz in the Negev. It was founded in 1946, and its members fought off an Egyptian attack during the War of Independence in 1948. (See also KIBBUTZ; NEGEV; WAR OF INDEPENDENCE.)

BEEROT YITZAK   Israeli farming village not far from Tel Aviv. The settlers of Beerot Yitzak originally built their settlement near Gaza. Many of them were killed fighting for their homes during the 1947-1949 War of Independence. After the war, they moved to the present village. (See also WAR OF INDEPENDENCE.)

BEERSHEBA (also spelled BEERSHEVA) City in the Negev, first founded about 6,000 years ago. The name means "well of the swearing." The Bible says that Abraham dug a well at Beersheba and made a pact there with the king of the Philistines. During biblical times Beersheba was an important town at the southern end of the Israelite nation. The saying "from Dan to Beersheba" means "the whole country."

Today Beersheba is a fast-growing city surrounded by desert. The Arab population fled the town during the War of Independence, and it was resettled by Jewish immigrants. Ben-Gurion University of the Negev was founded at Beersheba in 1965. (See also ABRAHAM; BEN-GURION UNIVERSITY OF THE NEGEV; DAN; NEGEV; PHILISTINES; WAR OF INDEPENDENCE.)

BEERSHEBA CAMEL MARKET Early every Thursday morning Bedouin come to Beersheba to sell camels as well as rugs, copper pots, and jewelry. It is a favorite place for tourists to buy souvenirs. (See also BEDOUIN; BEERSHEBA; TOURISM.)

BEGIN, MENACHEM (1913-   ) Sixth Prime Minister of Israel. Begin was born in Poland where he made his first political speech at the age of 12 as a member of Betar, a Zionist youth organization. He became the head of Betar in Poland and studied law in Warsaw. When the Russians invaded Poland in 1939, Begin was sent to a prison camp in Siberia. Three years later he was allowed to join the Polish army in Palestine.

In 1943 Begin became the commander of the Irgun, the Jewish underground terrorist organization fighting British rule in Palestine. Under his command, the Irgun killed British soldiers, planted bombs, and blew up part of the King David Hotel in Jerusalem. The British offered a reward of $30,000 for his capture. Begin's book, *The Revolt*, describes those days.

When Israel became a state in 1948, Begin founded the Herut (freedom) political party and became a member of the Israeli Knesset (legislature). Later Herut joined with other parties to form the Likud, and Begin remained its leader. He took a hard line against returning the lands Israel had occupied after the 1967 Six-Day War. Likud defeated the ruling Labor party in the 1977 elections and Menachem Begin became Prime Minister of Israel.

In November 1977, Prime Minister Begin welcomed President Anwar Sadat of Egypt to Jerusalem. Begin and Sadat met again in September 1978 at Camp David in the United States to discuss a peace treaty between their two countries. On March 26, 1979, the two leaders signed the first peace treaty between Israel and an Arab country.

Menachem Begin and Anwar Sadat shared the 1978 Nobel Peace Prize. (See also ADMINISTERED AREAS; BETAR; CAMP DAVID

Prime Minister Menachem Begin enjoys the French exhibition at the 1979 Jerusalem International Book Fair.

SUMMIT; CARTER, JIMMY; EGYPT; GREAT BRITAIN; HERUT; IRGUN; ISRAEL-EGYPT PEACE TREATY; KNESSET; LIKUD; PRIME MINISTER; SADAT, ANWAR; SIX-DAY WAR.)

BEHAR, NISSIM (1848-1931)   Educator born in Jerusalem where he was director of the Alliance Israelite school and introduced Hebrew as the school's language. He moved to New York in 1901. (See also HEBREW.)

BEILINSON, MOSHE (1889-1936)   Russian-born Hebrew journalist who lived in other parts of Europe and became a Zionist before settling in Palestine in 1924. He was a labor leader and an editor of *Davar,* the newspaper published by Histadrut, Palestine's labor federation. (See also DAVAR; HISTADRUT; ZIONISM.)

BEIN, ALEX (1903-   )   German-born writer who settled in Palestine in 1933. He wrote books about Palestine and a biography of Herzl, and was director of the Central Zionist Archives. (See also ARCHIVES.)

BEISAN see BET SHEAN

BEIT BERL   Organization founded in 1949 and named in honor of Berl Katzenelson, the labor leader. Beit Berl is the education and research bureau of the Israel Labor Party. It runs two high schools, a four-year college, a library, a sports center, and summer camps for young people. (See also EDUCATION; ISRAEL LABOR PARTY; KATZENELSON; BERL.)

BELKIND, ISRAEL (1861-1929)   Russian-born leader of BILU, a Zionist pioneering organization. Belkind went to Palestine in 1882 with the first group of BILU pioneers and helped establish the settlement of Rishon Le Zion. He founded the first Hebrew school in Jaffa and wrote textbooks in Hebrew, Russian, and Yiddish. (See also BILU; RISHON LE ZION; ZIONISM.)

BELVOIR   Crusader castle built high above the Jordan River in 1182 by the Christian order of the Knights Hospitaler. The castle has square towers and an inner and outer wall. (See also CRUSADES; JORDAN RIVER.)

BEN   Hebrew word meaning "son" or "son of" often used in names. For example, the name David Ben-Gurion means "David, son of a young lion." (See also BAR.)

BEN-AHARON, YITZHAK (1906-   )   Austrian-born politician and labor leader who went to Palestine in 1928. He was a member of the Israeli Knesset (legislature) and Secretary-General of Histadrut, the Israeli labor federation. Ben-Aharon suggested that the small labor parties join to form the Israel Labor Party which was the strongest political party in Israel until the 1977 elections. (See also HISTADRUT; ISRAEL LABOR PARTY; KNESSET; POLITICAL PARTIES.)

BEN-AMI, OVED (1905-   )   Native-born Israeli who was one of the founders of the city of Netanya and served as its mayor for 36 years. He helped bring the diamond industry to Israel and established its center in Netanya. (See also DIAMONDS; NETANYA.)

BEN-AMMI (pen name of MORDECAI RABINOWICZ) (1854-1932)   Russian-born writer who organized a Jewish group to defend against the pogroms (murder of Jews) in Odessa, Russia. Ben-Ammi went to Switzerland and then settled in Palestine in 1923. He wrote books in Russian and Yiddish urging Jews to cling to their Jewish culture.

BEN-ARI, MORDECHAI (1920-   )   Airline executive who was born in Eastern Europe, settled in Israel in 1940, and was a commanding officer in the Haganah (Jewish underground army). Ben-Ari became chairman of El Al Israel Airlines and introduced group air fares. (See also EL AL.)

BEN-ARI, URI (1925-   )   German-born soldier who went to Israel at the age of 14. Ben-Ari was a member of the Palmah (the striking force of the Jewish underground army) and fought in the

1948 War of Independence and in each of the following Israel-Arab wars. He commanded the tank division that liberated Jerusalem in the 1967 Six-Day War. In 1976 he was appointed Israeli consul in New York. (See also JERUSALEM; PALMAH; SIX-DAY WAR; WAR OF INDEPENDENCE.)

BEN-AVI, ITTAMAR (1882-1943)   Palestinian-born writer. He was the son of Eliezer Ben-Yehuda, the "father of modern Hebrew." Ben-Avi wanted Hebrew to be written in Latin letters (the same letters English uses) rather than Hebrew letters. He published a Hebrew newspaper written in Latin letters. (See also BEN-YEHUDA, ELIEZER; HEBREW.)

BEN ELIEZER, ARYE (1913-1970)   Russian-born soldier and politician who was brought to Palestine at the age of seven. Ben Eliezer joined the Betar youth movement and took part in the defense of Jerusalem during the 1929 and 1936 Arab riots. He was active in the Irgun (an underground Jewish defense organization), served in its High Command, and was imprisoned several times by the British for his activities. When Israel became a state in 1948, Ben Eliezer was one of the founders of the Herut political party and was elected as a Herut member of the Knesset (legislature). (See also ARAB RIOTS; BETAR; HERUT; IRGUN.)

BEN EZER, EHUD (1936-   )   Native Israeli author who has written novels, a children's book, short stories, and radio plays as well as a regular column for *Haaretz,* Israel's leading newspaper. (See also HAARETZ.)

BEN-GURION AIRPORT   Israel's international airport, it was formerly called Lod Airport, was established several miles southeast of Tel Aviv in 1936, and was taken over by Israel in 1948. In 1973 its name was changed from Lod Airport to honor David Ben-Gurion. Planes from 17 different countries carry almost two million passengers a year in and out of Ben-Gurion Airport. (See also BEN-GURION, DAVID.)

BEN-GURION, DAVID (name changed from GRUEN) (1886-1973) One of the founding fathers of Israel. He was born in Russian Poland where he learned about Zionism from his father. At the age of 14, Ben-Gurion and his friends formed a Zionist youth club. At 20, he went to Palestine to work the land as a pioneer. He helped to organize Bar Giora, a defense group of Jewish settlers.

Ben-Gurion was one of the founders of the Ahdut Ha-avoda (a Socialist political party) and was sent as its delegate to the 1920 Zionist Conference. Later, he was a founder of the Mapai Party. He was also an organizer of the Histadrut (Israel's labor federation) and was chairman of the Jewish Agency of the World Zionist Organization.

Prime Minister Ben-Gurion enjoying the freedom to pursue his scholarly work after his retirement.

In 1939 Great Britain issued the White Paper, which limited Jewish immigration to Palestine. At the time, Britain was also fighting against Germany in World War II. Ben-Gurion summed up the Zionist position: "We will fight the White Paper as if there were no war, and we shall fight the war as if there were no White Paper."

After the war, Ben-Gurion worked for the United Nations resolution that established the State of Israel in 1948. He became Prime Minister and Minister of Defense of the new government. As Minister of Defense, he organized the Israeli army that defeated the invading Arabs in the 1947-1949 War of Independence. As Prime Minister, he made Jerusalem the capital of Israel, welcomed thousands of Jewish immigrants to the country, and worked for the economic growth of Israel. He was Prime Minister from 1948 to 1953, and again from 1955 to 1963.

On leaving the government, Ben-Gurion retired to the small desert kibbutz of Sde Boker where he worked in the fields and wrote articles and essays. A collection of his writings is called *Rebirth and Destiny of Israel.* (See also AHDUT HA-AVODA; BAR GIORA; HISTADRUT; IMMIGRANTS; JERUSALEM; JEWISH AGENCY; MA-PAI; PRIME MINISTER; SDE BOKER; UNITED NATIONS; WAR OF INDE-PENDENCE; WHITE PAPER; WORLD ZIONIST ORGANIZATION; ZIONISM.

The Ben-Gurion University library (above) and the university administration building (below).

BEN-GURION MEMORIAL   Organization devoted to carrying on the ideas of David Ben-Gurion. It supports scientific study to benefit the Negev. The Memorial works with the Ben-Gurion University of the Negev and with other organizations, including the educational seminars (lectures) at Sde Boker. (See also BEN-GURION, DAVID; BEN- GURION UNIVERSITY OF THE NEGEV; NEGEV; SDE BOKER.)

BEN-GURION UNIVERSITY OF THE NEGEV   The Institute for Higher Education in the Negev was established in Beersheba, and in 1973 its name was changed to Ben-Gurion University of the Negev as a memorial to David Ben-Gurion. The university specializes in science and engineering, and one of its aims is to attract new immigrants to the Negev. In 1975 there were almost 3,000 students and about 700 teachers. Many of the teachers were "on loan" from the Hebrew University in Jerusalem. (See also BEERSHEBA; BEN-GURION, DAVID; HEBREW UNIVERSITY; NEGEV.)

BEN-HAIM, PAUL (name changed from FRANKENBURGER) (1897-   ) German-born composer who settled in Tel Aviv in 1933. Some of his music was inspired by Oriental folk songs.
    Ben-Haim has won a number of prizes for his symphonies, including the 1957 Israel Prize. (See also ISRAEL PRIZE.)

BEN-HORIN, ELIASHIV (1921-   ) Diplomat who has served at different times as Israel's ambassador to Germany, Belgium, Burma, and Venezuela.

BEN-HUR, NAHUM (1928-   ) Doctor who was educated at the Hebrew University-Hadassah Medical School, where he is now a professor. Dr. Ben-Hur is a specialist in plastic surgery. He has been given several awards for his work in rebuilding the faces of people hurt in accidents or wounded in war. (See also HADASSAH; HEBREW UNIVERSITY.)

BEN KOZIBA   see BAR KOKHBA

BEN PORAT, MIRIAM (1918-   ) Russian-born lawyer and judge who settled in Palestine in 1936. She studied law at the Hebrew University in Jerusalem, was the first woman public prosecutor (state lawyer) in Israel, and then became a district court judge. She also taught law at the Hebrew University. In 1978, Miriam Ben Porat was appointed a Justice of the Supreme Court of Israel. She is the first woman to hold that high office in any country of the world. (See also COURTS; HEBREW UNIVERSITY; JUDGES; SUPREME COURT.)

BEN SHEMEN   Youth village established in 1927 about 25 miles southeast of Tel Aviv. The village was the home of European children brought to Palestine in the Youth Aliyah (young people's immigration) of the 1930s. Ben Shemen has an agricultural school for young people and is also the site of the Herzl Forest. A moshav (farming village) of the same name is nearby. (See also AGRICULTURAL SCHOOLS; HERZL FOREST; MOSHAV; YOUTH ALIYAH; YOUTH VILLAGES.)

BEN YEHUDA, ELIEZER (name changed from PERELMANN) (1858-1922)   The father of modern Hebrew. Born in Lithuania, Ben Yehuda went to Paris where he became interested in Zionism and began to write articles arguing for a Jewish nation in Eretz Israel (Land of Israel) where Hebrew would be spoken. In 1881 he went to Jerusalem and devoted himself to making Hebrew the spoken language of the Jews of Palestine.

At that time Hebrew was mainly a sacred language used in prayer. It had no vocabulary for modern words like "soap" or "bicycle." Ben Yehuda began a giant Hebrew dictionary and invented the new Hebrew words needed by modern speakers. He was also the editor of several Hebrew magazines including *The Deer,* and was the founder and chairman of the Hebrew Language Council which later became the Hebrew Language Academy.

When his first son was born, Ben Yehuda insisted that the baby hear only Hebrew spoken. As a result, little Ben Zion became the first child in almost two thousand years to speak Hebrew as his native language.

Ben Yehuda completed the first five volumes of his Hebrew dictionary before he died of tuberculosis at the age of 64. The next eight volumes were finished by his wife, Hemda, from his notes. Funds came from the Ben Yehuda Memorial Trust. The last three volumes were published with the help of the Israeli government. (See also BEN YEHUDA, HEMDA; HEBREW; HEBREW LANGUAGE ACADEMY; ZIONISM.)

BEN YEHUDA, HEMDA (born POLA YANAS) (1869-1951) Second wife of Eliezer Ben Yehuda. She took over as editor of the magazine *The Deer* while her husband worked on his Hebrew dictionary. She traveled throughout Palestine and Europe to raise money for his publications. When Eliezer Ben Yehuda died, with only the first five volumes of his Hebrew dictionary finished, Hemda Ben Yehuda completed the next eight volumes. (See also BEN YEHUDA, ELIEZER.)

BEN-YOHANAN, ASHER (1929-   ) Composer and music teacher who was born in Greece and brought to Israel as a young child. Ben-Yohanan has written music for piano, violin, and other instruments, as well as music for a symphony orchestra.

BEN-YOSEF, REUVEN (name changed from REISS, ROBERT) (1937-   ) Writer who was born and educated in the United States and wrote his first book of poems in English. After settling in Israel in 1959, Ben-Yosef began to write poetry in Hebrew. He also translated a number of popular American books into Hebrew. (See also HEBREW.)

BEN ZAKKI, JOHANAN see JOHANAN BEN ZAKKAI

BEN-ZION, SIMHA (pen name of SIMHA ALTER GUTMANN) (1870-1932) Russian-born Hebrew writer who settled in Palestine in 1905. Besides writing stories, novels, and plays, Ben-Zion translated several famous German books into Hebrew.

BEN-ZVI, RACHEL YANAIT (1886-   ) Pioneer and educator. Russian-born Rachel Yanait went to Palestine as a pioneer in 1908. She worked the land and helped organize Hashomer, the Jewish Defense Group. She married Yitzhak Ben-Zvi in 1918. Rachel Yanait Ben-Zvi was a founder of the Hebrew High School in Jerusalem, a girl's agricultural training school, and a youth village. She was active in the labor movement and was responsible for the establishment of the Pioneer Women's organization in the United States. Her autobiography is called *Coming Home*. (See also AGRICULTURAL SCHOOLS; BEN-ZVI, YITZHAK; HASHOMER; PIONEER WOMEN; YOUTH VILLAGES.)

BEN-ZVI, YITZHAK (name changed from SHIMSHELEVITZ) (1884-1963) Second President of Israel. He was born in Russia where he joined the Poale Zion (a Socialist Zionist organization). Ben-Zvi went to Palestine in 1907 to work the land at Sejera, a pioneer village in Galilee. There, he became friends with David Ben-Gurion, and the two men became active in Hashomer, a group of Jewish "watchmen" who guarded the settlement against Arab raiders.

When Ben-Zvi and Ben-Gurion were thrown out of Palestine by the Turks during World War I, they went to the United States and organized Hehalutz, a pioneer youth movement whose members hoped to settle in Palestine. Returning to Palestine after the war, Ben-Zvi was one of the founders of the Ahdut Ha-avoda and Mapai political parties and was active in Histadrut, the Israel labor federation.

Ben-Zvi served as a member of the Israeli Knesset (legislature) and was elected President of Israel in 1952. He was also a scholar who published research in Jewish history. (See also AHDUT HA-AVODA; BEN-GURION, DAVID; HASHOMER; HEHALUTZ; KNESSET; MAPAI; POALE ZION; PRESIDENT.)

BENE AKIVA (also spelled BNEI AKIBA) The pioneering youth

President Ben-Zvi (Center) was host to Mrs. Franklin Delano Roosevelt at his home in Jerusalem on March 27, 1959. Mr. Ben-Zvi is describing a painting that hangs in his home.

organization of Hapoel Hamizrahi (a religious Zionist labor organization). Bene Akiva is named for the famous talmudic scholar, Rabbi Akiva, and its motto is "Religion and Labor." Its members must study at a yeshiva (religious school) for at least a year before they are trained to work in one of the movement's three cooperative farming settlements. (See also AKIVA BEN JOSEPH; HAPOEL HAMIZRAHI; YOUTH MOVEMENTS.)

BENE BERAK (also spelled BNAI BRAK)   A town about five miles northeast of Tel Aviv. It has a number of yeshivot (schools for religious studies) that draw students and scholars from all over the world. Modern Bene Berak was founded in 1924 by religious Jews from Poland. In the second century C.E. Bene Berak was the home of Rabbi Akiva's school. (See also AKIVA BEN JOSEPH; YESHIVA.)

BENE BERIT   Israeli moshav (farming village) founded in south Galilee in 1937. The land for the settlement was bought with money raised by the B'nai B'rith in the United States. (See also B'NAI B'RITH; MOSHAV; GALILEE.)

BENE BINYAMIN   An organization of farmers active in Palestine from 1921 to 1939. The Bene Binyamin founded the city of Netanya. (See also NETANYA.)

BENE DAROM   Israeli moshav (farming village) founded in 1949. The name means "sons of Darom" and it was settled by members of the Kephar Darom moshav who had to abandon their original settlement in 1948 during the War of Independence. (See also MOSHAV; WAR OF INDEPENDENCE.)

BENE ISRAEL   Jews of India. The Bene Israel claim as their ancestors eight Jewish families who fled persecution in Palestine in the second century B.C.E. and were shipwrecked near Bombay in India. In the 1700s a Jewish agent of the Dutch East India Company found them practicing a primitive form of Judaism and taught them about the Bible. Most of the Bene Israel immigrated to Israel after 1948. Although they were welcomed into the country, some Israelis questioned whether they were really Jews.

BENJAMIN   The youngest son of Jacob and his wife Rachel. Benjamin was the ancestor of the tribe of Benjamin, one of the Twelve Tribes of ancient Israel. When the Israelites occupied Canaan, the tribe of Benjamin settled the land between Ephraim and Judah. This land, which included Jerusalem, was finally divided between the kingdoms of Israel and Judah after the two countries had fought over it for many years. (See also CANAAN; ISRAEL, KINGDOM OF; JACOB; JUDAH, KINGDOM OF; TWELVE TRIBES.)

BENTOV, MORDEKHAI (name changed from GUTTGILD) (1900-   )   Polish-born labor leader who settled in Palestine in 1920. He was a Mapam Party member of the Israeli Knesset (legislature) and served as Minister of Development and Minister of Housing. Bentov was also the founder and editor of Mapam's daily newspaper, *Al Ha-Mishmar.* (See also KNESSET; MAPAM.)

BERGMAN, SAMUEL HUGO (1883-1975)   Czechoslovakian-born Zionist who settled in Palestine in 1920. He taught philosophy at the Hebrew University in Jerusalem and was the Director of the National and University Library. (See also HEBREW UNIVERSITY; NATIONAL AND UNIVERSITY LIBRARY.)

BERGMANN, ERNST DAVID (1900-1975)   Chemist who settled in Palestine in 1934 and became the Director of the Weizmann Institute of Science. (See also WEIZMANN INSTITUTE OF SCIENCE.)

BERIT IVRIT OLAMIT   World Hebrew Union. Organization founded in Berlin in 1931 and now based in Jerusalem. Its aim is to spread Hebrew language and culture. (See also HEBREW.)

BERIT SHALOM Jewish organization active in Palestine from 1926 to 1940. Under the leadership of Rabbi Magnes, Berit Shalom worked for peace between Arabs and Jews. It had a plan for a combined Arab-Jewish nation in Palestine. The organization's work was later taken over by Ihud. (See also BI-NATIONALISM; IHUD; MAGNUS, JUDAH LEON.)

BERIT TRUMPELDOR see BETAR

BERKOVITZ, YITZHAK DOV (1885-1967) Russian-born Hebrew writer who lived in the United States for 14 years before settling in Palestine in 1928. His stories, novels, and plays are about Jewish life in Europe and Jewish immigrants in the United States and Palestine. Besides writing novels such as *Menahem Mendel in Palestine,* Berkovitz translated the stories of his famous father-in-law, Sholem Aleichem, into Hebrew.

BERKOWITZ, HAZEL GREENWALD (1894-1977) American Hadassah (Women's Zionist organization) leader and photographer. Besides taking her own award-winning photographs of Israel, Hazel Berkowitz devoted herself to organizing the more than a quarter of a million pictures in Hadassah's pictorial library. This is the largest collection of photographs of Israel in the world. (See also HADASSAH.)

BERNADOTTE, FOLKE (1895-1948) Swedish diplomat and humanitarian who saw the Red Cross and the Scout movement as ways of building understanding between countries. In 1948 the United Nations appointed Count Bernadotte peacemaker between the warring Jews and Arabs in Palestine. Bernadotte arranged a truce and drew up a plan for peace. His peace plan would have given much Israeli land, including Jerusalem, to the Arabs. He was killed in Jerusalem by Jewish terrorists, and his plan died with him. Ralph Bunche took Bernadotte's place as peacemaker. (See also BUNCHE, RALPH; SCOUTING; UNITED NATIONS; WAR OF INDEPENDENCE.)

BERNSTEIN, LEONARD (1918-   ) American conductor and composer. Has conducted the Israel Philharmonic Orchestra in Israel and in the United States. (See also ISRAEL PHILHARMONIC ORCHESTRA.

BERNSTEIN, PERETZ (1890-1971) Zionist leader who was president of the Dutch Zionist organization before he settled in Palestine in 1936. Bernstein was a member of the Israeli Knesset (legislature) and served as Minister of Commerce and Industry. He was also the editor of the Tel Aviv daily newspaper *Ha-Boker.* (See also KNESSET; ZIONISM.)

BERNSTEIN-COHEN, MIRIAM (1895-   ) Actress and writer

who was born in Russia and brought to Israel at the age of 12 by her Zionist parents. She returned to Russia for several years to study medicine and to appear on the Russian stage before she settled permanently in Israel in 1921. During her long career as an actress, Miriam Bernstein-Cohen acted with the Habimah, Cameri, and a number of other theater groups. She has also written novels, short stories, and plays, and has translated Russian and English books into Hebrew. In 1975 she was awarded the Israel Prize. (See also CAMERI; HABIMAH; ISRAEL PRIZE.)

BERTINI, GARY (1927-   )   Russian-born conductor and composer who has led orchestras in Israel, the United States, France, Germany and other countries. Bertini is the main conductor of the Jerusalem Symphony Orchestra and the founder of the Israel Chamber Orchestra. He has written symphonies and ballet music as well as background music for plays and films. In 1978 he won the Israel Prize. (See also ISRAEL CHAMBER ORCHESTRA; ISRAEL PRIZE; MUSIC.)

BERTINORO, OBADIAH OF (also called YARE OF BERTINORO) (about 1450-1510)   Born in Italy, he traveled to Palestine in 1485 and founded a yeshiva (religious school) in Jerusalem. Although his descriptions of Palestine at that time are still remembered, Bertinoro is best known for his religious commentaries on the Talmud. (See also TALMUD; YESHIVA.)

BERUR HAYIL (also called BEN ZAKKAI)   Israeli farming settlement south of Tel Aviv founded in 1948. Oil was discovered nearby in 1957. The modern settlement is on the site of ancient Berur (also called Beror) where Rabbi Johanan Ben Zakkai had his school in the first century C.E. (See also JOHANAN BEN ZAKKAI; OIL.)

BET ALPHA (also spelled BEIT ALFA)   Israeli kibbutz founded in the Jezreel Valley in 1922. Near the kibbutz, archaeologists have uncovered a synagogue built in the sixth century C.E. The synagogue was restored by the Israeli government in 1960. It contains the most beautiful and complete mosaic floor in Israel. The floor pictures Abraham's sacrifice of Isaac, the four seasons, and the signs of the Zodiac. (See also ABRAHAM; ARCHAEOLOGY; JEZREEL VALLEY; KIBBUTZ; MOSAIC.)

BET ARABA (also spelled BETH HA-ARABAH)   Israeli kibbutz in the Araba Valley where vegetables were grown in spite of the large amount of salt in the soil. The settlement was destroyed by the Arabs during the 1948 War of Independence and the settlers later founded Kibbutz Gesher Haziz. (See also ARABA; GESHER HAZIZ; KIBBUTZ; WAR OF INDEPENDENCE.)

BET DAGAN (also spelled BEIT DAGON)   An ancient Philistine town named for their god, Dagon. Today it is a village three miles southeast of Tel Aviv. Most of the people living in Bet Dagan work in Tel Aviv. (See also PHILISTINES; TEL AVIV.)

BET EMEK (also spelled BETH HA-EMEK)   Israeli kibbutz founded northeast of Acre in 1949. (See also KIBBUTZ.)

The remains of a Roman theater in Bet Shean, in the northern part of Israel.

BET GUVRIN (also spelled BEIT GUVRIN)   Ancient town built in the Judean Hills in the first century B.C.E. It became a Roman town (named Eleutheropolis) in the first centuries of the Common Era, and several leading Jewish rabbis lived there. The town was rebuilt by the Crusaders in the twelfth century C.E. Today it is the site of an Israeli moshav (farming village). (See also CRUSADES; HISTORY; JUDEAN HILLS; MOSHAV; ROME.)

BET HATEFUTSOT   see JEWISH DIASPORA MUSEUM.

BET HORON (also spelled BEIT HORON)   Two ancient towns about 10 miles northwest of Jerusalem that have been the scene of many battles throughout the centuries. Judah the Maccabee defeated the Syrian army there in 166 B.C.E. (See also JUDAH THE MACCABEE.)

BET NETOPHA VALLEY (also spelled BEIT NETOFA)   Valley in lower Galilee behind the Nazareth hills. Part of the valley is a reservoir holding water being pumped from the Jordan River through the National Water Carrier to the dry Negev Desert. (See also NATIONAL WATER CARRIER; GALILEE; JORDAN RIVER; NEGEV; WATER.)

BET SHEAN (also spelled BETH SHAN; also called BEISAN) Ancient town where archaeologists have uncovered 18 different levels of occupation covering about 5,000 years. The town was occupied at different times by the Egyptians, Greeks, Jews, Romans, and Arabs. It was here that the Philistines fastened the body of King Saul to the wall after he was killed on nearby Mount Gilboa. Today tourists visiting Bet Shean can see Egyptian stelea (carved stone slabs), a Roman theater that seated 5,000 people, and a synagogue with a mosaic floor. (See also ARCHAEOLOGY; EGYPT; HISTORY; MOSAICS; MOUNT GILBOA; PHILISTINES; ROME; SAUL.)

BET SHEAN VALLEY   Valley in Israel near the Jordan border. The land is 850 feet below sea level near the Jordan River. The soil of the valley is fertile, but irrigation from the many springs in the area is needed to grow crops. The land in the Bet Shean Valley was bought from the Arabs in 1930 by the Jewish National Fund and settled by Jews in the late 1930s. (See also AGRICULTURE; IRRIGATION; JEWISH NATIONAL FUND.)

BET SHEARIM (also spelled BEIT SHE'ARIM)   Ancient city 12 miles from modern Haifa. It was built in the second century B.C.E. and destroyed in the fourth century C.E. In 170 C.E., Rabbi Judah Hanasi moved the Sanhedrin (Supreme Court) to Bet Shearim and the city became an important religious center. Rabbi Judah is said to be buried in the catacombs (underground tombs cut into the mountain) of Bet Shearim. Archaeologists have unearthed the catacombs, a large synagogue, and a number of other buildings. A moshav (farming village) of the same name, founded in 1936, is nearby. (See also ARCHAEOLOGY; CATACOMBS; JUDAH HANASI; SANHEDRIN.)

BET SHEMESH (also spelled BEIT SHEMESH) A town near Jerusalem that was important in biblical times. The biblical stories about Samson take place here, and the large cement factory in the modern town of Bet Shemesh is named for Samson. Archaeologists have uncovered the remains of the ancient city walls. (See also ARCHAEOLOGY.)

BET YERAH (also spelled BEIT YERAH) Ancient Canaanite city on the south shore of Lake Kinneret (Sea of Galilee). Archaeologists have found remains of people who lived at Bet Yerah more than 5,000 years ago. They have also uncovered a large synagogue from the fifth century C.E. containing a mosaic floor. Today there is an agricultural school at Bet Yerah. (See also AGRICULTURAL SCHOOLS; ARCHAEOLOGY; CANAAN; LAKE KINNERET; MOSAICS.)

BETAR (also spelled BETHAR) Ancient town five miles from Jerusalem. Betar is famous as the site of Bar Kokhba's last battle in the second Jewish revolt against Rome and his death in 135 C.E. (See also BAR KOKHBA, SIMEON; HISTORY; ROME.)

BETAR (also called the JOSEPH TRUMPELDOR LEAGUE) A nationalist youth movement established in 1923 and now associated with the adult Herut political party. Betar believes in Zionism without Socialism and in the value of discipline. Its members have founded several settlements in Israel. Betar is based in Israel where it has about 8,000 members (1975), but there are branches in America, Europe, and Australia. The Betar National Sports Organization takes part in soccer, basketball, and track-and-field events. (See also HERUT; SOCIALISM; SPORTS; TRUMPELDOR, JOSEPH; YOUTH MOVEMENTS; ZIONISM.)

BETHEL Ancient town ten miles north of Jerusalem that is mainly remembered as the biblical site of Jacob's dream (Genesis 28:10-12). It was here that God promised Jacob that the land he rested upon would be given to him and his descendants. Jacob then changed the name of the place from Luz to Bethel, which means "home of God." Archaeologists have uncovered the ruins of ancient Bethel. (See also ARCHAEOLOGY; JACOB.)

BETHLEHEM Ancient town about five miles south of Jerusalem. King David was born in Bethlehem and it is the scene of much of the biblical Book of Ruth. The town is holy to Christians as the place of birth of Jesus Christ. The Church of the Nativity was built over Christ's birthplace by the Roman emperor Constantine in 330 C.E. and has been rebuilt several times since then. Nearby is the Milk Grotto where Mary nursed the baby Jesus. Tourists can also see the Field of the Shepherd, where

Modern Bethlehem

the shepherds lay watching the first Christmas, and the Field of Ruth, where Ruth met Boaz. The Tomb of Rachel is at the entrance to the town.

When the boundaries of Israel were drawn in 1948, the town of Bethlehem became part of the country of Jordan. During the 1967 Six-Day War, Bethlehem was occupied by Israel and officially became an administered area. (See also ADMINISTERED AREAS; CHURCH OF THE NATIVITY; DAVID; JESUS; JORDAN; RACHEL, TOMB OF; SIX-DAY WAR; TOURISM.)

BETHLEHEM STAR   A flower with yellow petals that grows in the hills of Israel and blooms early in the winter.

BEVIN, ERNEST (1881-1951)   British politician. Bevin became the British Foreign Minister in 1945 while Britain still ruled Palestine under the Mandate. He continued the White Paper policy of restricting Jewish immigration into Palestine. When the Haganah and Irgun smuggled refugees into Palestine and attacked British troops, Bevin sponsored a plan to divide Palestine into Arab, Jewish, and British controlled sections. Finally he referred the Palestine problem to the United Nations. (See also

GREAT BRITAIN; HAGANAH; IRGUN; MANDATE; PARTITION; WHITE PAPER; UNITED NATIONS.)

BEZALEL MUSEUM   One of Israel's leading museums, located in Jerusalem. It was founded by Boris Schatz in 1906 as part of the Bezalel School of Arts and Crafts. The Bezalel Museum has a large collection of ancient and modern Jewish art, manuscripts, jewelry, and religious objects. In 1965 it became part of the Israel Museum in Jerusalem. (See also BEZALEL SCHOOL OF ARTS AND CRAFTS; ISRAEL MUSEUM; SCHATZ, BORIS.)

BEZALEL SCHOOL OF ARTS AND CRAFTS   School founded in 1906 in Jerusalem by the artist Boris Schatz. The school's aim was to create a national Jewish style of art based on traditional Jewish handicrafts. In 1969 the school's name was changed to the Bezalel Academy of Arts and Design. The academy gives four-year courses in fine arts, design, gold and silver making, and ceramics (pottery). Students wishing to attend the school must show talent in one of these fields on their entrance tests. (See also ART; SCHATZ, BORIS.)

BIALIK, HAYIM NAHMAN (1873-1934)   The greatest Hebrew poet of modern times. Bialik has been called the "poet of his people" and the "poet of the Hebrew Renaissance."

He was born in the Ukraine in Russia. His father died when he was seven years old, and the boy grew up in great poverty. Both the poverty of his childhood and his early love of nature are reflected in his poems. His first poem was published when he was 18 years old.

Bialik's poem "In the City of Slaughter" was written about the 1903 Kishineff pogrom (murder of Jews) and brought him fame. It also inspired many young European Jews to organize for self-defense and to emigrate to Palestine.

Bialik was important in reviving Hebrew as a spoken language and as a language of literature. He was the founder of the Devir publishing house, which still prints Hebrew books in Tel Aviv today.

In 1924 Bialik moved to Tel Aviv. There he created the Oneg Shabbat, a gathering held late Saturday afternoon for a lecture or a cultural event. His home in Tel Aviv is now a museum.

Besides writing poems, adult stories, and children's stories, Bialik edited a number of anthologies and translated Shakespeare and other great writers into Hebrew. The Bialik Prize for literature, the highest prize Israel can give a writer, is named in his honor. (See also BIALIK FOUNDATION; DEVIR; HEBREW; ONEG SHABBAT.)

BIALIK FOUNDATION (Hebrew, MOSAD BIALIK)   Jerusalem

publishing company named in honor of the poet Hayim Bialik. Its purpose is to encourage Hebrew writers to publish Hebrew books and to advance the Hebrew language. Besides having published over 600 different books, the Bialik Foundation has published a seven-volume *Hebrew Biblical Encyclopedia*. (See also BIALIK, HAYIM NAHMAN; HEBREW.)

A 1948 street scene in Camp Bejt Bialik near Salzburg, Austria. Bustling with refugees awaiting emigration to Palestine, this former Nazi concentration camp was renamed in Honor of Hayim Nahman Bialik, the famous Hebrew poet.

BIALIK PRIZE   Prize given each year by the City of Tel Aviv for achievement in literature. It was named in honor of Hayim Nahman Bialik, the famous Hebrew poet. The Bialik Prize is one of the highest honors an Israeli writer or poet can receive. Among the winners of the Bialik Prize was Shemuel Agnon, who also won the Nobel Prize for literature. (See also AGNON, SHEMUEL YOSEPH; BIALIK, HAYIM NAHMAN; PRIZES; LITERATURE; TEL AVIV.)

BIBLE   The sacred book of the Jewish and Christian religions. The Bible is made up of the Old Testament and the New Testament. Jews revere only the Old Testament, while Christians revere both.

The Old Testament is divided into three sections: Torah, Prophets, and Holy Writings. The first section, the Torah, is also called the Pentateuch or the Five Books of Moses. It states the laws that govern Jewish religious life. The Prophets contain 21 books which are divided into Early Prophets and Later Prophets. The 13 books of the Holy Writings are also called Hagiographa.

School children in Israel use the Bible to study the ancient history of their country. The Book of Genesis tells of God promising Abraham that the land of Israel (then called Canaan) would belong to him and his descendants. The next four books tell the story of Moses, who led the Israelites out of Egypt where they had been slaves. He gave them the Ten Commandments which became the foundation of the Jewish religion. The Book of Joshua (which begins the Prophets) describes the Israelites conquering the land of Canaan, and the Book of Judges tells how the Twelve Tribes of Israel were ruled when they settled in the Promised Land. The Books of Samuel and Kings tell of the Jewish kingdom under Saul, David, and Solomon, and its splitting into the kingdoms of Judah and Israel. This section of the Bible ends with the destruction of the Temple in Jerusalem and the Jewish exile in Babylon. The return to Israel is found in the Books of Ezra and Nehemiah, in the final section of the Bible. (See also ABRAHAM; BABYLONIAN EXILE; BIBLE STUDY; DAVID; EZRA; HISTORY; ISRAEL, KINGDOM OF; JESUS; JUDAH, KINGDOM OF; JUDGES; MOSES; NEHEMIAH; SAUL; SOLOMON; TEMPLE; TEN COMMANDMENTS; TORAH; TWELVE TRIBES.)

BIBLE STUDY   All Jewish children in Israel study the Bible as soon as they can read. Bible study is an important subject in both public schools and religious schools, taking up from 20 to 30 percent of a pupil's school time. School children learn Jewish history and culture from the Bible and are often taken on visits to historic places that were important in biblical times. High school students must pass a Bible test in order to graduate.

Jerusalem is a world center for scholarly Bible study and

research. The Hebrew University, the Rabbi Kook Institute, and the Pontifical Bible Institute—all in Jerusalem—are important in biblical research, as is Bar-Ilan University in Ramat Gan. The Israel Society for Biblical Research gives lectures throughout the country and publishes books and articles about the Bible. (See also BAR-ILAN UNIVERSITY; BIBLE; EDUCATION; HEBREW UNIVERSITY.)

Happy faces of Jerusalemites waiting for the gates of the Biblical Zoo to open.

BIBLICAL ZOO   Zoo founded in Jerusalem in 1939 by zoologist Aharon Shulov. It contains a complete collection of the 120 different animals, birds, and reptiles mentioned in the Bible. A sign on each animal's cage tells the animal's name, its native habitat, and where it is mentioned in the Bible.

BIKEL, THEODORE (1924-)   Actor and folk singer who was born in Austria, went to Israel as a young teenager, and acted with the Habimah Theater. Bikel has sung Jewish and Israeli folk songs in concerts all over the world. He now lives in the United States. (See also HABIMAH.)

BILLY ROSE SCULPTURE GARDEN   Part of the Israel Museum, in Jerusalem, where modern sculpture is displayed on outdoor terraces. The garden is named for American theater producer Billy Rose, who contributed money for it. (See also ISRAEL MUSEUM.)

Ruti Adania, zoo keeper at the Biblical Zoo in Jerusalem.

BILTMORE PROGRAM   Statement issued by the 1942 Zionist Conference held in New York's Biltmore Hotel. The Biltmore Program condemned the 1939 British White Paper (which limited Jewish immigration into Palestine) and called for the establishment of a Jewish State in Palestine. David Ben-Gurion was responsible for calling the Conference adopting the Biltmore Program. (See also BEN-GURION, DAVID; WHITE PAPER; WORLD ZIONIST ORGANIZATION; ZIONISM.)

BILU   A Zionist agricultural pioneering movement founded in

Kharkov, Russia, in 1882 by Jewish students. The name BILU comes from the initials of the Hebrew words meaning "House of Jacob, come, let us go!" BILU pioneers settling in Palestine made up the First Aliyah (wave of immigration). Although some of the young immigrants went to Jerusalem, others struggled to set up agricultural settlements. Some joined earlier settlers at Petah Tikva, while others founded new settlements at Rishon Le Zion and Gedera. (See also ALIYAH; GEDERA; PETAH TIKVA; RISHON LE ZION; ZIONISM.)

BI-NATIONALISM   Idea of setting up a joint Arab-Jewish State in Palestine as a way of solving the problems between the two peoples. Bi-nationalism was suggested by Rabbi Judah Magnes and the Berit Shalom society, but no Arabs and too few Jews supported the idea. (See also BERIT SHALOM, MAGNES, JUDAH LEON.)

BINYAMINAH   Village on the fertile Sharon plain founded in 1922 by the Palestine Jewish Colonization Association (PICA). Citrus fruits are the main crop grown at Binyaminah. (See also CITRUS; PALESTINE JEWISH COLONIZATION ASSOCIATION.)

BIRDS   About 100 species of birds live in Israel and another 250 species pass through the country during their yearly migration. The birds most commonly found in Israel are sparrows, larks, jays, doves, and swifts. Vultures are often seen near garbage dumps and eagles nest in the higher hills. (See also ANIMALS; INSECTS; REPTILES.)

BLOVSTEIN, RACHEL (1890-1931)   Hebrew poet who used the pen name of Rachel and is known as the poet of the Second Aliyah (wave of immigration into Palestine). She was born in Russia and went to Palestine as an agricultural pioneer in 1909. Many of her poems, including the best-known *Perhaps,* are about the land of Palestine and its pioneers. (See also ALIYAH.)

BLUM, LUDWIG (1891-1974)   Czechoslovakian-born painter who went to Palestine in 1923. Blum is known for his portraits.

BLUM, YEHUDA (1931-   )   Lawyer who was born in Czechoslovakia and went to Israel as a teenager. Blum is an expert on international law and has written books and articles on the subject. He is Israel's current (1980) ambassador to the United Nations. (See also UNITED NATIONS.)

BLUMENFELD, KURT YEHUDA (1884-1963)   Zionist leader who was President of the German Zionist Organization before he settled in Palestine in 1933. He worked with Keren Hayesod, the money-raising arm of the World Zionist Organization. (See also KEREN HAYESOD; WORLD ZIONIST ORGANIZATION; ZIONISM.)

B'NAI B'RITH   The name means People of the Covenant. A Jewish service organization with a half million members in 40 countries. The B'nai B'rith in Israel was founded in 1888 and had five thousand members in 1978. The organization works for Jewish rights throughout the world. (See COVENANT.)

BODENHEIMER, MAX ISADOR (1865-1940)   German-born Zionist leader who helped write the Basle Program (the basic program of Zionism) in 1897. Bodenheimer was an organizer of the Jewish National Fund and was its director for several years. He settled in Jerusalem in 1935. (See also BASLE PROGRAM; JEWISH NATIONAL FUND; ZIONISM.)

BODENHEIMER, SHIMON (1897-1959)   Zoologist who settled in Palestine in 1922. He taught at the Hebrew University in Jerusalem and was a director of the Agricultural Experimental Station at Rehovot. (See also AGRICULTURAL RESEARCH; HEBREW UNIVERSITY; VOLCANI INSTITUTE FOR AGRICULTURAL RESEARCH.)

BOOK FAIR   see JERUSALEM INTERNATIONAL BOOK FAIR

BOOK PUBLISHING   There are more than 150 publishers, 900 printers, and 300 booksellers in Israel. Most of the booksellers specialize in imported books. Every two years an international book fair is held in Jerusalem. (See also JERUSALEM INTERNATIONAL BOOK FAIR.)

BOOKS   The average Israeli reads ten books a year—more than the citizens of almost any other country of the world. About twelve million books are printed in Israel each year, and many more are imported from other countries. There are 750 public libraries, including libraries-on-wheels that travel to small communities. Hebrew Book Week is celebrated throughout the country each spring and an international book fair is held in Jerusalem every other year. (See also BOOK PUBLISHING; LITERATURE; JERUSALEM INTERNATIONAL BOOK FAIR.)

BOXING   The sport of boxing has become more popular in Israel since a number of fighters from the Soviet Union settled in the country in the 1970s. All boxing in Israel is amateur. Most boxing matches within the country are run by the Betar and Maccabi sports organizations. Israeli fighters have competed in international boxing matches. (See also BETAR; MACCABI; SPORTS.)

BOYS' TOWN   High school in Jerusalem founded in 1953 and supported by money raised by an American committee. Boys' Town provides academic, vocational, and religious training for

Jerusalem is a city with many bookstores. This popular bookstore is on the Via Dolorosa, in the Christian Quarter of the Old City.

teenage boys from all over Israel. In 1964 the school received an award for excellence from the government's Ministry of Education and Culture. (See also EDUCATION.)

BRANDEIS, LOUIS DEMBITZ (1856-1941)   Justice of the United States Supreme Court whose liberal legal decisions supported the interests of the American people against the demands of big business. Brandeis was president of the Zionist Organization of America and helped convince President Wilson to support the 1917 Balfour Declaration favoring a Jewish state in Palestine. He was also president of the World Zionist Organization but resigned his post after differences with Chaim Weizmann. Brandeis helped establish the Palestine Economic Corporation, and the Palestine Endowment Fund, two organizations devoted to building Palestine's economy. (See also BALFOUR DECLARATION; PALESTINE ECONOMIC CORPORATION; WEIZMANN, CHAIM; WORLD ZIONIST ORGANIZATION; ZIONISM.)

BRENNER, YOSEPH HAYIM (1881-1921)   Hebrew writer who

was born in the Russian Ukraine, where he had his first novels published. Brenner settled in Palestine in 1909, became a leader of the worker's movement, and was the editor of a Socialist journal while continuing to write fiction. His stories give a realistic picture of the Palestine of his day. His novel *Breakdown and Bereavement* was published one year before he was killed by Arabs near Jaffa.

BREUER, ISAAC (1883-1946)   German-born Orthodox rabbi who settled in Palestine in 1936. He was one of the founders of Agudat Israel, the world organization of Orthodox Jews. (See also AGUDAT ISRAEL.)

BRITAIN   see GREAT BRITAIN

BROADCASTING   Radio broadcasting in Israel began in 1936 when the British (then governing Palestine under the Mandate) established the Palestine Broadcasting Service. In 1948 Kol Israel, the Israeli radio system, took over and broadcast its first program—a reading of the Israeli Declaration of Independence. Today Kol Israel has five radio stations. Television did not come to Israel until 1968, and there is still only one channel. (See also KOL ISRAEL; TELEVISION.)

BROD, MAX (1884-1968)   Czechoslovakian-born writer who was famous in Germany before he settled in Palestine in 1939. Brod has written novels, books about religion, and a history of the Israeli War of Independence. He has also written music and was a director of the Habimah Theater Company in Tel Aviv. (See also HABIMAH.)

BRODETSKY, SELIG (1888-1954)   Zionist leader and mathematician born in Russia and educated in England. He was a leader of the World Zionist Organization and of the Jewish Agency. In 1949 Brodetsky went to Jerusalem to be president of the Hebrew University, but returned to England three years later. (See also HEBREW UNIVERSITY; JEWISH AGENCY; WORLD ZIONIST ORGANIZATION; ZIONISM.)

BRONZE AGE   The name used by archaeologists for a period in history during which people used bronze for tools and weapons. Tools of bronze, an alloy of copper and tin, were stronger and better than the copper tools previously used. The Bronze Age began about 3500 B.C.E. (See also ARCHAEOLOGY; IRON AGE.)

BUBER, MARTIN (1878-1965)   Religious philosopher whose ideas have influenced Christian as well as Jewish thought. In his books *I and Thou* and *Between Man and Man,* Buber spoke of religious faith as a dialogue (conversation) between man and

Martin Buber

God. He saw the Bible as a record of the dialogue between God and Israel.

Buber was born in Vienna, studied in Austria and Germany, and taught at the University of Frankfurt. He was an active Zionist with a strong interest in building a Jewish culture. Buber saw Zionism as a "holy way" for the Jewish people, rather than just a movement to establish a new country. In 1938 he settled in Palestine and became active in Ihud, an organization that worked for cooperation between Jews and Arabs. He was professor of religion at the Hebrew University in Jerusalem and was the first president of the Israel Academy of Science and Humanities. (See also BIBLE; HEBREW UNIVERSITY; IHUD; ISRAEL ACADEMY OF SCIENCES AND HUMANITIES; ZIONISM.)

BUDKO, YOSEPH (1888-1940)   Polish-born artist who lived in Berlin before settling in Jerusalem in 1933. The subjects of Budko's paintings and book illustrations were scenes of Jewish life in Eastern Europe and Palestine. He was the director of the Bezalel School of Arts and Crafts. (See also BEZALEL SCHOOL OF ARTS AND CRAFTS.)

BUNCHE, RALPH JOHNSON (1904-1971)   American diplomat. He served on the United Nations Palestine Commission and became its chief peacemaker after Count Bernadotte was assassinated. Bunche succeeded in arranging a settlement that ended the Arab-Jewish fighting of the 1947-1949 War of Independence. He won the Nobel Peace Prize for his work. (See also BERNADOTTE, FOLKE; UNITED NATIONS; WAR OF INDEPENDENCE.)

BURG, YOSEPH (1909-   )   German-born politician who settled in Palestine in 1939. He was a member of the Israeli Knesset (legislature) and served as Deputy Speaker, Minister of Health, and Minister of Social Welfare. (See also KNESSET.)

BURLA, YEHUDA (1886-1969)   Native Israeli writer whose novels deal with Sephardic and Oriental Jewish life in Palestine. He combined folk tales and realism in his books. (See also ORIENTAL JEWS; SEPHARDIM.)

BYZANTINE EMPIRE (also called BYZANTIUM)   By 400 C.E. the Roman Empire had broken into two parts. The eastern part, ruled from Constantinople, became the Byzantine Empire. At the height of its greatness, in the 500s C.E., the Byzantine Empire stretched from Arabia through Asia Minor, the Balkans, southern Italy and Spain, and also included Egypt and most of northern Africa. Over the next 900 years, the empire lost piece after piece of its territory to a series of invaders. Its end came when the Turks captured the capitol of Constantinople in 1453.

Palestine was part of the Byzantine Empire from the time it split off from the Roman Empire until 637 C.E. Many examples of Byzantine art and architecture have been found by archaeologists in Israel. (See also ARCHAEOLOGY; HISTORY; MOSAICS; ROME.)

C

CABALA see KABBALAH

CABINET The Israeli Basic Law of Government provides for a Cabinet (sometimes called the Government) made up of a Prime Minister and an unnamed number of other Ministers. The Cabinet is an arm of the Knesset (legislature) and is its main policymaking body. The Cabinet is responsible to the Knesset. It takes office on a vote of confidence from the Knesset and remains in power until the Knesset gives it a vote of no-confidence or until the Prime Minister resigns. Cabinet Ministers are usually members of the Knesset, but not always.

After an election, Israel's President appoints a member of the Knesset to form a new Cabinet. The person chosen is usually the leader of the party that received the most votes in the election. He or she becomes the Prime Minister and head of the Cabinet and chooses the other Ministers from a coalition of political parties. A large proportion of the Ministers chosen belong to the Prime Minister's party.

The first Cabinet had 17 Ministers. In 1974 there were 21 members of the Cabinet, including the Prime Minister, and the Ministers of Foreign Affairs, Agriculture, Commerce, Communications, Defense, Education and Culture, Finance, Health, Housing, Immigrant Absorption, Information, Interior, Justice, Labor, Religious Affairs, Social Welfare, Tourism, and Transport. (See also BASIC LAWS; GOVERNMENT; KNESSET; POLITICAL PARTIES; PRESIDENT; PRIME MINISTER.)

CAESAREA Ancient city founded by Herod the Great in 22 B.C.E. on the Mediterranean Sea coast between modern Haifa and Tel Aviv. Caesarea was the Roman capitol of Palestine and was its largest city for the first five hundred years of the Common Era. The 66 C.E. Jewish revolt against the Romans began here, and in 135 C.E. Rabbi Akiva was executed here during the Bar Kokhba revolt. Caesarea is also mentioned in the New Testament in connection with Saint Peter and Saint Paul. The city fell to the Arabs in 640 C.E., was a Crusader stronghold in the 1100s, and was destroyed by the Moslems in 1291.

Today Caesarea is an important tourist center. Archaeologists

Music lovers seated in an old reconstructed Roman amphitheater in Caesaria, overlooking excavated portions of this ancient Roman city.

have uncovered a Roman theater that is now used for outdoor concerts. In addition, tourists can visit a Roman aqueduct that brought water to the city, a Roman racetrack, a 1,400-year-old Byzantine mosaic floor, and the ruins of a Crusader cathedral and an ancient Jewish synagogue. (See also AKIVA BEN JOSEPH; ARABS; ARCHAEOLOGY; BAR KOKHBA, SIMEON; CRUSADES; HEROD I; HISTORY; MOSAICS; ROME; TOURISM.)

CAFTAN Tunic or ankle-length gown with long hanging sleeves that can be worn by a man or a woman. It is usually made of cotton and may be tied at the waist. The caftan is common in the Near East and North Africa and is worn by many Oriental Jews in Israel. (See also ORIENTAL JEWS.)

CAHAN, YAAKOV (also spelled COHEN) (1889-1960) Russian-born Hebrew poet who settled in Palestine in 1934. Cahan was active in the Bialik Foundation and the Hebrew Language Academy. He wrote epic poems and ballads as well as plays, novels, and folk tales. He is considered one of the most important modern Hebrew poets and twice won the Israel Prize for literature. (See also BIALIK FOUNDATION; HEBREW LANGUAGE ACADEMY; ISRAEL PRIZE; LITERATURE.)

CALENDAR, INTERNATIONAL   (also called GREGORIAN CALENDAR) The 365-day solar calendar used in the United States and most of the rest of the world. The international calendar is used in Israel, except for religious purposes. In some schools in Israel, teachers post the date each day of both the international and the Jewish calendar. (See also CALENDAR, JEWISH.)

CALENDAR, JEWISH   The calendar used for religious purposes and for setting holidays in Israel. The Jewish calendar is both lunar and solar. It is made up of 12 lunar months of 29 or 30 days each. Since these only total 353 or 354 days—about 11 days less than a solar year—an extra month (called second Adar) is added every third, sixth, eighth, and eleventh, fourteenth, seventeenth, and nineteenth year.

Each month of the Jewish calendar begins with the appearance of the new moon. The religious new year begins with the month of Tishri, although the first month, as mentioned in the Bible, is Nisan. The chart below shows the relationship between the Jewish calendar and the international calendar.

Jewish Month	Number of Days	International Months
Nisan	30	March-April
Iyyar	29	April-May
Sivan	30	May-June
Tammuz	29	June-July
Av	30	July-August
Elul	29	August-September
Tishri	30	September-October
Heshvan	29 or 30	October-November
Kislev	29 or 30	November-December
Tevet	29	December-January
Shevat	30	January-February
Adar	29 or 30	February-March

Adar Sheni (Second Adar) is added in leap years.

(See also CALENDAR, INTERNATIONAL; HOLIDAYS.)

CALENDAR, JULIAN   Old calendar still used by some Eastern Orthodox churches. Religious holidays set by the Julian calendar come 13 days later than the same holidays on the international (Gregorian) calendar. (See also CALENDAR, INTERNATIONAL; HOLIDAYS.)

CALENDAR, MOSLEM   The Moslem calendar is made up of twelve lunar months. Unlike the Jewish calendar, the Moslem calendar does not add an extra month in leap years to catch up with the solar year. Therefore, Moslem holidays fall about twelve days earlier each year according to the international calendar. For example, the Moslem holy month of Ramadan began on July 26 in 1979 and July 14 in 1980. (See also CALENDAR, INTERNATIONAL; CALENDAR, JEWISH; HOLIDAYS; MOHAMMED; RAMADAN.)

CALVARY   see GOLGOTHA

CAMERI   Israeli acting troup whose home theater is in Tel Aviv. The Cameri produces Hebrew translations of foreign plays as well as original plays by Israeli writers. (See also THEATER.)

CAMP DAVID SUMMIT   Meeting in September 1978 between Prime Minister Menachem Begin of Israel and President Anwar Sadat of Egypt. It was arranged by President Jimmy Carter of the United States. The meeting at Camp David, in the United States, resulted in an outline of a peace treaty between Egypt and Israel. The treaty was supposed to be signed in December 1978, but it took President Carter's trip to the Middle East in March 1979 to bring about the final signing. On March 26, 1979, Begin and Sadat signed the Israel-Egypt Peace Treaty in Washington, D.C., the first such treaty between the Jewish State and an Arab Country. (See also BEGIN, MENACHEM; CARTER, JIMMY; EGYPT; ISRAEL-EGYPT PEACE TREATY; SADAT, ANWAR.)

CANA (also called KEFAR KANNA)   Village about five miles from Nazareth in Galilee. It is sacred to Christians as the place where Jesus performed the miracle of changing water into wine at the wedding feast (John 2:2). There are several churches in the town including the Franciscan church which is said to be built on the site of the miracle. The population of Cana is all Christian. (See also CHRISTIANS, ISRAELI; GALILEE; JESUS.)

CANAAN   The land God promised to Abraham and his descendants. The biblical land of Canaan stretched along the coast of Palestine on both sides of the Jordan River, taking in modern Israel and part of modern Jordan. The Israelites invaded Canaan in the thirteenth century B.C.E., conquered the Canaanites in a series of wars, and settled down on the land. The land that had once belonged to the small Canaanite city-states was divided among the Twelve Tribes of Israel. (See also ABRAHAM; TWELVE TRIBES; COVENANT.)

CAPERNAUM (also called KEPHAR NAHUM)   Ancient town on Lake Kinneret (Sea of Galilee). It was the headquarters of the Roman army in Palestine when Jesus preached in the town's

The entrance to Capernaum, (also spelled Capharnaum and Kefar Nahum) on the northern side of the Kinneret Sea (Sea of Galilee).

synagogue. Jews lived in Capernaum until the city was buried in an earthquake in the sixth century C.E. Archaeologists have dug up a beautiful synagogue built in the third century C.E. They have also found flour mills and a large oil press that show how such stone implements were made and used in biblical times. (See also ARCHAEOLOGY; HISTORY; JESUS; LAKE KINNERET; ROME.)

CARLEBACH, AZRIEL (1908-1956)   German journalist who settled in Palestine in 1936. He was the founder and editor of the newspaper *Maariv*. (See also MAARIV.)

CARMEL CAVES   Two caves south of Haifa where human bones between 40,000 and 70,000 years old have been found. Archaeologists have named the ancient inhabitants of these caves Homo Carmelensis and believe that they were halfway between Neanderthal and modern man. (See also ARCHAEOLOGY; MOUNT CARMEL.)

CARMEL, MOSHEH (1911-)   Polish-born soldier and politician who settled in Palestine in 1924. Carmel fought with the Haganah (Jewish underground army) and later rose to the rank of Brigadier-General in the Israeli army. He became a member of the Israeli Knesset (legislature) and served as Minister of Communications. (See also HAGANAH; KNESSET.)

CARMEL, MOUNT   see MOUNT CARMEL

CARMELITE MONASTERY   Home of the Carmelites, a Christian order of monks. The monastery is perched near the top of Mount Carmel. The original monastery, built in the 1200s, was destroyed by the Saracens. The present building is only about 200 years old. (See also MOUNT CARMEL.)

CARMIEL   A new town about 12 miles from Acre in lower Galilee. Carmiel was founded in 1964 as part of a plan for Jewish development of the area. (See also DEVELOPMENT TOWNS; GALILEE.)

CAROB   An evergreen tree with red flowers that is native to Palestine. The sweet pulp of the carob pod is used as a substitute for chocolate.

CARTER, JIMMY (full name, JAMES EARL CARTER, JR.) (1924-   )
Thirty-ninth President of the United States. Carter was governor of the state of Georgia before he was elected President in 1976. He acted as mediator (peacemaker) between Israel and Egypt and invited Prime Minister Menachem Begin and President Anwar Sadat to the Camp David Summit in the United States in 1978 to discuss a peace treaty between their two countries. Later, when the peace treaty seemed stalled, President Carter flew to the

Prime Minister Menachem Begin and President Jimmy Carter.

Middle East to speak to the Israeli and Egyptian leaders. On March 26, 1979, Menachem Begin and Anwar Sadat signed the Israel-Egypt Peace Treaty in Washington, D. C., and Jimmy Carter signed as a witness. (See also BEGIN, MENACHEM; CAMP DAVID SUMMIT; EGYPT; ISRAEL-EGYPT PEACE TREATY; SADAT, ANWAR.)

CASTEL, MOSHE (1909-)   Jerusalem-born painter known for his colorful illustrations of Jewish religious life.

CATACOMB   Underground cemetery made up of a series of passageways lined with tombs on either side. Although the Christian catacombs in Rome are the most famous, the first catacombs were probably built in Palestine. Archaeologists have discovered large catacombs at Bet Shearim with tombs dating from the second through the fourth century C.E. (See also ARCHAEOLOGY; BET SHEARIM.)

CAVE OF ELIJAH   Cave at the foot of Mount Carmel that is holy to Jews, Christians, and Moslems. Jews claim that the Prophet Elijah hid here from the anger of King Ahab. Christians call the cave the School of the Prophet because Elijah is said to have taught there. Moslems have made the cave an official mosque. (See also AHAB; ELIJAH; MOUNT CARMEL.)

CAVE OF LETTERS In 1960 Yigael Yadin led an archaeological search of the Judean Desert caves where Bar Kokhba's followers barricaded themselves at the end of the 135 C.E. revolt against Rome. In the Cave of Letters, Yadin found about 50 letters and other documents along with the skeletons of Jewish warriors who had starved to death rather than surrender to the Romans. Among the letters were 15 military dispatches from "Simeon Bar Kokhba, Prince over Israel." Several of the dispatches were signed by Bar Kokhba himself. (See also ARCHAEOLOGY; BAR KOKHBA, SIMEON; HISTORY; WADI HEVER; YADIN, YIGAEL.)

CAVE OF MACHPELAH see MACHPELAH, CAVE OF

CAVE OF THE PATRIARCHS see MACHPELAH, CAVE OF

C.E. Abbreviation used after dates to stand for Common Era. It is the same as A.D., the abbreviation for *Anno Domini,* Latin words meaning "in the year of our Lord."

CHAGALL, MARC (1887-) Russian-born painter who has lived and worked in Paris since 1922. Chagall is world famous for his gay, colorful, and fantastic paintings of Jewish life. He has also created beautiful stained-glass windows for a number of public buildings throughout the world. His windows in the Hadassah Medical Center synagogue in Jerusalem picture the Twelve Tribes of Israel. (See also HADASSAH; TWELVE TRIBES.)

CHALUTZ see HALUTZ

CHANUKKAH see HANUKKAH

CHAVER (the plural is CHAVERIM) (also spelled HAVER) Hebrew word for "comrade." Although a young Israeli today may use the term "chaver" for a girl friend, boyfriend, or army buddy, it was most often used by the pioneers of the Second Aliyah (wave of immigration) to refer to their fellow *kibbutzniks* in their cooperative farming villages. (See also ALIYAH; KIBBUTZ.)

CHAZANOVITZ, JOSEPH (1844-1919) Lithuanian doctor and Zionist. Although Chazanovitz was active in Hibbat Zion (a Russian Zionist movement) he was never able to settle in Palestine. He devoted much of his life to collecting books for his dream of a central Jewish library in Jerusalem. His collection grew into the National and University Library in Jerusalem. (See also HIBBAT ZION; NATIONAL AND UNIVERSITY LIBRARY; ZIONISM.)

CHESS A popular game in Israel. The first countrywide chess competition was organized in 1929. In 1975 the Israel Chess Federation had 150 member chess clubs with about 2,000 players competing in official games. Thousands of other Israelis play chess just for fun.

CHIEF RABBINATE In 1920 the British (who then ruled Palestine under the Mandate) created a Chief Rabbinical Council headed by a Sephardic Chief Rabbi and an Ashkenazi Chief Rabbi. This council was "the sole authority on matters of Jewish law" with control over Jewish marriage, divorce, alimony, and wills. The Chief Rabbinate continued as the supreme religious body of the Jewish community when Israel became a state in 1948. Today it hears appeals from the lower rabbinical courts and is the final authority on all interpretations of religious law. (See also ASHKENAZIM; COURTS, RELIGIOUS; SEPHARDIM.)

CHOSROES II King of Persia who ruled 590-628 C.E. Chosroes' Persian army fought the Byzantine Empire and took Palestine from the Byzantines in 614 C.E. A year after Chosroes' murder in 628 C.E., the Persian army was driven out of Palestine by the Byzantines who held the country until 637 C.E. when they in turn were driven out by the Arabs. (See also ARABS; BYZANTINE EMPIRE; HISTORY; PERSIA.)

CHRISTIAN QUARTER Section of the Old City of Jerusalem that is the home of many Christian Arabs. The Via Dolorosa and the Church of the Holy Sepulchre are in the Christian Quarter. (See also ARABS, ISRAELI; CHRISTIANS, ISRAELI; HOLY SEPULCHRE; JERUSALEM; VIA DOLOROSA.)

CHRISTIANS, ISRAELI About 80,000 Christians live in Israel today and attend the 300 churches of the Catholic, Eastern Orthodox, and Protestant religions. Most of these Christians are Arabs as well, but there are also a number of Europeans and Armenians.

Israeli law guarantees Christians and all other non-Jews the right to celebrate their own Sabbath and religious holidays. It also provides religious education to their children if the parents wish. Since marriage, divorce, and child support are governed by religious law in Israel, Christians have 16 religious courts to decide such matters.

The Israeli Declaration of Independence pledged to safeguard the holy places of all religions. Today Christian pilgrims come to the Holy Land from all over the world to visit Christian shrines in Bethlehem, Nazareth, and Jerusalem. (See also ARABS; BETHLEHEM; COURTS, RELIGIOUS; EDUCATION; HOLIDAYS; JERUSALEM; JESUS; NAZARETH; RELIGION.)

CHRISTMAS Holiday celebrating the birth of Jesus Christ. It is observed in Christian churches throughout Israel on December 25 of each year. Special Christmas Eve and Christmas Day services are held in Shepherd's Field in Bethlehem. Eastern

An Arab-Christian wedding dinner being celebrated in Safed.

Orthodox churches that follow the Julian calendar celebrate Christmas 13 days later, on January 7th. (See also BETHLEHEM; CALENDAR, JULIAN; CHRISTIANS; HOLIDAYS.)

CHURCH OF THE HOLY SEPULCHRE   see HOLY SEPULCHRE

CHURCH OF THE NATIVITY   One of the oldest Christian shrines in the Holy Land and the oldest church in Israel still in use. The first Church of the Nativity in Bethlehem was built by the Emperor Constantine in 330 C.E., when his mother, Empress Helena, declared the site to be the place where the manger of Jesus' birth had stood. The present church in Bethlehem was built in the sixth century, and has been added to and restored many times since. A flight of stairs leads down from the church into a cave beneath, which Christians hold sacred as the birthplace of Christ. (See also BETHLEHEM; CONSTANTINE I; HELENA; JESUS.)

CHURCHILL WHITE PAPER   Statement issued by Winston Churchill when he served as British Colonial Secretary in 1922. It said that the aim of the Balfour Declaration of 1917 was to establish a Jewish national home, that Jews had a right to live in Palestine, and that the number of Jewish immigrants into the country should be limited only by what the country could absorb. (See also BALFOUR DECLARATION; CHURCHILL, WINSTON LEONARD SPENCER; GREAT BRITAIN.)

CHURCHILL, WINSTON LEONARD SPENCER (1874-1965)
Prime Minister of Britain, 1940-1945 and 1951-1955. As British
Colonial Secretary in 1922, he issued a statement (Churchill
White Paper) upholding the right of Jews to a national home in
Palestine. He opposed the 1939 White Paper which limited
Jewish immigration into Palestine. However, when Churchill
became Prime Minister in 1940, he continued the White Paper
restrictions rather than do anything that might interfere with
Britain's winning World War II. (See also CHURCHILL WHITE
PAPER; GREAT BRITAIN; WHITE PAPER.)

British Prime Minister Winston Churchill (left), chats with President Franklin D. Roosevelt aboard a British battleship during a
meeting at sea on August 10, 1941.

CHURGIN, PINKHOS (1884-1957) Founder of the Bar-Ilan
University at Ramat Gan. Churgin was a professor at the Yeshiva
University in New York, and dean of its Teacher's Institute. In
1955 he went to Israel to become Bar-Ilan's first president. (See
also BAR-ILAN UNIVERSITY.)

CIRCASSIANS Moslems who came to Palestine in the 1800s
from the Caucasus Mountains of Russia. The Circassians fought
on the side of the Jews in the 1947-1949 War of Independence, and
a number of their young men serve in the Israel Defense Forces or

the border police today. In 1975 there were about 1,200 Circassians in Israel, most of them living in two villages in Galilee. (See also DEFENSE FORCES; GALILEE; MOSLEMS, ISRAELI; POLICE; WAR OF INDEPENDENCE.)

CISTUS   A large pink flower that blooms in the spring in Israel. The fragrant gum of the cistus is called "myrrh" in the Bible.

CITADEL   see TOWER OF DAVID

CITIZENS' RIGHTS MOVEMENT   Small Israeli political party. It was founded in 1973 and elected three members to the Israeli Knesset (legislature) that year. (See also KNESSET; POLITICAL PARTIES.)

CITIZENSHIP   Any Jew who wishes to become a citizen of Israel has only to go to live there. A Jew receives all the rights of Israeli citizenship—including the right to vote and the obligation to serve in the armed forces—as soon as he or she is listed on the Population Register. Non-Jews must live in Israel for three years before applying for citizenship. Jews are allowed to remain citizens of their mother country (dual citizenship), but non-Jews must give up their previous citizenship. (See also DEFENSE FORCES; LAW OF RETURN; VOTING.)

CITRUS FRUIT   A group of subtropical (warm climate) fruits that includes the orange, grapefruit, lemon, lime, tangerine,

Oranges are the most common of the citrus fruits grown in Israel. They are shipped to markets all over the world.

Jaffa oranges are loaded onto a ship at the Port of Ashdod.

citron, and kumquat. Citrus fruit was unknown in ancient Israel and was probably introduced into the country between 1100 and 1500 C.E. Today it is Israel's most important agricultural crop and a very important export. In 1975 the country produced more than one and a half million tons of oranges and grapefruits. Most of this fruit was exported to Europe and the United States, either as it came from the tree or in the form of juice or juice concentrate. (See also AGRICULTURE; FOREIGN TRADE.)

CITY OF DAVID see JERUSALEM

CIVIL SERVICE People employed by the government of a country. The civil service does not include the legislature, judges, or the armed forces. The Israeli Civil Service Commission deals with hiring, training, promoting, and overseeing the efficiency of government workers. There are no civil service tests for jobs in Israel as there are in the United States. Instead new employees are appointed according to their training and ability. Top jobs are reserved for people with college educations. In 1975 the Israeli civil service had about 70,000 people working for the Ministries of Foreign Affairs, Defense, Agriculture, Commerce, Health, Social Welfare, etc. (See also GOVERNMENT.)

CLAUDIUS (full name TIBERIUS CLAUDIUS DRUSUS NERO GERMANICUS) (10 B.C.-54 C.E.) Roman emperor who ruled 41-54 C.E. Claudius took the Roman throne with the help of his friend Herod Agrippa. Claudius then approved Herod as king of Judea and gave him all the lands that had been ruled by his grandfather Herod the Great. When Herod Agrippa died, Claudius assigned Judea to the rule of a Roman procurator (governor) for a while, but later returned the northern part of the country to Herod's son. (See also HEROD AGRIPPA I; HEROD AGRIPPA II; HISTORY; JUDEA; ROME.)

CLIMATE Although Israel is a small country, its climate is varied. The Coastal Plain has hot and rather humid summers with daytime temperatures rising into the 90s. The winters there are warm and pleasant. The summer climate in the mountains produces hot days and cool evenings, and in the winter it is cold enough for a little light snow. Summer in the desert is hot and dry and the winter is very mild. It is warm enough to swim in the winter in Eilat and Tiberias.

There is almost no rain in Israel from May to October. November to April is called the "rainy season," but the rain really only falls for short periods. Most rainy days come in January and February. Rainfall is much heavier in the north than in the south of the country, although once in a while there is heavy enough rain in the desert to cause flash floods. (See also GEOGRAPHY; HAMSIN; WADI.)

COASTAL PLAIN Long strip of flat land running roughly north and south along the Mediterranean coast between the sea and the mountains. The Coastal Plain can be divided into three main sections: the Plain of Acre, from the Lebanon border to Mount Carmel; the Sharon Plain, from Mount Carmel to Tel Aviv; and the Southern Plains which end at the Negev Desert. The soil in the Coastal Plain is fertile, with a good supply of water coming from underground springs. The area has been inhabited from earliest times and was the site of a number of important ancient cities. (See also GEOGRAPHY; JEZREEL VALLEY; SHARON PLAIN.)

COHEN, ELIYHU BEN SAUL (code name ELI) (1924-1965) Egyptian-born Israeli secret agent. Cohen went to Damascus under an assumed Arab name, became friendly with high Syrian government officials, obtained important secret information from them, and radioed the information back to Israel. His activities went undiscovered for nine years, but he was finally arrested in 1965 and was hanged in a public square in Damascus.

COHEN, GEULA (1925-   ) Journalist and politician born in Tel Aviv. Geula Cohen is a member of the Israeli Knesset (legislature) and chairperson of its immigration committee. She also writes for the newspaper *Maariv*. (See also KNESSET; MAARIV.)

COHN, HAIM HERMANN (1911-   ) German-born judge who settled in Palestine in 1930. Cohn was appointed Attorney-General when Israel became a state in 1948 and later served as a Supreme Court judge. (See also SUPREME COURT.)

COINS There were no Jewish coins through most of biblical times. The shekel, which became the accepted coin among the Jews, was first commonly used under the Hasmonean kings in the second century B.C.E. The silver or bronze Hasmonean coins were engraved with Hebrew words and symbols. The coins of Herod the Great (37-4 B.C.E.) had Greek inscriptions and Herod's son, Philip, put the heads of Roman emperors on his coins. During the 66-70 C.E. revolt against Roman rule, the Jewish rebels issued silver shekels bearing ancient Hebrew inscriptions. Bar Kokhba's coins, used during the 132-135 C.E. revolt, had the Hebrew words "The liberation of Jerusalem" struck on top of existing Roman coins.

In modern times the British government, which ruled Palestine under the Mandate until 1948, introduced the pound as the standard money. Pounds were issued as paper money and were divided into coins called mils. Today the Israeli pound, which is also called the lira, is divided into 100 agorot. There are ½ and 1 lira coins and 1, 5, 10, and 25 agorot coins. (See also AGORA; BAR KOKHBA, SIMEON; HASMONEANS; HEROD I; HISTORY; ISRAELI POUND; LIRA; SHEKEL.)

COMMANDMENTS, TEN   see TEN COMMANDMENTS

CONFERENCE ON JEWISH MATERIAL CLAIMS   Organization founded in 1951 to obtain reparations (payment of damages) from Germany for the Jewish victims of the Nazi persecution. The Israeli government took part in the conference, although the $107 million finally settled on went to Jews living outside of Israel. (See also HOLOCAUST; REPARATIONS.)

CONSCRIPTION   Required military service in the armed forces of a country. In biblical times all men over the age of 20 were required to serve in the armies of the tribes of Israel and the king had the power to conscript the men of the country to fight for him. In modern Israel both men and women are drafted at age 18 to serve in the country's Defense Forces. (See also DEFENSE FORCES; NATIONAL SERVICE.)

CONSTANTINE I (also called CONSTANTINE THE GREAT) (about 288-337 C.E.)   Emperor of Rome who ruled 312-337 C.E. and made Christianity the official religion of the Roman Empire. Constantine and his mother, Helena, visited the Holy Land to find the places where Jesus was born, lived, and died. Constantine had churches built on the Christian holy sites. He built the original Church of the Holy Sepulchre in Jerusalem and the original Church of the Nativity in Bethlehem. (See also CHURCH OF THE NATIVITY; HELENA; HOLY SEPULCHRE; JESUS; ROME.)

COOPERATIVE   An association owned and operated by its members to enable them to buy, sell, or produce goods to their better advantage. The cooperative movement in Palestine began in the late 1800s with the vintners (winemakers) association at Rishon Le Zion and the Pardes citrus export society. The first kibbutzim and moshavim, two different kinds of agricultural cooperatives, were founded in the early 1900s and there are now hundreds of these cooperative agricultural settlements in Israel. Kupat Holim, a cooperative health fund, was established in 1913 and later became part of the Histadrut, the labor federation. The establishment of the Histadrut in 1920 extended the cooperative movement into many new fields. (See also HISTADRUT; KIBBUTZ; KUPAT HOLIM; MOSHAV; PARDES, HANNAH; RISHON LE ZION.)

COPPER   Reddish metal that is an excellent conductor of heat and electricity. Copper was mined in biblical times at Timna in the southern Negev Desert. Today modern copper mines are being worked near the ancient site of King Solomon's mines. Copper is also extracted from the water of the Dead Sea. (See also DEAD SEA WORKS; KING SOLOMON'S MINES; MINERALS; NEGEV.)

COPPER SCROLL   One of the ancient Dead Sea Scrolls discovered in 1952. It is made of copper and contains coded descriptions of hiding places of ancient treasure. The copper scroll is now in Amman, the capitol of Jordan. (See also DEAD SEA SCROLLS.)

CORN FLAG   A flower native to Israel that blooms a rosy red color and then darkens into a deep purple. The corn flag may be the lily of the field mentioned in the Bible.

COURTS   There are two kinds of courts in Israel: (1) civil courts which judge lawsuits and criminal cases under Israeli law, and (2) religious courts which rule on personal matters according to religious law. Israeli courts do not have juries. All court cases—whether civil or religious—are decided according to law by a judge or by a panel of judges.

The lowest civil courts are the Magistrates' Courts. They deal with less serious crimes and lawsuits that involve small amounts of money. Decisions of the Magistrates' Courts can be appealed to the District Courts. The five District Courts handle more serious crimes and larger lawsuits. The Supreme Court, the highest court in Israel, hears cases against the government and also judges appeals from the District Courts. All the lower courts are bound by the decisions of the Supreme Court. (See also COURTS, RELIGIOUS; JUDGES; SUPREME COURT.)

COURTS, RELIGIOUS   Each religious community in Israel has its own lower religious courts and a religious court of appeals to decide matters of personal status like marriage, divorce, adoption and support of children, and wills and inheritances. Eight Rabbinical Courts serve the Jewish community, with the Chief Rabbinate acting as a court of appeals. The Moslem religious courts (Sharia) serve most of Israel's Arabs. In addition, there are Druze religious courts and nine separate kinds of Christian religious courts for the different Catholic, Protestant, and Orthodox communities. (See also CHIEF RABBINATE; COURTS; RELIGION.)

COVENANT   God's promise in the Bible (Genesis 12:7) that the land of Canaan (much of it is now modern Israel) would be given to Abraham and his descendants. The Jewish people are often called the "People of the Covenant." (See also ABRAHAM; BIBLE; CANAAN.)

CRUSADES   A series of wars waged by the Christian rulers of Western Europe to take the Holy Land from the Moslems. There were seven Crusades from 1096 to 1291 c.e., of which the First and Third Crusades were the most important. The First Crusade drove the Moslems from part of Palestine, captured Jerusalem, and founded a Crusader kingdom that lasted for two hundred years.

The loss of Jerusalem to Saladin and his Moslem forces in 1187 led to the Third Crusade in which three European kings— Frederick Barbarossa of Germany, Philip Augustus of France, and Richard the Lionhearted of England—tried unsuccessfully to retake the city. The Crusaders moved their capitol to Acre and finally, in 1291, were driven from Palestine by the Turks.

The remains of Crusader forts and churches can be seen at Athlit, Belvoir, and other sites in Israel today. (See also ACRE; ATHLIT; BALDWIN I; BALDWIN II; BALDWIN III; BELVOIR; HISTORY; JERUSALEM; RICHARD I; SALADIN; TURKEY.)

CUKERMAN, YITZHAK (also called ANTEK) (1915-   )   One of the leaders of the Warsaw Ghetto uprising against the Nazis during World War II. After the war, Cukerman settled in Israel. (See also HOLOCAUST; NAZIS.)

CYPRESS   Cypress trees grew in Palestine in biblical times, and today, once again, many line the roads in parts of Israel. Some grow 50 to 60 feet tall and serve as windbreakers for citrus groves. (See also REFORESTATION.)

CYPRUS   Island nation in the Mediterranean Sea that is Israel's nearest non-Arab neighbor. The British built detention camps on Cyprus for Jews captured trying to enter Palestine from 1945 to 1948 in spite of the British rules against Jewish immigration. Today Israeli citizens who cannot marry under the religious laws governing marriage in Israel often go to Cyprus to marry. Such marriages are then considered legal in Israel. (See also ALIYAH; DETENTION CAMPS; IMMIGRANTS, ILLEGAL; MARRIAGE.)

CYRUS I (also called CYRUS THE GREAT) (about 600-529 B.C.E.) King of Persia who ruled 550-529 B.C.E. The Persians under Cyrus conquered the Babylonian Empire and ruled all the land from Egypt across Palestine and through Iran. Cyrus believed in allowing the conquered people in his empire return to their original homes. In 538 B.C.E. he issued a declaration permitting the Jews to return to Palestine from their exile in Babylon. (See also BABYLON; BABYLONIAN EXILE; HISTORY; PERSIA.)

D

DAGON   Ancient god of the Canaanites and Philistines. He was the god of the soil, and was supposed to make the plants grow. Shrines to Dagon at Ashdod, Bet Shean, and Gaza are mentioned in the Bible. (See also ASHDOD; BET SHEAN; CANAAN; GAZA; PHILISTINES.)

DALIYAH   Kibbutz founded in 1939 in the hills about 20 miles south of Haifa. People from all over Israel attend the National Folk Dancing Festival held at Daliyah every three years. (See also DANCE; KIBBUTZ.)

DAMARI, SHOSHANA   Folk singer who was born in Yemen and taken to Israel at the age of two. Since 1946 Shoshana Damari has given concerts in Israel and has toured many countries of the world. She has also made records and appeared in several films, including *Hatikva* and *Hill 24 Doesn't Answer*.

DAMASCUS GATE (Hebrew, SHAAR YAFO)   One of the eight gates in the wall around the Old City of Jerusalem. The Damascus Gate marks the beginning of the road leading to Damascus, the capital city of Syria. It is the most ornate and the busiest of the Old City gates. (See also JERUSALEM; WALLED CITIES.)

DAN   City at the northern limit of ancient Israel. The phrase "from Dan to Beersheba" meant the whole country. Dan was originally called Laish by the Phoenicians, but the name was changed by the tribe of Dan when they captured the city in the thirteenth century B.C.E. Archaeologists digging at Tel Dan have uncovered remains of the ancient city walls.

   A kibbutz of the same name, founded in 1939, is not far from the remains of ancient Dan. During the 1948 War of Independence, Kibbutz Dan fought off a heavy Syrian attack. (See also ARCHAEOLOGY; BEERSHEBA; DAN, TRIBE OF; KIBBUTZ; PHOENICIANS; WAR OF INDEPENDENCE.)

DAN REGION PROJECT   A sewage treatment project that treats the waste water of Tel Aviv for reuse in agriculture and industry. It is the largest and most advanced of the waste water treatment plants in Israel. The Dan Project has two main purposes: (1) to stop the pollution of Tel Aviv's beaches, and (2) to increase Israel's limited water supply. The first stage of the Dan Region Project was completed in 1975. By 1977 it was treating 20 million cubic meters (about 5½ billion gallons) of water a year. When the project is finished, it should be able to treat 130 million cubic meters (almost 35 billion gallons) of water. (See also METRIC SYSTEM; TEL AVIV; WATER.)

DAN, TRIBE OF One of the Twelve Tribes of Israel which claimed the fifth son of Jacob as its ancestor. When the Israelites conquered Canaan in the thirteenth century B.C.E., the tribe of Dan was given land south of Jaffa but was pushed back into the northern hills by the Amorites (a Canaanite tribe). (See also CANAAN; DAN; JACOB; TWELVE TRIBES.)

DANCE The hora—a lively circle dance that started in Israel's farming settlements in the 1920s—has become a kind of national dance. Folk dancing is a popular recreation throughout the country and Israelis celebrate national holidays with folk dances. Every three years a National Folk Dancing Festival is held in the village of Daliyah.

Israel's first professional dance company was the Inbal Dance Theater, founded in 1949, which performs folk dances of the Yemenite Jews. The Bat Dor Dance Theater performs both modern and classical dances. The Israel National Opera sometimes presents ballets, and foreign dance companies appear in Israeli theaters and at the yearly Israel Festival. (See also BAT DOR DANCE COMPANY; DALIYAH; INBAL DANCE THEATER; ISRAEL FESTIVAL; ISRAEL NATIONAL OPERA; MUSIC; THEATER.)

DA-OZ, RAM (1929-) German-born composer who was brought to Israel as a young child. Da-Oz fought in the 1948 War of Independence and was blinded. In spite of his handicap, he studied music and composed songs, instrumental music, and concertos. (See also WAR OF INDEPENDENCE.)

DAPHNAH (also spelled DAFNA) Kibbutz founded in the Huleh Valley in 1939. Trout are raised in large fish ponds at Daphnah. (See also FISH PONDS; HULEH VALLEY.)

DARIUS I (also called DARIUS THE GREAT) King of Persia who ruled 522-486 B.C.E. Darius ascended the throne of Persia after the death of Cyrus. Under Darius, the Jews that Cyrus had allowed to return to Palestine from their Babylonian exile were permitted to rebuild the Temple in Jerusalem. (See also BABYLONIAN EXILE; CYRUS I; HISTORY; PERSIA; TEMPLE.)

DAVAR Labor newspaper published daily by the Histadrut, the Israeli labor federation. Davar was founded in 1925 and its first

An Israeli dance group performs a traditional dance with oriental flavor.

editors were Berl Katznelson, Mosheh Beilinson, and Zalman Shazar. *Davar* also publishes a weekly newspaper for children. (See also BEILINSON, MOSHEH; HISTADRUT; KATZNELSON, BERL; SHAZAR, ZALMAN.)

DAVID   King of Judah and Israel who ruled from about 1000 to 960 B.C.E. His history is told in the Bible from I Samuel, Chapter 16, through I Kings, Chapter 2.

The Tomb of King David, located on Mount Zion in the south-western corner of the Old City outside of the city walls.

David became King Saul's armorbearer as a young man and later married Saul's daughter, Michal. When Saul and his sons were killed in battle, David was crowned king by the elders of his tribe of Judah. Within a few years he ruled all the tribes of Israel. In a series of wars, David captured Jerusalem and made it the capital of his kingdom, defeated the Philistines and took the land along the Mediterranean coast from them, and conquered large areas of what is now Syria and Lebanon. He built the largest and most powerful Jewish State that ever existed. David was a brave warrior, an excellent military commander, and a great king.

Many legends have grown up about King David. The account of his killing Goliath with a slingshot is one of the famous stories. Also, according to tradition, he wrote many of the

Psalms. (See also BIBLE; HISTORY; ISRAEL, KINGDOM OF; JUDAH, KINGDOM OF; PHILISTINES; SAUL.)

DAVID, CITY OF see JERUSALEM

DAVID, SHIELD OF see MAGEN DAVID

DAVID, STAR OF see MAGEN DAVID

DAVID, TOWER OF see TOWER OF DAVID

DAY OF ATONEMENT see YOM KIPPUR

DAYAN, DEBORAH (1891-1956) Russian-born pioneer and writer who settled in Palestine in 1913. She joined Palestine's first kibbutz and later was a founder of Nahalal, another farming settlement. Deborah Dayan wrote many short stories and was the editor of a women workers' magazine. She was married to Shemuel Dayan and was the mother of Moshe Dayan. (See also DAYAN, MOSHE; DAYAN, SHEMUEL; DEGANIA; KIBBUTZ; NAHALAL.)

DAYAN, MOSHE (1915-) Soldier and politician. Dayan was born at Degania, Israel's first kibbutz. At age 14 he joined the Haganah (underground army) and by 22 was second in command in Orde Wingate's commandos. Dayan was jailed by the British for these activities, but was later released to fight in Syria during World War II. He lost his left eye in the fighting and has since worn his famous black eye patch.

During the 1948 War of Independence Dayan was commander of the Jerusalem region. He is known for leading troops into battle by shouting "Follow me" instead of "Forward." In 1953 he became Chief of Staff of the Israel Defense Forces. He ran the 1956 Sinai War and then retired from the army to study law.

Dayan entered politics in 1959 by winning a seat in the Israeli Knesset (legislature) as a member of David Ben-Gurion's Mapai Party. He served as Minister of Agriculture in Ben-Gurion's Cabinet, as Minister of Defense under Golda Meir, and as Foreign Minister in Menachem Begin's government.

His autobiography, *Story of My Life*, was published in English in 1976. (See also BEGIN, MENACHEM; BEN-GURION, DAVID; DEGANIA; HAGANAH; KNESSET; MAPAI; MEIR, GOLDA; SINAI WAR; WAR OF INDEPENDENCE; WINGATE, CHARLES ORDE.)

DAYAN, SHEMUEL (1891-1968) Russian-born pioneer who settled in Palestine in 1908. Dayan was one of the founders of the villages of Degania and Nahalal, a leader of an organization of moshavim (farming villages), and a member of the Israeli Knesset (legislature). He was the father of Moshe Dayan. (See also DAYAN, MOSHE; DEGANIA; KNESSET; MOSHAV; NAHALAL.)

Moshe Dayan

Bathers in the Dead Sea need never fear drowning. The salt content is so rich that nothing except the heaviest object can sink.

DAYAN, YAEL (1939-)   Native-born Israeli writer. Her novels, which include *Dust* and *New Faces in the Mirror,* are about life in modern Israel. She is the daughter of Moshe Dayan. (See also DAYAN, MOSHE.)

DAYYAN (the plural is DAYYANIM)   The word means "judge" in Hebrew, but only refers to a judge of a rabbinical court. (See also COURTS, RELIGIOUS; JUDGES.)

DEAD SEA   Body of water on Israel's border with Jordan. The Dead Sea is 48 miles long, 11 miles wide, and covers an area of 395 square miles. It surface is 1,300 feet below sea level, which makes it the lowest spot on earth. Its name in Hebrew, *Yam Hamelah,* means "salt sea."

The millions of gallons of water flowing from the Jordan River into the Dead Sea each day have no way to escape. The hot sun evaporates the water and leaves the salt and minerals behind, making the Dead Sea five times as salty as the ocean. No fish or plants can live in it, and a person swimming in the water cannot sink. The minerals extracted from the water of the Dead Sea are an important export for Israel. (See also DEAD SEA WORKS; GEOGRAPHY; JORDAN; JORDAN RIVER.)

DEAD SEA SCROLLS   Rolls of parchment (paper made from animal skins) covered with ancient writing. The Dead Sea Scrolls were discovered in caves near the north end of the Dead Sea. A Bedouin looking for a lost animal found the first scrolls in 1947 and sold them to a dealer. Archaeologist Eliezer Sukenik heard about the scrolls, recognized how important they were, and finally managed to buy some of them for the Hebrew University. His son, Yigael Yadin, helped the Israeli government obtain other scrolls, and still more were found in an archaeological search of caves near Qumran. Today the Dead Sea Scrolls are displayed at the Israel Museum in the Shrine of the Book which was built especially to house them.

The Dead Sea Scrolls contain two complete copies of the Book of Isaiah and pieces of other Books of the Bible. These are one thousand years older than any other existing Hebrew text of the Bible. Other scrolls, dating from the second century B.C.E. through the first centrury C.E., describe life in Palestine during those years. The Temple Scroll is a detailed description of the Temple in Jerusalem, and the Manual of Discipline Scroll gives the rules governing a religious sect thought to be the Essenes. (See also ARCHAEOLOGY; BIBLE; ESSENES; HEBREW UNIVERSITY; ISAIAH; ISRAEL MUSEUM; QUMRAN; SUKENIK, ELIEZER LIPA; TEMPLE; TEMPLE SCROLL; YADIN, YIGAEL.)

DEAD SEA WORKS   Company formed in 1952 to continue the

Valuable salt dredged from the Dead Sea is piled high on its shore, later to be transported to processing centers.

This enlarged fragment of the Dead Sea Scrolls is on display at the
Shrine of the Book, in Jerusalem.

work of the earlier Palestine Potash Company. The Dead Sea Works extracts minerals like potash, phosphates, and copper from the waters of the Dead Sea for use in agriculture and industry. During the 1970s about a million tons of potash a year were produced at the plant at Sodom and sold on the world market. The Israeli government owns most of the shares in the Dead Sea Works. (See also DEAD SEA; FOREIGN TRADE; MINERALS; NOVOMEYSKY, MOSHE; POTASH; SODOM.)

DEBORAH (twelfth century B.C.E.)   Israelite Judge and prophetess. She was the only woman Judge. After rallying the tribes of Israel to fight the Canaanites, she called Barak to command the armies, and went with him to the army stronghold on Mount Tabor. The Israelites swept down to defeat the Canaanite armies in what is now called the Jezreel Valley. The story of the battle is told in Chapter 4 of the Book of Judges, and Deborah's song of victory makes up Chapter 5. (See also BARAK BEN ABINOAM; BIBLE; CANAAN; JEZREEL VALLEY; JUDGES; MOUNT TABOR.)

DECALOGUE   see TEN COMMANDMENTS

DECLARATION OF INDEPENDENCE (also called DECLARATION OF THE ESTABLISHMENT OF THE STATE OF ISRAEL)   On May 14, 1948 (the 5th of Iyar, 5708 on the Jewish calendar) the provisional (temporary) government headed by David Ben-Gurion met in the Tel Aviv Museum hall with the Chief Rabbis and representatives of the Jewish Agency, the Zionist Organization, the Haganah, and other Jewish groups. Ben-Gurion read the Declaration which said in part:

We, members of the People's Council, representatives of the Jewish community of Eretz-Israel and of the Zionist movement, are here assembled on the day of termination of the British Mandate over Eretz-Israel and, by virtue of our natural and historic right and on the strength of the resolution of the United Nations General Assembly, hereby declare the establishment of a Jewish State in Eretz-Israel. To be known as the State of Israel.

The Declaration was unanimously adopted and the new nation was born.

Independence Day is celebrated on the fifth of Iyar each year in Israel. (See also BEN-GURION, DAVID; CALENDAR, JEWISH; CHIEF RABBINATE; HAGANAH; INDEPENDENCE DAY; JEWISH AGENCY; MANDATE; UNITED NATIONS; WORLD ZIONIST ORGANIZATION; ZIONISM.)

DEFENSE FORCES (also called ZAHAL)   The Defense Forces were established by the provisional (temporary) Israeli government in May of 1948 during the War of Independence. It was made up of members of the Haganah and the other underground

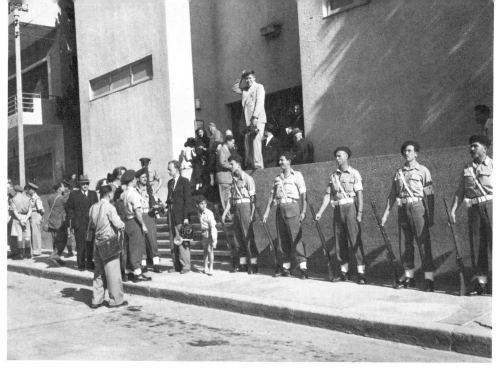

Women as well as men serve in Israel's defense forces. Here, women soldiers are preparing their rifles before going out to the firing range.

organizations that had fought the British during the Mandate, and of veterans of the World War II Jewish Brigade.

Today the Defense Forces have a small core of career officers, but most of its strength comes from the men and women drafted for National Service. There is also a large Reserve. All Jewish young men and most young women serve two to three years of National Service and then go into the Reserve. Druze and Circassians are also drafted, and many Moslems and Christians volunteer.

The Israel Defense Forces are made up of land, air, and sea branches. All three sections are commanded by a combined General Staff headed by a Chief-of-Staff. The land forces include Infantry, Paratroops, Artillery, Intelligence, Military Police, Nahal, and Gadna. (See also CIRCASSIANS; CONSCRIPTION; DRUZE; GADNA; HAGANAH; JEWISH BRIGADE; MANDATE; NAHAL; NATIONAL SERVICE; WAR OF INDEPENDENCE.)

DEGANIA (also spelled DEGANYAH) The first kibbutz in Palestine, sometimes called the "mother of kibbutzim." It was founded in 1909 by a European workers' group on swamp land south of Lake Kinneret (Sea of Galilee). The land was bought from Persian owners who called the place "the death spot" because malaria killed so many settlers. In 1920 Degania's sister kibbutz, Degania Beth, was formed rather than let the original settlement grow too large. During the 1948 War of Independence the men and women of Degania, fighting alongside Haganah forces, threw back the invading Syrian army. Today Degania is a showplace of the kibbutz movement. Its Gordon Museum of Natural History is named for A.D. Gordon, one of its early members. (See also GORDON, AHARON DAVID; HAGANAH; KIBBUTZ; MALARIA; WAR OF INDEPENDENCE.)

DEMOCRACY A system of government in which the people of a country hold the political power. In a pure democracy, such as ancient Athens, each person speaks for himself or herself. In a modern representational democracy, as in the United States or Israel, the people vote in a free election for their representatives in the government. The Israeli Knesset (legislature) is elected by all the people of the country according to a system of proportional representation, and the country's Prime Minister is chosen from among the members of the Knesset. (See also GOVERNMENT; KNESSET; PRIME MINISTER; PROPORTIONAL REPRESENTATION.)

DEPARTMENT OF ANTIQUITIES Israeli government department responsible for protecting archaeological sites and ancient remains. The most important sites are also cared for by the National Parks Authority. The Department of Antiquities conducts archaeological surveys and maps new finds. It also oversees the work of all archaeologists digging in Israel. (See also ARCHAEOLOGY; NATIONAL PARKS.)

DESALINIZATION The process of converting sea water into fresh water. Since Israel suffers from a water shortage while the Mediterranean Sea stretches along its western border, it is natural for the Israelis to be pioneers in desalinization. Experiments are being conducted to find the cheapest and most practical methods of removing the salt from the sea water, and several experimental plants are now in operation. Two large desalinization plants, which use the flash evaporation method, are supplying fresh water to the southern city of Eilat and a new plant is being built on the Mediterannean at Ashdod. The Eilat desalinization plant produces electricity as well as fresh water, and the Ashdod project will have a nuclear power plant to produce energy in addition to the water. (See also ASHDOD; EILAT; WATER.)

DETENTION CAMPS Prisons set up by the British to hold "illegal" Jewish immigrants caught trying to enter Palestine in the early 1940s. Beginning in 1940 these immigrants were held in Athlit, but from 1946 to 1948 most were sent to the Mediterranean island of Cyprus. (See also ALIYAH; ATHLIT; CYPRUS; IMMIGRANTS, ILLEGAL.)

DEVELOPMENT TOWNS   New towns built or developed in Israel since it became a nation in 1948. In building these towns away from the populated Coastal Plain, the government tried to distribute population and industry throughout the country. Each development town has its own industry and many of them also serve as market and cultural centers for the agricultural villages around them. Afula, Ashdod, Lod, and Beersheba are among the development towns. (See also COASTAL PLAIN.)

DEVIR   Company publishing Hebrew books founded in Berlin in 1922 by the famous poet Hayim Bialik and two other writers, Yehoshua Ravnitzky and Shemarya Levin. In 1924 Devir moved to Tel Aviv where it continues to print Hebrew literature and scholarly books. (See also BIALIK, HAYIM NAHMAN; LEVIN, SHEMARYA; RAVNITZKY, YEHOSHUA HANA.)

DIAMONDS   Israel's most important industrial import. In 1975 more than one-third of the diamonds sold throughout the world and four-fifths of the world's medium-sized stones were cut and polished in Israel. Israel is second only to Belgium as the world's diamond center, and the largest diamond exchange in the world is at Ramat Gan near Tel Aviv. Raw diamonds are imported into Israel from South Africa, cut and polished in Netanya, and then shipped to the United States to be sold worldwide. (See also FOREIGN TRADE; NETANYA; RAMAT GAN.)

DIMONA (also spelled DIMONAH)   City established in 1955 in the Negev about 20 miles southeast of Beersheba. Today it has a number of industries of its own, although many of the people living there are employed at the Sodom Dead Sea Works. A nuclear research center at Dimona conducts experiments in desalinization (removing salt from sea water) and nuclear energy. (See also DESALINIZATION; NEGEV; NUCLEAR ENERGY; SODOM.)

DINITZ, SIMCHA (1929-   )   Diplomat who was born in Tel Aviv and studied political science in the United States. Dinitz served in the Israeli embassy in Washington and in 1973 was appointed ambassador to the United States. He has also lectured to many American groups.

DINUR, BEN ZION (name changed from DINABURG) (1884-1973)   Historian born in the Ukraine in Russia. Dinur settled in Palestine in 1921, taught Jewish history at the Hebrew University in Jerusalem, wrote books and articles on history, and was the editor of *Zion,* the magazine of the Israel Historical Society. He was elected to the Israeli Knesset (legislature) and later served as Minister of Education and Culture. (See also HEBREW UNIVERSITY; KNESSET; ZION.)

DIVORCE There is no civil divorce in Israel. All divorces must be granted by a religious court. People who were divorced in a civil court in another country cannot legally remarry in Israel. (See also COURTS, RELIGIOUS; MARRIAGE.)

DIZENGOFF, MEIR (1861-1936) Zionist, born in Bessarabia in Russia, who became the first Mayor of Tel Aviv. Dizengoff settled in Palestine in 1905. He was one of the founders of Tel Aviv. In 1909 he laid the cornerstone of the new city in the sand dunes outside of Jaffa. Building Tel Aviv then became his life's work. He served as its mayor for 12 years, helped plan its housing and streets, brought industry to the city, and founded its first museum. One of the main streets and shopping areas of Tel Aviv is named in his honor. (See also JAFFA; TEL AVIV; ZIONISM.)

DIZENGOFF STREET One of the main streets of Tel Aviv. It is a popular place to sit at a sidewalk cafe and watch the crowds of people pass by. The street is named in honor of Meir Dizengoff, the first Mayor of Tel Aviv. (See also DIZENGOFF, MEIR; TEL AVIV.)

A view of Dizengoff in 1980, after the famous square was reconstructed.

Dizengoff Street is one of the busiest streets in Tel Aviv. Such scenes at outdoor cafes are common throughout the year.

DOME OF THE ROCK (also called MOSQUE OF OMAR) Gold-domed Moslem mosque in Jerusalem. The original mosque, built in 690 C.E. after the Caliph Omar conquered Jerusalem, still stands. This beautiful eight-sided building is lined with marble and blue-green tiles. The rock at the center of the mosque is holy to both Jews and Moslems. Jews call the rock "Even Shetiyah" and believe that it was the place on Mount Moriah where Abraham prepared to sacrifice his son Isaac. King David built an altar on that spot and it was there that Solomon erected the Temple. Moslems believe that Mohammed rose to heaven on his winged horse from the rock. (See also ABRAHAM; DAVID; EVEN SHETIYAH; MOUNT MORIAH; TEMPLE.)

DOR Ancient Phoenician city on the Mediterranean coast. Dor was an Israelite city under King David, was captured by the Assyrians in the eighth century B.C.E., and was occupied by the Crusaders in the 1100s C.E. Today it is a small beach resort. (See also ASSYRIA; CRUSADES; DAVID; HISTORY; PHOENICIANS.)

DORI, YAAKOV (name changed from DOSTROVSKI) (1889-1973) Soldier and engineer. Dori was a leader of the Haganah (underground army) for years and became its head in 1939. When the Haganah was made into the Israel Defense Forces in 1948, Dori was appointed its Chief-of-Staff. His engineering background qualified him for the position of president of the Technion in Haifa when he retired from the armed forces. (See also DEFENSE FORCES; HAGANAH; TECHNION.)

DORMITION MONASTERY Church and home of the Christian order of the Benedictines built on Mount Zion in the early 1900s. Christians believe that the Dormition Monastery is on the spot where the Virgin Mary fell into an eternal sleep. (See also MOUNT ZION.)

DOSH see GARDOSH, KARIEL

DREIDEL A spinning top used in a game played by Jewish children during the Hanukkah holidays. The original dreidel was marked with initials for the Hebrew words, "A great miracle happened there." In Israel, when the Jewish State was established, the words were changed to "A great miracle happened here." (See also HANUKKAH.)

DRUYANOW, ALTER (1870-1938) Russian-born writer who settled in Palestine in 1923. He was active in Hibbat Zion (a Zionist movement) in Russia and later wrote its history. He was also the editor of *Ha-olam*, a Zionist magazine. (See also HA-OLAM; HIBBAT ZION; ZIONISM.)

The Dome of the Rock is the third holiest mosque in Islam. Mecca is
the holiest spot and Medina is second.

A view of the Dome of the Rock showing Muslim faithfuls in prayer
at one of the smaller outdoor prayer sites.

DRUZE   Arabic-speaking people who practice a special form of the Moslem faith that they are forbidden to discuss with outsiders. Each April twenty-fifth, the Druze go on a pilgrimage to the tomb of their Prophet Shueib (the biblical Jethro, father-in-law of Moses) near the Horns of Hittin in lower Galilee.

In 1975 there were 38,000 Druze living in Israel in 18 villages in Galilee and on Mount Carmel. They are an independent people who maintain their own lifestyle. Israeli Druze have their own schools and their own religious courts. Many Druze fought beside the Israelis in the 1948 War of Independence and now, at their own request, their young men are drafted into the Israel Defense Forces. (See also COURTS, RELIGIOUS; EDUCATION; GALILEE; MOUNT CARMEL; NATIONAL SERVICE; RELIGION; WAR OF INDEPENDENCE.)

DUNAM   Land in Israel is measured in dunams. One dunam is about a quarter of an acre. (See also METRIC SYSTEM.)

DUNG GATE (Hebrew, SHAAR HAASHPOT)   One of the eight gates in the wall around the Old City of Jerusalem. In ancient times garbage was removed from the city through the Dung Gate. (See also JERUSALEM; WALLED CITIES.)

E

EASTER Christian holiday celebrated on the Sunday after the first full moon following the vernal equinox (first day of spring). The Eastern Orthodox churches, which still use the older Julian calendar, celebrate the holiday later. Easter Sunday marks the resurrection (rising from the dead) of Jesus Christ. It ends the 40-day fast of Lent that began on Ash Wednesday. (See also CALENDAR, JULIAN; CHRISTIANS; GOOD FRIDAY; HOLIDAYS; JESUS; PALM SUNDAY.)

EBAN, ABBA SOLOMON (also spelled EVEN) (1915-) Politician born in Capetown, South Africa, and educated in England. He was a brilliant student, graduating from Cambridge University with first class honors in Latin, Greek, Hebrew, Arabic, and other oriental languages. During World War II Eban served in the British army and was sent to Jerusalem. After the war he made Jerusalem his home, worked in the political department of the Jewish Agency, and represented the Agency in the 1940 United Nations debate on establishing a Jewish State.

When Israel became a nation in 1948, Eban continued to serve the new government. He was Israel's representative in the United Nations and her ambassador to the United States. He was elected to the Israeli Knesset (legislature) and served as Minister of Education and Culture in Prime Minister Ben-Gurion's Cabinet, Deputy Prime Minister under Levi Eshkol, and Foreign Minister in both Eshkol's and Golda Meir's governments.

Eban was also president of the Weizmann Institute of Science and established the Institute's international science conferences. He has written a number of books, including a history of the Jews called *My People*. (See also BEN-GURION, DAVID; CABINET; ESHKOL, LEVI; JEWISH AGENCY; KNESSET; MEIR, GOLDA; UNITED NATIONS; WEIZMANN INSTITUTE OF SCIENCE.)

ECCE HOMO ARCH Arch over the Via Dolorosa in the Old City of Jerusalem. It is believed that this is the place where Pontius Pilate showed Jesus to the crowd before the Crucifixion and said, *"Ecce homo"* (Latin for "Behold the man"). (See also JERUSALEM; JESUS; VIA DOLOROSA.)

ECONOMY Israel has a mixed economy with government-owned corporations, cooperative associations, and private business existing side by side. The government controls all water and electric production and about half of the transportation and communications. It also invests in private and cooperative companies, regulates imports and exports, and plans for the economy as a whole. The Histadrut (General Federation of Labor) is very active in the field of cooperatives. Its members own newspapers and construction and industrial companies, as well as running agricultural marketing cooperatives. In spite of the importance of the government and the Histadrut in the economy, private business accounts for more than half of all goods and services produced in Israel. (See also COOPERATIVES; ELECTRICITY; FOREIGN TRADE; HISTADRUT; WATER.)

EDOM (also called IDUMEA)   Ancient country in Palestine located between the Dead Sea and the Gulf of Eilat. The Edomites and the Israelites were often at war. King David conquered Edom in the tenth century B.C.E., but it later regained its independence. When John Hyrcanus again conquered the country in the second century B.C. E., he forced the Edomites to become Jews. From then on they were considered part of the Jewish people. (See also DAVID; HYRCANUS, JOHN.)

Abba Eban (standing), Israel's first Ambassador to the U.S., listens in on the first meeting of President Harry Truman with David Ben-Gurion (right), Israel's first Prime Minister.

The Ecce Homo Arch (foreground) on the Via Dolorosa. The words
ecce homo, in Latin, mean "here is the man." According to legend
Jesus was given to the Romans on this spot.

EDUCATION   Education is considered very important in Israel. A large part of the government's budget is spent on schooling and the Ministry of Education and Culture oversees all schools. All children between the ages of five and fifteen must attend school, although their parents can decide whether to send them to general or religious schools. Many religious Jews choose to send their children to yeshivot (religious schools), and Arab and Druze children usually attend their special schools. Education is free until age fifteen and there are special grants to help poor children continue school after age fifteen.

Many Israeli three and four-year-olds go to nursery schools. All five-year-olds must attend kindergarten. Children whose immigrant families speak a different language at home are taught to speak Hebrew in kindergarten. This is important because all their later schooling will be in Hebrew. Arab children, however, are taught in Arabic.

Students attend elementary school for six years. They learn to read and write and they study arithmetic, social studies, science, citizenship, and Bible. Bible study is an important subject in state schools as well as in religious schools. Students also begin to

Vocational training is an important part of education in Israel. Here, a student is learning to use a machine lathe at a vocational training center.

study a foreign language in elementary school—usually English, although some schools teach French.

Secondary education is divided into two three-year schools, similar to American junior high and high schools. There are academic, vocational, and agricultural secondary schools. Students attending academic secondary schools often plan to go on to university study. They must pass examinations in five subjects to receive the matriculation certificate (diploma) needed to enter a university. Vocational and agricultural school students usually go directly into the work world when they graduate.

Israel has seven universities. Both the large Hebrew University in Jerusalem and Tel Aviv University offer a very wide range of studies. The smaller Haifa University specializes in the humanities, while Ben-Gurion University of the Negev is mainly an engineering school. The Technion is Israel's institute of technology and the Weizmann Institute is a science center. Bar-Ilan University is known for religious studies.

Israel's large number of new immigrants pose a special educational problem. Some of these immigrants received little or no education in their native lands. Others come well educated but know no Hebrew. Young immigrants who are drafted into the Defense Forces get intensive training in Hebrew. Draftees who do not have an elementary school education must also study school subjects. Other immigrants can attend an ulpan, a special school teaching Hebrew language and culture. (See also AGRI-CULTURAL SCHOOLS; ARABIC; BAR-ILAN UNIVERSITY; BEN-GURION UNIVERSITY; BIBLE STUDY; BOOKS; HAIFA UNIVERSITY; HEBREW; HEBREW UNIVERSITY; NATIONAL SERVICE; PHYSICAL EDUCATION; TECHNION; TEL AVIV UNIVERSITY; ULPAN; WEIZMANN INSTITUTE; YESHIVA.)

EFROS, ISRAEL (1890-   )   Hebrew poet. Born in Poland, Efros went to the United States in 1906. Besides writing poetry, he translated Shakespeare into Hebrew and Bialik's Hebrew poems into English. He also taught at Dropsie College and Hunter College. In 1954 Efros settled in Israel where he taught at Tel Aviv University. (See also BIALIK, HAYIM NAHMAN; TEL AVIV UNIVERSITY.)

EGYPT   Country in northeast Africa that borders Israel. Its capital is Cairo. Egypt covers an area of 386,000 square miles and has a population of 38,900,000 (1977). Most Egyptians are Moslems and speak Arabic.

Civilization began early along the Nile River. By 3100 B.C.E. the kingdoms of lower Egypt and upper Egypt were united under one Pharaoh (king). The united kingdom conquered Palestine,

Syria, and Ethiopia in the 1500s B.C.E. and established a powerful empire that lasted for 500 years. In 525 B.C.E. Egypt was conquered by Persia. It was then ruled in turn by the Greeks, Romans, Arabs, and British. In 1922, modern Egypt again became an independent nation.

Egypt was one of the Arab countries that refused to accept the existence of the new State of Israel in 1948. The Egyptian army advanced through the Sinai Desert into Israel and nearly reached Tel Aviv before being turned back. The Egyptian-Israeli armistice that ended the War of Independence in 1949 only held for six years before war between the two states broke out again. The fighting of the 1956 Sinai War lasted for a week, during which time Israel occupied most of the Sinai and the Gaza Strip. Under pressure from the United Nations Israel later withdrew. In May 1967 President Nasser of Egypt announced that his country was ready for a total war to destroy Israel. This resulted in the June 1967 Six-Day War, which ended with the defeat of the Egyptian armies. On October 6, 1973 Egyptian forces again invaded Israel, but the Yom Kippur War, too, ended with the Egyptians being driven back.

In November 1977 President Anwar Sadat (who had succeeded President Nasser in 1970) surprised the world by going to Jerusalem to talk peace with Israel, where he met with Israeli Prime Minister Begin. Sadat and Begin met again at Camp David, in the United States, and on March 26, 1979 the Israel-Egypt Peace Treaty was signed in Washington, D.C. The other Arab countries denounced Egypt for making peace with Israel. Most of them broke off trade and diplomatic relations with Egypt. (See also CAMP DAVID SUMMIT; GAZA STRIP; ISRAEL-EGYPT PEACE TREATY; NASSER, GAMAL ABDUL; SADAT, ANWAR; SINAI; SINAI WAR; SIX-DAY WAR; WAR OF INDEPENDENCE; YOM KIPPUR WAR.)

EGYPT-ISRAEL PEACE TREATY see ISRAEL-EGYPT PEACE TREATY

EHUD One of the biblical Judges. Ehud killed the king of Moab and led the Israelites into battle to destroy the Moabite armies and retake the land of Moab for Israel. His story is told in the biblical Book of Judges, Chapter 3. (See also BIBLE; JUDGES; MOAB.)

EICHMANN, ADOLPH (1906-1962) Nazi general who organized the murder of a million and a half Jews in Eastern Europe during World War II. Eichmann hid in Argentina after the war, but was tracked down by Israeli agents and brought to Israel for trial. More than a hundred witnesses from many countries appeared at Eichmann's trial in 1961. They told of the horrors of the concentration camps. The Eichmann trial attracted the attention of the whole world and reminded the world of how the Jews had

Adolph Eichmann (in glass booth) on trial in Jerusalem.

suffered during the Holocaust. Eichmann was hanged in 1961 for his crimes against humanity. (See also HOLOCAUST; NAZIS.)

EILAT (also spelled ELATH and ELAT)   Port on the Gulf of Eilat that is Israel's most southern city. Eilat was founded in 1949 and grew rapidly after the 1956 Sinai War opened the Gulf of Eilat to Israeli shipping. Today many of Israel's exports to Africa and the Far East are shipped from Eilat. The city is at the southern end of Israel's oil pipeline and is also the site of a desalinization plant turning sea water into fresh water. Because of its hot climate and location on the sea, Eilat is a popular winter beach resort. Its

Children's Forest contains a tree planted for every child born in Eilat. (See also DESALINIZATION; EILAT, GULF OF; OIL; PORTS; RE-FORESTATION; SHIPPING; SINAI WAR.)

EILAT, GULF OF (also called GULF OF AQABA)   Long thin body of water at the southern tip of Israel. It is 117 miles long, but only 9 miles wide. The Gulf of Eilat is bounded by Egypt, Jordan, Saudi Arabia, and Israel, and serves as Israel's southern outlet to the Indian Ocean. Ships leaving the port of Eilat sail down the Gulf of Eilat, into the Red Sea, and on into the Indian Ocean. (See also EILAT; SHIPPING.)

EIN (also spelled EN)   The Hebrew word for "well" or "spring." Since ancient Palestinian towns were often founded near a well or oasis, "Ein" is common as part of place-names in Israel.

EIN DOR (also spelled EN DOR)   Kibbutz founded in 1948 on the site of the biblical town of En Dor. (See also KIBBUTZ.)

EIN GANNIM (also spelled EN GANNIM)   First moshav (farming village where the workers share the profits) in Israel. It was founded in 1908 by members of Hibbat Zion (a Russian Zionist group) on land a few miles east of Tel Aviv. Today Ein Gannim is part of the city of Petah Tikva. (See also MOSHAV; PETAH TIKVA.)

EIN GEDI (also spelled EN GEDI)   Oasis in the Judean Desert near the western shore of the Dead Sea. The name refers to the spring that pours down the rock mountainside into a clear pool. Ein Gedi was praised in the *Song of Songs* in the Bible. Nearby are the caves where David hid from Saul. The town was one of Bar Kokhba's strongholds in the 132-135 C.E. revolt against Rome.

Ein Gedi is an important archaeological site. Five different towns built on top of each other have been uncovered. Among the most interesting finds are a Roman public bath from the time of Bar Kokhba and a Byzantine synagogue with a beautiful mosaic floor bearing the words, "Peace in Israel."

In 1953 a kibbutz was founded near the ancient site. The settlers grow flowers for the European market. (See also ARCHAE-OLOGY; BAR KOKHBA, SIMEON; BYZANTIUM; DAVID; FLOWERS; HISTO-RY; KIBBUTZ; MOSAICS; ROME; SAUL.)

EIN GEV (also spelled EN GEV)   Village founded in 1937 on the eastern shore of Lake Kinneret (Sea of Galilee). It was the only Jewish settlement in that area in 1948 and stood up to repeated Syrian attacks during the War of Independence. Today the settlers grow tropical fruits, and fish in the lake. Ein Gev is the home of the annual Passover Music Festival which draws performers and audiences from all over the world. (See also LAKE KINNERET; MUSIC; WAR OF INDEPENDENCE.)

A natural waterfall at Ein Gedi.

EIN HAROD (also spelled EN HAROD)   One of the largest kibbutzim in Israel. Ein Harod was founded on swampland in the Jezreel Valley in 1921. The swamps were drained and the settlement grew rapidly. Today, besides flourishing crops, dairies, and workshops, it boasts a theater, an art gallery, and the Beit Sturman Museum of natural history and archaeology. Ein Harod is really two neighboring communities, having divided in 1956 because of political differences among the members. Near the kibbutz is the Ma'ayan Harod National Park which contains the Spring of Harod where the Bible says that Gideon gathered his army before the battle with the Midianites. (See also GIDEON; JEZREEL VALLEY; KIBBUTZ; NATIONAL PARKS.)

EIN HASHOFET (also spelled EN HA-SHOPHET)   Kibbutz founded by American pioneers in 1937 in the hills about 15 miles south of Haifa. Its name means "spring of the judge" and honors United States Supreme Court Justice Louis Brandeis for his Zionist Activities. Ein Hashofet has a small archaeological museum and a theater where plays are produced during the summer season. (See also BRANDEIS, LOUIS DEMBITZ; KIBBUTZ.)

EIN HOD (also spelled EN HOD)   Artists' village in the Carmel hills 14 miles south of Haifa. Ein Hod is sponsored by the Israeli government, but is run by the artists themselves. A cooperative art gallery sells paintings, sculpture, pottery, silver, and tapestries made in the village. (See also ARTISTS' COLONY.)

EIN KAREM (also spelled EN KAREM)   Suburban village west of Jerusalem. Ein Karem was the birthplace of John the Baptist. It contains both the Church of John the Baptist and the Church of the Visitation which marks the spot where the Virgin Mary is said to have visited John's mother. Near Ein Karem archaeologists have uncovered an early Israelite High Place used for worship before the Temple was built in Jerusalem. (See also ARCHAEOLOGY; HIGH PLACE; JERUSALEM; JOHN THE BAPTIST; TEMPLE.)

EIN NETAFIM (also spelled EN NETAPHIM)   Outpost in the Sinai near Eilat. Ein Netafim was once an important stop for caravans of merchants traveling between Asia and Africa. (See also SINAI.)

EITAN, RAPHAEL (1929-   )   Soldier who was born and educated in Israel and who joined the Palmah (striking force of the Jewish underground army) at the age of 17. Eitan fought in each of the Israeli-Arab wars and was wounded in the 1948 War of Independence and again in the 1967 Six-Day War. He was a paratrooper and parachuted into battle from airplanes. He became chief paratroop officer and then rose to the rank of Chief-of-

Staff of the Israeli Defense Forces. (See also DEFENSE FORCES; PALMAH; SIX-DAY WAR; WAR OF INDEPENDENCE.)

EKRON   The most northern of the five Philistine cities in ancient Palestine. It stood between Jerusalem and what is now Tel Aviv. Ekron was captured by the Assyrians in the eighth century B.C.E. and was a large Jewish village in the 200s C.E. The farming village of Mazkeret Batyah, founded in 1883, stands on the ancient site. (See also ASSYRIA; PHILISTINES.)

EL AKSA MOSQUE (also spelled EL AQSA)   Silver-domed Moslem mosque in the Old City of Jerusalem built in the eighth century C.E. by the Caliph Abd el-Malik. It has been partly destroyed by earthquakes and invasions and rebuilt and repaired many times, but sections of the original building still remain. King Abdullah of Jordan was murdered in the El Aqsa Mosque in 1951.

The mosque is believed to be built on the site of the palace of the kings of Judah, and a stairway leads down from the mosque into King Solomon's stables. (See also ABDULLAH IBN HUSSEIN; JERUSALEM; JUDAH, KINDGOM OF.)

The interior of the richly carpeted El Aksa Mosque, where the moslems of Jerusalem gather in large numbers for the Friday prayer service.

EL AL The national airline of Israel. El Al was established in 1948 and has grown as Israel's tourist industry has increased. Today the airline links Tel Aviv and Jerusalem with four continents and carries more than half the passengers flying in and out of Ben-Gurion Airport. Since Israeli planes have been targets of Arab terrorist attacks, strict security measures are taken on all flights. (See also BEN-GURION AIRPORT; TOURISM.)

EL ARISH (also spelled AL ARISH) City on the Mediterranean coast in northern Sinai. El Arish is the capital of the Sinai. The city (along with the rest of the Sinai peninsula) was occupied by Israel during the 1967 Six-Day War. In May of 1979, El Arish and all the land in the Sinai west of the city was returned to Egypt under the terms of the Israel-Egypt Peace Treaty. (See also ISRAEL-EGYPT PEACE TREATY; SINAI; SIX-DAY WAR.)

ELAH King of Israel who succeeded his father Baasha and ruled 886-885 B.C.E. Elah was killed by one of his own captains during a war against the Philistines. (See also BAASHA; ISRAEL, KINGDOM OF; PHILISTINES.)

ELAMITES Ancient people who lived in biblical times in what is now Iran.

ELATH see EILAT

ELATH, ELIHU (name changed from EPSTEIN) (1903-) Russian-born diplomat who settled in Palestine in 1925 and worked for the Jewish Agency. Elath was the first Israeli ambassador to the United States and later was ambassador to Great Britain. He also served as president of the Hebrew University in Jerusalem. (See also HEBREW UNIVERSITY; JEWISH AGENCY.)

ELAZAR, DAVID (1925-1976) Yugoslavian-born soldier who settled in Palestine in 1940. Elazar fought in the 1967 Six-Day War and was responsible for Israel's capturing the Golan Heights. He became Commander-in-Chief of the army in 1972, but resigned two years later because of criticism that the army was not properly prepared for the 1973 Yom Kippur War. (See also DEFENSE FORCES; GOLAN HEIGHTS; SIX-DAY WAR; YOM KIPPUR WAR.)

ELAZARI-VOLCANI, YITZHAK (name changed from WILKANSKI) (1880-1955) Lithuanian-born soil and crop expert who settled in Palestine in 1908. Volcani believed that a farming settlement should plant a variety of crops rather than concentrating on only one crop. He worked with the World Zionist Organization to set up a number of experimental farms and founded an experimental agricultural station that later became the Volcani Institute for Agricultural Research at Rehovot. (See also AGRI-

David Elazar

CULTURE; AGRICULTURAL RESEARCH; VOLCANI INSTITUTE; WORLD ZIONIST ORGANIZATION.)

ELEAZAR (also called AURAN) (died 163 B.C.E.)   Hasmonean soldier and brother of Judah the Maccabee. Eleazar was killed in battle during the second century B.C.E. Maccabean revolt against the Syrians. (See also HASMONEANS; HISTORY; JUDAH THE MACCABEE; MACCABEE; SYRIA.)

ELEAZAR BEN JAIR (died 73 C.E.)   Zealot leader. When the 66-70 C.E. Zealot revolt against Roman rule in Palestine began to fail, Eleazar led the remaining Jewish army and their families to the fortress of Masada. They held out through a long Roman siege and finally killed themselves rather than surrender. (See also HISTORY; ROME; ZEALOTS.)

ELEAZAR BEN SIMON   Zealot leader in the 66-70 C.E. Jewish revolt against Roman rule of Palestine. Eleazar played an important part in defeating the Roman army that Cestius Gallus led to Jerusalem to try to put down the revolt. (See also HISTORY; ROME; ZEALOTS.)

ELECTED ASSEMBLY   see ASEFAT HANIVHARIM

ELECTRICITY   Generators that produce electricity can be powered by diesel engines, by steam turbines, by water power, or by nuclear energy. Palestine's first electric power plant, built in 1923 at Tel Aviv, was diesel powered. The first steam-driven power plant was built at Haifa in 1934. A plan to harness the Jordan River for water power to produce electricity was suggested as early as 1921, and the dam and power plant at Naharayim on the Jordan River were completed in 1932. (The Naharayim plant was destroyed by the Arabs during the 1948 War of Independence.) No nuclear-powered plants have been built as of 1978, but one is planned at Ashdod.

In 1923 the British (who then ruled Palestine under the Mandate) gave the Palestine Electric Company, under the direction of Pinhas Rutenberg, the right to build and operate the country's electric generating plants. In 1955 the Israeli government took over the company and changed its name to the Israel Electric Company. Today the Israel Electric Company operates under the direction of the government Ministry of Development, which is responsible for producing and distributing the country's electricity. All generating plants in Israel are hooked into one national power grid. (See also ASHDOD; GREAT BRITAIN; JORDAN RIVER; NUCLEAR ENERGY; PALESTINE ELECTRIC COMPANY; RUTENBERG, PINHAS.)

ELECTRONICS INDUSTRY   The manufacture of electric and electronic equipment is a new, but fast-growing, industry in Israel. After the 1967 Six-Day War, the government encouraged industry to produce the electronic equipment needed for defense so it would not have to depend on imports from other countries. By 1971 the industry had doubled its production. It now exports electronic equipment for telephones and military uses to other countries. (See also FOREIGN TRADE.)

ELIJAH   Biblical prophet who lived in the kingdom of Israel during the rule of Ahab. When Jezebel, Ahab's wife, brought the worship of Baal to Israel, Elijah denounced Ahab and killed the prophets of Baal on Mount Carmel. Elijah was forced to flee from Ahab's anger and hide in a cave, but he returned to denounce the king again for killing one of his subjects in order to take his vineyard. Elijah's prophesies of Ahab's destruction are described in the biblical first Book of Kings. (See also AHAB; BAAL; BIBLE; CAVE OF ELIJAH; ISRAEL, KINGDOM OF; JEZEBEL.)

ELIMELEKH   In the Book of Ruth, the father-in-law of Ruth and husband of Naomi. He was a native of Bethlehem who moved to Moab during a period of famine.

ELISHEVA (pen name of YELIZAVETA ZHIRKOVA) (1888-1949) Russian-born poet who settled in Palestine in 1925. Elisheva's first poems were written in Russian, but she soon began to write in Hebrew.

EL-KUDS   Arabic name for Jerusalem.

ELMALEH, ABRAHAM RAPHAEL (also spelled ALMALIAH) (1885-1947)   Jerusalem-born writer and leader of the Sephardic community. Elmaleh compiled an Arabic-Hebrew dictionary and a French-Hebrew dictionary and wrote books about the life and history of Sephardic Jews. He also served in the first Israeli Knesset (legislature). (See also KNESSET; SEPHARDIM.)

ELON   Settlement in western Galilee founded in 1938 as a defense post against Arab raids from Lebanon. (See also GALILEE; LEBANON.)

ELON MOREH   A hilltop about one mile from Nablus (the biblical Shechem). In Genesis 12:6 God promised to give the land (it was then called Canaan, and later, Palestine) to Abraham and his descendants. In 1979, when Elon Moreh was part of the West Bank of Israel, a Jewish settlement was built there and this caused much tension between Arabs and Jews. In October 1979 the Israel Supreme Court ruled that this settlement was illegal.

EMEK   Hebrew for "valley" or "plain." "The Emek" usually refers to the Jezreel Valley. (See also JEZREEL VALLEY.)

EMEK HEFER   see HEFER VALLEY

EMEK JEZREEL   see JEZREEL VALLEY

EMEK ZEBULUN   see ZEBULUN VALLEY

EMMAUS   Ancient city near Jerusalem. It was near Emmaus that Judah the Maccabee fought the Syrians during the 167 B.C.E. Jewish revolt. Christians remember Emmaus as the place where Jesus appeared to his followers on the third day after his death. The Romans called the city Nicopolis. Today there is only a small village on the site. (See also JESUS; JUDAH THE MACCABEE; ROME.)

ENGEL, YOEL (1868-1927)   Russian-born composer who settled in Tel Aviv in 1924. He was the founder of the Moscow Society for Jewish Folk Music and his own compositions show the influence of folk music. His children's songs are still popular in Israel. The Engel Prize, named in his honor, is given each year in Tel Aviv to an outstanding composer or musician.

ENGLISH   Hebrew and Arabic are the official languages of Israel, but English is taught in most elementary schools from the fifth grade on. Much of the reading in universities is in English. Street signs in the cities are in English as well as in Hebrew and Arabic. (See also ARABIC; EDUCATION; HEBREW.)

ENTEBBE RAID   In July of 1976 Palestinian terrorists hijacked an airplane on its way from Israel to Paris. They flew the plane to Entebbe Airport in Uganda, Africa. The terrorists held 105 passengers hostage (most of whom were Israeli citizens) and threatened to kill them unless a number of terrorists were freed from jails in Israel and other countries. Shortly before the deadline for murder, Israeli soldiers carried out a daring raid on Entebbe Airport. Three hostages and the ground commander of the raid were killed in the fighting, but the other soldiers and the hostages flew safely back to Israel. The raid showed the world that Israel was determined to protect its people against terrorism. (See also PALESTINE LIBERATION ORGANIZATION; TERRORISM.)

EPHRAIM   Ancient Israelite tribe descended from Ephraim, the younger son of Joseph. When King Solomon died around 920 B.C.E., not everyone liked his son Rehoboam who succeeded him, and Palestine split into the northern kingdom of Israel and the southern kingdom of Judah. Since Jeroboam, the first king of the northern kingdom of Israel, was of the tribe of Ephraim, his country was often called the House of Ephraim. (See also HISTORY; ISRAEL, KINGDOM OF; JEROBOAM; JOSEPH; JUDAH, KINGDOM OF; SOLOMON; TWELVE TRIBES.)

EPIPHANY   Christian holiday celebrated in Catholic, some Eastern Orthodox, and Protestant churches throughout Israel on January 6th. Epiphany marks the visit of the three Magi (kings) to the infant Jesus. Some of the Eastern Orthodox churches celebrate Epiphany on Christmas Day. (See also CHRISTIANS; CHRISTMAS; HOLIDAYS; JESUS.)

EPSTEIN, YITZHAK (1862-1943)   Russian-born Hebrew writer and teacher who settled in Palestine in 1919. Epstein wrote many articles about the Hebrew language and published a textbook describing his direct method of teaching Hebrew. He believed in cooperation between Arabs and Jews and was one of the founders of Berit Shalom, an organization that worked for a joint Arab-Jewish state in Palestine. (See also BERIT SHALOM; HEBREW.)

EPSTEIN, ZALMAN (1860-1936)   Russian-born Zionist and writer who emigrated to Palestine in 1925 and wrote about Zionist problems and Hebrew language and literature. (See also HEBREW; ZIONISM.)

EREL, SHLOMO (name changed from EHRLICH, SIEGUSH) (1916-   )   Diplomat who was secretary of Habonim (a Zionist youth group) in his native Germany before settling in Israel in 1937. Over the years Erel has represented the Jewish Agency and the Israeli government in missions to the United States, Canada, and several South American countries. (See also HABONIM; JEWISH AGENCY.)

Shlomo Erel

ERETZ YISRAEL   Hebrew for "land of Israel."

ESHKOL, LEVI (name changed from SHKOLNIK) (1895-1969)
Third Prime Minister of Israel. He was born in the Ukraine in
Russia and settled in Palestine in 1914. Eshkol worked as a
farmhand at the settlement of Petah Tikva, served in the Jewish
Legion during World War I, and after the war was one of the
founders of Kibbutz Degania Beth.

Eshkol became an expert on land settlement and helped plan
and develop Jewish settlements in the Jezreel and Hefer valleys.
At the same time he raised money and bought arms for the
Haganah (Jewish underground army). He also organized immigration of Jews from Nazi Germany into Palestine. When Israel
became a state in 1948 and large numbers of immigrants poured
into the country, Eshkol was the head of the Jewish Agency's
settlement department, which helped the new immigrants to find
homes and establish new lives.

He was elected as a Mapai Party member of the Israeli Knesset
(legislature), served as Minister of Finance in David Ben-
Gurion's government, and succeeded Ben-Gurion as Prime Minister in 1963. Eshkol's strength as Prime Minister was his ability
to get Israelis of different political views to work together.
During his six years in office Israel reopened diplomatic relations with Germany, fought the Six-Day War, and struggled to
establish secure national borders. (See also BEN-GURION, DAVID;
CABINET; DEGANIA; HAGANAH; HEFER VALLEY; IMMIGRANTS;
KNESSET; JEWISH AGENCY; JEWISH LEGION; JEZREEL VALLEY; MAPAI;
PETAH TIKVA; PRIME MINISTER; SIX-DAY WAR.)

ESSENES   Ancient Jewish monklike religious sect that existed in Palestine from the second century B.C.E. to the second century C.E. The Essenes believed in the immortality of the soul. They opposed slavery, the sacrifice of animals, and the ownership of private property. They lived lives of discipline and poverty. The Manual of Discipline, one of the ancient Dead Sea Scrolls, is believed to describe the rules governing the lives of the Essenes. (See also DEAD SEA SCROLLS.)

ESTHER   Biblical heroine who became the wife of King Ahasuerus of Persia. When Haman, the evil adviser to the king, decided to kill all the Jews of Persia, Queen Esther pleaded with Ahasuerus to permit the Jews to defend themselves. The king agreed and the Jews were saved. Haman was hanged, and the feast of Purim was established to celebrate the event. Purim is celebrated every year with a feast and the reading of the Megillah (the biblical Book of Esther). (See also BIBLE; HAMAN; PURIM.)

ETHNARACH   Title meaning "ruler of a people" in Greek. It was given to Simon the Hasmonean by the people of Judea. (See also SIMON THE HASMONEAN.)

ETHRONGES   (also spelled ATHRONGAIOS) (first century B.C.E.)   One of the five brothers who led a Jewish revolt against the Romans in 4 B.C.E. Ethronges was captured after defeating a Roman force at Emmaus. (See also ROME.)

ETTINGER, AKIVA JACOB (1872-1945)   Soil expert who settled in Palestine in 1918. Ettinger was interested in developing new kinds of agricultural settlements. He planned some of the villages in the Jezreel Valley and was the founder of Kiryat Anavim, the first agricultural settlement in the hills rather than on the flat Coastal Plain. He wrote several books about his agricultural work. (See also AGRICULTURE; JEZREEL VALLEY; KIRYAT ANAVIM.)

ETZION BLOCK   see GUSH ETZION

EUCALYPTUS   Evergreen tree native to Australia that was introduced into Palestine in the 1870s. Eucalyptus were planted by the early Jewish settlers on the Coastal Plain because they drew off the water and helped drain the swamps where malaria-carrying mosquitos lived. Eucalyptus trees grow throughout Israel today and are valued for their shade and as windbreaks. (See also COASTAL PLAIN; MALARIA; REFORESTATION.)

EUPHRATES RIVER   One of the two rivers that enclose the Tigris-Euphrates Valley in what is now Iraq. The fertile land between the rivers was called Mesopotamia in ancient times and gave rise to the world's earliest civilizations. The Euphrates is the more western of the two rivers. It marked the furthest border of the Jewish empire under King Solomon in the tenth century B.C.E. (See also FERTILE CRESCENT; MESOPOTAMIA; SOLOMON.)

EVEN   Hebrew word meaning "s⁺one." It is part of some place names in Israel.

EVEN SHETIYAH   Hebrew name for the large rock at the center of the Moslem mosque called the Dome of the Rock. *Even shetiyah* means "stone of foundation" and Jewish legend says that it is the rock on which the world was founded. It is also said to be the place where Abraham prepared to sacrifice his son Isaac and the site where the Ark of the Covenant was placed in the First Temple. (See also ABRAHAM; ARK OF THE COVENANT; DOME OF THE ROCK; TEMPLE.)

EVEN YEHUDA   Agricultural village on the Sharon Plain near Netanya founded in 1932 by members of Bene Binyamin, a Palestinian farmers' organization. It is named for Eliezer Ben Yehuda, the "father of modern Hebrew." (See also BEN YEHUDA, ELIEZER; SHARON PLAIN.)

EXODUS   The flight of the Israelites from slavery in Egypt around the thirteenth century B.C.E. The Book of Exodus describes the Israelites' preparations to leave Egypt, their departure, their 40 years of wandering in the desert, and their crossing of the Jordan River into Palestine. Each spring the Passover holiday celebrates the anniversary of the Exodus. (See also BIBLE; EGYPT; PASSOVER; SINAI.)

EXODUS 1947   Ship used by the Haganah (underground army) to bring Jewish refugees into Palestine in 1947. The British (who ruled Palestine under the Mandate) had forbidden more Jewish immigration and therefore seized the ship. Three Jews were killed in the battle and the rest forced to go back to Germany. The seizure of the *Exodus 1947* helped to show the world the need for a Jewish homeland in Palestine. (See also GREAT BRITAIN; HAGANAH; IMMIGRANTS, ILLEGAL; MANDATE.)

EYTAN, WALTER (1910-   )   German-born diplomat who settled in Palestine in 1946. He was the Israeli ambassador to France and wrote *A Diplomatic History of Israel.*

EZEKIEL (sixth century B.C.E.)   Biblical prophet who was exiled to Babylon in 586 B.C.E. and prophesied over a period of 22 years. The Book of Ezekiel describes his foreseeing the fall of Jerusalem. When Jerusalem was destroyed, Ezekiel said that the Jews would repent the sins that brought about the disaster and that the

Temple would be rebuilt. (See also BABYLONIAN EXILE; BIBLE; JERUSALEM; TEMPLE.)

EZION GEBER   Ancient city at the northern end of the Gulf of Eilat. Ezion Geber was an important port during King Solomon's reign in the tenth century B.C.E. Archaeologists have uncovered remains of the ancient port. (See also ARCHAEOLOGY; EILAT, GULF OF; SOLOMON.)

EZRA (fifth century B.C.E.)   Jewish priest and reformer of Jewish life in ancient Palestine. When the Jews returned from the Babylonian exile in the sixth century B.C.E., they abandoned many of their laws and traditions. In 458 B.C.E. Ezra returned to Jerusalem with Nehemiah and a group of Jewish exiles. The Book of Ezra in the Bible tells how he established a new order in Jerusalem and persuaded the Jews to keep the Torah (religious law), observe the Sabbath, and refuse to marry gentiles. (See also BABYLONIAN EXILE; BIBLE; NEHEMIAH; TORAH.)

F-G

FAITH BLOCK   see GUSH EMUNIM

FARBSTEIN, JOSHUA HESHEL (1870-1948)   Polish Zionist who was president of the Zionist Organization of Poland before he settled in Palestine in 1931 and worked for the Jewish Agency. (See also JEWISH AGENCY; ZIONISM.)

FARHI, ESTORI (also spelled PARHI) (about 1280-1355) Medieval French explorer who traveled throughout Palestine before he settled in Bet Shean. He published a book in 1322 that described the geography, natural history, towns, and ancient sites of Palestine of that period. (See also BET SHEAN.)

FARMING   see AGRICULTURE

FEDAYEEN (also spelled FEDAYIN)   In Arabic the name means "those who sacrifice themselves for the homeland." Fedayeen are Arab terrorists who attack Israeli border settlements, plant bombs in Israeli cities, and highjack planes as they try to drive the Jews into the sea. Most fedayeen are recruited from Arab refugee camps into commando organizations like Al Fatah and the Popular Front for the Liberation of Palestine. (See also AL FATAH; PALESTINE LIBERATION ORGANIZATION; PALESTINIAN REFUGEES; POPULAR FRONT FOR THE LIBERATION OF PALESTINE)

FEINBERG, AVSHALOM (1886-1917)   One of the founders (the other was Aaron Aaronson) of NILI, an underground group working to free Palestine from the Turks during World War I. Feinberg was killed by Bedouins in the Sinai Desert in 1917 while on a mission to Egypt to establish contact with the British. When his body was found 50 years later by Israeli soldiers, a palm tree was growing from a date pit he had had in his pocket. (See also AARONSON, AARON; NILI; SINAI.)

FEISAL IBN HUSSEIN (1885-1933)   King of Iraq who ruled 1921-1933. In 1919 Feisal signed an agreement with Chaim Weizmann, the Zionist leader, pledging friendship between the Arab and Jewish peoples and declaring himself in favor of Jewish immigration into Palestine. However, politics soon changed Feisal's attitude. He adopted the usual Arab anti-Zionism line, although he was not active in the fight against a Jewish State in Palestine. (See also WEIZMANN, CHAIM; ZIONISM.)

FEIWEL, BERTHOLD (1875-1937) Austrian Zionist leader who settled in Palestine in 1933. Feiwel helped Theodor Herzl organize the First Zionist Conference in Basle, Switzerland, in 1897 and was an editor of the Viennese Zionist newspaper *Die Welt.* In the 1920s he directed the Keren Hayesod (Zionist money-raising organization) in London. (See also HERZL, THEODOR; KEREN HEYESOD; WORLD ZIONIST ORGANIZATION; ZIONISM.)

FELAFEL A popular food sold at street stands in Israel's cities. Felafel is made of mashed chickpeas shaped into balls, deep fried, and put in a pocket of flat pita bread with sliced raw vegetables and tahina (sesame) sauce. (See also PITA; TAHINA.)

A felafel stand in Tel Aviv.

FELLAH (the plural is FELLAHEEN or FELLAHIN) Arab farmer who works his land himself. Fellaheen in Israel usually own their own small farms or belong to a village group that works all the village's land in turn. Fellaheen in Arab countries are more likely to rent their land from an absentee landlord. (See also ARABS.)

FERTILE CRESCENT An area of fertile land in the Middle East that produced some of the greatest civilizations of ancient times. The fertile crescent arches from Palestine to ancient Meso-

A felafel stand in Haifa. Felafel is enjoyed by Arabs, Jews, and tourists.

potamia and includes the valleys of the Jordan, the Tigris, and the Euphrates rivers. The area is now part of modern Israel, Lebanon, Syria, Turkey, and Iraq. (See also MESOPOTAMIA.)

FICHMAN, YAAKOV (1881-1958)   Russian-born Hebrew poet, writer, translator, and editor who settled in Palestine in 1925. The poems in his book *Corner of the Field* describe the beauty of the Palestinian countryside.

FISH PONDS   About one-third of the fish eaten in Israel each year comes from large fish ponds. The first experimental ponds were built in 1938 and the Israelis have since become world experts in fish breeding. Carp is the fish most often bred in the kibbutz ponds on the Coastal Plain. When the swamps of the Huleh Valley were drained in the 1950s, the excess water was used in establishing fish ponds. (See also COASTAL PLAIN; HULEH VALLEY; KIBBUTZ.)

FLAG   Israel's flag is white with a broad blue horizontal stripe near the top and near the bottom, and a blue Magen David (Star of David) in the center. The colors are said to have come from the blue and white of the traditional Jewish prayer shawl. This flag was originally adopted by the World Zionist Organization and became the official flag of Israel on October 28, 1948. (See also MAGEN DAVID; WORLD ZIONIST ORGANIZATION.)

FLOWERS   Fresh cut flowers are becoming an important agricultural export. Flowers are grown in greenhouses and out of doors throughout the year. Roses, gladiolas, and carnations are among the flowers grown in Israel and shipped by air to European and American markets. (See also AGRICULTURE; CLIMATE; FOREIGN TRADE; NEGEV.)

At Kibbutz Nes Ammim, a Christian kibbutz north of Acco, beautiful roses are grown in hothouses. The roses are exported to various parts of Europe.

FOOL'S HAT   see KOVEH TEMBEL

FOOTBALL   The British and Israeli name for the sport Americans call soccer. (See also SOCCER.)

FOREIGN AID PROGRAM   Since Israel is still a developing nation, it feels a special obligation to help other developing nations in Africa, Asia, Latin America, and the Mediterranean area. Israeli experts visit developing nations to share their agricultural, engineering, and health skills; and citizens of these nations come to Israel for training. As many as ten thousand students from developing countries study in Israel each year.

FOREIGN TRADE   The United States and the Common Market

of Western Europe account for about 80% of Israel's foreign trade. Israel's main exports are polished diamonds (most of which go to the United States), citrus fruit, textiles, and chemicals; the main imports are raw diamonds, consumer goods, and fuel. The Israeli government regulates foreign trade by means of licenses, taxes, and subsidies. (See also CITRUS FRUIT; DIAMONDS; ECONOMY; ELECTRONICS; FLOWERS; MINERALS; TEXTILES.)

FOREST OF THE MARTYRS A forest of six million trees planted outside of Jerusalem in memory of the six million Jews killed by the Nazis during World War II. (See also HOLOCAUST; NAZIS; REFORESTATION.)

FRANKEL, AVRAHAM HALEVI (1891-1965) German mathematician who settled in Palestine in 1929 and taught mathematics at the Hebrew University in Jerusalem. (See also HEBREW UNIVERSITY.)

FREIER, RECHA (1892-   ) German-born teacher and founder of Youth Aliyah. When Hitler came to power in Germany in 1933, Recha Freier formed the Society for Youth Aliyah, an organization devoted to bringing groups of Jewish young people out of Germany and settling them in villages in Palestine. She persuaded Henrietta Szold to take charge of the organization of Youth Aliyah while she formed the groups for immigration from Europe. In 1941 Recha Freier settled in Palestine and continued working with poor children. (See also NAZIS; SZOLD, HENRIETTA; YOUTH ALIYAH.)

FRIEDMANN, DAVID ARYE (1889-1957) Russian-born critic who settled in Palestine in 1925 and wrote many articles about Hebrew and world literature.

FRUMKIN, ARYE LEIB (1845-1916) Lithuanian-born rabbi and Palestinian pioneer. Frumkin was among the settlers who founded the village of Petah Tikva in 1882, building the first house in the settlement and establishing a yeshiva (religious school). He is remembered for his book, *History of the Sages of Jerusalem*. (See also PETAH TIKVA.)

FRUMKIN, ISRAEL DOV (1850-1914) Russian-born Hebrew journalist whose family moved to Palestine when he was nine. He was the editor of *Havatzelet*, Jerusalem's second modern newspaper, for 40 years. Frumkin invited Eliezer Ben Yehuda to come to Palestine to help him edit the paper. (See also BEN YEHUDA, ELIEZER; HAVATZELET.)

GAD One of the Twelve Tribes of Israel whose ancestor was Gad, the seventh son of Jacob. The tribe of Gad were important warriors during the rules of Saul and David in the eleventh and tenth centuries B.C.E. (See also DAVID; JACOB; SAUL; TWELVE TRIBES.)

GADNA   An abbreviation of the Hebrew words *geduday noar,* meaning "youth battalion." Gadna was set up by the Haganah (the Jewish underground army) in 1939 as a youth army. It was taken over by the Israeli government in 1949. Today, Gadna is the youth corps of the Israel Defense Forces that trains boys and girls ages 14 to 18 in service to their country. It is an educational organization similar to the Scouts that stresses physical education and citizenship. Gadna's members plant forests, help in archaeological digs, and work the soil in border agricultural settlements. The corps is divided into army, navy, and air sections. (See also DEFENSE FORCES; HAGANAH; YOUTH MOVEMENTS.)

GAHAL   Coalition of the Liberal and Herut political parties. Gahal was formed in 1965 and elected 26 out of the 120 members of the Israeli Knesset (legislature) that year. In 1973 Gahal added some small parties to its coalition, changed its name to Likud, and took 39 Knesset seats in the next election. (See also HERUT; KNESSET; LIBERAL PARTY; LIKUD; POLITICAL PARTIES.)

GALILEE   Geographical area in the extreme north of Israel. Upper Galilee is the highest section of Israel. It receives more rainfall than any other part of the country and its mountains are covered with plants and trees. Throughout history upper Galilee has been a remote and undeveloped area. Until 1960 its only city was Safed.

Lower Galilee is hilly, rather than mountainous, and has a number of fertile valleys. It was the center of Jewish life in Palestine after the destruction of the Second Temple in the first century C.E. and contains many important historic sites. Nazareth, the home of many Chrisitan Israelis, is in Galilee. (See also NAZARETH; SAFED; TEMPLE.)

GALILEE, SEA OF   see LAKE KINNERET

GALILEE SKULL   Stone age skull found in a cave west of Lake Kinneret (Sea of Galilee) in 1925. The skull has features of Neanderthal man as well as of modern man and is thought to be a link between the two.

GALILI, ISRAEL (1911-   )   Russian-born politician and soldier who was brought to Palestine at the age of four. Galili was a leader of the Haganah (underground Jewish army) and helped form the Palmah, Haganah's striking force. He was one of the founders of the Mapam political party and served as a member of the Israeli Knesset (legislature). (See also HAGANAH; KNESSET; MAPAM; PALMAH.)

GAN Hebrew word meaning "garden." It is part of some place-names in Israel.

GAN SHMUEL Kibbutz on the Sharon Plain. Gan Shmuel began with the planting of a grove of citrus trees in 1896. (See also CITRUS FRUIT; KIBBUTZ; SHARON PLAIN.)

GAN YAVNE Moshav (farming village) south of Tel Aviv founded in 1931 by American Zionists. It has since grown into a small city. (See also MOSHAV.)

GAON (plural GEONIM) The Hebrew word means "his eminence." The great Jewish scholars who lived in Babylonia from the sixth to the twelfth centuries. This was the period following the talmudic era which ended about 500 C.E. The geonim were not only the heads of the great colleges (yeshivot) of that period, but were also very influential in the political life of the community. They represented the Jews before the civil authorities.

Jewish life was centered in Babylonia during these centuries. Although there were academies of learning in Palestine, and their leaders were also called "geonim," these men carried little influence.

The two main academies in Babylonia were Sura and Pumbedita, named for the cities in which they were housed. The first geonim to occupy the exalted office were: Mar Hanan, the first gaon of Pumbedita, who took office in 589; and Mar bar Huna, the first gaon of Sura, who took office in 591.

GARDEN OF GETHSEMANE see GETHSEMANE

GARDOSH, KARIEL (pen name DOSH) (1921-) Hungarian-born cartoonist who settled in Israel in 1948. Dosh's political cartoons appear regularly in *Maariv*, an Israeli newspaper. (See also MAARIV.)

GARSTANG, JOHN (1876-1956) British archaeologist who was the director of the Palestine Department of Antiquities in the 1920s and led archaeological expeditions at Ashkelon, Jericho, and Hazor. (See also ARCHAEOLOGY; ASHKELON; HAZOR; JERICHO.)

GATE OF FLOWERS see HEROD'S GATE

GATE OF THE MUGHRABINS Small entrance on the south side of the Western Wall in Jerusalem. In ancient times the Western Wall was part of the outer wall of the Temple and the Gate of the Mughrabins led into the Temple court. (See also TEMPLE; WESTERN WALL.)

GATH   One of the five ancient Philistine cities on the Coastal Plain of Palestine. The city was captured by King David in the tenth century B.C.E. Nothing remains of it today. (See also DAVID; COASTAL PLAIN; PHILISTINES.)

GAVISH, YESHAYAHU (1925-   )   Native Israeli soldier who commanded the southern front during the 1967 Six-Day War. Gavish retired from the Defense Forces and became head of Koor Metals, a company that is part of Israel's largest group of industries. (See also DEFENSE FORCES; KOOR INDUSTRIES; SIX-DAY WAR.)

One of the gates leading to the Temple Mount.

GAZA   The most important of the five ancient Philistine cities on the coast of Palestine. Gaza was the busiest trade center of biblical times. It was here that Samson was blinded and pulled down the temple to the god Dagon (Judges 16:21-30). Gaza was captured by the Assyrians in 720 B.C.E., by the Persians in 521 B.C.E., became a Helenistic city under Alexander the Great, and later became a Roman commercial town. Today it is the main city of the Gaza Strip, one of the territories administered by Israel since the 1967 Six-Day War. (See also ASSYRIA; DAGON; GAZA STRIP; HELENISM; HISTORY; PERSIA; PHILISTINES; ROME; SIX-DAY WAR.)

GAZA STRIP   Narrow strip of land running 22 miles up the Mediterranean coast from the Israel-Egypt border. The Gaza Strip remained in Egyptian hands at the end of the War of

Independence in 1948 and served as a base for fedayeen (Arab terrorists) raids into Israel. It was occupied by Israel for a short time after the 1956 Sinai War and was captured again in the 1967 Six-Day War. Since 1967 the Gaza Strip has been one of the administered areas governed by Israel. By the terms of the 1979 Israel-Egypt Peace Treaty, the Palestinian Arabs in the Gaza Strip will be given self-rule by 1980. However, the treaty left the final fate of the Gaza Strip and of the Israeli settlements in the area to be worked out in the future. (See also ADMINISTERED AREAS; FEDAYEEN; ISRAEL-EGYPT PEACE TREATY; PALESTINIANS; SINAI WAR; SIX-DAY WAR; WAR OF INDEPENDENCE.)

GAZOZ STANDS Street stands in Israel's cities that sell cold drinks, candy, and pretzels. (See also CLIMATE; MITZ.)

GEDALIAH Governor of Judah who ruled over Palestine after the First Temple was destroyed in 586 B.C.E. Most Jews had been exiled to Babylon. (See also BABYLONIAN EXILE; JUDAH, KINGDOM OF.)

GEDERA Town about 15 miles south of Tel Aviv founded in 1884 by ten BILU pioneers. It was the first settlement in the area. In the late 1970s it had a population of nearly 6,000. (See also BILU.)

GEDUD HA-AVODA (English, LABOR BATTALION) Pioneering group in Palestine in the 1920s. The Labor Battalion was run as a commune, with its members sharing all the work and putting any earnings into a treasury to be doled out to the members as needed. They built many roads and founded the settlements of Ein Harod and Tel Yosef. (See also EIN HAROD; TEL YOSEF.)

GELBER, NATHAN MICHAEL (1891-1966) Austrian-born historian who was secretary of the Austrian Zionist Organization before he settled in Palestine in 1933. He wrote books on Jewish history and a history of Zionism. (See also ZIONISM.)

GEMARA see TALMUD

GENERAL ZIONISTS Political party founded in 1931. The General Zionists believed that the needs of the Jewish nation and the Jewish people as a whole had to be put above the needs of any particular group or class. In 1948 a section of the General Zionists broke away to become the Progressive Party, but in 1965 the two groups joined again to form the Liberal Party. (See also LIBERAL PARTY; POLITICAL PARTIES; PROGRESSIVE PARTY.)

GEOGRAPHY Israel is a small Middle Eastern country located between Asia and Africa. The Mediterranean Sea lies along its west coast and it has a southern outlet to the Red Sea through the

Gulf of Eilat. It is bordered on the north, west, and south by Lebanon, Syria, Jordan, and Egypt.

Israel's 1948 borders gave it a land area of about 8,000 square miles, but the territories occupied in 1967 bring the total area to about 35,000 square miles. The highest point in the country is the 3,692-foot peak of Mount Meron, and the lowest point is the Dead Sea whose surface is 1,300 feet below sea level. The main river is the Jordan River, and the two largest lakes are the Dead Sea and Lake Kinneret (Sea of Galilee).

Northern Israel is divided into three main regions: the Coastal Plain, the Highlands, and the Jordan Valley. The level Coastal Plain, which runs north-south along the Mediterranean coast, is the most fertile and most heavily populated part of the country. Haifa and Tel Aviv are located on the Coastal Plain as are a large number of smaller cities and agricultural villages. The Highlands, which include Galilee and Samaria, are much less fertile and therefore less populated. However, the Jezreel Valley, which runs through the Highlands, is an important agricultural area. The Jordan Valley marks Israel's eastern border.

Southern Israel is extremely dry. Although the Negev accounted for almost two-thirds of Israel's area before the 1967 Six-Day War, only about 3% of the country's population lived there. Today the Negev is being developed and its main cities, Beersheba and Eilat, are growing rapidly. (See also COASTAL PLAIN; DEAD SEA; GALILEE; GAZA STRIP; GOLAN HEIGHTS; HEFER VALLEY; JEZREEL VALLEY; JORDAN RIVER; JORDAN VALLEY; JUDEAN HILLS; LAKE KINNERET; MEDITERRANEAN SEA; NEGEV; SAMARIA; SHARON PLAIN; SINAI DESERT; WEST BANK.)

GERSON-KIWI, EDITH (1908-   )   German-born music expert who settled in Jerusalem in 1933. She was in charge of the archives of Jewish and Oriental music at the Hebrew University in Jerusalem. (See also ARCHIVES; HEBREW UNIVERSITY.)

GESHER   Kibbutz founded in the Jordan Valley in 1939. The settlement held off heavy Iraqi attacks during the 1948 War of Independence, but most of its buildings were destroyed and had to be rebuilt later. (See also KIBBUTZ; WAR OF INDEPENDENCE.)

GESHER BNOT YAAKOV   Bridge over the Jordan River in upper Galilee that linked Syria and Israel. The Haganah (Jewish underground army) blew up the bridge in 1946 as part of a campaign to destroy all bridges connecting Israel with the Arab countries. Fourteen Jewish soldiers were killed in the action. (See also GESHER HAZIV; HAGANAH.)

GESHER HAZIV   Kibbutz founded in 1949 in upper Galilee by Jewish pioneers forced to abandon Kibbutz Bet Araba during the

1948 War of Independence. Gesher Haziv, which means "Bridge of Splendors," was named for the 14 Haganah (Jewish underground army) soldiers killed blowing up a nearby bridge over the Jordan River in 1946. (See also BET ARABA; GALILEE; GESHER BNOT YAAKOV; HAGANAH; WAR OF INDEPENDENCE.)

GETHSEMANE   The Garden of Gethsemane lies in eastern Jerusalem at the foot of the Mount of Olives. Jesus used to meet his followers there and it is also the place where he found shelter after the Last Supper. The large and beautiful Church of All Nations now stands in Gethsemane. (See also GARDEN OF GETH-SEMANE; JERUSALEM; JESUS; MOUNT OF OLIVES.)

The Church of Gethsemane (also called the Church of the Agony), with its beautiful gardens, at the base of the Mount of Olives. It was rebuilt in 1924 with contributions from many countries and has therefore also been called Church of All Nations. Built over the Grotto of Agony where, according to Christian tradition, after the Last Supper Jesus was betrayed by his disciple Judas.

GEVAT   Kibbutz founded in the Jezreel Valley in 1926 by Polish immigrants who helped drain the valley's swamps. (See also JEZREEL VALLEY; KIBBUTZ.)

GEZER   Ancient city about halfway between Jerusalem and modern Tel Aviv. Gezer was first built about 6,000 years ago and was an important Canaanite town between the twentieth and fourteenth centuries B.C.E. It was a stronghold of King Solomon in the tenth century B.C.E. The Gezer Calendar, dug up by archaeologists on the site, dates from Solomon's time. Gezer was a Helenistic city when Simon the Hasmonean captured it in the second century B.C.E., built a fortress and a palace, and made it the second most important Jewish city (after Jerusalem) in Palestine. Today a kibbutz founded by members of the Youth Aliyah (young people's immigration) stands near the ancient site. (See also ARCHAEOLOGY; CANAAN; GEZER CALENDAR; HELENISM; HISTORY; KIBBUTZ; SIMON THE HASMONEAN; SOLOMON; YOUTH ALIYAH.)

GEZER CALENDAR   Tenth century B.C.E. stone tablet dug up by archaeologists at Gezer in the early 1900s. The Gezer Calendar is the oldest known Hebrew inscription. It contains seven lines of writing which list the agricultural seasons of the year. The original tablet is in the Istanbul Archaeological Museum in Turkey, but a reproduction can be seen in the Israel Museum in Jerusalem. (See also ARCHAEOLOGY; GEZER; ISRAEL MUSEUM.)

GIBBEATH BENJAMIN (also called TELL AL-FUL)   Ancient city three miles north of Jerusalem that was the central town of the biblical tribe of Benjamin. The town was rebuilt by King Saul in the eleventh century B.C.E. and was the site of his royal palace. It declined after his death. (See also BENJAMIN; SAUL; TWELVE TRIBES.)

GIBEON   Ancient city four miles northwest of Jerusalem that was built in the twelfth century B.C.E. and destroyed in the Babylonian conquest of the eighth century B.C.E. Gibeon is mentioned many times in the Bible. Archaeologists have uncovered the pool of Gibeon described in the Second Book of Samuel. (See also ARCHAEOLOGY; BABYLON; BIBLE.)

GIDEON (also called JERUBAAL) (twelfth century B.C.E.)   Warrior of the tribe of Manasseh and Judge of Israel for 40 years. He defeated the Midianites in battle and killed their kings. Gideon was offered the throne of Israel, but refused it. The biblical Book of Judges, Chapters 6-8, tells his story. (See also BIBLE; JUDGES; TWELVE TRIBES.)

GIDONA   Moshav (farming village) founded in the Jezreel Valley in 1949. It is named for Gideon, the Judge of Israel who gathered his army nearby to fight the Midianites in the twelfth century B.C.E. (See also GIDEON; JEZREEL VALLEY; MOSHAV.)

GIHON   Spring in the Kidron Valley near Jerusalem where Solomon was anointed king of Israel in the tenth century B.C.E. (See also ISRAEL, KINGDOM OF; KIDRON VALLEY; SOLOMON.)

GILADI, ISRAEL (1886-1918)   Russian-born pioneer who went to Palestine in 1905. Giladi was one of the founders and leaders of Hashomer, the "Jewish watchmen" organization. He also helped found the settlement of Kefar Giladi which bears his name. (See also HASHOMER; KEFAR GILADI.)

GINNEGAR   Kibbutz founded in the Jezreel Valley in 1922 by members of the Third Aliyah (wave of immigration). The Balfour Forest is nearby. (See also ALIYAH; BALFOUR FOREST; JEZREEL VALLEY; KIBBUTZ.)

GINNOSAR   Kibbutz founded in 1937 on the western shore of Lake Kinneret (Sea of Galilee). Yigal Allon was one of its founders. (See also ALLON, YIGAL; KIBBUTZ; LAKE KINNERET.)

GIVAT   Hebrew word meaning "hill of" that is sometimes part of place-names in Israel.

GIVAT ADA   Agricultural village about 20 miles south of Haifa named for the wife of Baron Edmond de Rothschild whose money supported the settlement when it was founded in 1903. Givat Ada absorbed many new immigrants in the 1950s. (See also ROTHSCHILD, EDMOND DE.)

GIVAT BRENNER   One of the largest of the kibbutzim in Israel, Givat Brenner was founded in 1928 about 15 miles south of Tel Aviv. Today it has industry as well as farming and also runs a large and popular guest house for tourists. (See also KIBBUTZ; TOURISM.)

GIVAT HAVIVA   School for training youth leaders founded in 1951 at the foot of the Samaria Mountains in western Israel. The school also has an Institute for Jewish-Arab studies. (See also EDUCATION.)

GIVATAYIM   Town between Tel Aviv and Ramat Gan formed in 1942 by uniting five suburbs of Tel Aviv. It has a cultural center and a swimming pool. (See also TEL AVIV.)

GLUECK, NELSON (1900-1971)   American archaeologist who directed the American School of Oriental Research in Jerusalem. Glueck did an archaeological survey of the Negev and was the discoverer of King Solomon's mines at Ezion Geber. (See also ARCHAEOLOGY; EZION GEBER; KING SOLOMON'S MINES; NEGEV.)

GLICKSTEIN, MOSHE YOSEPH (1878-1939)   Russian-born Hebrew writer and editor who settled in Palestine in 1919. Glickstein wrote for and edited several newspapers in Russia and Palestine before becoming the editor of the Tel Aviv daily

Rabbi Nelson Glueck (center), president of Hebrew Union College, delivering the benediction at the 1961 inaugural ceremony in which John F. Kennedy (left) was inaugurated President of the United States and Lyndon B. Johnson Vice-President.

newspaper *Ha-aretz,* a post he held for 15 years. (See also HA-ARETZ.)

GOITEIN, SHELOMO DOV (1900-   )   German-born historian who settled in Palestine in 1923 and taught history at the Hebrew University in Jerusalem. (See also HEBREW UNIVERSITY.)

GOLAN HEIGHTS (also spelled GAULAN)   Plateau overlooking upper Galilee that runs for 40 miles north-south along the Israel-Syria border and is about 10 miles wide. The Syrians held the Golan Heights after the 1948 War of Independence and used it as a military zone from which to shell Israeli settlements in the upper Jordan Valley. When Israel occupied the Golan Heights in the 1967 Six-Day War, it became one of the administered areas. The area is very lightly populated. About five thousand Druze live in five villages near Mount Hermon in the north and some new settlements have been established by young Israelis since 1967. (See also ADMINISTERED AREAS; DRUZE; SIX-DAY WAR; SYRIA; WAR OF INDEPENDENCE.)

GOLD, ZEEV (1889-1956)   Polish-born rabbi and Zionist leader who served as president of the Mizrahi (a religious Zionist organization) in the United States before he settled in Palestine in 1935. Rabbi Gold was a member of the executive committee of the Jewish Agency and president of the Mizrahi World Organization. (See also JEWISH AGENCY; MIZRAHI; ZIONISM.)

GOLDBERG, LEA (1911-1970)   Russian-born Hebrew poet who settled in Palestine in 1935. Her poetry is often sad, but contains a ray of hope. Besides writing poetry, Lea Goldberg was a drama critic and taught literature at the Hebrew University in Jerusalem. (See also HEBREW UNIVERSITY.)

GOLDEN BOOK   Roll of honor kept at the Jewish National Fund headquarters in Jerusalem. Names are written in the book along with the amount raised for the Fund. (See also JEWISH NATIONAL FUND.)

GOLDEN GATE (Hebrew, SHAAR HARAHAMIM)   One of the eight gates in the wall around the Old City of Jerusalem. The Golden Gate is the only one of the eight that is no longer open to the public. It is also known as the Mercy Gate. (See also JERU-SALEM; WALLED CITIES.)

GOLDMANN, NAHUM (1894-   )   Russian-born Zionist leader who lived in the United States and Switzerland. Goldmann was president of the World Jewish Congress, joint chairman of the Jewish Agency, and president of the World Zionist Organization. He helped arrange the 1952 reparations agreement in which Germany agreed to pay the Jews for their suffering under the Nazis. (See also JEWISH AGENCY; REPARATIONS; WORLD JEWISH CONGRESS; WORLD ZIONIST ORGANIZATION; ZIONISM.)

GOLDSTEIN, ISRAEL (1896-   )   American-born rabbi who did most of his Zionist work in the United States before he settled in Israel in 1960. Rabbi Goldstein was president of the American Jewish Congress, served on the executive committee of the Jewish Agency, and was chairman of the Keren Hayesod (Palestine Foundation Fund). (See also JEWISH AGENCY; KEREN HAYESOD; ZIONISM.)

GOLGOTHA (also called CALVARY)   Skull-shaped hill where Jesus Christ was crucified. Christian tradition says that Golgotha lies inside the Church of the Holy Sepulchre in Jerusalem. (See also HOLY SEPULCHRE, CHURCH OF; JESUS; VIA DOLOROSA.)

GOLOMB, ELIYAHU (1893-1945)   Russian-born founder of the Haganah, the Jewish underground army in Palestine. Golomb went to Palestine in 1909 and was in the first graduating class of the Herzliya High School in Tel Aviv. During World War I, he smuggled arms into Palestine for Hashomer (the "Jewish watchmen" organization) and later served in the Jewish Legion. He helped found the Haganah and the Palmah (Haganah's striking force) and was the head of Haganah from 1931 to his death. During World War II, Golomb directed "illegal" Jewish immigration into Palestine. (See also HAGANAH; HASHOMER; HERZLIYA

HIGH SCHOOL; IMMIGRANTS, ILLEGAL; JEWISH LEGION; PALMAH.)

GOMORRAH   One of the two ancient Palestinian cities (the other was Sodom) whose destruction for its wickedness is described in the Book of Genesis, Chapter 19. The exact location of Gomorrah is not known. (See also SODOM.)

GOOD FRIDAY   Holiday celebrated in Christian churches throughout Israel on the Friday before Easter. It marks the crucifixion of Jesus Christ. A special funeral service is held in the Church of the Holy Sepulchre in Jerusalem. (See also CHRISTIANS; EASTER; HOLIDAYS; HOLY SEPULCHRE, CHURCH OF; JESUS.)

GOOR, YEHUDA (name changed from GRAZOVSKY) (1862-1950) Russian-born inventor of a direct method of teaching Hebrew. He settled in Palestine in 1887. Goor also wrote Hebrew textbooks and a Hebrew dictionary. (See also HEBREW.)

GORDON, AHARON DAVID (1856-1922)   Russian-born philosopher who became the spiritual leader of the kibbutz movement in Palestine. He was 48 years old when he settled in Palestine to work as a farmhand at Petah Tikva, Rishon Le Zion, and Degania. Gordon preached what he called "the religion of labor." He believed that men and women should work the soil to get close to nature. He also believed that the land and the tools to work it should be owned by the workers. His ideas had great influence on the settlers who came to Palestine in the Second Aliyah (wave of immigration) in the early 1900s, (See also ALIYAH; DEGANIA; KIBBUTZ; PETAH TIKVA; RISHON LE ZION.)

GORDON, SAMUEL LOEB (pen name SHALAG) (1865-1933) Russian-born Hebrew writer and teacher who settled in Palestine in 1924. He wrote poetry, textbooks, and school editions of the Bible, and edited magazines for young people.

GORDONIA   Pioneer scouting movement named for Aharon David Gordon. It was founded in Poland in 1925 and spread to other European countries, America, and Palestine. Its members founded several settlements in Israel. Gordonia is now part of Habonim, the world organization of youth movements. (See also GORDON, AHARON DAVID; HABONIM; YOUTH MOVEMENTS.)

GOREN, SHLOMO (1918-   )   Ashkenazic Chief Rabbi of Israel. Goren was the chaplain of the Israel Defense Forces and served as Chief Rabbi of Tel Aviv before he was elected as one of Israel's two Chief Rabbis in 1972. (See also ASHKENAZIM; CHIEF RABBINATE; DEFENSE FORCES.)

GOVERNMENT   Israel is a democratic country with a government more like the British than the American system. It has no written constitution, but there are "basic laws" that carry the same force as a constitution.

The legislative body is the Knesset. All Israelis over the age of 18 have the right to vote for members of the Knesset. Voters cast their ballots for a party's list of candidates. Members of the Knesset are elected from the lists by a system of proportional representation. This system is necessary because Israel has a large number of political parties.

The President of Israel is elected for a five-year term. Although he is the official head of the country, he has very little real power. His office is mostly ceremonial.

The Prime Minister is the country's real chief executive. He or she is also a member of the Knesset, usually the head of the most powerful political party. The Prime Minister chooses members of the Cabinet to head the various Ministries (government departments) from a coalition of parties.

Israel's courts are unusual because there are two different court systems—civil and religious. There are no juries in Israel, and all court cases are decided by judges.

Local city and regional governments are elected by the same system of proportional representation as the Knesset. Israel is divided into six administrative districts. The District Officers represent the central government on the local level. (See also BASIC LAWS; CABINET; CITIZENSHIP; CIVIL SERVICE; COURTS; COURTS, RELIGIOUS; JUDGES; KNESSET; LOCAL GOVERNMENT; POLITICAL PARTIES; PRESIDENT; PRIME MINISTER; PROPORTIONAL REPRESENTATION; STATE COMPTROLLER; VOTING.)

GRADENWITZ, PETER (1910-   )   German-born music expert who settled in Palestine in 1936. Gradenwitz was the president of the Israel Musicological Society and wrote several books on music including *The Music of Israel.*

GRANOTT, ABRAHAM (1890-1962)   Russian-born Zionist and soil expert who settled in Palestine in 1922. Granott was managing director of the Jewish National Fund and was a member of the Israeli Knesset (legislature). He also taught agriculture at the Hebrew University in Jerusalem and wrote a number of books on land use in Palestine. (See also AGRICULTURE; HEBREW UNIVERSITY; JEWISH NATIONAL FUND; ZIONISM.)

GREAT ASSEMBLY (Hebrew, KENESET GEDOLAH)   A group of 120 of the leading Jewish scholars of the early Second Temple Period (about the fifth and fourth centuries B.C.E.) who decided matters of religion and law. When the modern Israeli Knesset (legislature) was organized, it was given 120 members in memory of the Great Assembly. (See also KNESSET.)

GREAT BRITAIN   Island nation off the coast of Western Europe. Great Britain is made up of England, Scotland, Wales, and Northern Ireland which together have an area of about 95,000 square miles and a population of 56 million (1977). Its capitol is London. Although Great Britain is a small nation, its empire covered large parts of the world until the mid-1900s. It ruled Palestine from 1918 to 1948.

In 1917 General Edmund Henry Allenby led a British army into Palestine. Palestine was then a possession of Turkey, one of the Central Powers who were fighting against Britain and the other Allied Powers in World War I. In the same year, British Foreign Secretary Balfour issued a statement, known as the Balfour Declaration, which said that Britain favored a national home for the Jewish people in Palestine.

World War I ended in 1918 with British troops in possession of Palestine. The 1920 San Remo Peace Conference resolved that the Balfour Declaration be made part of the peace treaty with Turkey and that Great Britain be given the Mandate for Palestine. (A Mandate was an order from the League of Nations for a country to govern a territory conquered in World War I.) The Mandate was made official by the League of Nations in 1922.

Britain's rule of Palestine was not logical. It promised Jews a Jewish National Home, and it supported Arab nationalists who opposed the presence of Jews in Palestine. Gradually the policy began to lean more and more toward the Arabs. The Passfield White Paper, issued after the Arab riots of 1929, blamed Jewish settlement in Palestine for the riots. The Peel Commission, which investigated Arab unrest in Palestine in 1935, recommended partition (dividing) of the country into Arab and Jewish states.

Britain's anti-Zionist policy became even stronger in 1939 when the White Paper was issued to limit Jewish immigration and land purchase in Palestine. The White Paper was particularly harsh because many Jewish refugees from Nazism in Europe had no other place to go. Many Jewish immigrants entered Palestine illegally during World War II.

World War II ended in 1945 with Great Britain still governing Palestine and still not able to balance the conflicting Jewish and Arab claims to the country. Several conferences were called to try to solve the problem. They were unsuccessful and the British finally submitted the Palestine issue to the United Nations. The General Assembly of the United Nations voted on November 19, 1947, to establish a Jewish State in part of Palestine. On May 14, 1948, the British Mandate for Palestine ended and the new State of Israel was born. (See also ALLENBY, EDMUND HENRY; ARAB RIOTS; BALFOUR DECLARATION; HISTORY; HOLOCAUST; IMMIGRANTS, ILLE-

GAL; LEAGUE OF NATIONS; NAZIS; PARTITION; PASSFIELD WHITE PAPER; PEEL COMMISSION; SAN REMO CONFERENCE; UNITED NATIONS; WHITE PAPER; ZIONISM.)

GREEN ONIONS see BATZAL YAROK

GREENBERG, AHARON YAAKOV HALEVI (1900-1963) Zionist leader who helped found Bene Akiva (a religious pioneering youth organization) in Poland before settling in Palestine in 1935. Greenberg was a member of the Israeli Knesset (legislature) and served as its Deputy Speaker. (See also BENE AKIVA; KNESSET; ZIONISM.)

GREENBERG, URI ZVI (1894-   ) Austrian-born Yiddish poet who began to write in Hebrew when he settled in Palestine in 1923. Greenberg's fiery poetry mirrored his political belief in a fighting Jewish youth reestablishing the kingdom of Israel. He supported Jewish underground movements fighting the British rule in Palestine, and was elected as a Herut Party member of the first Knesset (legislature) when Israel became a state in 1948. Uri Greenberg won both the Bialik Prize and the Israel Prize for his poetry. (See also BIALIK PRIZE; HERUT; ISRAEL PRIZE; KNESSET; LITERATURE.)

GROSSMAN, MEIR (1888-1964) Russian-born Zionist leader who helped establish the Jewish Legion during World War I. He was one of the founders of the Revisionists, a Zionist group that believed in putting political pressure on the British (who ruled Palestine under the Mandate) for more Jewish settlements. Grossman settled in Palestine in 1934 and became a member of the executive committee of the Jewish Agency. He also wrote articles for Yiddish newspapers in Europe, the United States, and Palestine, and founded Palestine's first English language newspaper, the *Palestine Bulletin*. (See also GREAT BRITAIN; JEWISH AGENCY; JEWISH LEGION; REVISIONISM; ZIONISM.)

GRUNBAUM, YITZHAK (1879-1970) Writer who was a Zionist leader in Poland before he settled in Palestine in 1934 and became a member of the executive committee of the Jewish Agency. Grunbaum was one of the Jewish Agency leaders arrested by the British (who were then ruling Palestine) in 1946. He retired from politics soon after Israel became a state in 1948 to write books on Polish and Zionist history and to edit the *Encyclopedia of the Diaspora*. (See also GREAT BRITAIN; JEWISH AGENCY; ZIONISM.)

GRUNER, DOV (1912-1947) Hungarian-born soldier who settled in Palestine in 1940. He fought in the Jewish Brigade of the British army during World War II. After the war, Gruner joined the Irgun (underground group fighting British rule in Palestine) and took part in a raid on the Ramat Gan police station. He was wounded, captured by the British, and was executed in Acre Prison in 1947. (See also ACRE PRISON; GREAT BRITAIN; IRGUN; JEWISH BRIGADE.)

GULF OF AQABA   see EILAT, GULF OF

GULF OF EILAT   see EILAT, GULF OF

GUNZBERG, PESAH (1894-1947)   Hebrew writer who settled in Palestine in 1922 and published stories and poems as well as translated English and Scandinavian literature into Hebrew.

GUNZBERG, SHIMON (1890-1944)   Hebrew poet who settled in Palestine in 1933. He is best known for his biblical poem, *The Love of Hosea.*

General Motta Gur

GUR, MORDECHAI (nickname, MOTTA)   Soldier who became known for his daring when he commanded the paratroop group that captured the northern outskirts of Jerusalem during the 1967 Six-Day War. Gur rose to the rank of Lieutenant-General and was appointed Chief-of-Staff of the Israel Defense Forces in 1974. (See also DEFENSE FORCES; JERUSALEM; SIX-DAY WAR.)

GUSH EMUNIM (English, FAITH BLOCK)   A group of Orthodox Jews who believe that the West Bank rightfully belongs to Israel. Its leader is Rabbi Moshe Levinger. Gush Emunim claims the right to establish scttlements in the West Bank with or without the approval of the Israeli government. This has led to clashes between group members and the Israeli soldiers sent to stop the settlements. (See also WEST BANK.)

GUSH ETZION (also spelled GUSH EZION)   Area of Jewish settlements in the Judean hills between Jerusalem and Hebron that was taken over by Jordan during the 1948 War of Independence. Gush Etzion was occupied by Israel again in the 1967 Six-Day War and Israeli pioneers soon moved back to reestablish settlements in the area. (See also KEFAR ETZION; SIX-DAY WAR; WAR OF INDEPENDENCE.)

GUSH HALAV   Ancient town north of Safed in upper Galilee that was fortified by the Zealots during the first century C.E. revolt against Rome. Tombs and ruins of a second century C.E. synagogue still remain. Today Gush Halav is an Arab town called Jish. (See also GALILEE; HISTORY; ROME; ZEALOTS.)

GUTMAN, NAHUM (1898-   )   Russian-born writer and artist who was brought to Palestine at the age of seven by his writer-father, Simhah Ben-Zion. Gutman studied art at the Bezalel School of Arts and Crafts. He is known for his book illustrations and was the first person to write and illustrate Hebrew children's books in Palestine. In 1978 he won the Israel Prize for his work. (See also BEN-ZION, SIMHAH; BEZALEL SCHOOL OF ARTS AND CRAFTS; ISRAEL PRIZE.)

GYROS   see SHWARMA

H

HA-ARETZ Israel's leading newspaper. *Ha-aretz,* which means "the land," was founded in Jerusalem in 1919 and moved to Tel Aviv in 1937. It was the first Hebrew daily published in Palestine after World War I and is Israel's oldest newspaper still being published. *Ha-aretz* is not connected with any political party and is known for its independence. It publishes a magazine for young people in its Friday edition. (See also GLICKSON, MOSHE; SCHOCKEN, GERSHOM.)

HA-ARETZ MUSEUM One of Tel Aviv's leading museums whose name means "museum of the land." It is made up of several small museum buildings in a park in the Ramat Aviv suburb, where exhibits devoted to glass, coins, pottery, Jewish history, and anthropology (study of mankind) are shown. The science and technology building has special exhibits for young people. (See also TEL AVIV.)

HABERMAN, ABRAHAM MEIR (1901-) German-born writer, librarian, and historian who settled in Palestine in 1934 and taught medieval Hebrew literature at the Hebrew University in Jerusalem. (See also HEBREW UNIVERSITY.)

HABIMAH Hebrew theater company whose name means "the stage." Habimah was founded in Moscow in 1918, moved to Tel Aviv in 1928, and now performs in its own 1,200-seat theater in Tel Aviv. It was made the official National Theater of Israel in 1958 and the Israeli government supports it when necessary. Habimah performs Hebrew plays written in Israel as well as Hebrew translations of foreign-language plays. (See also TEL AVIV; THEATER.)

HABONIM Organization of Zionist youth pioneers whose name means "the builders." Habonim was founded in Great Britain in 1929 and spread until it became a worldwide organization with about 20,000 members between the ages of 10 and 23. Its headquarters are in Tel Aviv. Former members of Habonim have founded more than 20 kibbutzim in Israel. Habonim's youth workshops give high school graduates from other countries a chance to live and work on an Israeli kibbutz for a year. (See also KIBBUTZ; YOUTH MOVEMENTS; ZIONISM.)

HACOHEN, DAVID (1898-   ) Son of Mordecai Hacohen. David Hacohen was active in the Histadrut (Israel's labor federation), served in the Israeli Knesset (legislature), and was Israel's ambassador to Burma. (See also HACOHEN, MORDECAI; HISTADRUT; KNESSET.)

HACOHEN, MORDECAI BEN HILLEL (name changed from MARCUS KAHAN) (1856-1936) Russian-born writer and Zionist leader who settled in Palestine in 1907. Hacohen was the only delegate at the First Zionist Conference in 1897 to address the meeting in Hebrew. He was one of the founders of Tel Aviv, organized a credit union and a writers' organization, wrote many books on Jewish and Zionist subjects, and published his memoirs. (See also HEBREW; TEL AVIV; WORLD ZIONIST ORGANIZATION; ZIONISM.)

HADASSAH   The Women's Zionist Organization of America. Hadassah was founded in 1912 by Henrietta Szold. Its aims were to encourage Jewish life in America and to raise the standard of health in Palestine. By the late 1970s Hadassah was the largest Zionist organization in the world with 360,000 members in the United States and Puerto Rico.

Hadassah's medical work in Palestine began in 1912 with two trained nurses treating children's eye diseases. It went on to establish hospitals and clinics throughout the country that have become part of the Israeli health care system.

The Hadassah Medical Center opened on Mount Scopus in 1939. Today the Hadassah-Hebrew University Medical Center in Ein Karem has a medical school, a dental school, a nursing school, a 600-bed hospital, and facilities to treat 250,000 outpatients a year; and the rebuilt Mount Scopus center has a 300-bed hospital. The Medical Center synagogue at Ein Karem boasts Marc Chagall's beautiful stained glass windows.

The Hadassah-Israel Education Service was established in 1942. It runs a high school and a community college in Jerusalem as well as a vocational guidance center to help young people find the work they are suited for.

Hadassah has been active in the Youth Aliyah (youth immigration to Palestine) movement since it was started by Recha Freier in 1934. It has helped 135,000 young people from 80 countries settle in Israel.

Hashahar, which means "the dawn," is Hadassah's youth program. It teaches young Americans about Israel and organizes work-study-travel trips to Israel. (See also CHAGALL, MARC; EDUCA-

TION; FREIER, RECHA; HEALTH; HEBREW UNIVERSITY; SZOLD, HENRI-
ETTA; YOUTH ALIYAH; ZIONISM.)

HADASSIM   Agricultural school founded on the Sharon Plain
in 1947 by the Canadian Hadassah (Women's Zionist Organization). The school teaches farming methods to about 500 students
a year. (See also AGRICULTURAL SCHOOLS; EDUCATION; HADASSAH;
SHARON PLAIN.)

HADERA (also spelled HEDERAH)   City founded on the swampy
Sharon Plain in 1890 by Russian immigrants of the First Aliyah
(first wave of immigration). Almost half of the early settlers died
from malaria until the swamps were drained by digging ditches
and planting eucalyptus trees. By the late 1970s Hadera had a
population of about 35,000. It grows citrus fruit, produces lum-
ber from its eucalyptus trees, and has a paper mill and a tire
factory. (See also ALIYAH; CITRUS FRUIT; EUCALYPTUS; MALARIA;
SHARON PLAIN.)

HADRIAN (full name PUBLIUS AELIUS HADRIANUS) (76-138 C.E.)
Roman emperor who ruled 117-138 C.E. In 130 C.E. Hadrian
visited Palestine and ordered Jerusalem rebuilt as a Roman city
to be called Aelia Capitolina. This led the Jews to revolt against
Rome under the leadership of Simeon Bar Kokhba. After the
Roman army put down the revolt in 135 C.E., Hadrian forbade
Jews to practice their religion or to enter the rebuilt city of Aelia
Capitolina. Jewish leaders who refused to obey the law were
killed. Among those executed was Rabbi Akiva. (See also AELIA
CAPITOLINA; AKIVA BEN JOSEPH; BAR KOKHBA, SIMEON; HISTORY;
ROME.)

HAGANAH Underground Jewish army whose name means
"defense." The Haganah was founded in 1920. It grew from a
group of Jewish units protecting individual settlements against
Arab attacks into a national army that later became the Israel
Defense Forces.

   Although only 200 Haganah members defended Jerusalem
during the 1920 Arab riots, the organization expanded rapidly
after the 1929 riots. When the Arabs attacked the British (who
were ruling Palestine under the Mandate) as well as Jews during
the 1936-1939 Arab revolt, the British government organized a
"legal" Jewish police force that was actually run by Haganah. A
British army officer, Captain Charles Wingate, trained the Special Night Squads that later became the Palmah (Haganah's
striking force). By 1939 the Haganah was a nationwide, well-
organized, Jewish army with a General Staff directing the training, arms, operations, and intelligence departments.

   In answer to the British 1939 White Paper limiting Jewish

immigration into Palestine, the Haganah began to smuggle thousands of "illegal" immigrants into the country. Although the Haganah cooperated with the British to win World War II, and although many of its members fought in the Jewish Brigade of the British army, as soon as the war ended in 1945 the Haganah clashed with the British over the question of Jewish immigration. The Jewish army raided a refugee camp, fought British ships trying to stop "illegal" immigration, attacked British military bases, and blew up 11 bridges. After British counterattacks and arrests in 1946, the Haganah stopped fighting the British and devoted itself to smuggling Jewish immigrants into Palestine. However, attacks on the British were continued by the Irgun and the Stern Group, organizations that had split off from the Haganah in the early 1930s.

On May 14, 1948, Israel became a nation. The British troops moved out and Arab armies attacked the new nation from all sides. Haganah (now called the Israel Defense Forces) took the offensive, occupied the land given to Israel by the United Nations, and turned back the Arab armies in the War of Independence. (See also ARAB RIOTS; DEFENSE FORCES; GREAT BRITAIN; HISTORY; IMMIGRANTS, ILLEGAL; IRGUN; JEWISH BRIGADE; MANDATE; PALMAH; SPECIAL NIGHT SQUADS; STERN GROUP; WAR OF INDEPENDENCE; WHITE PAPER; WINGATE, CHARLES ORDE.)

HAGGADAH (the plural is HAGGADOT)   Book read at the Passover Seder (holiday feast). The Haggadah tells the story of the Exodus of the Jews from slavery in Egypt. It also contains prayers, old folk songs, and the four questions asked by the youngest child at the Seder. (See also EXODUS; PASSOVER; SEDER.)

HAIFA   Israel's major port and third largest city. Haifa was an important Jewish town in 1100 C.E. before it was conquered and largely destroyed by the Crusaders. The modern city developed when Haifa was chosen as the final station on the railway line to Damascus. The British built a deep-sea harbor on the Mediterranean Sea in Haifa Bay; an oil refinery and a cement factory were built near the harbor; the Technion (Institute of Technology) was founded, and Jewish immigrants arrived in large numbers. By the time Israel became a state in 1948, Haifa was a city of 128,000 people.

Haifa is built on three levels up the slopes of Mount Carmel. The lowest level is the port and industrial center. Ships from all over the world bring goods into Haifa harbor. The port was the main gateway for Jewish immigrants arriving in Israel both before and after 1948. The next level holds the business districts, with its shops and offices, as well as middle-class apartment houses. On the highest level, well up Mount Carmel, are luxury

hotels and the homes of the wealthy people. Israel's only subway connects the different levels of the city.

Haifa has two universities (the Technion and Haifa University), several museums, a municipal theater and symphony orchestra, and excellent beaches. It is the center of the Bahai religion, and its beautiful Bahai Shrine and gardens are a popular tourist attraction. (See also BAHAI SHRINE; CRUSADES; HAIFA UNIVERSITY; IMMIGRANTS; KHOUSHI, ABBA; MOUNT CARMEL; PORTS; SHIPPING; TECHNION; TOURISM.)

HAIFA MUNICIPAL THEATER   The first theater group in Israel organized by a city. The Haifa Theater was founded in 1961. It started out with a grant of money from the city of Haifa and with its own modern theater for performances. (See also HAIFA; THEATER.)

HAIFA UNIVERSITY   University established by the city of Haifa in 1963 with help from the Hebrew University of Jerusalem. Since the Technion (Institute of Technology) is nearby, Haifa University concentrates on the humanities and social sciences, although it also has schools of education and social work. In 1975 the university had about 500 teachers and 3,600 students. (See also EDUCATION; HEBREW UNIVERSITY; TECHNION.)

HAKHSHARA   Hebrew word meaning "preparation." A training program, particularly in farming, for pioneers planning to settle in Palestine.

HAKIBBUTZ HAARTZI   Organization of cooperative farming settlements founded in 1927. Although other kibbutz organizations allow different political opinions among its members, Hakibbutz Haartzi has insisted that its members accept the political ideas of Hashomer Hatzair, its founding organization. Hashomer Hatzair believes that the kibbutz is the way to fulfill the Zionist ideal, to further the struggle between social classes, and to build a Socialist society. Members of Hakibbutz Haartzi were active in Israel's struggle for independence in the 1930s and 1940s. They founded the first "stockade and tower" settlements, smuggled in "illegal" immigrants, and fought in the Palmah (commando units of the underground Jewish army). In the 1970s the organization had 71 member kibbutzim with a population of over 30,000 people. Its members are supporters of the Mapam political party. (See also HASHOMER HATZAIR; IMMIGRANTS, ILLEGAL; KIBBUTZ; MAPAM; PALMAH; STOCKADE AND TOWER; ZIONISM.)

HAKIBBUTZ HADATI   Organization of religious kibbutzim founded in 1934. Hakibbutz Hadati believes in combining Orthodox Jewish religious life with the kibbutz ideals of equal-

The port of Haifa is the busiest port in Israel.

Haifa University

ity, cooperation, and labor. In the 1970s the organization had 13 member kibbutzim with a population of 4,000 people. Many of its new members come from the Bene Akiva youth movement. Hakibbutz Hadati makes its political views known through the National Religious Party in the Israeli Knesset (legislature). (See also BENE AKIVA; KIBBUTZ; KNESSET; NATIONAL RELIGIOUS PARTY.)

HAKIBBUTZ HAMEUHAD Organization of kibbutzim founded in 1927 by Kibbutz Ein Harod. It believes that a kibbutz should be a large settlement open to all who wish to join, that it should absorb new immigrants, and that it should have industry as well as agriculture. Hakibbutz Hameuhad was active during Israel's struggle for independence in the 1930s and 1940s, particularly in the Palmah (commando units of the Jewish underground army). It believes that Israel's natural borders include the administered areas occupied in the 1967 Six-Day War, and it established the first new kibbutz in the Golan Heights after the war. In the 1970s the organization had 62 member kibbutzim with a population of 26,000 people. Its members support the Israel Labor political party. (See also ADMINISTERED AREAS; EIN HAROD; GOLAN HEIGHTS; ISRAEL LABOR PARTY; KIBBUTZ; PALMAH; SIX-DAY WAR.)

HAKOAH Jewish sports organization whose name means "strength." It was active in Vienna, Austria, from 1909 to 1930. It was reestablished in Palestine in 1942. Hakoah is now an Israeli soccer organization. (See also SOCCER; SPORTS.)

HALPERN, GEORGE (1878-1962) German-born businessman and Zionist leader who settled in Palestine in 1933. Halpern was a founder of the Keren Hayesod (Palestine Foundation Fund), a director of Bank Leumi Le-Israel (Israel's leading commercial bank), and one of the founders of the Palestine Electric Company. (See also BANK LEUMI LE-ISRAEL; KEREN HAYESOD; PALESTINE ELECTRIC COMPANY; ZIONISM.)

HALPERN, YEHIEL MIKHAEL (1860-1919) Russian-born Palestine pioneer. Halpern settled in Palestine in 1887 and was a founder of the settlments of Hadera and Nes Tziyona. He organized the first Jewish workers' union in Palestine and helped organize Hashomer, the Jewish "watchmen" who guarded their settlements against Arab raids. (See also HADERA; HASHOMER; NES TZIYONA.)

HALPRIN, ROSE LURIA (1895-1978) American Zionist leader who lived in Palestine for five years in the 1930s. Rose Halprin was president of Hadassah (Women's Zionist Organization of America) and helped plan and finance the Hadassah-Hebrew University Medical School and the Mount Scopus Hospital. She served on the executive committee of the Jewish Agency and was one of its representatives at the United Nations debate on establishing the State of Israel. (See also HADASSAH; JEWISH AGENCY; UNITED NATIONS; ZIONISM.)

HALUKKA   A Hebrew word meaning "division." It refers to money collected from Jews throughout the world that was later divided among the poor religious Jews in Palestine to enable them to spend their lives in prayer and study. Most of the money collected between 1600 and 1900 went to support the Jews and Jewish religious institutions of the four "holy cities": Jerusalem, Safed, Tiberias, and Hebron. (See also HEBRON; JERUSALEM; SAFED; TIBERIAS.)

HALUTZ (the plural is HALUTZIM)   Hebrew word for "pioneer" used to refer to Jews who went to Palestine to reclaim and work the land. Halutzim built settlements under the most difficult conditions and worked for the good of the community rather than for personal gain. The halutz— the man or woman with the plow and the gun—is the Israeli ideal. (See also HEHALUTZ.)

HAMAN   Evil adviser to King Ahasuerus of Persia who tried to have all the Jews in the kingdom killed. The holiday of Purim celebrates Esther's saving the Jews. The Book of Esther in the Bible tells the complete story. (See also ESTHER; PURIM.)

HAMAT GADER   Hot springs near the Jordan River south of Lake Kinneret (Sea of Galilee). The springs were famous in Roman times and archaeologists have found the remains of a third-century Roman theater nearby. Hamat Gader was in the demilitarized zone between Israel and Jordan, but was occupied by Israel in the 1967 Six-Day War. (See also ARCHAEOLOGY; ROME; SIX-DAY WAR.)

HAMEIRI, AVIGDOR (name changed from FEUERSTEIN) (1890-1970)   Hungarian-born Hebrew poet and novelist who settled in Palestine in 1921. Hameiri's poems, stories, and novels are about the horrors of war, the fate of the Jews, and life in Palestine. His collection of stories, *The Great Madness,* tells of his experiences as a Hungarian soldier and Russian prisoner in World War I. Hameiri was a leading Israeli writer who was awarded the Bialik Prize for his writing. (See also BIALIK PRIZE; LITERATURE.)

HAMEIRI, MOSHE (name changed from OSTROWSKI) (1885-1947)   Russian-born rabbi who was brought to Palestine as a child. Hameiri was one of the founders of Mizrahi (a religious Zionist organization) in Palestine. He also founded the Mizrahi Teachers Seminary in Jerusalem and taught there for 27 years. (See also MIZRAHI.)

HAMSIN (also spelled KHAMSIN)   A very hot dry wind that may blow across Israel from the eastern deserts for days at a time in the spring and fall. The temperature often rises above 100 degrees during a hamsin and the wind may carry fine bits of desert sand, covering everything with a film of gray dust. (See also CLIMATE.)

HANKIN, YEHOSHUA (1864-1945)   Russian-born pioneer who settled in Palestine in 1882. Hankin was a land buyer for the Jewish National Fund and for the Jewish Colonization Association. For more than 50 years he bought land and planned settlements throughout Palestine, particularly in the Jezreel Valley (also called the Emek). He became known as the "Redeemer of the Emek." (See also JEWISH COLONIZATION ASSOCIATION; JEWISH NATIONAL FUND; JEZREEL VALLEY.)

HANOAR HAOVED   The largest of all youth movements in Israel. Its name means "working youth." It is the youth group of the Histadrut, Israel's labor federation. Hanoar Haoved, founded in 1924, grew in numbers in 1959, when it joined forces with another youth group. By 1978 it had about 100,000 Jewish and non-Jewish members between the ages of 10 and 18. The organization runs study groups and outings, and teaches young people practical skills for use in trades or on the farm. It also tries to improve wages and working conditions for young people holding jobs. (See also HISTADRUT; YOUTH MOVEMENTS.)

HANOAR HATZIYONI   A pioneering youth movement whose name means "Zionist youth." Founded in Eastern Europe in the 1930s, its members developed kibbutzim in Palestine and helped form the Progressive political party when Israel became a state. Today Hanoar Hatziyoni is a small youth group (two thousand members in 1978) with its headquarters in Tel Aviv. (See also KIBBUTZ; PROGRESSIVE PARTY; YOUTH MOVEMENTS.)

HANUKKAH (also spelled HANUKAH and CHANUKKAH)   Jewish holiday celebrating Judah the Maccabee's victory over the Syrians in 164 B.C.E. and the reopening of the Temple in Jerusalem to Jewish worship. Hanukkah is celebrated for eight days beginning on the twenty-fifth day of the Hebrew month Kislev which usually falls in the month of December. Candles are lit each night in a menorah (eight-branched candle holder) in remembrance of the small jar of oil that miraculously burned for eight days in the Temple. There are parties, games are played with a *dreidel* (spinning top), and gifts are given to the children.

Hanukkah is both a religious and a national holiday in Israel. A giant menorah burns on the roof of the Knesset (legislature) and on other public buildings. Youth groups organize torchlight parades. A torch lit at the tombs of the Maccabees at Modiin is

carried by relay runners to Jerusalem. (See also CALENDAR, INTER-
NATIONAL; CALENDAR, JEWISH; DREIDEL; HOLIDAYS; JUDAH THE
MACCABEE; MACCABEES; MENORAH; MODIIN; TEMPLE.)

HAOVED HADATI Religious workers' organization allied
with Histadrut, the Israel labor federation. Haoved Hadati works
for the rights of religious workers within Histadrut. (See also
HISTADRUT.)

HAOVED HATZIYONI The General Zionist Workers' section
of Histadrut, Israel's labor federation. Haoved Hatziyoni was one
of the groups that formed the Progressive political party. (See
also HISTADRUT; PROGRESSIVE PARTY.)

HAPOEL The largest sports organization in Israel. It was
founded in 1925 as part of Histadrut, Israel's labor federation. In
1979 Hapoel had 110,000 members in 875 clubs. It sponsors sports
events and cross-country marches, invites athletes from other
parts of the world to compete in Israel, and organizes sports and
recreational activities in the places where people work. In 1975
Hapoel held its tenth countrywide sports festival to mark its
fiftieth birthday. Athletes from all over Israel competed at the
festival and there were organized exercises and folk dancing for
everyone attending. (See also HISTADRUT; SPORTS.)

HAPOEL HAMIZRAHI Organization of religious workers
founded in 1922 as part of the Mizrahi (religious Zionist) movement. It aims to build a nation of workers founded on Jewish
religious law. Hapoel Hamizrahi was active as a separate political party until it united with the Mizrahi Party in 1955. Now it is
mainly a labor union that protects the rights of religious workers. It also runs an agricultural cooperative of over 70 villages.
Hapoel Hamizrahi's youth group is Bene Akiva. (See also BENE
AKIVA; MIZRAHI; POLITICAL PARTIES; TORAH.)

HAQIQAT AL-AMR Arabic language weekly newspaper first
published in Tel Aviv in 1937. Until Israel became a state in 1948,
the aim of *Haqiqat al-Amr* was to explain the Jewish position in
Palestine to the Arabs. Now it is concerned with the interests of
Israeli Arabs. The paper runs a special column for school children. (See also ARABS.)

HAREUVENI, EPHRAIM (1881-1953) Russian-born botanist
(plant expert) who settled in Palestine in 1906 and taught at the
Hebrew University in Jerusalem. Hareuveni founded a museum
of biblical plants that was later transferred to the Hebrew University. (See also HEBREW UNIVERSITY.)

HARLAP, YAAKOV MOSHE (1883-1951) Jerusalem-born rab-

A kindergarten class sponsored by Hapoel Hamizrachi Women's Organization that was funded by the Ilana Branch Brooklyn, New York.

bi and writer who founded a yeshiva (religious school) to study those religious laws that could only be observed by people living in the Holy Land.

HARMAN, AVRAHAM (1914-) British-born diplomat who settled in Palestine in 1940. Harman served as an Israeli delegate to the United Nations, as a member of the executive committee of the Jewish Agency, and as Israel's ambassador to the United States. In 1968 he became president of the Hebrew University in Jerusalem. (See also HEBREW UNIVERSITY; JEWISH AGENCY; UNITED NATIONS.)

HARZFELD, ABRAHAM (1888-) Russian-born labor leader who settled in Palestine in 1914. Harzfeld represented the interests of farmers in the Histadrut, Israel's labor federation. He played an important part in establishing new agricultural settlements, particularly the "stockade and tower" settlements in the Negev. He also served as a member of the Israeli Knesset (legislature). (See also HISTADRUT; KNESSET; NEGEV; STOCKADE AND TOWER.)

HASHILOAH Hebrew literary monthly magazine founded by Ahad Haam in Odessa in Russia in 1896 and published in

Jerusalem from 1920 to 1927. Although it had only about 2,000 readers a month, *Hashiloah* had a great influence on the Hebrew literature of its time. One of its editors was the poet Hayim Nahman Bialik. (See also AHAD HAAM; BIALIK, HAYIM NAHMAN.)

HASHOMER Jewish defense organization whose name means "watchman" in Hebrew. Hashomer was founded in 1909 in lower Galilee to protect the new Jewish settlements from Arab raiders. Its leader was Israel Shohat. Hashomer was a small organization that never had more than 100 members at any one time, but it set an example of bravery that inspired other Jews. When the Haganah (the Jewish underground army) was founded in 1920, Hashomer became part of the Haganah. (See also GA-LILEE; HAGANAH; SHOHAT, ISRAEL.)

HASHOMER HATZAIR Zionist youth organization founded in Eastern Europe in 1913. Its members began settling in Palestine during the Third Aliyah (third wave of immigration) in 1919 to 1921 and founded a number of kibbutzim. An organization of its kibbutzim, called Hakibbutz Haartzi, was established in 1927. Hashomer Hatzair insists that all its members accept its political ideals, which includes the acceptance of a Socialist society. It was pro-Russian until the 1960s, but Russian support of the Arabs has changed its attitude somewhat. In 1948 Hashomer Hatzair became part of the Mapam political party. Its youth group now has about 12,000 members in Israel and works closely with the Israel Arab Pioneering Youth Movement. (See also ALIYAH; HAKIBBUTZ HAARTZI; KIBBUTZ; MAPAM; YOUTH MOVE-MENTS.)

HASIDIM Members of a Jewish religious movement called *Lasidism*, which was in Eastern Europe in the middle 1700s by Rabbi Israel Baal Shem Tov. Hasidim form a close community around their leader, known as the *rebbe* or *zaddik*. The *rebbe* is seek as a holy man whose prayers bring his followers closer to God and who can bring God's blessings to the members of his community. Hasidic worship is joyful and is often expressed in singing and dancing.

The first hasidim to go to Palestine settled in Jerusalem and Safed in the 1770s. By 1900, several hasidic communities in Palestine had their own synagogues and schools. Hasidim were among the founders of the Israeli towns Bene Berak, Kiryat Ata, and Kefar Habad. Today there is also a Hasidic community in a section of the city of Netanya. (See also BENE BERAK; JEWS, ISRAELI; KEFAR HABAD; NETANYA.)

HASMONEANS A line of Jewish rulers of Palestine during the

A group of Hasidim in Mea Shearim section of Jerusalem engage in a lively debate after leaving a meeting.

first and second centuries B.C.E. founded by Mattathias of Modiin. Mattathias and his five sons (who included Judah the Maccabee and Simon the Hasmonean) led a successful revolt against Syrian rule in 166-164 B.C.E. Judah was killed in the revolt, but Simon became high priest and leader of the Jewish State from 142 to 135 B.C.E. Simon was succeeded by his son John Hyrcanus (135-104) and his grandson Alexander Jannaeus (104-76) who took the title of king. In 63 B.C.E. Aristobulus II and Hyrcanus II, two rivals for the Jewish throne, appealed to the Roman general Pompey for help. Pompey occupied Jerusalem and put an end to the Hasmonean rule of Palestine. (See also ALEXANDER JANNAEUS; ARISTOBULUS II; HISTORY; HYRCANUS, JOHN; HYRCANUS II; JUDAH THE MACCABEE; MACCABEES; MATTATHIAS; MODIIN; POMPEY; ROME; SIMON THE HASMONEAN; SYRIA.)

HATENUAH HAMEUHEDET   Israeli pioneer youth movement that was founded in 1945 and became part of the Habonim youth organization in 1951. (See also HABONIM; YOUTH MOVEMENTS.)

HATIKVAH Zionist song that became the national anthem of Israel. *Hatikvah* means "the hope" in Hebrew, and tells of the yearning of Jews to return to Palestine. The words were written in 1889 by Naphtali Imber to an existing folk melody. The Israel Philharmonic Orchestra played *Hatikvah* at the May 14, 1948 ceremony declaring Israel a Jewish nation. (See also DECLARA-TION OF INDEPENDENCE; IMBER, NAPHTALI; ISRAEL PHILHARMONIC ORCHESTRA.)

HATKVAH Fruit of the cactus plant. It is often sold cut and peeled at street stands in Israel's cities. The cactus fruit is also called a sabra. (See also SABRA.)

HATZEVI Hebrew word meaning "the deer." The first modern political magazine to be published in Palestine. It was published in Hebrew by Eliezer Ben Yehuda (the father of modern Hebrew) in the late 1800s and preached the rebirth of Hebrew as a spoken language. (See also BEN YEHUDA, ELIEZER.)

HATZOFE (also spelled HA-TZOPHEH) Israeli daily newspaper founded in Jerusalem in 1937 and now published in Tel Aviv. *Hatzofe* is the newspaper of the Mizrahi (religious Zionist) political movement. It prints articles on religious subjects as well as the usual material found in newspapers. In 1970 it had a circulation of 11,000. (See also MIZRAHI.)

HAUSNER, GIDEON (1915-) Austrian-born lawyer and judge who was brought to Palestine as a child. Hausner served as Attorney-General of Israel and was chief prosecutor against Adolph Eichmann at the Nazi's trial in Israel for war crimes. Hausner also taught at the Hebrew University in Jerusalem and was a member of the Israeli Knesset (legislature). (See also EICHMANN, ADOLPH; HEBREW UNIVERSITY; KNESSET.)

HAVATZELET Hebrew word meaning "the lily." One of the first Hebrew magazines in Palestine. It was published by Israel Frumkin in the late 1800s and opposed Zionist settlements in Palestine. (See also FRUMKIN, ISRAEL DOV.)

HAVER see CHAVER

HAVLAGA Hebrew word meaning "self-restraint." Havlaga was the policy of the Jewish Agency and the Haganah (Jewish underground army) during the Arab revolt of 1936-1939 in Palestine. Jews defended themselves against Arab attacks but did not retaliate by attacking Arabs. (See also ARAB RIOTS; HAGANAH; JEWISH AGENCY.)

HAYCRAFT COMMISSION Group appointed by the British

government (who ruled Palestine under the Mandate) to investigate the Arab riots of 1921. The commission's report was anti-Zionist and said that the growing Jewish settlement in Palestine was a major cause of the Arab riots. (See also ARAB RIOTS; GREAT BRITAIN; ZIONISM.)

HAZAZ, HAYIM (1897-1973)   Russian-born Hebrew writer who settled in Palestine in 1931. Hazaz's novels were realistic and described Jewish life in Russia, Yemen, and Palestine. Several of his novels and his play *The End of the Days* have been translated into English. Hazaz was awarded both the Bialik and the Israel prizes for literature. (See also BIALIK PRIZE; ISRAEL PRIZE; LITERATURE.)

HAZOR   Ancient town in upper Galilee about ten miles north of Safed. Hazor was the leading Canaanite town in Galilee when Joshua conquered Canaan in about the fourteenth century B.C.E. King Solomon rebuilt and fortified the town as a base for his chariot troops. In the ninth century B.C.E. King Ahab built a new city on the site and constructed the largest water system in ancient Israel. The city was conquered and destroyed by the Assyrians in 732 B.C.E.

Hazor is one of the largest and most important archaeological sites in Israel. It covers an area of over 200 acres and several archaeological expeditions, led by Yigael Yadin, have uncovered 21 layers of ruins showing that human occupation goes back 2,700 years. Among the finds are Canaanite and Israelite temples and altars, fortress walls and gates, a pottery workshop, underground tombs, statues, and pottery. There is a museum on the site and tourists can walk down the steps to the cistern where water was stored in King Ahab's time. (See also AHAB; ARCHAEOLOGY; ASSYRIA; CANAAN; GALILEE; HISTORY; JOSHUA; SOLOMON; TOURISM; YADIN, YIGAEL.)

HAZOREA   Kibbutz (cooperative farming village) in the Jezreel Valley founded in 1936. Hazorea contains the Wilfred Israel Museum of art and archaeology. (See also JEZREEL VALLEY; KIBBUTZ.)

HEALTH   The Israeli Ministry of Health oversees health care in the country. It licenses doctors and dentists, enforces health and safety laws, and guards against pollution of air, water, and food. The Ministry of Health also operates government hospitals, clinics, mother-and-child health stations, and school health services. About one-third of all hospitals and two-thirds of the mother-and-child health stations in Israel are run by the government. The rest are operated by Kupat Holim, Hadassah, and other organizations.

Kupat Holim is the health insurance fund of the Histadrut (Israel's labor federation). It provides medical and dental care in its own hospitals, clinics, health stations, and drugstores. All Histadrut members and their families belong to Kupat Holim since some of their union dues goes to pay for their health insurance. About 70% of Israel's population belongs to Kupat Holim.

The Hadassah Medical Organization, sponsored by the Women's Zionist Organization of America, runs the Hadassah-Hebrew University Medical Center and the rebuilt Mount Scopus Center in Jerusalem. Malben, paid for by the American Jewish Distribution Committee, cares for the aged, the chronically sick, and the handicapped. Magen David Adom (Red Shield of David) operates first-aid services and blood banks. The Israel Anti-Tuberculosis League and the Israel Cancer Society fight tuberculosis and cancer respectively.

Israel is very concerned about the health of its children. There are about 750 mother-and-child health stations throughout the country. These care for mothers before and after their children are born, vaccinate children against disease, and generally keep Israel's children healthy. There is also a school health program for older children. (See also HADASSAH; KUPAT HOLIM; MAGEN DAVID ADOM; MALBEN.)

HEBREW   The language in which most of the Bible was written and the official language of Israel. Hebrew is a Semitic language written from right to left with an alphabet of 22 letters. Vowel sounds appear under the letters, but are usually left out in magazines, newspapers, and books, since all but beginners can read without vowels.

Hebrew was the only spoken and written language of the Jews until the Babylonian Exile in the sixth century B.C.E. when Jews began to use Aramaic as their everyday language. Hebrew died out as a spoken language by the second century C.E., although it continued to be an important written language for Jewish literature through the Middle Ages and right up to modern times.

Modern Hebrew began in the late 1800s when Jewish pioneers started to settle in Palestine. The man most responsible for the rebirth of Hebrew as a spoken language was Eliezer Ben Yehuda. Biblical Hebrew had only about 7,700 words. Although new words had been added by writers through the centuries, Hebrew did not have the vocabulary to express many modern ideas. Ben Yehuda spent his life coining new words and compiling a huge Hebrew dictionary. He organized the Hebrew Language Council (which later became the Hebrew Language Academy) to help him with this task. Today a modern Hebrew dictionary contains over 50,000 words. (See also ARAMAIC; BEN YEHUDA, ELIEZER; HEBREW LANGUAGE ACADEMY; SEMITIC LANGUAGES.)

HEBREW LANGUAGE ACADEMY   In 1953 the Israeli Knesset (legislature) recognized the old Hebrew Language Council, founded by Eliezer Ben Yehuda, as an official government agency and changed its name to the Hebrew Language Academy. The Academy has 18 members who determine the proper spelling and grammar of Hebrew. It also prepares dictionaries and coins new words. (See also BEN YEHUDA, ELIEZER; HEBREW.)

HEBREW UNION COLLEGE   Religious college founded in Cincinnati, Ohio, in 1875. The school now has three campuses in the United States and one in Jerusalem. The Jerusalem center, called the Nelson C. Glueck School of Biblical Archaeology, is for advanced study in the history and archaeology of the Holy Land. Besides holding classes, the Glueck School runs archaeological digs at Tel Dan. (See also ARCHAEOLOGY; EDUCATION; GLUECK, NELSON; TEL DAN.)

HEBREW UNIVERSITY   The largest university in Israel. Establishing a university in Palestine was an important Zionist goal. Land was bought on Mount Scopus, a hill north of Jerusalem, and foundation stones for the first buildings were laid by Zionist leader Chaim Weizmann in 1918. The university opened in 1925. When the Mount Scopus buildings fell into Arab hands after the 1948 War of Independence, a new campus was built at Givat Ram in western Jerusalem. After Mount Scopus was recaptured in the 1967 Six-Day War, it again became the main center of the university

The Hebrew University has departments of science, social science, humanities, law, pharmacy, dentistry, agriculture, education, library science, social work, and medicine. The Hadassah hospital serves as its teaching hospital. In 1978 the university had sixteen thousand students, about three thousand of whom came from other countries to study. The university has extension courses for Israeli students who cannot travel to Jerusalem. It has also helped develop Haifa University and the Ben-Gurion University of the Negev. The Hebrew University is a research as well as a teaching center. It carries out important research in medicine and agriculture. (See also BEN-GURION UNIVERSITY OF THE NEGEV; HADASSAH; HAIFA UNIVERSITY; SIX-DAY WAR; WAR OF INDEPENDENCE; WEIZMANN, CHAIM; ZIONISM.)

HEBRON   One of the oldest towns in Palestine, Hebron has been inhabited continuously for more than 5,000 years. It lies 18 miles south of Jerusalem in the center of vineyards and olive groves. The Book of Genesis tells of Abraham buying a cave in the field of Machpelah at Hebron as a burial place for his family. The city was David's early capital and the place where he was coronated king of Israel. Jews have lived in Hebron throughout its history and it was one of the four holy cities of Palestine. In the 1800s it had a Jewish population of about 1,500 people, many of whom studied at Hebron's yeshivot (religious schools). The Arabs killed many of the town's Jewish inhabitants in the 1929 riots; the rest fled. Jews only settled in Hebron once again after the 1967 Six-Day War. (See also ABRAHAM; ARAB RIOTS; BIBLE; DAVID; MACHPELAH, CAVE OF; SIX-DAY WAR.)

HECHT, JOSEPH (1894-   ) Russian-born Haganah (Jewish underground army) leader who settled in Palestine in 1914. Hecht was in charge of Jewish defense in Palestine during the 1929 Arab riots. (See also ARAB RIOTS; HAGANAH.)

HEFER VALLEY (also called EMEK HEPHER) Plain on the coast between Haifa and Tel Aviv. When the Jewish National Fund bought the swampy land in 1929, it was infested with malaria-carrying mosquitoes. Today the swamps have been drained and there are over 40 agricultural settlements flourishing in the fertile Hefer Valley. The first and largest of these villages is Kefar Vitkin. (See also KEFAR VITKIN; MALARIA.)

HEHALUTZ Youth organization whose name means "the pioneer." The first Hehalutz group was founded in the United States in 1915 by David Ben-Gurion and Yitzhak Ben-Zvi. American and European groups combined into a world organization in 1924. The organization trained halutzim (pioneers) to settle in Palestine in new or established agricultural villages, to work the land, and to defend their settlements against attack. Hehalutz and the allied youth movements of Gordonia, Habonim, Ben Akiva, and Hashomer Hatzair brought supplies to the pioneers who built Palestine between World War I and the birth of the State of Israel in 1948. (See also BENE AKIVA; BEN-GURION, DAVID; BEN-ZVI, YITZHAK; GORDONIA; HABONIM; HALUTZ; HASHOMER HATZAIR; YOUTH MOVEMENTS.)

HEICHAL SHLOMO (also spelled HECHAL SHLOMO) Religious center in Jerusalem that is the seat of the Chief Rabbinate of Israel. Heichal Shlomo also houses a synagogue, a religious research center, a museum, a library, and archives. The center is financed by the Israeli government. (See also ARCHIVES; CHIEF RABBINATE; JERUSALEM.)

HELENA (about 247-327 C.E.) Mother of Constantine the Great (the first Roman emperor to become a Christian). Helena traveled to the Christian holy places in Palestine and founded several churches including the original Church of the Holy Sepulchre in Jerusalem and the Church of the Nativity in Bethlehem. (See also CHURCH OF THE NATIVITY; CONSTANTINE; HOLY SEPULCHRE.)

HELETZ (also spelled HELEZ)   Moshav (farming village) on the Coastal Plain founded in 1950 by immigrants from Yemen. The Heletz oil fields are nearby. (See also COASTAL PLAIN; HELETZ OIL FIELDS; MOSHAV.)

HELETZ OIL FIELDS (also spelled HELEZ)   Israel's main oil fields. Heletz is near the Mediterranean coast, about 30 miles south of Tel Aviv. Oil was discovered there in 1955. Although the oil wells of the Heletz fields produce from half a million to a million and a half barrels of crude oil a year, that is only a small part of the oil Israel needs. The rest must be imported from other countries. (See also OIL.)

HELLENISM   The form of ancient Greek culture that spread through the Mediterranean countries and the Middle East after the end of the fourth century B.C.E. Archaeological remains in Israel from the third century B.C.E. through the early centuries C.E. show a strong Hellenistic influence in art and architecture. (See also ARCHAEOLOGY.)

HEN (abbreviation of HEL NASHIM, meaning "women's army"). The women of Hen often serve their military service by working as teachers, welfare workers, or nurses in isolated settlements inside Israel. Women soldiers also free men to fight by doing clerical and communications jobs. (See also DEFENSE FORCES; NATIONAL SERVICE.)

HEPTAPEGON   see TABGHA

HEROD I (also called HEROD THE GREAT) (73-4 B.C.E.)   King of Judea from 40 to 4 B.C.E. Herod was appointed king of Judea by the Roman Senate and captured Jerusalem with the help of Roman troops. Rome gave him a free hand to run his country's internal affairs, but he was not allowed to make foreign policy. To secure his position as king among his Jewish subjects, Herod married Mariamne (a Hasmonean princess) and killed many of his political rivals. He ruled Judea with a firm hand. Taxes were high during his rule, but he increased the country's trade and added to its wealth. He replaced the old Temple in Jerusalem with a magnificent new building, and founded the cities of Caesarea and Sabaste (Samaria). Although people outside of Palestine thought of Herod as an excellent king and a protector of the Jews, many of his own people hated him because of his friendliness toward Rome. (See also CAESAREA; HISTORY; JUDEA; ROME; SAMARIA; TEMPLE.)

HEROD AGRIPPA (10 B.C.E.-44 C.E.)   King of Judea who ruled 37-44 C.E. Herod Agrippa was appointed king by the Roman emperor. He respected the religion of his Jewish subjects and improved the Temple in Jerusalem that his grandfather, Herod I, had rebuilt. When he died, Agrippa's kingdom became part of the Roman province of Syria. (See also HEROD I; JUDEA; ROME; TEMPLE.)

HEROD'S GATE (Hebrew, SHAAR HORDUS)   One of the eight gates in the wall around the Old City of Jerusalem. Herod's Gate is also called the Gate of Flowers. (See also JERUSALEM; WALLED CITIES.)

HERUT   Israeli political party whose name means "freedom." Herut was founded in 1948 by veterans of the Irgun (an underground fighting group) and was joined by members of the Union of Zionist Revisionists. Herut believes that Israel should occupy its "historical boundaries," which include the land occupied in the 1967 Six-Day War. Its economic policy favors free enterprise rather than government control of business and industry. In 1965 Herut allied itself with the Liberal Party to form Gahal, and in 1973 added some small parties to the alliance to form Likud. In 1977 Likud defeated the Labor Party that had ruled Israel since it became a state in 1948. Herut's leader, Menachem Begin, became Israel's sixth Prime Minister. (See also BEGIN, MENACHEM; GAHAL; IRGUN; ISRAEL LABOR PARTY; KNESSET; LIBERAL PARTY; LIKUD; POLITICAL PARTIES; PRIME MINISTER; REVISIONISTS.)

HERZL, THEODOR (1860-1904)   Father of Political Zionism. Born in Budapest in Hungary, he studied law in Vienna, Austria, but soon gave it up to become a writer and journalist. He wrote a number of plays that were produced in Europe, who served as editor of the *Neue Freie Press*, a liberal Viennese newspaper.

Herzl became concerned with the problem of Jews living in Europe who were facing anti-Semitism (prejudice against Jews). In 1895 he wrote *The Jewish State*, a book in which he said that the only solution to the Jewish problem was the establishment of a Jewish State and mass Jewish immigration to the new country. His book *Old-New Land*, written in 1902, urged that a new Jewish society be created in Palestine, built on tolerance and cooperation between its peoples, and the most advanced science and technology.

Herzl devoted much of his life to working for a Jewish State in Palestine. He called the First Zionist Conference which met in 1897 in Basle, Switzerland, and established the World Zionist Organization. He became president of the Zionist organization and traveled to many countries to meet with world leaders and

Theodor Herzl

plead the case for a Jewish State. He went to Turkey, Palestine, Germany, Russia, Great Britain, and Italy, and met with Sultan Abdul Hamid, Kaiser Wilhelm II, Russian Minister Von Plehve, British Foreign Secretary Chamberlain, and the Pope.

Herzl died at the age of 44. He was buried in Vienna, but his body was moved to Mount Herzl in Jerusalem in 1949. (See also BASLE PROGRAM; MOUNT HERZL; WORLD ZIONIST ORGANIZATION; ZIONISM.)

HERZL FOREST   Forest at Hulda, about 15 miles southeast of Tel Aviv, planted in honor of Theodor Herzl. The first trees, planted in 1905, were olives and almonds, but pine trees proved easier to grow in the soil of the area. (See also ALMOND; HERZL, THEODOR; JERUSALEM PINE; OLIVES; REFORESTATION.)

HERZLIA HIGH SCHOOL (also called HERZLIYAH GYMNASIUM) First high school in Palestine to teach all classes in Hebrew. It was founded in 1905 in Jaffa, named in honor of Theodor Herzl, and moved to its own building in the new city of Tel Aviv in 1909. Herzlia High School published the first Hebrew textbooks in mathematics and the sciences and coined new Hebrew words for these subjects. (See also EDUCATION; HEBREW; HERZL, THEODOR.)

HERZLIYA   Town on the Mediterranean coast north of Tel Aviv that was named in honor of Theodor Herzl. Herzliya was founded in 1924 in an area that grew citrus fruit. It has grown into a small city and is a leading beach resort today. (See also HERZL, THEODOR.)

HERZOG, CHAIM (1918-   )   Polish-born soldier and diplomat. Herzog fought in the battle for Latrun during the 1948 War of

dem° wackeren Mitstreiter
Dr S. R. Landau

DER

Th. Herzl

JUDENSTAAT.

VERSUCH

EINER

MODERNEN LÖSUNG DER JUDENFRAGE

VON

THEODOR HERZL

DOCTOR DER RECHTE.

LEIPZIG und WIEN 1896.
M. BREITENSTEIN'S VERLAGS-BUCHHANDLUNG
WIEN, IX., WÄHRINGERSTRASSE 5.

Reproduktion des Umschlagblattes der Original-Broschüre
„Der Judenstaat" mit Widmung.

The original copy of Herzl's book *Der Judenstaat,* in which
he stated his views about a Jewish State. The book is
dedicated to Dr. Landau, his collaborator.

Independence and later became the head of the Israel Military Intelligence. After retiring from the armed forces, he served as Israel's ambassador to the United Nations. He is the son of Isaac Halevi Herzog. (See also HERZOG, ISAAC HALEVI; LATRUN; UNITED NATIONS; WAR OF INDEPENDENCE.)

HERZOG, ISAAC HALEVI Polish-born rabbi who served as Chief Rabbi of the Irish Free State before he was elected Ashkenazi Chief Rabbi of Palestine in 1936. Herzog was a founder of the Mizrahi (religious Zionist) movement in England. He was a scholar who spoke 12 languages and wrote a number of books, including *The Main Institutions of Jewish Law.* (See also ASHKENAZIM; CHIEF RABBINATE; MIZRAHI.)

HERZOG, JACOB (1921-1972) Irish-born diplomat who served as Israel's minister to the United States and as ambassador to Canada. He was the son of Isaac Halevi Herzog. (See also HERZOG, ISAAC HALEVI.)

HEVER HAKEVUTZOT Organization of small kibbutzim founded in 1926. In 1951 Hever Hakevutzot joined with a group of kibbutzim that broke away from the Hakibbutz Hameuhad organization to form a new group called Ihud Hakevutzot Veha-Kibbutzim. (See also HAKIBBUTZ HAMEUHAD; IHUD HAKEVUTZOT VEHA-KIBBUTZIM.)

HEZEKIAH Son of Ahaz and one of the greatest kings of Judah. He ruled 720-692 B.C.E. Hezekiah threw out the idols of the Assyrian kings his father had allowed to be placed in the Temple. He fortified Jerusalem and joined with neighboring states in an uprising against Assyria. The Assyrians invaded Judah but did not occupy Jerusalem. Hezekiah was forced to pay a large tribute to Assyria and to give 43 of Judah's towns to the Philistines. However, he recaptured the towns after the Assyrian army left. (See also AHAZ; ASSYRIA; HISTORY; JUDAH, KINGDOM OF; PHILISTINES; TEMPLE.)

HIBBAT ZION Zionist movement organized in Russia after the pogroms (murder of Jews) of 1801. The name means "love of Zion." Other such groups were started in Poland, Rumania, Austria, and Great Britain. Hibbat Zion's slogan was "To Palestine" and it bought land in Palestine on which its members built farming settlements. At first, much of the money to buy the land and support the settlements came from Baron Edmond de Rothschild. In 1887 the different Hibbat Zion groups joined together in an organization called Hoveve Zion, and in 1897 Hoveve Zion joined the newly founded World Zionist Organization. (See also ROTHSCHILD, EDMOND DE; WORLD ZIONIST ORGANIZATION; ZIONISM.)

HIGH COMMISSIONER FOR PALESTINE   Head of the British government of Palestine from 1918 to 1948. The High Commissioner had the power to appoint public officials, to pass any laws he felt were necessary for the peace and order of Palestine, and to control public land. (See also GREAT BRITAIN; MANDATE.)

HIGH PLACE   Ancient place of worship. A Canaanite High Place was an altar, a pillar, or a sacred tree placed on top of a hill. The Israelites also worshipped at High Places in Palestine from the time they occupied the country until King Solomon built the Temple in Jerusalem in the tenth century B.C.E. Archaeologists have found the remains of a number of High Places in Israel. (See also ARCHAEOLOGY; CANAAN; SOLOMON; TEMPLE.)

HIGH PRIEST   Chief priest in the Temple in ancient Jerusalem. There were 18 high priests during the existence of the First Temple; about 60 served in the Second Temple. During the first and second centuries B.C.E., the positions of high priest and king were often held by the same person. (See also TEMPLE.)

HILLEL (first century B.C.E.)   One of the two great scholars of his time (the other was Shammai). Hillel was born in Babylonia, went to Palestine as a young man to study in Jerusalem, and founded a religious school called Bet Hillel. When asked by a non-Jew to explain the ideals of Judaism in a few words, he answered, "What you yourself do not like, do not do to another. That is the whole Law. Everything else is only an explanation of it." Hillel's descendants were among the great scholars and leaders of Israel for the next 600 years. (See also SHAMMAI.)

HIRSCH, MAURICE DE (1831-1896)   German-born banker who later lived in Paris. During his lifetime Baron de Hirsch gave over $100 million to Jewish causes. He founded and financed the Jewish Colonization Association (ICA) to help Jews establish agricultural settlements in Argentina. Theodor Herzl tried unsuccessfully to convince Baron de Hirsch to support Jewish settlement in Palestine. However, after the Baron's death ICA did finance some Palestinian settlements. (See also HERZL, THEODOR; JEWISH COLONIZATION ASSOCIATION.)

HISTADRUT   General Federation of Labor of Israel. Next to the government, Histadrut is the most powerful organization in Israel. More than half of Israel's population—including workers, professional people, farmers, and housewives—belong to it. All are also members of Kupat Holim, Histadrut's health insurance service. They can also take advantage of the labor federation's vocational training or adult education classes, its cultural and recreational activities (such as art shows and folk dancing), or join Hapoel, Histadrut's sports organization.

When Histadrut was founded in 1920, Palestine was a backward country. Besides protecting workers' rights on the job, the labor federation had to create jobs for its members and provide them with housing and health services. That is why, unlike union labor organizations in most other countries, Histadrut operates businesses and industries that account for almost a quarter of the goods and services produced in Israel. All Histadrut members are also part of Hevrat Ovdim, the General Cooperative Association, which owns and operates factories, building and construction companies, trucking firms, a bank, a publishing house, and two newspapers, and has a part interest in a shipping firm and an airline. Tnuva, Histadrut's agricultural marketing cooperative, sells over two-thirds of the crops grown in the country. (See also AGRICULTURE; DAVAR; ECONOMY; HAPOEL; INDUSTRY; KUPAT HOLIM.)

HISTADRUT HA-OVEDIM HALEUMIT   Israeli non-Socialist labor organization founded in 1934. It had 88,000 members in 1975 and is allied with the Herut political party. Histadrut Haovedim Haleumit operates the second largest health insurance fund in Israel. (See also HEALTH; HERUT.)

HISTORY   The biblical history of the Jews in Israel began in the seventeenth century B.C.E. when Abraham entered the land of Canaan which God promised to him and his descendants. Famine drove Abraham's grandson, Jacob, to Egypt where the Jews were held as slaves for several generations until Moses led them back to the Promised Land. The Israelite tribes conquered the land of Canaan during the thirteenth to eleventh centuries B.C.E. and established the first Jewish kingdom under Saul in about 1020. David extended the kingdom and made Jerusalem its capital. His son, Solomon, built the First Temple in Jerusalem. After Solomon's death the kingdom split into two—Israel in the north and Judah in the south.

The two Jewish kingdoms lived side by side, sometimes as allies and sometimes at war, until the Assyrians conquered Israel in 722 B.C.E. and the Babylonians conquered Judah in 586. The Temple was destroyed and most of the Jews were forced into exile. They were allowed to return and rebuild the Temple after the Persians conquered Babylon in 538.

The Jewish State was fairly independent for the next four centuries although it was first part of the Persian Empire, and then the Greek Empire. During the Greek period, the Syrians dominated Palestine and attempted to Hellenize (impose Greek culture) the Jews and destroy their religion. This led to the successful Jewish revolt of 167 B.C.E. led by Judah the Maccabee, and to the establishment of the line of Hasmonean kings in 165 B.C.E.

Jewish independence came to an end when two rivals to the Hasmonean throne appealed to the Roman general Pompey for help. Rome moved in and took control of Judea (the Roman name for Israel). The Jews revolted against Roman rule in 66 C.E. and again in 132 C.E. under Bar Kokhba, but both revolts were cruelly put down and Palestine remained a Roman colony.

When the Roman Empire split into two parts in the fourth century C.E., Palestine was ruled by the eastern part, known as the Byzantine Empire. In 640 B.C. Palestine was conquered by the Arabs who held it until the Crusader (Christian European knights) invasion of 1099. The Crusaders were driven out by the Egyptian Mamelukes in 1291. The Mamelukes were in turn defeated in 1518 by the Turks who ruled Palestine until the British captured it in 1918, during World War I.

The Jews had been driven out of their homeland by one conqueror after another. By 1880 only 25,000 Jews lived in four cities of Palestine. Beginning in 1882, groups of young Jews from Europe, inspired by the Zionist ideal, began to settle in Palestine. They established new agricultural villages and reclaimed the land. By the time Britain was given the League of Nations Mandate to govern Palestine in 1922, there were 90,000 Jews in the country.

The years of the British Mandate saw increasing Jewish immigration to Palestine. The Jewish community built villages and cities, established schools and hospitals, and formed an army for self-defense. Although, in the Balfour Declaration of 1917, the British government declared itself in favor of a Jewish homeland in Palestine, it did nothing to help create a Jewish State. Instead it tried to limit Jewish immigration into the country.

In 1947 the fate of Palestine was referred to the United Nations, and on May 14, 1948 the State of Israel was created. The Arab nations surrounding Israel immediately attacked, but Israel drove them back as they battled for independence. The Arabs tried to destroy the Jewish State three more times—in the Sinai War of 1956, the Six-Day War of 1967, and the Yom Kippur War of 1973—but they were driven back each time and Israel emerged from the wars holding considerable land outside of its 1948 boundaries.

As soon as Israel became a state in 1948, it opened its doors to Jews from all over the world. More than 676,000 new immigrants poured into the country during the first three years of its existence. (See also ABRAHAM; ALIYAH; ARABS; ASSYRIA; BABYLON; BAR KOKHBA, SIMEON; BYZANTINE EMPIRE; CANAAN; CRUSADES; DAVID;

GREAT BRITAIN; HASMONEANS; HELLENISM; IMMIGRANTS; ISRAEL,
KINGDOM OF; JACOB; JUDAH, KINGDOM OF; JUDAH THE MACCABEE;
JUDEA; LEAGUE OF NATIONS; MAMELUKES; MANDATE; MOSES; PERSIA;
ROME; SAUL; SINAI WAR; SIX-DAY WAR; SOLOMON; SYRIA; TEMPLE;
TURKEY; UNITED NATIONS; WAR OF INDEPENDENCE; YOM KIPPUR
WAR.)

HITLER, ADOLPH (1889-1945)   Dictator of Germany from 1933
to 1945. Hitler was born in Austria, served in the German army
during World War I, helped form the Nazi party, and became the
party's leader. Under Hitler's dictatorship, the German armies
conquered most of Europe during World War II (1939-1945).
Hitler gave the orders for the Nazis to murder six million Jews in
Germany and the occupied countries. When it became clear in
1945 that Germany was about to lose the war, Hitler killed
himself in Berlin. (See also HOLOCAUST; NAZIS.)

HOD HASHARON   Town on the Sharon Plain formed in 1924
by combining three earlier settlements. It grows citrus fruits and
other crops and has several small industries. (See also SHARON
PLAIN.)

HOD, MORDEKHAI (1926-   )   Native-born Israeli soldier who
fought with the Haganah (Jewish underground army) and later
became Commander of the Israel Air Force. Hod commanded the
successful air strike against the Arab air forces in the 1967 Six-Day
War. (See also DEFENSE FORCES; HAGANAH; SIX-DAY WAR.)

HOLIDAYS   The Israeli Work and Rest Hours Law of 1951 states
that Jewish workers have their day of rest on the Jewish Sabbath
(Saturday) and vacations on the Jewish holidays. Religious and
national holidays in Israel are set by the Jewish calendar. The
same holiday falls on a different day of the international calendar
each year. Holidays begin at sundown on the evening before the
day of the holiday, and end at sundown 24 hours later. Trains,
buses, and streetcars stop running during the Sabbath and religious holidays in most Israeli cities. Haifa is an exception.

Although the official holidays of Israel are Jewish, the law
guarantees every other religious community (Christian, Moslem,
Druze, etc.) the right to observe its own weekly rest day and its
own holidays. (See also CALENDAR, INTERNATIONAL; CALENDAR,
JEWISH; RELIGION; SABBATH.)

HOLOCAUST   Word meaning complete destruction by fire.
"The Holocaust" is the term used to describe the murder of six
million Jewish men, women, and children in Europe during
World War II (1939-1945). When the Nazis (National Socialist
party) gained power in Germany in the 1930s, they began to

In April 1945, U.S. third Army troops liberated the inmates at the Buchenwald concentration camp in East Germany, where more than 50,000 had died. Most of these homeless and stateless refugees found homes in Israel.

A piece of sculpture on the grounds of Yad Vashem, symbolic of the Holocaust. Concentration camps were surrounded by barbed wire and many people were killed in futile attempts to escape.

persecute the country's Jews. At first the Nazis took away the Jews' citizenship papers, homes, and possessions. Later most German Jews were sent to concentration camps and were killed. During World War II, Germany conquered most of Europe. The Nazis rounded up the Jews in the occupied countries and sent them to concentration camps, such as Buchenwald, Auschwitz, and Dachau. There they were worked to death, or gassed to death, and their bodies burned in ovens. (See also HOLOCAUST; NAZIS; YAD VASHEM.)

HOLOCAUST DAY Israeli holiday in remembrance of the martyrs and heroes who died under Nazi oppression in the 1930s and 1940s. There are wreath-laying ceremonies at Yad Vashem (the Jerusalem monument to the Nazi victims) and all Jewish places of entertainment are closed. Holocaust Day falls on the twenty-seventh of Nissan on the Jewish calendar (April-May on the international calendar). (See also CALENDAR, INTERNATIONAL; CALENDAR, JEWISH; HOLIDAYS; HOLOCAUST; NAZIS; YAD VASHEM.)

HOLON City two miles south of Tel Aviv formed in 1940 by joining several suburbs of Tel Aviv. Holon is an important industrial center with hundreds of factories and workshops. About half of the Samaritans (a small religious sect) in Israel live in a section of Holon. (See also SAMARITANS; TEL AVIV.)

HOLY SEPULCHRE Church in Jerusalem in what is believed to be the site of Golgotha (also called Calvary), the hill where Jesus Christ was crucified, buried, and rose from the dead. The first Church of the Holy Sepulchre was built in the fourth century C.E. by the Roman emperor Constantine and his mother, Helena. The present church was originally built by the Crusaders in 1149, but most of it has been destroyed and restored several times since. The Holy Sepulchre is considered by many Christians to be the holiest place on earth. (See also CHRISTIANS; CONSTANTINE; CRUSADES; GOLGOTHA; HELENA; JESUS.)

HORA Popular folk dance of Israel. The hora originated in Eastern Europe and was brought to Palestine by Jewish immigrants. It is danced in a circle with each dancer resting his or her outstretched arms on the shoulders of the next person in the circle. Many Israeli composers have written hora music. (See also DANCE.)

HOROWITZ, DAVID (1889-) Polish-born economist who went to Palestine in 1920 as part of a group of young pioneers. Horowitz was the director of the Jewish Agency's economic department, head of the Israeli government Department of Finance, and the governor of the Bank of Israel. He also wrote several books on economics in Palestine and Israel. (See also BANK OF ISRAEL; JEWISH AGENCY.)

HOS, DOV(1894-1940)   Russian-born labor leader who settled in Palestine in 1906. Hos was one of the founders of the Histadrut (Israel's labor federation), represented Palestinian Jewish labor at conferences in Europe and the United States, and was a leader of the Haganah (Jewish underground army). He was deputy mayor of Tel Aviv until his death in an automobile accident. (See also HAGANAH; HISTADRUT; TEL AVIV.)

HOUSHI, ABBA   see KHOUSHI, ABBA

HOVEVE ZION   see HIBBAT ZION

HUBERMAN, BRONISLAW (1882-1947)   One of the finest violinists of his time. Huberman was born in Poland and gave concerts throughout Europe. In 1936 he founded the Palestine Symphony Orchestra (now called the Israel Philharmonic Orchestra) and invited musicians from leading European orchestras to join. By doing so, he saved the lives of many talented musicians who might have died under Nazi oppression in Europe. (See also ISRAEL PHILHARMONIC ORCHESTRA; MUSIC; NAZIS.)

HULATA   Kibbutz founded on the shore of Lake Huleh in 1936 and moved to its present site in the Huleh Valley in 1946. Hulata was under Arab fire during the 1948 War of Independence. (See also HULEH VALLEY; WAR OF INDEPENDENCE.)

HULDAH   Kibbutz about 15 miles south of Tel Aviv founded as a research and training farm on land bought by the Jewish National Fund in 1907. The original settlement was attacked during the Arab riots of 1929. Although the settlers and members of Haganah (Jewish underground army) bravely defended the village, they were driven out. The new settlement, founded in 1930, was an important base of Israeli forces fighting to free Jerusalem during the 1948 War of Independence. The Herzl Forest is near Huldah. (See also AGRICULTURAL RESEARCH; ARAB RIOTS; HAGANAH; HERZL FOREST; JEWISH NATIONAL FUND; KIBBUTZ; WAR OF INDEPENDENCE.)

HULEH VALLEY (also spelled HULA)   Valley in upper Galilee that was covered by a swamp filled with malaria-carrying mosquitoes. Many of the settlers in the early 1900s suffered greatly, and many died of malaria. The swamps were drained in an operation that began in 1951 and took seven years to complete. Large ponds for raising fish were built and the drained land was planted with fruit trees, cotton, and rice. Today the Huleh Valley is one of the most fertile areas of Israel and its fishponds supply much of the fish eaten in the country. (See also FISHPONDS; GALILEE; GEOGRAPHY; MALARIA.)

HUMUS   Popular Israeli dish served as the first course of a meal, or as a snack. Humus is a paste made of mashed chickpeas and spices. It is served cold and eaten by scooping it up with pieces of pita bread. (See also PITA.)

HUSSEIN (1935-   )   King of Jordan who has ruled since 1952. Although Hussein kept Jordan out of the 1956 Sinai War, his army invaded Israel in the Six-Day War of 1967. As a result of its defeat in the Six-Day War, Jordan lost the West Bank to Israel.

Hussein is considered a moderate Arab leader and has not agreed with the Arab terrorist groups and their violence. However, he favors the establishment of an Arab-Palestinian State and considers the Palestine Liberation Organization (P.L.O.) the legal voice of the Arabs of Palestine. (See also JORDAN; PALESTINE LIBERATION ORGANIZATION; SINAI WAR; SIX-DAY WAR; WEST BANK.)

HUSSEINI, HAJJ AMIN (1893-1974)   Jerusalem-born Arab leader who was appointed Mufti (judge of Moslem law) of Jerusalem in 1921 by the British who then ruled Palestine under the Mandate. Husseini organized the 1936 Arab riots in Palestine. Because the riots were directed against the British as well as the Jews, he was exiled from the country. He went to Germany and during World War II helped Hitler in his efforts to exterminate the Jews. When Israel became a state in 1948, Husseini tried to set up an Arab government of Palestine in the Gaza Strip, but failed. (See also ARAB RIOTS; GAZA STRIP; GREAT BRITAIN.)

HYRCANUS, JOHN (second century B.C.E.)   High priest and king of Judea who ruled 135-104 B.C.E. He was the son of Simon the Hasmonean. Although early in his rule Hyrcanus was forced to give up a number of cities to Syria, he soon recaptured them and expanded the Jewish State. He conquered the Edomites and overran Samaria and Galilee. He built up the country's trade and put down an uprising of the Pharisees, a religious political party that opposed his policies. By the end of Hyrcanus' rule Judea was a strong and independent nation. (See also EDOM; GALILEE; HIGH PRIEST; HISTORY; PHARISEES; SAMARIA; SIMON THE HASMONEAN; SYRIA.)

HYRCANUS II (first century B.C.E.)   High priest of Judea 78-40 B.C.E. Hyrcanus II was the son of Alexander Jannaeus and Salome Alexandra. Upon their mother's death, Hyrcanus and his brother Aristobulus fought to rule Judea. They appealed to the Roman general Pompey to resolve the dispute. Pompey sided with Hyrcanus and confirmed him as high priest, but the appeal marked the beginning of the end of an independent Jewish nation. Roman control of the country grew until Judea became a

This gift box was handmade for King Hussein of Jordan by artistic binder Persekian in his shop near the New Gate, in the Old City of Jerusalem. The king presented it to Pope Paul VI during his visit to Jerusalem in 1964.

Roman colony. Hyrcanus was later accused of treason by King Herod and was executed. (See also ALEXANDER JANNAEUS; ARISTO-BULUS; HEROD; HIGH PRIEST; POMPEY; ROME; SALOME ALEXANDRA.)

I

IDELSON, BEBA (1895-1976)   Russian-born labor leader who settled in Palestine in 1926. Beba Idelson was active in the fight for women's rights. She was one of the founders and leaders of the Moetzet Hapoalot (Israel's council of women workers) and worked with the Pioneer Women. As a member and Deputy Speaker of the Israeli Knesset (legislature) she helped pass the Equal Wage Law and the National Insurance Act for Housewives. She also wrote many articles on the problems of working women. (See also KNESSET; MOETZET HAPOALOT; PIONEER WOMEN.)

IDUMEA see EDOM

IHUD   Organization founded in Palestine in 1942 to foster cooperation between Arabs and Jews. *Ihud* means "unity" in Hebrew. Ihud took over the work of Berit Shalom and urged a combined Arab-Jewish State in Israel. (See also BERIT SHALOM.)

IHUD HAKEVUTZOT VEHA-KIBBUTZIM   Organization of kibbutzim formed in 1951 by the union of the Hakibbutz Hameuhad and the Hever Hakevutzot organizations. Most of its members support the Mapai political party. In the 1970s it had 76 member kibbutzim with a total population of 27,000 people. (See also HAKIBBUTZ HAMEUHAD; HEVER HAKEVUTZOT; MAPAI.)

ILANIYAH (name changed from SEJERA)   Moshav (farming village) in lower Galilee. Ilaniyah, founded as an agricultural training farm in 1899, was the first modern Jewish settlement in lower Galilee and was the center of the Jewish labor movement in Palestine. The first workers' cooperative was founded at Ilaniyah. Hashomer, the Jewish "watchmen" self-defense organization, also started there. During the 1948 War of Independence, Ilaniyah held out against heavy Arab attack. (See also GALILEE; HASHOMER; MOSHAV; WAR OF INDEPENDENCE.)

IMBER, NAPHTALI HERZ (1856-1909)   Austrian-born Hebrew poet who lived in several European countries and visited Palestine before he finally settled in the United States. Although he published several books of Zionist poetry, Imber is best known for writing the words to *Hatikvah,* Israel's national anthem. (See also HATIKVAH.)

IMMIGRANT CAMPS   Providing for the huge number of immigrants that poured into Israel after it became a state in 1948 was a difficult task. At first the immigrants were housed in temporary camps. Since there were no jobs for them in or near the camps, they had to be supported by the government or by the Jewish Agency. There were 35 such temporary immigrant camps holding 95,000 people in 1950 when the Israeli government began to set up *maabarot,* tent villages near towns or cities where the immigrants could find work. Some of these tent villages were meant to be temporary, while others were the beginnings of new settlements. By 1954, *maabarot* were being replaced by work villages. New immigrants were sent directly to the villages where they would live permanently. They were given jobs reclaiming the land while they built their own houses and learned the necessary farming skills. By the end of the 1950s all the temporary immigrant camps had been closed or turned into permanent settlements. (See also IMMIGRANTS; JEWISH AGENCY.)

IMMIGRANTS   Since its birth in 1948, Israel has been open to any Jew who wanted to settle there. By the end of 1951 Israel's population had more than doubled; 750,000 immigrants had entered the country. These were survivors of the Nazi oppression in Europe, as well as entire Jewish communities that poured in from the the neighboring Arab countries. Between 1955 and 1957, 165,000 Jews from Morocco, Tunisia, and Poland immigrated to Israel; in the early 1960s 215,000 more came from North Africa and Eastern Europe; and after 1967 immigrants came mainly from the Americas, Western Europe, and the Soviet Union. In all, Israel absorbed more than one and a half million new citizens in its first 25 years.

   During the first three years of statehood it was very hard for Israel to provide housing and employment for the large numbers of immigrants. Temporary camps were set up to house the newcomers. Since many of them could not work or could not find jobs, they were supported by the government and the Jewish Agency. However, conditions soon improved. By 1954 immigrants were being settled in villages where they were taught to build houses and farm the land. Today new immigrants often spend their first months in Israel in an absorption center learning Hebrew while they are helped to find homes and jobs. (See also ALIYAH; IMMIGRANT CAMPS; IMMIGRANTS, ILLEGAL; JEWISH AGENCY; LAW OF RETURN; ULPAN.)

IMMIGRANTS, ILLEGAL   Although a few Jewish immigrants

entered Palestine without permits before 1938, large scale "illegal" immigration did not begin until that year. The British (who ruled Palestine under the Mandate) limited Jewish immigration into the country at the same time that Jews were fleeing the Nazi menace in Europe. As a result, Jewish immigrants had to be smuggled into Palestine by the Haganah, Irgun, and Palmah (Jewish underground organizations). Ships sailed from Europe and passengers were secretly unloaded on the beaches of Palestine by night. Immigrants who were caught were either deported to Europe or sent to detention camps. Several ships, including the *Struma* and *Patria,* were sunk. In spite of the difficulties, between 1938 and 1948 about 120,000 "illegal" immigrants either reached Palestine or were held in Cyprus and entered Israel as soon as it became a nation. (See also ALIYAH; CYPRUS; DETENTION CAMPS; EXODUS 1947; GREAT BRITAIN; HAGANAH; IMMIGRANTS; MANDATE; NAZIS; PALMAH; PATRIA; STRUMA.)

INBAL DANCE THEATER   Dance company whose name means "clapper of a bell." Inbal was founded in 1949 by Sara Levi-Tannai, who was its director and choreographer (creator of dances). The company combines dancing, singing, and acting in its versions of folk dances of the Yemenite Jews. Besides being popular in Israel, Inbal has toured many countries of the world. (See also DANCE; LEVI-TANNAI, SARA; ORIENTAL JEWS.)

INDEPENDENCE DAY (Hebrew, YOM HA-ATZMAUT)   National holiday in Israel celebrating the signing of the Declaration of Independence on Iyyar 5, 5708 in the Jewish calendar (May 14, 1948). The holiday begins the evening before with a ceremony on Mount Herzl, and there are fireworks, parties, and dancing. Independence Day itself is celebrated with picnics, trips, sports, and other events, including the International Bible Contest for Jewish Youth. Israel's President gives a reception for foreign diplomats, and the Israel Prize is awarded for literature, music, art, science, and social science. (See also CALENDAR, INTERNATIONAL; CALENDAR, JEWISH; DECLARATION OF INDEPENDENCE; HOLIDAYS; ISRAEL PRIZE; MOUNT HERZL.)

INDEPENDENT LIBERAL PARTY   see PROGRESSIVE PARTY

INDUSTRY   There was almost no industry in Palestine before 1918, and modern industry, with its large factories, did not begin until World War II (1939-1945). Between 1950 and 1972, Israel's industry grew to nine times its World War II size. Factories were built, more consumer goods were produced for Israeli use, and foreign trade grew. This rapid growth took place in spite of Israel's lack of natural resources and raw materials. The govern-

On Mount Herzl, a
Guard of Honor
rehearses for the
Independence Day
parade (above).
Soldiers practice
for the Indepen-
dence Day parade
(right).

ment played a large part in developing the country's industries.

Today most consumer goods bought by Israeli citizens are produced in Israel. Israeli products are sold in foreign countries at ten times the rate they were in the 1950s. Polished diamonds and processed citrus fruits are the most important exports. Other important industries that produce products for use in Israel as well as for foreign trade are electronics, textiles and clothing, and minerals. (See also AGRICULTURE; CITRUS FRUIT; DIAMONDS; ELECTRONICS; FOREIGN TRADE; MINERALS; TEXTILES.)

INSECTS   There are about 7,000 species of insect in Israel. Bees, wasps, and many kinds of butterflies are common. Swarms of desert locusts sometimes attack crops, as do scale insects. Beetles can harm fruit trees. Flies, which are a serious health problem throughout the rest of the Middle East, are under good control in Israel. The mosquitoes that caused malaria in the early Palestinian settlements have been completely wiped out. (See also ANIMALS; BIRDS; MALARIA; REPTILES.)

IRAN   see PERSIA

IRGUN (full name IRGUN ZVAI LEUMI)   Jewish underground military organization formed in Palestine in 1931. Whereas the Haganah (the underground Jewish army) followed the more moderate Jewish Agency policy of defense against the Arabs (which aimed at avoiding retaliation or revenge), the Irgun believed in retaliation. Its symbol was a hand holding a rifle over the map of Palestine.

Before the issuance of the British White Paper of 1939, which limited Jewish immigration into Palestine, Irgun's attacks were directed against the Arabs. After 1939 it attacked the British as well. It also was active in smuggling "illegal" immigrants into the country. Menachem Begin (later Israel's sixth Prime Minister) became Irgun's leader in 1943.

In 1945 the Irgun joined forces with the Haganah and the Stern Group to blow up bridges and railway lines and to attack the British. When the British retailiated in 1946, the Jewish Agency decided to stop the attacks. The Haganah went along with the decision, but the Irgun and the Stern Group did not. The Irgun blew up British army headquarters, kidnapped British army officers, and broke into Acre prison to free Irgun members being held there.

The Irgun had between three thousand and five thousand members, but few were full-time soldiers. Most led normal lives when not actually participating in a military operation. When Israel became a state in 1948, Irgun's members joined the Defense Forces and fought in the War of Independence. Most of them also joined the Herut political party. (See also ACRE PRISON; BEGIN, MENACHEM; DEFENSE FORCES; GREAT BRITAIN; HAGANAH; HERUT; HISTORY; IMMIGRANTS, ILLEGAL; JEWISH AGENCY; STERN GROUP; WAR OF INDEPENDENCE; WHITE PAPER.)

IRON AGE   The name used by archaeologists for a period in history in which people used iron for tools and weapons. Iron was stronger and better than the bronze previously in use. An army with iron weapons had a great advantage over an army equipped only with bronze ones. King Saul, fighting the Philistines toward the beginning of the Iron Age in the eleventh century B.C.E., was defeated because the Philistines had more iron weapons. (See also ARCHAEOLOGY; BRONZE AGE; HISTORY; PHILISTINES; SAUL.)

IRRIGATION   Bringing water to farmland that does not have enough rainfall. Since rain does not fall in Israel in the summer, and since there is not enough rain in the south of the country even in the winter, about half of Israel's crops are grown on irrigated lands. Water for irrigation is brought to the south from Lake Kinneret (Sea of Galilee) and the Jordan River in the north through the giant National Water Carrier system. Although the National Water Carrier increased the water supply for agriculture six times over, water remains a problem. New types of irrigation are being tried to save water, including trickle irrigation which drips water slowly along rows of plants. (See also AGRICULTURE; CLIMATE; NATIONAL WATER CARRIER; WATER.)

ISAIAH (eighth century B.C.E.)   Biblical prophet. Isaiah was active in the public affairs of the kingdom of Judah, supporting King Hezekiah in removing the pagan idols and altars from the Temple in Jerusalem. Isaiah opposed treaties with other nations; he believed Jews should trust completely in God. He prophesied that the Jews would be punished for their sins, but would not be destroyed. His prophesies are recorded in the Book of Isaiah. (See also BIBLE; HEZEKIAH; JUDAH, KINGDOM OF; TEMPLE.)

ISHMAEL   Son of the biblical patriarch Abraham and the Egyptian maid Hagar. Ishmael was the ancestor of the Arab tribes. (See also ABRAHAM; ARABS.)

ISRAEL ACADEMY OF SCIENCES AND HUMANITIES
Organization of Israel's top scientists and scholars established in 1961. The Academy has 50 members elected for life. Its main purpose is to encourage work in the sciences and the humanities (literature, art, social science, etc.). It also publishes articles and books, advises the government on research, and represents Israel at international conferences of scholars.

A modern irrigation system brings water from the North to a kibbutz in the Galilee.

ISRAEL BONDS The Israel Bond Organization was founded in 1951 to raise money to help build Israel's economy. Almost four and a half billion dollars worth of bonds have been sold to two million people in 20 countries. The money has been used to drain swamps and reclaim land, to build large projects like the National Water Carrier and the port of Ashdod, to establish new industries and help old ones to grow, and to create jobs for Israel's large number of new immigrants. (See also ASHDOD; ECONOMY; IMMIGRANTS; INDUSTRY; LAND RECLAMATION; NATIONAL WATER CARRIER.)

ISRAEL BROADCASTING SERVICE see BROADCASTING and KOL ISRAEL

ISRAEL CHAMBER ORCHESTRA Group founded in 1965 by the composer Gary Bertini. The orchestra began by playing only chamber music (music performed by a small group of musicians in a private room or small auditorium). Today it also presents full-scale operas. (See also BERTINI, GARY; MUSIC.)

ISRAEL DEFENSE FORCES see DEFENSE FORCES

ISRAEL-EGYPT PEACE TREATY The first peace treaty between Israel and an Arab country. The moves toward peace began with Egypt's President Anwar Sadat making a visit to Jerusalem in November 1977 and addressing the Israeli Knesset (legislature). Israel's Prime Minister Menachem Begin visited Egypt soon after. In September 1978, at the invitation of President Carter of the United States, Begin and Sadat met at Camp David in the United States to work out a plan for peace between their two countries. Although there were difficulties and delays, the Israel-Egypt Peace Treaty was signed in Washington, D.C., on March 26, 1979.

By the terms of the treaty, Israel and Egypt were to exchange ambassadors and open trade and diplomatic relations. Israel promised to pull its soldiers out of the western half of the Sinai peninsula within nine months, and to remove all its troops and settlements from Sinai within three years. Egypt promised to allow Israeli ships to use the Suez Canal and to sell Israel oil from the Sinai oil fields. The treaty also promised self-rule to the Palestinian Arabs on the West Bank and the Gaza Strip. (These are two of the administered areas occupied by Israel in the 1967 Six-Day War.) However, the final fate of these areas was left to be worked out in the future. (See also ADMINISTERED AREAS; BEGIN, MENACHEM; CAMP DAVID SUMMIT; CARTER, JIMMY; EGYPT; GAZA STRIP; PALESTINIANS; SADAT, ANWAR; SINAI; SUEZ CANAL; WEST BANK.)

ISRAEL ELECTRIC CORPORATION   see ELECTRICITY

ISRAEL FESTIVAL   Festival of music and drama held in Israel every July and August. Concerts, plays, and dances are performed by Israeli and foreign companies in Jerusalem, Tel Aviv, Caesarea, and Ein Gev. Some of the world's finest performers appear at the festival and both Israelis and tourists flock to see them. (See also MUSIC; THEATER; TOURISM.)

ISRAEL INSTITUTE OF TECHNOLOGY   see TECHNION

ISRAEL, KINGDOM OF   The northern and larger of the two kingdoms (the other was Judah) into which Solomon's Jewish empire split after his death around 920 B.C.E. Israel was sometimes called Samaria, after the city that became its capital. It was also called House of Ephraim, after the tribe which produced its kings. The first king of Israel was Jeroboam, who led the revolt of the northern tribes against Solomon's son Rehoboam. Jerobaom ruled 933-912 B.C.E. The other kings of Israel were: Nadab (912-911), Baasha (911-888), Elah (888-887), Zimri (887), Omri (887-876), Ahab (876-853), Ahaziah (853), Jehoram (853-843), Jehu (843-816), Johoahaz (816-800), Jehoash (800-785), Jeroboam II (785-745), Zechariah (744), Shallum (743), Menahem (743-736), Pekahiah (736-735), Pekah (735-730), Hoshea (730-721).

Throughout its more than 200-year history, Israel was often at war with Judah, Syria, and other neighboring countries. It was finally conquered by the Assyrians in 721 B.C.E. (See also ASSYRIA; EPHRAIM; HISTORY; JEROBOAM I; JUDAH, KINGDOM OF ; REHOBOAM; SOLOMON; SYRIA.)

ISRAEL LABOR PARTY   Political party formed in 1968 by a union of the Mapai, Rafi, and Ahdut Ha-avoda parties. In 1969 the Israel Labor Party entered an alliance with Mapam, although Mapam remained a separate party. All of Israel's Prime Ministers until Menachem Begin were members of the Israel Labor Party or one of the parties that formed it. (See also AHDUT HA-AVODA; MAPAI; MAPAM; POLITICAL PARTIES; RAFI.)

ISRAEL LAND DEVELOPMENT COMPANY (name changed from PALESTINE LAND DEVELOPMENT COMPANY) Company founded by the World Zionist Organization in 1908. Its purpose was to buy land from the Arabs for the Jewish National Fund, and to develop the land for settlement. The company provided the land for the settlements of Ein Harod, Nahalal, Tel Yosef, and many others. Nearly half the land owned by Jews in Palestine when Israel became a state in 1948 had been bought through the Palestine Land Development Company. (See also JEWISH NATIONAL FUND; WORLD ZIONIST ORGANIZATION.)

ISRAEL LOTTERY (Hebrew, MIFAL HAPAYIS) Lottery founded in 1951. Its original aim was to raise money for hospitals. Now it also helps to support mother-and-child health centers as well as junior and senior high schools. In addition, it gives grants for medical research. (See also HEALTH.)

ISRAEL MUSEUM A group of museums in Jerusalem. The Israel Museum includes the Bezalel Museum's collection of Jewish religious objects, the Billy Rose Sculpture Garden with statues by modern sculptors like Rodin, Moore, and Lipchitz, the Bronfman Biblical and Archaeological Museum, and the Shrine of the Book. The Shrine of the Book was built to house the Dead Sea Scrolls, ancient manuscripts found in caves near Qumran in the late 1940s. (See also BEZALEL MUSEUM; BILLY ROSE SCULPTURE GARDEN; DEAD SEA SCROLLS; SHRINE OF THE BOOK.)

ISRAEL NATIONAL OPERA Opera company founded in Tel Aviv in 1947. It gives about 300 opera and ballet performances a year. Many of the operas are sung in Hebrew. (See also DANCE; MUSIC.)

ISRAEL PHILHARMONIC ORCHESTRA (name changed from PALESTINE SYMPHONY ORCHESTRA) Orchestra founded in 1936 by Bronislaw Huberman, the famous violinist. Sixty of the orchestra's original 72 musicians were talented Jews rescued by Huberman from the Nazi menace in Europe. The first performance was conducted by Arturo Toscanini. Today the Israel Philharmonic's home is the three-thousand-seat Mann Auditorium in Tel Aviv, but it gives concerts throughout the country and travels on tours to other parts of the world. Important foreign musicians and conductors often visit Israel to perform with the Philharmonic. (See also HUBERMAN, BRONISLAW; MUSIC; NAZIS; TEL AVIV.)

ISRAELI POUND The unit of money of the State of Israel. The abbreviation for the pound is IL. One Israeli pound is called a "lira" in Hebrew. There are ½- and 1-pound coins, and bills of 5, 10, 50, and 100 pounds. The pound is divided into 100 agorot. The Israeli pound is also the legal currency of the administered areas, the land occupied by Israel in the 1967 Six-Day War. (See also ADMINISTERED AREAS; AGORA.)

ISRAEL PRIZE Awards given each year on Independence Day by the Israeli government Ministry of Education and Culture for outstanding work in a number of fields including literature, art, architecture, science, social science, Jewish studies, and medicine. (See also ART; INDEPENDENCE DAY; LITERATURE; MUSIC; PRIZES.)

ISRAEL SCOUT FEDERATION   see SCOUTING

ISRAEL, STATE OF   Country in the Middle East on the eastern shore of the Mediterranean Sea, established on May 14, 1948. It covers an area of 8,000 square miles (34,500 square miles including the land occupied in the 1967 Six-Day War) and has a population of 3,550,000 (1977). About 85% of the population is Jewish and the rest are Moslems and Christians. Israel's capital is Jerusalem. Besides Jerusalem, the three largest cities are Tel Aviv, Ramat Gan, and Haifa, which is the country's major port. The government is a representative democracy and the economy is mixed, part socialist and part capitalist. (See also ADMINISTERED AREAS; AGRICULTURE; CLIMATE; DEFENSE FORCES; ECONOMY; EDUCATION; FOREIGN TRADE; GEOGRAPHY; GOVERNMENT; HEALTH; HISTADRUT; HISTORY; INDUSTRY; POPULATION; RELIGION; SOCIAL SERVICES; WATER.)

ISSACHAR   The third largest of the biblical Twelve Tribes of Israel. Issachar was the fifth son of Jacob. When the Israelites conquered Canaan in the thirteenth century B.C.E., the tribe of Issachar was given the land between Mount Tabor and the Jordan River. (See also CANAAN; JACOB; JORDAN RIVER; MOUNT TABOR; TWELVE TRIBES.)

J

JABEL MUSA (also spelled JEBEL MUSSA)   The 7,360-foot-high mountain in the southern Sinai Desert that is thought to be the mountain described in the Bible where God gave Moses the Ten Commandments. At the foot of Mount Sinai is St. Catherine's Monastery, one of the oldest churches in the world. It contains a beautiful sixth century C.E. mosaic ceiling. It was under Israeli control from 1967 to 1979 and was returned to Egypt after the Israeli-Egyptian Peace Treaty was signed in March 1979. (See also BIBLE; ISRAEL-EGYPT PEACE TREATY; MOSAICS; MOSES; SINAI; TEN COMMANDMENTS.)

JABNEEL (also spelled YAVNEEL)   Founded in 1901, Jabneel was one of the first Jewish settlements in Galilee. Because it was often attacked by Arab raiders in the early days, the settlement was a base for Hashomer, the Jewish "watchmen" self-defense organization. By the late 1970s Jabneel had grown into a farming village supporting 1,500 people. (See also GALILEE; HASHOMER.)

JABNEH (also spelled YAVNE) (biblical name JABNEEL)   Ancient city about ten miles south of modern Tel Aviv. Jabneh was the center of Jewish learning after the destruction of the Temple in Jerusalem in 70 C.E. The Sanhedrin moved to Jabneh and Johanan Ben Zakkai opened a school there. The town was resettled in 1948, and in the late 1970s had a population of over 10,000. A large yeshiva (religious school) stands on a hill near the modern town in the same place as Rabbi Ben Zakkai's academy. (See also JOHANAN BEN ZAKKAI; SANHEDRIN; TEMPLE.)

JABOTINSKY, VLADIMIR (1880-1940)   Russian-born Zionist leader and writer. During World War I, Jabotinsky pushed for a Jewish Legion in the British army and served with it when it was formed. He founded the first Haganah (Jewish underground army) group in Jerusalem and led it against the Arabs during the 1920 riots.

After serving on the executive committee of the World Zionist Organization and disagreeing with its moderate policies, Jabotinsky formed the World Organization of Revisionists. The Revisionists demanded a stronger stand against the actions of the

British government of Palestine, and worked for the establishment of a Jewish State on both sides of the Jordan River.

Jabotinsky urged "illegal" Jewish immigration into Palestine, and smuggling in immigrants became an important activity of the Revisionists after 1936. He also supported Jewish retaliation and revenge for Arab attacks, and became the supreme commander of the Irgun. Although he died of a heart attack in the United States, Jabotinsky's body was later moved to Mount Herzl in Jerusalem. (See also ARAB RIOTS; HAGANAH; IMMIGRANTS, ILLEGAL; IRGUN; JEWISH LEGION; MOUNT HERZL; REVISIONISM; WORLD ZIONIST ORGANIZATION; ZIONISM.)

JABOTINSKY INSTITUTE Organization founded in Tel Aviv in 1935 to collect Zionist and Revisionist documents. Its archives (collection of documents) can be used by scholars and university students, and its museum is open to the public. (See also ARCHIVES; JABOTINSKY, VLADIMIR; REVISIONISM; TEL AVIV; ZIONISM.)

JACOB One of the three patriarchs of Israel. His twelve sons were the ancestors of the twelve Israelite tribes. (See also PATRIARCHS; TWELVE TRIBES.)

JACOBY, HANOKH (1909-) German-born musician and composer who settled in Jerusalem in 1934 and wrote music for orchestra and chorus.

JAFFA (also called YAFO) Ancient town that is now part of the twin city of Tel Aviv-Yafo. Jaffa is mentioned as a Canaanite town in Egyptian documents of the sixteenth century B.C.E. In King Solomon's time (tenth century B.C.E.) its natural harbor on the Mediterranean Sea received goods for inland Jerusalem. The cedars of Lebanon for Solomon's Temple in Jerusalem came by sea to Jaffa. The city was held by the Phoenicians and then by the Greeks until it was captured by Simon the Hasmonean in about 140 B.C.E and was made into a Jewish city. The Romans burned Jaffa during the 66-70 C.E. Jewish revolt. It was the first city taken by the Crusaders when they invaded Palestine in 1088 C.E.

Tel Aviv was a small suburb of Jaffa in 1909; today Jaffa is really a part of Tel Aviv. Most of Jaffa's population is Jewish since most of the Arabs fled during the 1948 War of Independence. One section of the old city is an artists' colony where arts and crafts are sold in colorful shops on winding streets. Jaffa's Archaeological Museum shows objects found in that area that date back to the Stone Age. (See also ARTISTS' COLONY; CANAAN; CRUSADES; HISTORY; PHOENICIANS; ROME; SIMON THE HASMONEAN; SOLOMON; TEL AVIV; TEMPLE; WAR OF INDEPENDENCE.)

JAFFA GATE (Hebrew, SHAAR YAFO) One of the eight gates in the wall around the Old City of Jerusalem. It marks the Jerusalem end of the road from Jaffa on the Mediterranean coast. Goods arriving by ship in Jaffa's port were transported down the Jerusalem-Jaffa road and into Jerusalem through the Jaffa Gate. (See also JAFFA; JERUSALEM; WALLED CITIES.)

JAFFE, LEIB (also spelled YOFFE) (1876-1948)   Zionist leader who was active in the Russian Zionist organization before he settled in Palestine in 1920. Jaffe worked for Keren Hayesod (Palestine Foundation Fund) and became its managing director. He was killed when the Keren Hayesod building was bombed during the 1948 War of Independence. (See also KEREN HAYESOD; WAR OF INDEPENDENCE; ZIONISM.)

JAMAL PASHA, AHMED (1872-1922)   Turkish soldier and politician who commanded the Turkish army in Palestine during World War I (1914-1918). He forced many Jewish settlers to leave the country and persecuted those who remained. After the British conquered Palestine in 1918, Jamal Pasha went to Russia where he was assassinated a few years later. (See also HISTORY; TURKEY.)

JAMMER, MOSHE (1915-   )   German-born scientist who settled in Palestine in 1935. Jammer taught physics at the Hebrew University in Jerusalem and later at Bar-Ilan University at Ramat Gan. In 1966 he became president of Bar-Ilan. (See also BAR-ILAN UNIVERSITY; HEBREW UNIVERSITY.)

JANCO, MARCEL (1895-   )   Hungarian-born painter who was a leader of the Dada art movement in Europe before he fled to Palestine in 1940. Janco founded the artists' colony in Ein Hod. His paintings portray Israel's people and land. (See also ART; EIN HOD.)

JARBLUM, MARC (1887-   )   Polish-born writer who was active in the Zionist movements in Poland, Russia, and France, and was president of the Zionist Federation of France before he settled in Israel in 1953. He served on the executive committee of the Histadrut (Israel's federation of labor) and wrote many books about Palestine, Soviet Jews, and the fight against the Nazis in Europe. (See also HISTADRUT; NAZIS; ZIONISM.)

JDC (abbreviation of AMERICAN JEWISH JOINT DISTRIBUTION COMMITTEE)   Organization founded in the United States in 1914 to provide food for the Jews who were starving in Palestine under Turkish rule. Since its founding the JDC has spent more than a billion dollars helping European Jews overcome the disasters of two world wars and the Nazi oppression. After Israel became a state in 1948, the JDC was active in bringing European refugees to the new country. Its "Operation Magic Carpet" flew the Jewish population of Yemen to Israel. Today JDC's Malben program cares for many of the aged and handicapped people in Israel. (See also MALBEN; NAZIS; OPERATION MAGIC CARPET.)

JEHOAHAZ (also spelled JOAHAZ)   King of Israel who ruled 815-800 B.C.E. He had little power because much of Israel was controlled by the neighboring country of Aram. (See also ARAMEANS; ISRAEL, KINGDOM OF.)

JEHOIACHIN   King of Judah who ruled for only three months in 597 B.C.E. before being forced into exile in Babylon. (See also BABYLONIAN EXILE; JUDAH, KINGDOM OF.)

JEHOIADA   High priest in Jerusalem in the ninth century B.C.E. When King Ahaziah and his family were assassinated, Jehoiada saved his baby son, Joash, and put him on the throne of Israel. Jehoiada influenced Joash to forbid the worship of Baal and to restore the Temple in Jerusalem. (See also AHAZIAH; BAAL; HIGH PRIEST; ISRAEL, KINGDOM OF; JOASH; TEMPLE.)

JEHOIAKIM (name changed from ELIAKIM)   King of Judah who ruled 608-598 B.C.E. During his reign Judah was first controlled by Egypt and then by Babylon. (See also BABYLON; EGYPT; JUDAH, KINGDOM OF.)

JEHORAM (also called JORAM)   King of Israel who ruled 853-842 B.C.E. He fought wars against the neighboring lands of Moab and Aram. (See also ARAMEANS; ISRAEL, KINGDOM OF; MOAB.)

JEHORAM (also called JORAM)   King of Judah who ruled 850-843 B.C.E. His wife, Athaliah, persuaded him to bring the worship of Baal to Judah. During Jehoram's reign the Philistines invaded Israel and plundered Jerusalem. (See also ATHALIAH; BAAL; JUDAH, KINGDOM OF; JERUSALEM; PHILISTINES.)

JEHOSHAPHAT   King of Judah who ruled 874-820 B.C.E. Jehoshaphat was the first king of Judah to sign a treaty with the neighboring Jewish kingdom of Israel. Judah and Israel fought together against Aram and Moab. (See also ARAMEANS; ISRAEL, KINGDOM OF; JUDAH, KINGDOM OF; MOAB.)

JEHU   King of Israel who ruled 842-814 B.C.E. Jehu revolted against King Jehoram and murdered him and his family in order to take the throne. Under Jehu's rule Israel lost much of its land to Aram. (See also ARAMEANS; ISRAEL, KINGDOM OF; JEHORAM.)

JENIN (biblical name, EIN GANNIM)   Arab town on the West Bank. Jenin was a center of Arab fanatics in the 1930s and a base for Arab attacks on Jewish settlements in the Jezreel Valley. It became part of Jordan during the 1948 War of Independence and was occupied by Israel in the 1967 Six-Day War. (See also SIX-DAY WAR; WAR OF INDEPENDENCE; WEST BANK.)

JEREMIAH (seventh to sixth centuries B.C.E.) Biblical prophet who spoke out against the ungodliness of the Jews from 628 to 586 B.C.E. When Jeremiah prophesied that Babylon would conquer Judah, King Jehoiakim ordered his arrest and Jeremiah had to go into hiding. He was put in prison during King Zedekiah's rule for predicting the fall of Jerusalem and calling for surrender. The story of his life and his prophesies is told in the biblical Book of Jeremiah. (See also BABYLON; BIBLE; JEHOIAKIM; JUDAH, KINGDOM OF; ZEDEKIAH.)

JERICHO Ancient city in the Jordan Valley about 15 miles east of Jerusalem. Jericho is the oldest city in Israel and one of the oldest in the world. Archaeologists have uncovered 23 levels of human occupation going back to 7,000 B.C.E.

When the Israelites invaded Canaan in about the thirteenth century B.C.E., Jericho fell to Joshua's forces and was given to the tribe of Benjamin. It was later deserted and then resettled after the Jews returned from the Babylonian exile in the sixth century B.C.E.

In the first century B.C.E. King Herod erected a new town at Jericho with a splendid palace. Another beautiful palace was

The main street in modern Jericho.

Women of Jericho wash clothes in a brook much as they did in biblical days.

built by the Caliph Hishman in the eighth century c.e. when the Arabs occupied the city. The Crusaders conquered the town in 1099 c.e. and it was deserted for about six hundred years after they were driven out in 1187. Modern Jericho has only been built during this century.

Among the most interesting remains uncovered by archaeologists at Jericho are human skulls more than eight thousand years old. These skulls were covered with clay molded to look like faces. Visitors to the ancient site can see the remains of Herod's palace, the Caliph's palace, Crusader sugar mills, and a fourth century c.e. synagogue with a lovely mosaic floor. (See also ARCHAEOLOGY; BABYLONIAN EXILE; BENJAMIN; CANAAN; CRUSADES; HEROD I; HISTORY; JOSHUA; MOSAICS.)

JEROBOAM I Member of the tribe of Ephraim who became king of Israel and ruled 930-910 b.c.e. Jeroboam led an unsuccessful revolt against King Solomon and had to flee to Egypt. When Solomon died and his son Rehoboam took the throne, the northern tribes broke away and formed the kingdom of Israel with Jeroboam as their king. As king he encouraged pagan shrines for the worship of bulls at Bethel and Dan. (See also EPHRAIM; HISTORY; ISRAEL, KINGDOM OF; REHOBOAM; SOLOMON.)

JEROBOAM II King of Israel who ruled 784-744 b.c.e. He recaptured all of Israel's land that was in the hands of the Arameans and conquered some of their cities as well. Israel was at its strongest under Jeroboam's rule, but declined after his death. (See also ARAMEANS; ISRAEL, KINGDOM OF.)

JERUSALEM Capital of Israel. It is located 2,700 feet above sea level in the Judean hills and it had a population of 355,000 people in 1976. The Israeli government buildings, the Hebrew University, and many religious shrines of the Jewish, Christian, and Moslem religions lie in Jerusalem. The city has been the spiritual center of the Jewish people for three thousand years.

Jerusalem first became the capital of the Jewish nation when King David captured it in 1000 b.c.e. His son, Solomon, enlarged the city and built the Temple. When Solomon's empire split in two after his death, Jerusalem became the capital of the southern kingdom, Judah.

Babylon destroyed Jerusalem in 586 b.c.e. and exiled its people. When the Jews were allowed to return 50 years later, they rebuilt the city and the Temple. Jerusalem remained the Jewish capital through Persian, Greek, Hasmonean, and Roman rule until 70 c.e. when it was conquered and destroyed by the Roman emperor, Titus. After that, Jerusalem was ruled by foreign con-

Jaffa Street at night. The oldest and busiest street in Jerusalem.

querors for almost two thousand years until modern Israel was born in 1948.

The 1947 United Nations resolution creating modern Israel also made Jerusalem into an international city so that members of all religions would be able to visit their holy places. However, the fierce fighting of the 1948 War of Independence ended with Jordan holding the old part of Jerusalem and Israel holding the new city. For 19 years Jerusalem was divided by barbed wire barricades. In 1967, during the Six-Day War, Israel captured the Old City and reunited Jerusalem, offering free access to all holy places for all people.

The most holy site in Jerusalem for Jews is the Western Wall, the only remaining part of the wall that protected the ancient Temple. For Christians the holiest place is the Church of the Holy Sepulchre where Jesus Christ was crucified and buried. Moslems worship at the Dome of the Rock and the El Aqsa Mosque. In addition to synagogues, churches, mosques, and other religious shrines, Jerusalem has many places of historical interest, of which the Antonia fortress, the Tower of David, and the pool of Siloam are only a few. Tourists can also visit several museums including the Israel Museum, the Hebrew University and other educational institutions, the Knesset and other government buildings, the Hadassah Medical Center, the Biblical Zoo, and a number of parks. (See also ANTONIA; BABYLON; BIBLICAL

A view of Jerusalem showing the Dome of the Rock in the foreground and some of Israel's more recent structures in the background.

ZOO; DAVID; DOME OF THE ROCK; EL AQSA MOSQUE; HADASSAH; HASMONEANS; HEBREW UNIVERSITY; HISTORY; HOLY SEPULCHRE; ISRAEL, STATE OF; ISRAEL MUSEUM; JESUS; JUDAH, KINGDOM OF; JUDEAN HILLS; KNESSET; SILOAM; SIX-DAY WAR; SOLOMON; TEMPLE; TITUS; TOWER OF DAVID; WESTERN WALL; WAR OF INDEPENDENCE.)

JERUSALEM CROWFOOT   A small yellow flower that grows in rocky soil in Israel. It looks rather like a buttercup.

JERUSALEM DAY   Holiday celebrated in Israel on the 28th of Iyyar (early June on the international calendar) to mark the day during the 1967 Six-Day War when the two divided halves of Jerusalem were united again. Jerusalem Day begins with a thanksgiving service at the Western Wall. Torches are lit at the Wall in memory of the Israeli soldiers who died in the battle for Jerusalem. (See also CALENDAR, INTERNATIONAL; CALENDAR, JEWISH; JERUSALEM; SIX-DAY WAR; WESTERN WALL.)

JERUSALEM INTERNATIONAL BOOK FAIR   Since 1963, an international book fair has been held in Jerusalem every other year at the Jerusalem Convention Center (Binyanei Ooma). At the ninth book fair in April 1979, 43 different nations were represented and 40,000 books were on display. At each fair the municipality of Jerusalem presents a literary award to a writer whose work expresses the idea of "the freedom of the individual in society." The first prize was awarded to Bertrand Russell in 1963. In 1979 it was awarded to Sir Isaiah Berlin. (See also BOOKS; PRIZES.)

JERUSALEM PINE (also called ALEPPO PINE)   Evergreen tree native to Israel. During the past century many forests of pine trees have been planted in Israel, especially in mountain areas. The Herzl Forest near Huldah is mainly pine trees. (See also HERZL FOREST; REFORESTATION.)

JERUSALEM POST (name changed from PALESTINE POST) Israel's leading English language daily newspaper. The *Jerusalem Post* was founded in 1932 by Gershon Agron who was its editor until 1955. During the years that the British ruled Palestine under the Mandate, the *Post* called for opposing British policies without violence. Today the paper is not connected with any political party. It publishes daily and weekend editions in Israel and puts out a special weekly edition that is airmailed to readers in other countries. (See also AGRON, GERSHON; GREAT BRITAIN; MANDATE; NEWSPAPERS.)

Teddy Kollek awards Sir Isaiah Berlin the Jerusalem Prize for literary achievement (1979).

JERUSALEM PRIZE   Prize given every other year by the city of Jerusalem to the writer whose work "best expresses the idea of freedom of the individual in society." It is an international prize that has not yet been awarded to an Israeli writer. The 1979 winner of the Jerusalem Prize was an Englishman, Sir Isaiah Berlin. (See also PRIZES.)

JERUSALEM SALVIA   A reddish flower that blooms in Israel in April. The Jerusalem salvia is a member of the mint family.

JESUS (also called JESUS CHRIST and JESUS OF NAZARETH) (about 4 B.C.E.-29 C.E.)   Founder of the Christian religion. Christians believe that Jesus was the Son of God who came to save the world, that he was crucified and rose again, and that he will return to judge mankind. His life and teachings are described in the Gospels of Matthew, Mark, Luke, and John of the New Testament.

The cave in Bethlehem where Jesus was born is guarded by an Israeli soldier.

Jesus was born in Bethlehem. His mother was Mary, wife of the carpenter Joseph of Nazareth. At the age of 30 Jesus began to preach, teaching people to "love the Lord thy God with all thy heart and thy neighbor as thyself." After preaching for three years, he went to Jerusalem where he threw the money-changers out of the Temple. Pontius Pilate, the Roman governor of Palestine, saw Jesus as a threat to Roman rule in the country. Jesus was arrested, tried for treason on a charge of calling himself the Messiah, and crucified. The Gospels say that three days later his tomb was found empty and an angel announced that Jesus had been resurrected. (See also BETHLEHEM; BIBLE; CHRISTIANS, ISRAELI; GETHSEMANE; GOLGOTHA; HOLY SEPULCHRE; JERUSALEM; MESSIAH; NAZARETH; ROME; TEMPLE; VIA DOLOROSA.)

JETHRO, FEAST OF (also called NEBI SHU 'AIB)   Three-day holiday celebrated in April by the Druze (a religious sect) in Israel. Jethro was the father-in-law of Moses and the ancestor of the Druze. During the holiday, the Druze visit Jethro's shrine in Hittim in western Galilee. (See also DRUZE; GALILEE; HOLIDAYS.)

JEWISH AGENCY (full name JEWISH AGENCY FOR ISRAEL)   In 1922 the League of Nations Mandate for Great Britain to govern Palestine also called for a Jewish agency to advise and cooperate with the British in "matters that may affect the establishment of a Jewish national home and the interests of the Jewish population of Palestine." In accordance with the Mandate, the Jewish Agency was set up by the World Zionist Organization in 1929.

The Jewish Agency worked for a Jewish homeland in Palestine, taking its case to the British government in London, to the League of Nations, and appealing to world opinion. It represented the Jews of Palestine in their dealings with the British government when it ruled the country. Before 1948 it was the equivalent of the Jewish government of Palestine, setting the political policies of the Jews, helping immigrants settle in farming villages and towns, and providing some social services.

When Israel became a state in 1948, the Jewish Agency gave up most of its political activities and concentrated on Jewish immigration and settlement in Israel. It worked closely with the Israeli government in organizing immigration and helping immigrants become part of the life of their new country. It cared for children and young people and educated them in Youth Aliyah centers. Since 1948, the Jewish Agency has brought more than one and a half million immigrants into Israel and founded 500 villages. (See also GREAT BRITAIN; HISTORY; IMMIGRANTS; LEAGUE OF NATIONS; MANDATE; YOUTH ALIYAH; WORLD ZIONIST ORGANIZATION.)

JEWISH BRIGADE Infantry unit of Jewish soldiers in the British army during World War II. Although the Jewish Agency called for the establishment of a Jewish fighting force as early as 1939, the Jewish Brigade was not formed until 1944. Before 1944, the 130,000 Palestinian Jews who volunteered for military service with the Allies mainly served in an Arab-Jewish Palestinian regiment on guard duty in the Middle East. In 1944-1945 the Jewish Brigade fought in Italy and later helped rescue the Jewish survivors of the Nazi concentration camps. When Israel became a state in 1948, many veterans of the Jewish Brigade served in the new Israel Defense Forces. (See also DEFENSE FORCES; JEWISH AGENCY.)

JEWISH COLONIAL TRUST First bank of the World Zionist Organization. The Jewish Colonial Trust was established in 1899 to help Jewish settlement in Palestine. It gave credit to new settlers and invested in new companies like the Palestine Electric Company. (See also WORLD ZIONIST ORGANIZATION.)

JEWISH COLONIZATION ASSOCIATION (also called ICA) Organization founded by Baron Maurice de Hirsch in 1891 to help European Jews settle in South America. In 1899, ICA took over a number of agricultural settlements that had been founded in Palestine with money from Baron Edmond de Rothschild. The support of these colonies was handed over to the Palestine Jewish Colonization Association (PICA) in 1924, but since then ICA has been active in founding other settlements and supporting agricultural training and research in Israel. (See also HIRSCH, MAURICE DE; PALESTINE JEWISH COLONIZATION ASSOCIATION; ROTHSCHILD, EDMOND DE.)

JEWISH DEFENSE LEAGUE (J.D.L) Organization founded in New York by Rabbi Meir Kahane. The Jewish Defense League's slogan is "Never again." This refers to the Holocaust that killed six million European Jews during World War II. The J.D.L.'s aim is to protect Jews and Jewish rights through "direct action," which can include violence. It also encourages all Jews— particularly American Jews—to immigrate to Israel. (See also HOLOCAUST; KAHANE, MEIR.)

JEWISH DIASPORA MUSEUM (also called BET HATEFUTSOT) Tel Aviv museum that opened in 1978. It was conceived in the 1950s by Dr. Nahum Goldmann, and is devoted to the history and culture of Jews throughout the world during the past 2,500 years. The Jewish Diaspora Museum has many audio-visual exhibits, including slide shows, dioramas, a computer to answer visitor's questions, and a "Chronoscope" show on Jewish history. (See also TEL AVIV.)

Beth Hatefutsoth (the Museum of the Diaspora), Tel Aviv's newest museum, where an unusually beautiful and graphic panorama of Jewish history has been created.

JEWISH LEGION Military unit of Jewish volunteers from Palestine, the United States, and Canada who fought alongside the British during World War I to free Palestine from Turkey. Vladimir Jabotinsky and Joseph Trumpeldor pushed for a Jewish fighting unit in 1914, but the British would only permit a nonfighting group called the Zion Mule Corps. However, the Jewish Legion was finally formed in 1917 and took part in the final attacks on the Turkish army in Palestine in 1918. (See also GREAT BRITAIN; HISTORY; JABOTINSKY, VLADIMIR; TRUMPELDOR, JOSEPH; TURKEY.)

JEWISH NATIONAL FUND Organization founded in 1901 to buy and reclaim land in Palestine. The land bought by the Jewish National Fund remained the property of the Jewish people and was only leased to the settlers on 49-year leases which could be renewed. The first land purchases were made in 1905. During the 1920s the Fund bought large tracts of land in the Jezreel Valley, the Zebulun Valley, and the Hefer Valley. By the time Israel became a state in 1948, the Jewish National Fund had bought more than 235,000 acres of land in Palestine.

Today over 90% of Israel's land is owned either by the goverment or by the Jewish National Fund. Since 1948 the Fund has concentrated more on developing land than buying it. It has drained swamps and reclaimed over 200,000 acres of land. It has planted 105 million trees and built 2,000 miles of roads. (See also HEFER VALLEY; JEZREEL VALLEY; LAND OWNERSHIP; LAND RECLAMATION; REFORESTATION; ZEBULUN VALLEY.)

JEWISH QUARTER Section of the Old City of Jerusalem. Archaeological excavations have shown that Jews lived in this part of Jerusalem as early as the seventh century B.C.E. The

Ramban (Nahmanides) Synagogue, built in the 1200s C.E. and opened again to Jewish worship after the 1967 Six-Day War, is in the Jewish Quarter. The most famous synagogue in the Jewish Quarter is the Hurva Synagogue. It was built by Jews from Poland who came to Palestine in 1701. Their leader was Rabbi Yehuda HeHasid. In 1720, when the group could not pay their debts to the Moslems from whom they borrowed money, their land was confiscated and the synagogue was destroyed. It was rebuilt and destroyed several times in later years, hence the name Hurva (from the Hebrew word *hurban*) which means "destruction" in Hebrew. (See also ARCHAEOLOGY; JERUSALEM; SIX-DAY WAR.)

JEWS, ISRAELI The name "Jew" comes from the Hebrew word *Yehudi* which means "a person from Judah." (Judah was the Jewish kingdom in southern Palestine that existed from about 920 to 586 B.C.E.)

Israel is predominantly a Jewish State. About 85% of its people are Jews. Since government and religion are not kept separate in Israel as they are in the United States, Jewish religious holidays are also celebrated as national holidays and buses and trains do not run in every city on the Jewish Sabbath and on holidays. Non-Jews have their rights to observe their own Sabbath and holidays guaranteed by law. There are almost six thousand synagogues in the country and Bible study is an important subject in Israeli public schools. Jewish dietary laws are observed in the Israel Defense Forces and in most restaurants. Rabbinical courts decide matters like marriage and divorce for all Jewish citizens of Israel. (See also ASHKENAZIM; BIBLE STUDY; COURTS, RELIGIOUS; DEFENSE FORCES; HOLIDAYS; JUDAH, KINGDOM OF; ORIENTAL JEWS; POPULATION; SEPHARDIM.)

JEZEBEL (died 843 B.C.E.) As the wife of Ahab, king of Israel, Jezebel was able to introduce the worship of Baal into the country. Her murder during Jehu's revolt was seen as just punishment for her sins. (See also AHAB; BAAL; ISRAEL, KINGDOM OF; JEHU.).

JEZREEL Ancient city near Mount Gilboa in the northwest of Israel. Jezreel was the site of King Ahab's palace and the place where his wife Jezebel was killed in the ninth century B.C.E. An agricultural village founded in 1948 stands near the ancient site. (See also AHAB; JEZEBEL.)

JEZREEL VALLEY (also called EMEK JEZREEL or the EMEK) Israel's largest and most fertile valley. It runs for 17 miles east-west between the mountains of Galilee and Samaria. Most of the Jezreel Valley was swampland filled with malaria-carrying mos-

quitoes when the Jewish National Fund bought the land in 1921. The land was drained and cooperative agricultural villages were built by Third Aliyah (wave of immigration) pioneers from Eastern Europe. Among the early settlements were Ein Harod, Nahalal, and Ginnegar. The Jezreel Valley has since become one of the most densely settled rural areas in Israel. Afula is its main city. (See also AFULA; ALIYAH; EIN HAROD; GEOGRAPHY; GINNEGAR; JEWISH NATIONAL FUND; MALARIA; NAHALAL.)

JOASH (also spelled JOHOASH)   King of Judah who ruled 836-797 B.C.E. The high priest Jehoiada rescued the baby Joash when his grandmother Athaliah murdered the rest of the family in order to seize the throne of Judah. Six years later Jehoiada murdered Athaliah and put Joash on the throne. During Joash's rule the Baal cult was banned and the Temple was restored. When the Arameans invaded Judah, Joash bribed them with a large sum of money. (See also ARAMEANS; ATHALIAH; BAAL; HIGH PRIEST; JOHOIADA; JUDAH, KINGDOM OF; TEMPLE.)

JOASH (also spelled JEHOASH)   King of Israel who ruled 800-785 B.C.E. Joash recaptured a number of towns his father Jehoahaz had been forced to give to the Arameans. In a war with the neighboring Jewish kingdom of Judah, Joash defeated King Amaziah in battle and conquered Jerusalem. (See also AMAZIAH; ARAMEANS; ISRAEL, KINGDOM OF; JEHOAHAZ; JUDAH, KINGDOM OF.)

JOFFE, ELIEZER LIPA (1882-1942)   Russian-born agricultural pioneer who settled in Palestine in 1910. Joffe was one of the founders and directors of Tnuva, the marketing cooperative for farming products run by Histadrut (Israel's labor federation). He was also the editor of two agricultural magazines and published several books on agriculture. (See also AGRICULTURE; HISTADRUT.)

JOFFE, HILLEL (1864-1936)   Russian-born doctor who settled in Palestine in 1891. He fought the malaria and other diseases that beset the early Palestinian pioneers and established a hospital at Zikhron Yaakov. (See also MALARIA; ZIKHRON YAAKOV.)

JOHANAN BEN ZAKKAI (first centrury C.E.)   Palestinian scholar who was the most admired rabbi of his time. Johanan Ben Zakkai founded the yeshiva (religious school) at Jabneh that became the center of Jewish scholarship after the fall of Jerusalem in 70 C.E. He was the teacher of Rabbi Akiva. (See also AKIVA BEN JOSEPH; JABNEH.)

JOHN OF GISCALA (also called JOHANAN) (first century C.E.)   Military leader during the 66-70 C.E. Jewish revolt against the Roman rule of Palestine. John was one of the leaders of the

A view of the Jezreel Valley as seen from Mount Tabor.

defense of Jerusalem. He was captured after the Roman general Titus conquered Jerusalem and died in prison. (See also ROME; TITUS.)

JOHN THE BAPTIST (early first century C.E.)   Palestinian religious figure who preached the coming of the Messiah and who baptized Jesus Christ. John was executed by Herod Antipas, the ruler of Galilee. (See also ANTIPAS, HEROD; JESUS; MESSIAH.)

JOHN THE BAPTIST DAY   Christian holiday celebrating the birthday of John the Baptist on June 24 in churches throughout Israel. Special services are held at Ein Kerem where John was born. (See also CHRISTIANS; EIN KEREM; HOLIDAYS; JOHN THE BAPTIST.)

JOHNSON, LYNDON BAINES (1908-1973)   Thirty-sixth President of the United States. In 1956, while he was a U.S. Senator, Johnson opposed President Dwight D. Eisenhower's plan for action against Israel after the Sinai War. Johnson was elected President in 1963. During his term of office, he upheld Israel's right to strong borders that could be defended and he sold Israel jet planes for defense. He also helped create the United States-Israel study program for desalinization (removing of salt) of sea water. (See also DESALINIZATION; SINAI WAR.)

JOKNEAM   Ancient Canaanite town in the Jezreel Valley. A modern settlement was founded near the ancient site in 1935. (See also CANAAN; JEZREEL VALLEY.)

JONATHAN (also called APPHUS)   Ruler of Judea 161-142 B.C.E. Jonathan was the brother of Judah the Maccabee and took over the leadership of the Jews after Judah's death in 160 B.C.E. Jonathan was a practical politician who managed to set up an independent Jewish state that lasted for almost a hundred years under Hasmonean rule. (See also HASMONEANS; JUDAH THE MACCABEE.)

JORDAN (name changed from TRANSJORDAN)   Middle Eastern country across the Jordan River from Israel. Jordan has a population of 2,860,000 (1977) of whom 94% are Moslems and 6% Christians. It covers an area of 37,700 square miles (counting the land occupied by Israel in the 1967 Six-Day War). Its capital and largest city is Amman.

During biblical times Jordan was known as Edom and Moab. It was part of the Jewish kingdom of David in the tenth century B.C.E. Like the rest of Palestine, the land that is now Jordan was ruled in turn by Romans, Byzantines, Arabs, Crusaders, Mamelukes, and Turks. It was taken from the Turks by the British in 1918 during World War I. In 1921 Palestine was divided. The eastern part (which later became Israel) was ruled by the British; the western part became the kingdom of Transjordan under King Abdullah.

When Israel became a state in 1948, Jordan joined other Arab countries in invading the Jewish State. At the end of the War of Independence, Jordan held the West Bank and the Old City of Jerusalem. King Hussein, who succeeded the assassinated Abdullah in 1953, was considered a moderate Arab leader. However, he attacked Israel in the 1967 Six-Day War, and this time lost the West Bank and Jerusalem. (See also ABDULLAH IBN HUSSEIN; DAVID; EDOM; GREAT BRITAIN; HISTORY; HUSSEIN; ISRAEL, STATE OF; JERUSALEM; JORDAN RIVER; MOAB; SIX-DAY WAR; TURKEY; WAR OF INDEPENDENCE; WEST BANK.)

JORDAN RIVER   The major river of Palestine. It flows from Mount Hermon in the north to the Dead Sea in the south. The Jordan River is over 200 miles long counting all its bends, but only 87 miles long measured in a straight line. Part of the river lies inside Israel, part forms the border with Jordan, and part is the 1967 cease-fire line between Israel and Jordan. In 1964 Israel began to draw water from the Jordan River and sent it through the National Water Carrier to irrigate fields in the dry south of the country. (See also DEAD SEA; GEOGRAPHY; IRRIGATION; JORDAN; NATIONAL WATER CARRIER; SIX-DAY WAR; WATER.)

JORDAN VALLEY (also called EMEK HA-YARDEN)   Fertile valley formed by the Jordan River. The valley has a hot climate and grows tropical crops irrigated with water from the Jordan River. (See also CLIMATE; GEOGRAPHY; IRRIGATION; JORDAN RIVER.)

JOSEPH   Biblical figure. The son of Jacob and Rachel. Joseph was sold into slavery in Egypt but later rose to become viceroy of Egypt. The tribes of Ephraim and Manasseh were the descendants of Joseph. (See also BIBLE; CANAAN; EPHRAIM; HISTORY; MANASSEH; TWELVE TRIBES.)

JOSEPH BEN GORION (first century C.E.)   Military leader in Jerusalem during the 66-70 C.E. Jewish revolt against the Roman rule of Palestine. (See also HISTORY; ROME.)

JOSEPH, DOV (also spelled YOSEPH) (1899-   )   Canadian-born lawyer who went to Palestine during World War I to serve in the Jewish Legion and settled in Jerusalem in 1921. He was on the executive committee of the Jewish Agency and was jailed by the British (who then governed Palestine) for a time. When Israel became a state in 1948, Joseph was elected to the Knesset (legislature) and served in the Cabinet at different times as Minister of Trade, Minister of State, and Minister of Justice. (See also

CABINET; GREAT BRITAIN; JEWISH AGENCY; JEWISH LEGION; KNES-
SET.)

JOSEPHTHAL, GIORA (1912-1962) German-born Zionist
leader who organized the Youth Aliyah (young people's immigration to Palestine) in Germany before he settled in Palestine in
1938. After World War II, Josephthal helped arrange German
reparations (repayments) to Israel for Jewish suffering and loss of
property under the Nazis. He was active in the Mapai political
party, was elected to the Israeli Knesset (legislature), and served as
Minister of Labor and Minister of Housing and Development.
(See also KNESSET; MAPAI; REPARATIONS; YOUTH ALIYAH; ZIONISM.)

JOSEPHUS FLAVIUS (about 37-95 C.E.)   Soldier and historian.
During the 66-70 C.E. Jewish revolt against Roman rule in
Palestine, Josephus became the Jewish military governor of
Galilee. When the Romans attacked Galilee and besieged his
garrison in the fortress of Jotapata, Josephus defected to the
Romans. He found favor with the Roman Emperor Vespasian
and lived the rest of his life in Rome. Josephus' books are our
main source of information about the history of the Jews in the
first centuries B.C.E. and C.E. His most important books were *The
Jewish Antiquities,* a history of the Jews from the creation of the
world to the beginning of the war with Rome, and *The Jewish
War,* which describes the 66-70 C.E. revolt. (See also GALILEE;
HISTORY; ROME; VESPASIAN.)

JOSHUA (fifteenth century B.C.E.)   Biblical military leader. After
the death of Moses, Joshua led the Israelite tribes in their conquest of the land of Canaan. The Book of Joshua in the Bible
describes how he crossed the Jordan River, defeated the kings of
the south and the kings of the north, and divided their land
among the Twelve Tribes of Israel. (See also BIBLE; CANAAN;
MOSES; TWELVE TRIBES.)

JOSIAH   King of Judah who ruled 637-608 B.C.E. During his
reign Judah was a strong and prosperous country. Josiah banned
the worship of pagan idols and reformed Judaism according to a
book of religious law discovered in the Temple. He entered the
war between Egypt and Assyria on the Assyrian side and was
killed in battle at Megiddo. (See also ASSYRIA; EGYPT; JUDAH,
KINGDOM OF; MEGIDDO; TEMPLE.)

JOTAPATA   Ancient fortified town in Galilee where Jewish
forces under Josephus were besieged by the Romans during the
Jewish revolt of 66-70 C.E. (See also HISTORY; JOSEPHUS FLAVIUS;
ROME.)

**The source of the Jordan River in Upper Galilee. The waters pour
forth from the mountainside and begin their long journey through
the Sea of Galilee (Kinneret) to the Dead Sea.**

JOTHAM   King of Judah who ruled 751-735 B.C.E. He fought and defeated the neighboring Ammonites. Judah was prosperous under his rule. (See also JUDAH, KINGDOM OF.)

JUDAH   Fourth son of Jacob and Leah. The tribe of Judah was given the largest area of land in the south of Canaan when the Israelites conquered the country in the thirteenth century B.C.E. King David was a member of the tribe of Judah. (See also CANAAN; DAVID.)

JUDAH HANASI (about 135-220 C.E.)   Scholar who was the political and religious leader of the Jews of Palestine in the late second and early third century C.E. He used much of his vast wealth to support other scholars in the study of the Torah (Jewish religious law). Rabbi Judah Hanasi headed a group of important scholars in preparing the Mishnah, the codification (collection and organization) of Jewish law. (See also MISHNAH; TORAH.)

JUDAH, KINGDOM OF   The southern and smaller of the two kingdoms (the other was Israel) into which King Solomon's Jewish empire split after his death in 920 B.C.E. It was a poorer and less important country than Israel, but its capital city, Jerusalem, contained the Temple that was the center of the Jewish religion. Judah was more stable than Israel; it was involved in fewer foreign wars and its kings were overthrown less often. The kings of Judah were: Rehoboam (933-917 B.C.E.), Abijam (917-915), Asa (915-875), Jehoshaphat (875-851), Jehoram (851-844), Ahaziah (844-843), Athaliah (843-837), Joash (837-798), Amaziah (798-780), Azariah (also called Uzziah) (780-740), Jotham (740-735), Ahaz (735-720), Hezekiah (720-692), Manasseh (692-638), Amon (638-637), Josiah (637-608), Johoahaz (608), Jehoiakim (608-598), Jehoiachin (598-597), and Zedekiah (597-586 B.C.E.). In 586 B.C.E. Judah was conquered by Babylon and many Jews were sent into exile. (See also BABYLON; BABYLONIAN EXILE; HISTORY; ISRAEL, KINGDOM OF; JERUSALEM; SOLOMON; TEMPLE.)

JUDAH THE GALILEAN (died 6 C.E.)   Founder of the Zealots, a Jewish political party which said that God was the only ruler of the Jewish people. Judah was killed by the Romans when he opposed their rule of Palestine. (See also HISTORY; ROME; ZEALOTS.)

JUDAH THE MACCABEE (died 160 B.C.E.)   Jewish military hero who took over the leadership of the Jewish revolt against the Syrians in 167 B.C.E. on the death of his father, Mattathias. Judah conquered Jerusalem in 164, threw the statue of Jupiter out of the Temple, and reopened the Temple to Jewish worship. (The

Hanukkah holiday celebrates the event.) Soon after, the Syrians granted the Jews freedom of worship, but Judah and his men continued to fight for political freedom as well. Judah was killed in 160 B.C.E. in the battle of Elasa. The fight went on under his brothers, Jonathan and Simon the Hasmonean, who succeeded in establishing an independent Jewish state under Hasmonean rule. (See also HANUKKAH; HASMONEANS; HISTORY; JONATHAN; MACCABEE; MATTATHIAS; SELEUCIDS; SIMON THE HASMONEAN; SYRIA.)

JUDEA   The Roman name for the southern part of Palestine. Judea had roughly the same borders as the kingdom of Judah and contained the city of Jerusalem. For about 100 years after Rome conquered Judea in 63 B.C.E. it permitted the Jewish kings of the country a reasonable amount of control over their internal affairs. For example, Herod, who ruled Judea from 73 B.C.E. to 4 B.C.E., was a powerful king although he owed his appointment to the throne to Rome. However, later Judea became a Roman colony, had its name changed to Palestina, and was ruled by a Roman governor called a procurator. (See also HEROD I; HISTORY; JUDAH, KINGDOM OF; PROCURATOR; ROME.)

The rolling hills of the Jordan Valley. In the Book of Psalms they are described as "mountains that prance like rams."

JUDEAN DESERT   Eastern slope of the Judean Hills. The Judean Desert runs from below Jerusalem south to the Dead Sea. At its highest point in the north, the desert is 3,000 feet above sea level; at its lowest point near the Dead Sea in the south, it is 1,300 feet below sea level. There are many caves in its area. The Dead Sea Scrolls were found in a cave near Qumran in the Judean Desert. (See also DEAD SEA; DEAD SEA SCROLLS; GEOGRAPHY; JUDEAN HILLS; QUMRAN.)

JUDEAN HILLS (also called JUDEAN MOUNTAINS)   Mountain range in central Palestine. The Judean Hills are part of a large mountainous area that runs north and south through most of the length of Israel. The Judean Hills connect the northern mountains of Samaria with the highlands of the Negev in the south. Jerusalem is in the Judean Hills. (See also GEOGRAPHY; NEGEV; SAMARIA.)

JUDELEVITZ, DAVID (also spelled YUDELEVITZ) (1863-1943) Rumanian-born pioneer who settled in Palestine in 1882. He became a teacher at Rishon Le Zion, wrote textbooks in Hebrew, and helped establish the first Hebrew kindergarten in Palestine. (See also RISHON LE ZION.)

JUDGES   During early biblical times, priests, prophets, and tribal leaders also acted as judges. Later special courts were set up and judges were appointed by the kings. Many of these judges were also priests. During the Second Temple period (about 450 B.C.E. to 70 C.E.) the Sanhedrin (a group of priests and scholars) acted both as lawmakers and judges.

In modern Israel judges to the Magistrates Courts, the District Courts, and the Supreme Court are appointed by the President of Israel from a list of qualified people gathered by a special nominating committee. These appointments are particularly important because Israeli courts do not have juries and all cases are decided by judges. Judges of religious courts are appointed by the President from the list prepared for him by the nominating committee of the religion involved. (See also COURTS; COURTS, RELIGIOUS; PRESIDENT; SANHEDRIN.)

JUDITH   Beautiful heroine who saved the Jews from the Assyrians. The Assyrian general, Holofernes, was besieging the city of Bethulia. The city was ready to surrender when Judith went down to the Assyrian camp. Holofernes was attracted to Judith and invited her to a feast. Judith cut off his head while he slept after the feast, and the rest of the Assyrians fled. Her story is told in the Book of Judith, one of the books of the Apocrypha. (The Apocrypha is part of the Catholic Bible, but not the Jewish or Protestant Bible.) (See also ASSYRIA; BIBLE.)

K

KABAK, AHARON AVRAHAM (1880-1944)   Russian-born writer who settled in Jerusalem in 1911. Kabak wrote a series of novels about people involved in the Zionist movement in the early 1900s. (See also ZIONISM.)

KABBALAH (also spelled CABALA)   Jewish beliefs and traditions about the mysteries of creation and the nature of God. Kabbalah is often called Jewish mysticism. The earliest Palestinian Kabbalists were Rabbi Johanan Ben Zakkai (a first century C.E. scholar) and Rabbi Simeon Bar Yohai (a second century C.E. scholar). Simeon Bar Yohai is said to be the author of the *Zohar*, the Bible of the Kabbalists. Each year Kabbalists visit his grave at Meron on Lag B'Omer, the day he is believed to have died. (See also LAG B'OMER; JOHANAN BEN ZAKKAI; SIMEON BEN YOHAI; LURIA, ISAAC.)

Still donning talis and tefilin after their morning prayers, these students of the Kabbalah devote an hour to study in the Ari Synagogue, in Safed.

KAHANA, AVRAHAM (1874-1946)   Scholar who left Russia to settle in Palestine in 1923. Kahana wrote a Bible commentary, a Hebrew-Russian dictionary, and many articles on Jewish history and literature.

KAHANE, MEIR (1932-   )   American rabbi who became the founder and leader of the Jewish Defense League, an organization that uses "direct action" to protect Jews and Jewish rights. Kahane encourages all Jews to emigrate to Israel, and did so himself in 1971. (See also JEWISH DEFENSE LEAGUE.)

KALWARISKI-MARGOLIS, HAYIM (1868-1947)   Russian-born pioneer and soil expert who settled in Palestine in 1895. In his early years in Palestine, he bought land for the Jewish Colonization Association and helped found new agricultural settlements. Later he became a champion of cooperation between Jews and Arabs and worked through the Berit Shalom and the Ihud organizations for a Jewish-Arab State in Palestine. (See also BERIT SHALOM; IHUD; JEWISH COLONIZATION ASSOCIATION.)

KAMINSKI, JOSEPH (1903-1972)   Violinist and composer who played in the Warsaw String Quartet in his native Poland before going to Palestine in 1937 to join the Palestine Symphony Orchestra. (See also ISRAEL PHILHARMONIC ORCHESTRA.)

KAPLAN, ELIEZER (1891-1952)   Russian-born labor leader who worked in the Zionist movement in Europe before he settled in Palestine in 1923. Kaplan was on the executive committee of the Jewish Agency, was active in the Histadrut (Israel's labor federation), and served as Israel's first Minister of Finance. (See also HISTADRUT; JEWISH AGENCY; ZIONISM.)

KAPLANSKY, SHELOMO (1884-1950)   Polish-born educator and Zionist leader who settled in Palestine in 1912. Kaplansky was active in the work of the Jewish National Fund, the Jewish Agency, and the Histadrut (Israel's labor federation) before he became the director of the Technion (Institute of Technology) in Haifa in 1932. (See also HISTADRUT; JEWISH AGENCY; JEWISH NATIONAL FUND; TECHNION; ZIONISM.)

KARAITES   A Jewish religious sect founded in the eighth century C.E. by Anan Ben David. The Karaites hold to the strict letter of the Written Law of the Bible and reject all Oral Law, interpretations, and traditions. In 1978 about 10,000 Karaites lived in Israel, most of them in or near Ramla. Karaite men serve in the Israel Defense Forces, but their women are excused on religious grounds. There has been a question of whether Karaites are really Jews or are a separate religion. This is an important question when a Karaite and a Jew want to marry, because people of different religious persuasions cannot be married in Israel. (See also ANAN BEN DAVID; BIBLE; DEFENSE FORCES; MARRIAGE; RAMLA; RELIGION.)

KARKUR   Moshav (farming settlement) founded on the Sharon Plain in 1926. Karkur became part of the village of Pardes Hannah in 1969. (See also PARDES HANNAH.)

KARNI, YEHUDA (1884-1946)   Hebrew poet who left his native Russia to settle in Palestine in 1921 and write many poems about Jerusalem. Karni won the Bialik Prize in 1944. (See also BIALIK PRIZE.)

KASTEIN, JOSEPH (pen name of JULIUS KATZENSTEIN) (1890-1946)   German-born writer who lived in Switzerland before settling in Palestine in 1934. Kastein was known for his articles about outstanding Jews. He also wrote fairy tales, novels, plays, and a history of the Jews called *Jerusalem: The Story of a Land.*

KATZENELSON, AVRAHAM (1888-1956)   Russian-born doctor who settled in Palestine in 1924. Katzenelson headed the Zionist Organization's health committee and later became the director of Israel's Ministry of Health. (See also WORLD ZIONIST ORGANIZATION.)

KATZENELSON, BERL (1887-1944)   Labor leader who moved from Russia to Palestine in 1909 and became active in the labor movement. After serving in the Jewish Legion during World War I, Katzenelson helped establish Histadrut (Israel's federation of labor). In 1925 he founded *Davar*, the first daily newspaper of the workers' movement in Palestine, and was its editor until his death. He wrote many articles on Socialist Zionism and stressed the importance of labor and self-defense. He supported "illegal" Jewish immigration into Palestine and the struggle for a Jewish State. Katzenelson was one of the founders of the Mapai political party. (See also DAVAR; HISTADRUT; IMMIGRANTS, ILLEGAL; JEWISH LEGION; MAPAI; SOCIALISM; ZIONISM.)

KATZNELSON, RACHEL   see SHAZAR, RACHEL KATZNELSON

KATZIR, AHARON (name changed from KATCHALSKY) (1913-1972)   Russian-born scientist who was brought to Palestine at the age of 12. Katzir taught chemistry at the Hebrew University in Jerusalem and was the president of the Israel Academy of Sciences and Humanities. He was killed in a terrorist attack at Lod (now Ben-Gurion) Airport. Aharon Katzir was the brother of Ephraim Katzir, Israel's fourth President. (See also HEBREW UNIVERSITY; ISRAEL ACADEMY OF SCIENCES AND HUMANITIES; KATZIR, EPHRAIM.)

KATZIR, EPHRAIM (name changed from KATCHALSKY) (1916-   )
Scientist who was brought to Palestine from Russia at the age of
six. He attended public school in Jerusalem and studied science
at the Hebrew University. As a student, Katzir was a member of
the Haganah (Jewish underground army) and later headed Haganah's science corps before becoming chief scientist of Israel's
Ministry of Defense. He directed the biophysics department of
the Weizmann Institute of Science and established the Institute as
a world center for research into proteins. He was a founding
member of the Israel Academy of Science and Humanities and,
among other prizes, won the Israel Prize for natural science.

In 1973 Katzir was elected Israel's fourth and youngest President. Although the post of President is largely honorary, Katzir
has spoken out on public affairs. (See also HAGANAH; HEBREW
UNIVERSITY; ISRAEL ACADEMY OF SCIENCE AND HUMANITIES; ISRAEL
PRIZE; PRESIDENT; WEIZMANN INSTITUTE OF SCIENCE.)

KAUFMANN, RICHARD YITZAK (1887-1954)   German-born
architect and town planner who settled in Palestine in 1920.
Kaufmann planned the streets and buildings for a number of
settlements in the Jezreel Valley, including Nahalal and Ein
Harod, and also designed the plans for new sections of Jerusalem
and Ramat Gan. (See also EIN HAROD; JERUSALEM; NAHALAL;
RAMAT GAN.)

KAUFMANN, YEHEZKEL (1889-1963)   Scholar who was born
in Russia, settled in Palestine in 1920, and became professor of
Bible studies at the Hebrew University in Jerusalem. Kaufmann
wrote many books, including the eight-volume *A History of the
Israelite Faith*. (See also BIBLE STUDY; HEBREW UNIVERSITY.)

KEDESH   Ancient site in upper Galilee that was important in
biblical times. Archaeologists have found five levels of human
occupation, the oldest dating back to the Bronze Age. (See also
ARCHAEOLOGY; BRONZE AGE; GALILEE.)

KEFAR (also spelled K'FAR or KEPHAR)   Hebrew word meaning
"village," used as part of a number of place-names in Israel.

KEFAR BARUKH   Village founded in the Jezreel Valley in 1926.
It was named for Barukh Kahana, the first Jew to will his entire
fortune to the Jewish National Fund to be used to establish an
agricultural settlement. (See also JEWISH NATIONAL FUND; JEZREEL
VALLEY.)

KEFAR BIRIM   Archaeological site in upper Galilee. Kefar
Birim contains a well-preserved synagogue dating from the third
or fourth century C.E. (See also ARCHAEOLOGY; GALILEE.)

KEFAR BLUM Kibbutz (cooperative farming settlement) founded in the Huleh Valley in 1943. Besides farming, Kefar Blum has a number of industrial workshops and a popular tourist guesthouse. (See also HULEH VALLEY; KIBBUTZ; TOURISM.)

KEFAR DANIEL Farming village near Tel Aviv founded in 1949 by veterans of Israel's War of Independence. (See also WAR OF INDEPENDENCE.)

KEFAR ETZION Village in the Hebron hills founded in 1943 by settlers from Poland. Kefar Etzion is one of the four settlements in the Gush Etzion (Etzion Block) occupied by Jordan during the 1948 War of Independence and retaken by Israel in the 1967 Six-Day War. It was reestablished as an Israeli kibbutz (cooperative farming village) after 1967 by children and friends of the original pioneers. (See also GUSH ETZION; JORDAN; KIBBUTZ; SIX-DAY WAR; WAR OF INDEPENDENCE.)

KEFAR GILADI Kibbutz founded in 1916 in upper Galilee by members of Hashomer (Jewish "watchmen" self-defense organization). In 1920 Kefar Giladi and the neighboring settlement of Tel Hai were attacked by Arabs and the Jews were forced to abandon the villages temporarily, but their brave defense helped convince the League of Nations to include the Huleh Valley in the land that later became Israel. Today Tel Hai is part of Kefar Giladi. The settlement is a showplace of farming methods, and has a popular tourist guesthouse. (See also HULEH VALLEY; KIBBUTZ; LEAGUE OF NATIONS: TEL HAI; TOURISM.)

KEFAR HABAD Village between Jerusalem and Tel Aviv founded in 1949 by Hasidic Jews from Russia. The settlement has a yeshiva (religious school) and several vocational schools. (See also EDUCATION.)

KEFAR HABONIM Village on the Mediterranean coast south of Haifa founded in 1949 by English-speaking veterans of the Israeli War of Independence. (See also WAR OF INDEPENDENCE.)

KEFAR HANASI Kibbutz (cooperative farming village) in upper Galilee named for Chaim Weizmann, the first President (Nasi) of Israel. It was founded in 1948 when the heavy fighting of the War of Independence was still going on in the area. (See also GALILEE; KIBBUTZ; WAR OF INDEPENDENCE; WEIZMANN, CHAIM.)

KEFAR HAROE Village founded in the Hefer Valley in 1934. Its school combines religious studies with agricultural training. (See also EDUCATION; HEFER VALLEY.)

KEFAR HASIDIM Village in the Zebulun Valley near Haifa founded by a group of elderly Hasidic Jews from Poland. Under the leadership of their two rabbis, the old Jews drained swamps, built houses, and planted crops. (See also ZEBULUN VALLEY.)

KEFAR HITTIN Village in lower Galilee founded in 1936 after several attempts to establish a settlement on the site had failed. Kefar Hittin was the first moshav shitufi (semi-cooperative farming village) in Israel. It stands near the Horns of Hittin where the Crusaders (European Christian knights) were defeated by Saladin in 1187 C.E. and were driven out of Palestine. Also near the village is the tomb of Jethro, the holy place of the Druze (a Moslem religious sect). (See also CRUSADES; DRUZE; GALILEE; JETHRO, FEAST OF; MOSHAV; MOSHAV SHITUFI; SALADIN.)

KEFAR KANNA   see CANA

KEFAR MONASH Village founded in the Sharon Plain in 1946 by veterans of World War II. (See also SHARON PLAIN.)

KEFAR NAHUM   see CAPERNAUM

KEFAR SAVA (also spelled KFAR SABA) City about eight miles north of Tel Aviv. Although land for the village was bought in 1892, it was not settled until 1903. The settlement was destroyed in 1918 during the fighting of World War I and again in the Arab riots of 1921. It grew rapidly in the late 1920s and by the late 1970s had a population of over 30,000 people. The city's economy is devoted mainly to growing citrus fruit, but it also has other industries. (See also ARAB RIOTS; CITRUS FRUIT.)

KEFAR SHITUFI Another name for a moshav shitufi, a semi-cooperative farming village. (See also MOSHAV; MOSHAV SHITUFI.)

KEFAR SHMARYAHU Village on the Sharon Plain founded in 1937 by immigrants from Germany. (See also SHARON PLAIN.)

KEFAR SILVER Agricultural school about 25 miles south of Tel Aviv near Ashkelon. The school was founded in 1952 by the Zionist Organization of America. (See also AGRICULTURAL SCHOOLS.)

KEFAR SZOLD Village in upper Galilee named for Henrietta Szold, the founder of Hadassah (American women's Zionist organization). Kefar Szold was established in 1942 and came under heavy Syrian attack during the 1948 War of Independence. The villagers kept the Syrian forces from breaking through into the Huleh Valley. (See also GALILEE; HULEH VALLEY; SZOLD, HENRIETTA; WAR OF INDEPENDENCE.)

KEFAR TRUMAN Village southeast of Tel Aviv founded in

1949 by veterans of the Palmah, the striking force of the Haganah (Jewish underground army). The village was named for the American President, Harry Truman. (See also HAGANAH; PALMAH.)

KEFAR VITKIN   Village founded in the Hefer Valley in 1933 on land bought by the Jewish National Fund and reclaimed by draining swamps. Today Kefar Vitkin is the largest moshav in Israel. (See also HEFER VALLEY; JEWISH NATIONAL FUND; MOSHAV.)

KEFAR YASSIF   Village near Acre where an ancient mosaic floor with Jewish symbols can still be seen. Today the village is inhabited by Druze (a Moslem religious sect) and Christian Arabs. (See also DRUZE; MOSAICS.)

KEFIYAH   Head scarf worn by Arab men. It protects the neck and most of the face from the sun. The kefiyah is held in place by an *agal,* a twist of black wool. (See also ABEYAH.)

KENESET GEDOLAH   see GREAT ASSEMBLY

KENNEDY MEMORIAL AND PEACE FOREST   Memorial and forest honoring American President John F. Kennedy. The Kennedy Memorial building is built in the shape of a tree trunk on a mountain top in the Judean Hills near Jerusalem. The

Admirers of President John F. Kennedy contributed to the erection of this Kennedy Memorial, in Jerusalem. The structure consists of 51 spokes, representing the 50 states and the District of Columbia.

nearby Peace Forest contains about five million trees. Many of the trees have been planted by visiting Americans, including United States senators and congressmen and members of the Kennedy family. (See also JUDEAN HILLS; REFORESTATION.)

KEREN HAYESOD (English, PALESTINE FOUNDATION FUND)   A fund established by the World Zionist Organization in 1920 to raise money for the development of a Jewish national home in Palestine. Keren Hayesod is the money-raising arm of the Jewish Agency. Until Israel became a state in 1948, the fund provided money for the Jewish Agency to establish settlements, run schools, and protect the Jewish community. After the State of Israel took over many of these jobs, Keren Hayesod continued to raise money for bringing immigrants to Israel and helping them get settled. Between 1948 and 1975 it raised over $3 billion from Jews in 70 countries to be used for immigration, housing, welfare, health, education, and agricultural settlements in Israel. About 65% of the money was collected in the United States by the United Jewish Appeal. (See also IMMIGRANTS; JEWISH AGENCY; UNITED JEWISH APPEAL; WORLD ZIONIST ORGANIZATION; YOUTH ALIYAH.)

KEREN KAYEMET LE-ISRAEL   see JEWISH NATIONAL FUND

KESTENBURG, LEO (1882-1962)   Czechoslovakian-born pianist who settled in Tel Aviv in 1939 and became the artistic director of the Palestine Symphony Orchestra. (See also ISRAEL PHILHARMONIC ORCHESTRA.)

KEVUTZA (the plural is KEVUTZOT)   Cooperative farming settlement whose members share the work and the gains equally. Originally a kevutza was a small settlement with limited membership and a kibbutz was a larger village, but now any such community is usally called a kibbutz. (See also KIBBUTZ.)

KHAMSIN   see HAMSIN

KHOUSHI, ABBA (also spelled HOUSHI) (1898-1969)   Austrian-born labor leader who settled in Palestine in 1920. Khoushi was a member of the executive committee of the Histadrut (Israel's federation of labor) and secretary of the Haifa Labor Council. He served in the Israeli Knesset (legislature), but left in 1951 to become Mayor of Haifa, a post he held until his death in 1969. During his years as Mayor, Khousi improved the city greatly. He played an important part in building Haifa's Municipal Theater, Haifa University, and many parks and playgrounds. (See also HAIFA; HISTADRUT; KNESSET.)

KIBBUTZ (the plural is KIBBUTZIM)   A kind of cooperative farm-

At Kibbutz Lavi, near Tiberias, synagogue furniture is manufactured for use in Israel and overseas.

Kibbutz Sde Boker, in the Negev, specializes in raising poultry.

ing settlement first tried in Palestine in 1909 when 12 young pioneers founded Degania near Lake Kinneret (Sea of Galilee) and shared the work and earnings equally. Today there are almost 250 kibbutzim in Israel.

A kibbutz may have as few as 50 members (called *kibbutzniks*) or as many as several thousand. It may only farm the land or it may have industry as well. But all kibbutzim are run on the principles of equality and cooperation. All property is owned by the kibbutz, which provides its members with food, laundry, housing, education, health care, etc. Kibbutzniks also receive small personal allowances for clothing and hobbies. Work is shared equally and is assigned by a committee elected by the members. Jobs are assigned according to the work that needs to be done, the skills of the workers, and the workers' preferences— but all kibbutz members take turns at the less liked jobs like dishwashing. Food is cooked in the kibbutz kitchen and served in the community dining hall. Children are raised and educated together with members of their own age group under the care of a *metapelet* (nurse/teacher). However, there are also strong ties between parents and children. Entertainment, music, and social life are provided by the members themselves in the kibbutz's social and cultural center.

A kibbutz is a pure democaracy. All members belong to a general assembly that makes the major decisions for the community. Committees elected by the general assembly make the necessary day by day decisions in running the kibbutz. Although only about 3% of Israel's population lives in kibbutzim, the ideals of the kibbutz have had a great influence on the country and have attracted attention thoughout the world. (See also DEGANIA; METAPELET.)

The oldest resident of Kibbutz Kefar Ruppin. A member since 1935, he was an immigrant from Czechoslovakia.

KIBBUTZNIK A member of a kibbutz, a cooperative farming settlement. (See also KIBBUTZ.)

KIDRON VALLEY Valley in East Jerusalem between the old section of the city and the Mount of Olives. The Kidron Valley contains several ancient burial places including Absalom's Tomb. (See also ABSALOM; JERUSALEM; MOUNT OF OLIVES.)

KILOGRAM (called KILO for short) A unit of weight in the metric system of measurement. Food in Israel is weighed and sold by the kilo. One kilo is equal to 2.2 pounds. There are 1,000 grams to a kilo. (See also METRIC SYSTEM.)

KILOMETER Road distances in Israel are measured in kilometers. One kilometer is about six-tenths of a mile. (See also METRIC SYSTEM.)

KIMRI, DOV (name changed from MELLER) (1889-1961) Austrian-born writer who settled in Palestine in 1908 and wrote romantic novels about life in Israel.

KING SOLOMON'S MINES Mines near Timna in the southern Negev Desert where copper was dug and smelted during the reign of King Solomon, 3,000 years ago. Black slag (mining waste) heaps can still be seen at the ancient site. Today, copper is again being mined in the Negev not far from King Solomon's mines. (See also COPPER; NEGEV; SOLOMON.)

KINNERET Farming settlement on the southwest shore of Lake Kinneret (Sea of Galilee). An experimental training farm was founded at Kinneret in 1908, and 12 of the farmers trained there left the farm to found Degania, Israel's first kibbutz (cooperative farming settlement). Kinneret is now a flourishing agricultural village with popular tourist hotels and restaurants. (See also AGRICULTURE; DEGANIA; KIBBUTZ; LAKE KINNERET.)

KINNERET, LAKE see LAKE KINNERET

KIRYAT Hebrew word meaning "city of." It is used as part of a number of Israeli place-names.

KIRYAT ANAVIM Kibbutz founded near Jerusalem in 1920 by Akiva Ettinger, the soil expert, and pioneers from Eastern Europe. It was the first Jewish agricultural settlement in the hills. Before that all settlements had been built on the level Coastal Plain. During the 1948 War of Independence Kiryat Anavim held out against repeated Arab attacks. (See also COASTAL PLAIN; ETTINGER, AKIVA; WAR OF INDEPENDENCE.)

KIRYAT ATA (also called KEFAR ATTA) City near Haifa founded in 1925 by religious Zionists from Poland. It was destroyed during the Arab riots of 1929, but was rebuilt soon after. Kiryat Ata is the home of the Ata textile factories and other industries. In 1979 it had a population of nearly 30,000. (See also ARAB RIOTS; TEXTILES.)

KIRYAT BIALIK   Town in the Zebulun Valley founded in 1934 and named for the poet Hayim Nahman Bialik. Kiryat Bialik was part of a development plan for the area around Haifa Bay. Each house has its own garden and some houses have small farms. (See also BIALIK, HAYIM NAHMAN; ZEBULUN VALLEY.)

KIRYAT BINYAMIN   Settlement near Haifa that is now part of the city of Kiryat Ata. (See also KIRYAT ATA.)

KIRYAT GAT   A development town about 30 miles south of Tel Aviv founded in 1956 to serve as the central city of the Lachish region. The farm products grown in the surrounding agricultural settlements are processed in Kiryat Gat. The town has cotton gins and textile plants and houses Israel's largest sugar refinery. (See also AGRICULTURE; DEVELOPMENT TOWNS; LACHISH REGION; TEXTILES.)

KIRYAT MOTZKIN   Town near Haifa founded by middle-class settlers from Eastern Europe in 1948. Many of its inhabitants work in Haifa. (See also HAIFA.)

KIRYAT ONO   Town near Tel Aviv founded in 1939. After Israel became a state in 1948, large housing projects were built in Kiryat Ono to take care of the wave of new settlers. In 1979 the town had a population of almost 20,000 people, many of whom work in Tel Aviv. (See also TEL AVIV.)

KIRYAT SEPHAR   Magazine founded in 1924 and published four times a year by the National and University Library. The publication lists books and articles of interest to librarians. (See also NATIONAL LIBRARY.)

KIRYAT SHEMONA   Town in upper Galilee settled by Jews in 1949 after the Arabs had abandoned it in the 1948 War of Independence. Kiryat Shemona has often been shelled by Arab artillery from nearby Lebanon. In April of 1974 Arab terrorists attacked the town and killed 18 people, most of them women and children. (See also GALILEE; LEBANON; TERRORISM; WAR OF INDEPENDENCE.)

KIRYAT TIVON   Town founded near Haifa in 1937. Kiryat Tivon is now a popular resort town with hotels, campsites, and a youth hostel.

KIRYAT YEARIM (also spelled KIRIATH JEARIM)   Biblical site where the Ark of the Covenant was kept for 20 years before King

David brought it to Jerusalem. A youth village of the same name now stands near the ancient site and the Arab village of Abu Gosh is across the road. (See also ABU GOSH; ARK OF THE COVENANT; DAVID; YOUTH VILLAGES.)

KISHON, EPHRAIM (1924-) Hungarian-born writer who settled in Israel in 1949. Kishon has written a number of humorous books about life in Israel, including the popular *Look Back Mrs. Lot.*

KISHON RIVER River in the Jezreel Valley. Although the Kishon River is 27 miles long, only the last eight miles hold water all year. The rest of the river fills and overflows during heavy rains. This flooding created the swamps of the Jezreel Valley, which were drained in the 1920s. A dam built in 1955 now holds the Kishon's flood waters for irrigation. (See also GEOGRAPHY; IRRIGATION; JEZREEL VALLEY.)

KISSINGER, HENRY A. (1923-) German-born professor who served as an adviser to three American Presidents before becoming Secretary of State under President Nixon. In 1975 Kissinger helped bring about an agreement between Israel and Egypt, in which Israel returned some of the Sinai land taken in the 1967 Six-Day War. This was one of the steps that led to peace between Israel and Egypt. (See also ISRAEL-EGYPT PEACE TREATY; SINAI; SIX-DAY WAR.)

KLARMAN, JOSEPH (1909-) Zionist leader who moved to Palestine from Russia in 1940. Klarman was a member of the executive committee of the Jewish Agency, helped organize "illegal" Jewish immigration from Eastern Europe to Palestine, and headed the World Zionist Organization's Youth Aliyah (young people's immigration) Department. (See also IMMIGRANTS, ILLEGAL; JEWISH AGENCY; YOUTH ALIYAH; WORLD ZIONIST ORGANIZATION.)

KLAUSNER, JOSEPH GEDALIA (1874-1958) Lithuanian-born scholar and writer who settled in Palestine in 1919 and taught literature and history at the Hebrew University in Jerusalem. Klausner wrote hundreds of scholarly articles and published a number of books, including *A History of Modern Hebrew Literature.* He was also the editor of the *Encyclopedia Hebraica* and a winner of the Israel Prize. (See also HEBREW UNIVERSITY; ISRAEL PRIZE.)

KNESSET The Parliament (legislature) of Israel. The Knesset has a single house of 120 members elected by all the citizens of Israel under a system of proportional representation. The voters choose from candidate lists of the different political parties, and

The Knesset, in Jerusalem, where the 120-member Israeli parliament convenes.

the members of the Knesset are elected according to the number of votes each list receives. Candidates must be 21 years of age, and military men and government employees must resign from their jobs before running for office. Knesset members serve a four-year term, but a majority of its members may call a new election before the end of the four years.

The Knesset meets three days a week for about eight months each year. Deliberations are held in Hebrew with a translation into Arabic. When a bill is introduced into the Knesset, it is discussed, and then sent off to one of ten committees to be put into final form. It is then presented once again to the Knesset where it is read, possibly changed, read again, and voted on. If a majority of the members present vote for a bill, it becomes law. The law cannot be overruled by the Supreme Court as in the American system of government, nor can it be vetoed by the Prime Minister or President.

The Knesset elects Israel's President and must approve its Cabinet. After an election, the President calls on a member of the Knesset (usually the head of the party receiving the most votes) to

The entrance to the Knesset as seen through the heavy sculptured gates symbolizing the barbed wire of the concentration camps.

take the job of Prime Minister and form a Cabinet (also called a Government). The new Prime Minister must then present his Cabinet choices to the Knesset for a vote of approval. Even after the Cabinet is approved, the Knesset may dissolve it at any time by giving it a vote of no-confidence.

The Knesset building in Jerusalem was built in 1966 with money donated by James R. Rothschild. It is a beautiful example of modern architecture, with mosaics and tapestries designed by the artist Marc Chagall. (See also ARCHITECTURE; CABINET; CHAGALL, MARC; COURTS; DEMOCRACY; GOVERNMENT; JERUSALEM; POLITICAL PARTIES; PRESIDENT; PRIME MINISTER; PROPORTIONAL REPRESENTATION; VOTING.)

KOL ISRAEL (also called ISRAEL BROADCASTING SERVICE) Government-operated radio broadcasting system with its headquarters in Jerusalem. Kol Israel (whose name means "Voice of Israel") has five networks (stations). Network A broadcasts news, music, special events, and educational programs in Hebrew. Network B provides entertainment and broadcasts special programs in simple Hebrew for new immigrants. It also carries commercials. Network C sends shortwave broadcasts in 11 languages to other countries. Network D's programs are in Arabic and are aimed at Arabs in Israel and in neighboring countries. There is also one television channel. Political parties are given free radio and television time before elections. (See also ARABIC; BROADCASTING; HEBREW; MUSIC; POLITICAL PARTIES.)

KOL, MOSHE (name changed from KOLODNY) (1911-   ) Russian-born politician who settled in Palestine in 1932 and was one of the founders of the Progressive political party. He was a member of the Israeli Knesset (legislature), served as Minister of Tourism, and wrote several books about education in Israel. (See also KNESSET; PROGRESSIVE PARTY.)

KOLLEK, THEODORE (TEDDY) (1911-   ) Austrian-born politician who settled in Palestine in 1934. He was one of the founders of the village of Ein Gev. Kollek was Israel's minister to the United States, headed the Israeli tourist board, helped build the country's tourist industry, and founded the Israel Museum, but he is best known as Mayor of Jerusalem. Since his election as Mayor in 1965, he has devoted all his energy to governing, building, and improving Jerusalem. His autobiography, *For Jerusalem,* published in 1978, describes his life and his work in Jerusalem. (See also EIN GEV; ISRAEL MUSEUM; JERUSALEM; TOURISM.)

Teddy Kollek

KOOK, AVRAHAM YITZHAK (1865-1935)   Scholar from Eastern Europe who settled in Palestine in 1904 and became rabbi of

Jaffa. In 1921 he was chosen Ashkenazi Chief Rabbi of Palestine, a post he held until his death. Rabbi Kook spoke out for the right of the Jewish people to a homeland in Palestine. His writings called for a return of the Jews to Palestine and the observance of Jewish law and religion in the new country. He founded a yeshiva (religious school) that taught the ideal of a rebirth of the Jewish people through a union of Zionism and religion. (See also ASHKENAZIM; CHIEF RABBINATE; RABBI KOOK FOUNDATION; ZIONISM.)

KOOR INDUSTRIES Israel's largest group of industries. The 130 companies and plants belonging to the Koor Group manufacture metals, chemicals, glass, building materials, electronic equipment, and many other products. About 11% of the products used by Israelis are made by companies belonging to the Koor Group. Koor also trades all over the world and accounts for 18% of Israeli products sold in foreign markets. (See also INDUSTRY; FOREIGN TRADE.)

KOTEL MAARAVI see WESTERN WALL

KOVEH TEMBEL (English, FOOL'S HAT) Hat that looks like a sailor's hat with the brim turned down. It is popular in Israel, particularly in farming villages, where it is worn as protection against the hot sun.

KOVNER, ABBA (1918-) Russian-born Hebrew writer who was a leader of the Jewish fighters in the Vilna Ghetto during World War II before he escaped to Palestine. He fought in the Israel Defense Forces during the 1948 War of Independence. Kovner has written stories, novels, and poems, mostly about his war experiences. (See also WAR OF INDEPENDENCE.)

KRAUSE, ELIYAHU (1878-1962) Soil expert who moved to Palestine from Russia in 1901 and helped establish the first cooperative of Jewish farmers at Sejera (later called Ilaniyah). Krause became the director of the Mikveh Israel Agricultural School and changed the language in which classes were taught from French to Hebrew. (See also HEBREW; ILANIYAH; MIKVEH ISRAEL.)

KRINITZI, ABRAHAM (1886-1969) Russian-born industrialist and politician who settled in Palestine in 1906 and built the country's first sawmill. Krinitzi was one of the founders of Ramat Gan, became its first Mayor, and helped build it from a small farming settlement into a city of 120,000 people. While he was Mayor, the Ramat Gan Stadium, Israel's largest sports stadium, was built and Bar-Ilan University was established. (See also BAR-ILAN UNIVERSITY; RAMAT GAN.)

KUMRAN   see QUMRAN

KUMSITZ   A yiddish word that means "come and sit." It is used in Israel to mean an informal party or get-together.

KUPAT HOLIM   Health insurance fund of Histadrut, Israel's labor federation. All Histadrut members and their families (almost three-quarters of Israel's population) get their medical and dental care through Kupat Holim. Their health insurance is partly paid for by their union dues. New immigrants to Israel get free health insurance for six months. In 1978 Kupat Holim ran about 1,120 medical clinics, 120 dental clinics, 230 mother-and-child health stations, hospitals with over 4,200 beds, plus drugstores, laboratories, rest homes, and a medical research center. Five smaller health funds also work with Kupat Holim. (See also HEALTH; HISTADRUT.)

L

LABOR   see HISTADRUT

LABOR BATTALION   see GEDUD HA-AVODA

LACHISH (also spelled LAKHISH)   Ancient Canaanite city about 25 miles southwest of Jerusalem. Lachish was captured by the Israelites in the thirteenth century B.C.E. and later became part of the kingdom of Judah. The city fell to the Assyrians after a fierce battle in 701 B.C.E. and was destroyed by the Babylonians in 586 B.C.E. Archaeologists have uncovered the remains of a temple destroyed during the Israelite invasion of Canaan and the ruins of the city built by the Israelites. They also found pieces of broken pottery with messages in Hebrew written on them. (See also ARCHAEOLOGY; ASSYRIA; BABYLON; CANAAN; HISTORY; JUDAH, KINGDOM OF; LACHISH LETTERS.)

LACHISH LETTERS   Twenty-one messages written in Hebrew on potsherds (pieces of pottery) by Jewish military commanders during the sixth century B.C.E. Babylonian invasion of Judah. Archaeologists dug up the potsherds at the site of the ancient city of Lachish. Besides the history they reveal, the Lachish letters are important to scholars studying ancient Hebrew writing. (See also ARCHAEOLOGY; BABYLON; JUDAH, KINGDOM OF; LACHISH.)

LACHISH REGION   An area of planned villages and farms around the central city of Kiryat Gat on the Coastal Plain. The development of the region was begun in 1955. By the late 1970s there were 60 villages in the area and 70,000 acres of farms raising dairy cattle and growing cotton, sugar beets, and other crops. (See also COASTAL PLAIN; DEVELOPMENT TOWNS; KIRYAT GAT.)

LACHOVER, YERUHAM FISHEL (1883-1947)   Polish-born scholar who settled in Palestine in 1927 and wrote a history of modern Hebrew literature.

LAG B'OMER   Jewish holiday whose name means "thirty-third day of the Omer." It is celebrated thirty-three days after the *Omer* (a thanksgiving offering of the first barley the farmers harvested) was brought to the Temple in Jerusalem on the second day of Passover. Lag B'Omer is also called the Scholar's Festival to celebrate the end of a plague that killed many students of Rabbi Akiva in the second century C.E.

The holiday falls on the eighteenth of Iyyar on the Jewish calendar (April or May on the international calendar). In Israel, bonfires are lit on the eve of Lag B'Omer and there is singing and dancing round the fires. Schools are closed for the holiday and young people take part in archery contests. Trips are taken to the tomb of Rabbi Simeon Ben Yohai in Meron. (See also AKIVA BEN JOSEPH; CALENDAR, INTERNATIONAL; CALENDAR, JEWISH; HOLIDAYS; MERON; OMER; PASSOVER; SIMEON BEN YOHAI; TEMPLE.)

LAHAT, SHLOMO (1927-) Soldier and politician who was brought to Israel from Germany as a young child. Lahat studied law at the Hebrew University in Jerusalem and took military training in the United States. He holds the rank of Major-General in the Israel Defense Forces Reserve and is the current (1978) Mayor of Tel Aviv. (See also DEFENSE FORCES; HEBREW UNIVERSITY; TEL AVIV.)

LAKE KINNERET (also called LAKE TIBERIAS and SEA OF GAL-ILEE) Lake in northeastern Israel. It is 13 miles long and 7 miles wide. Lying 685 feet below sea level, it is the lowest freshwater lake in the world. There is good fishing in the lake, and the farming villages along its shores grow bananas, dates, and other crops that need a warm climate. The town of Tiberias, on its western shore, is a winter resort. Water is carried from Lake Kinneret through the National Water Carrier to irrigate dry land in the south of Israel. (See also CLIMATE; GEOGRAPHY; JORDAN RIVER; NATIONAL WATER CARRIER; TIBERIAS.)

LAMDAN, YITZHAK (1899-1954) Russian-born Hebrew poet who settled in Palestine in 1920. His best-known poem, *Masada,* is about the pioneers who settled the harsh land of Palestine in the 1920s.

LAMEL SCHOOL Officially known as the Simon Edler von Lamel's Stiftung, it was the first modern Jewish school in Palestine. It was founded in 1855 in Jerusalem with money given by Elise Herz, daughter of Austrian merchant Simon Edler von Lamel. At first the classes were taught in German, but after eight years Hebrew was made the school's official teaching language. (See also EDUCATION; HEBREW.)

LAND OWNERSHIP The Jewish National Fund was established by the World Zionist Organization in 1901 to buy land in Palestine for Jewish settlement. In 1920 the World Zionist Organization adopted the principle that all land bought should be the property of the Jewish nation. When Israel became a state in 1948, the government also took over ownership of the lands abandoned by Arabs when they left the country. Two years later the Israeli Knesset (legislature) passed a law that said that no land owned by the government, except certain areas in cities, could be sold to private persons. Today 92% of Israel's land is owned by the government and overseen by the Israel Land Authority. The land is leased to the people living on it for 49-year periods. (See also JEWISH NATIONAL FUND; WORLD ZIONIST ORGANIZATION.)

LAND RECLAMATION   Much of the land of Palestine had been neglected for centuries and needed to be restored to good condition to make it fit for settlement and agriculture. The first Jewish settlers in the 1880s began to drain swamps, remove rocks, and build terraces for vineyards. By the late 1970s over 200,000 acres of land had been reclaimed for growing crops; 150,000 more acres had been planted with forests; and more land reclamation was planned. Swamps in the Huleh, Jezreel, and Zebulun valleys were drained to expose the fertile land. Land in the hills was cleared of rocks and was terraced to stop the soil from washing away. Salty soil in the Araba Valley and the Negev was washed with large amounts of water. Water for irrigation was brought to the dry land of Southern Israel. The reclaimed land was planted with grain, vegetables, fruit trees, and vineyards. (See also AGRICULTURE; IRRIGATION; REFORESTATION.)

LANDAU, MOSHE (1912-   )   Polish-born lawyer who settled in Palestine in 1933. He was made a judge of the Haifa District Court and then a judge of the Israeli Supreme Court. Landau was the judge at the trial of Adolph Eichmann, the Nazi war criminal. (See also COURTS; JUDGES.)

LASKER-SCHULER, ELSE (1876-1945)   German poet who was well-known in her native land before she settled in Palestine in 1936. She drew the illustrations for her books.

LASKOV, HAIM (1919-   )   Soldier who fought in the Israeli War of Independence, commanded Israel's tanks during the Sinai War, and became Chief-of-Staff of the Defense Forces before he retired to run the government Harbor Authority. (See also DEFENSE FORCES; PORTS; SINAI WAR; WAR OF INDEPENDENCE.)

LATRUN   Site of a monastery at the foot of the Judean Hills. Many Jews struggling to free Palestine from British control in the 1940s were arrested and held at Latrun. During the 1948 War of Independence, Jewish forces tried to capture Latrun in order to open the road between Tel Aviv and Jerusalem. When they failed, they had to build a new section of road around it. (See also GREAT BRITAIN; WAR OF INDEPENDENCE.)

LAVI Kibbutz founded in lower Galilee in 1949 by religious pioneers from England. They have developed a fine furniture manufacturing facility, and they export their products. (See also GALILEE; KIBBUTZ.)

LAVON, PINHAS (name changed from LUBIANIKER) (1904-1976) Polish-born labor leader who settled in Palestine in 1929 and became Secretary-General of Histadrut (Israel's labor federation). Lavon was elected to the Israeli Knesset (legislature) as a member of the Mapai political party and served as Minister of Agriculture and Minister of Defense. A disagreement between Lavon and Prime Minster Moshe Sharett about Israel's defense policy led to a split in the Mapai Party in 1954. (See also CABINET; HISTADRUT; KNESSET; MAPAI; SHARETT, MOSHE.)

LAVRY, MARC (1903-1967) Latvian-born composer who settled in Palestine in 1935. Lavry was one of Israel's best-known composers. He wrote many different kinds of music, including popular songs and the operas *Dan the Guard* and *Tamar*. He was also music director of the *Kol Zion la-Gola* radio station. (See also KOL ISRAEL; MUSIC.)

LAW OF RETURN Law passed by the Knesset (legislature) in 1950 as a written statement of the Israeli policy of accepting all Jews who wanted to settle in the country. Any Jewish immigrant automatically becomes a citizen of Israel with all rights and duties as soon as he or she enters the country and is listed in the Population Register. Only known criminals who may be a danger to the country or Jews working against the Jewish people can be refused citizenship. (See also CITIZENSHIP.)

LEAGUE OF NATIONS Organization of nations established in 1919 as a result of the treaty that ended World War I. The purposes of the League of Nations were (1) to prevent war, and (2) to solve some of the world's social and economic problems through cooperation between countries. One of the League's agencies, the Mandate Commission, was set up to oversee the government of the former colonies of the defeated nations of Germany and Turkey. The Mandate Commission appointed Great Britain to rule Palestine (which had belonged to Turkey). Although the League of Nations gave Great Britain the Mandate to govern Palestine, it had little authority over the actions of Britain. (See also GREAT BRITAIN; MANDATE; TURKEY.)

LEBANON Middle Eastern country on Israel's northern border. Its capital is Beirut, and its official language is Arabic. Lebanon has an area of 4,015 square miles and a population of 3,055,000 people (1977). Its people are divided into Moslems and Christians, and clashes between the two groups grew into civil war in 1958 and again in 1975.

In 1948 Lebanon joined the rest of the Arab countries in invading Israel. But most of the later conflict between Israel and Lebanon has been an outgrowth of Palestinian terrorists using bases in Lebanon for raids into Israel. Israel's response was to reciprocate with raids on terrorist bases. After a terrorist attack on an Israeli bus in 1978, Israel invaded southern Lebanon to wipe out the bases. Israeli troops pulled out a week later when the United Nations sent a peacekeeping force into the area. (See also TERRORISM; UNITED NATIONS; WAR OF INDEPENDENCE.)

LEHI   see STERN GROUP

LEVANON, MORDEKHAI (1901-1968)   Hungarian-born artist who settled in Palestine in 1921 and painted many scenes of Jerusalem.

LEVIN, SHEMARYA (1867-1935)   Writer and Zionist leader who spoke out for Jewish rights in the Russian Parliament and was forced to flee to Germany. Levin helped build the Zionist movement in Germany and the United States, worked for the Keren Hayesod (Palestine Foundation Fund), and was one of the founders of the Haifa Technion. He fought for Hebrew as the teaching language of the Technion and was one of the founders—with the poet Hayim Nahman Bialik—of Devir, a Hebrew publishing company. Levin settled in Palestine in 1924 and wrote several books, including his memoirs. (See also BIALIK, HAYIM NAHMAN; DEVIR; KEREN HAYESOD; TECHNION; ZIONISM.)

LEVIN, YITZAK MEIR (1894-1971)   Religious leader who was president of Agudat Israel (a world organization of Orthodox Jews) in Poland before he settled in Palestine in 1940. Although Levin had earlier been opposed to the Zionist struggle for a Jewish state, he signed the Israeli Declaration of Independence, was elected to the Knesset (legislature), and served as Minister for Social Welfare. (See also AGUDAT ISRAEL; DECLARATION OF INDEPENDENCE; KNESSET.)

LEVI-TANNAI, SARA   Native Israeli choreographer (creator of dances). Sara Levi-Tannai is the founder and director of the Inbal Dance Theater. She is a Yemenite by birth and has used her background to help her create dances based on Yemenite folk dances. In 1962 she received an award in Paris for best choreographer of the year. (See also INBAL DANCE THEATER.)

LEVONTIN, ZALMAN DAVID (1856-1940)   Russian-born Zionist who worked with Theodor Herzl in Europe before he went to Palestine in 1882. He helped establish the settlement of Rishon

LeZion. Levontin was the founder of the Anglo-Palestine Bank (which later became Bank Leumi LeIsrael) and served as its director for more than 20 years. He also wrote Zionist booklets and magazine articles. (See also BANK LEUMI LE-ISRAEL; HERZL, THEODOR; RISHON LE ZION; ZIONISM.)

LIBERAL PARTY   Political party formed in 1965 by a union of the General Zionists and the Progressive Party. It stood for free trade and private enterprise, and was mainly supported by businessmen. In 1965 the section of the Liberal Party that had previously been the General Zionists joined with Herut to form the Gahal bloc. The former Progressive Party did not join Gahal, but became the Independent Liberal Party. (See also GAHAL; GENERAL ZIONISTS; HERUT; POLITICAL PARTIES; PROGRESSIVE PARTY.)

LIFSCHITZ, EFRAIM (1909-   )   Polish artist who lived in Paris before he settled in Israel in 1935. Lifschitz began to paint while still a child. He has had many one-man shows in Israel and his paintings have also been shown in the United States and Europe. He is a member of the artists' colony in Safed. (See also ARTISTS' COLONY.)

LIKUD   Voting bloc of political parties formed in 1973 when Gahal (which had been created by the union of Herut and the Liberal Party in 1965) joined with several smaller parties. Likud elected 39 members to the Israeli Knesset (legislature) in the 1974 election. In 1977 Likud's support made it possible for Menachem Begin to become first Prime Minister of Israel who did not come from a labor party. (See also BEGIN, MENACHEM; GAHAL; KNESSET; POLITICAL PARTIES; PRIME MINISTER.)

LINDHEIM, IRMA LEVY (1886-   )   American-born Zionist leader who was president of Hadassah (a women's organization) in the United States before settling in Palestine in 1933. There, she continued to work for Hadassah, the Jewish National Fund, and Histadrut (Israel's labor federation). (See also HADASSAH; HISTADRUT; JEWISH NATIONAL FUND.)

LION'S GATE (Hebrew, SHAAR HAAROYOT)   One of the eight gates in the wall around the Old City of Jerusalem. It gets its name from the lions carved above the gate. The Lion's Gate is the only entrance to the Old City from the east. It leads into the Via Dolorosa, the street along which Jesus carried his cross to his crucifixion. The gate is also known as St. Stephan's (Stephen's) Gate. (See also JERUSALEM; VIA DOLOROSA; WALLED CITIES.)

LIRA   see ISRAELI POUND

LITER   A unit of liquid measurement in the metric system.

Liquids in Israel, including milk and gasoline, are sold by the liter. A liter is a little more than a quart. (See also METRIC SYSTEM.)

LITERATURE Eliezer Ben Yehuda's work in developing Hebrew into a modern spoken language brought about a new growth of Hebrew literature. European Jewish writers began to produce Hebrew poems, stories, and novels about life in Europe and the dream of a new life in a Jewish homeland. Many of these writers settled in Palestine, and by the 1930s Palestine was the center of Hebrew literature.

The two great writers of this period were Hayim Nahman Bialik and Shemuel Yoseph Agnon. Bialik's poems expressed the spirit of the Jewish people and called for Jews to take their place among the nations of the world. Agnon's novels, based on Jewish tradition, won him worldwide fame and the Nobel Prize for literature. Other important writers were the novelist Hayim Hazaz, and the poets Saul Tschernichowsky and Natan Alterman.

The establishment of the State of Israel in 1948 changed Hebrew literature. Although some older writers like Agnon continued to write about the past, many new writers turned their attention to the present and the future. S. Yizhar was the first native Israeli novelist to deal with the problems of the new nation. Soon there was a whole group of writers, like Amos Oz, who were born in Israel, spoke Hebrew as their native language, and whose books formed a part of a new native Israeli literature. (See also AGNON, SHEMUEL YOSEPH; ALTERMAN, NATAN; BEN YEHUDA, ELIEZER; BIALIK, HAYIM NAHMAN; BOOKS; HAZAZ, HAYIM; HEBREW; OZ, AMOS; TSCHERNICHOWSKY, SAUL; YIZHAR, S.)

LITVINOVSKY, PINHAS (1894-) Artist who settled in Palestine from Russia in 1919 and produced many colorful modern paintings.

LIVNEH, ELIEZER (name changed from LIEBENSTEIN) (1902-) Russian-born writer and politician who settled in Palestine in 1920, went to Germany in the 1930s to organize Jewish immigration to Palestine, and became head of the Political Department of the Haganah (Jewish underground army). Livneh was elected to the Israeli Knesset (legislature) but resigned after several years. He wrote political articles and pamphlets, many of which criticized the government. (See also HAGANAH; KNESSET.)

LLOYD GEORGE, DAVID (1863-1945) Prime Minister of Great Britain from 1916 to 1922 and liberal member of the British Parliament for over 50 years. Lloyd George was Prime Minister in 1917 when the Balfour Declaration was issued favoring a Jewish national home in Palestine. At the San Remo Conference of 1920 he worked to have the Balfour Declaration included in the peace treaty with Turkey, and for Great Britain to be given the Mandate to govern Palestine. Later, Lloyd George spoke out against British rule in Palestine, particularly against the White Paper of 1939 which limited Jewish immigration into the Holy Land. (See also BALFOUR DECLARATION; GREAT BRITAIN; HISTORY; MANDATE; SAN REMO CONFERENCE; WHITE PAPER.)

LOCAL GOVERNMENT   Local government in Israel includes the municipal councils and mayors of large cities, the local councils of towns and villages, and the regional councils of rural areas. These councils are elected by the people by a system of proportional representation. They deal with health, education, sanitation, fire protection, etc., in their communities. A group of councils may form a union to look after hospitals, secondary schools, agricultural services, etc.

The Ministry of the Interior of the central government oversees the local councils and helps them in land and town planning, settlement of immigrants, and voter registration. The country is divided into six administrative districts, each with a District Officer responsible to the Ministry of the Interior. These District Officers serve as links between the local council and the central government. (See also GOVERNMENT; PROPORTIONAL REPRESENTATION.)

LOCKER, BERL (1887-1972)   Austrian-born Zionist who worked for Poale Zion (a Socialist Zionist organization) in Austria, Holland, and the United States before settling in Palestine in 1936. Locker was on the executive committee of the Jewish Agency and later was elected to the Israeli Knesset (legislature). He was married to Dina Malka Locker, the writer. (See also JEWISH AGENCY; KNESSET; LOCKER, DINA MALKA; POALE ZION; ZIONISM.)

LOCKER, DINA MALKA   Yiddish writer who was born in Austria, married Berl Locker there in 1910, and moved to Palestine with him in 1936. She wrote more than ten books of poems, plays, and criticism. (See also LOCKER, BERL.)

LOD (also called LYDDA)   City 13 miles east of Tel Aviv. Ancient Lod was the home of many Jews who returned from the exile in Babylon in the fifth century B.C.E. It became an important center of Jewish trade and learning after the destruction of Jerusalem in 70 C.E., but most of the Jews of the city were killed during a revolt against Roman rule in 352 C.E. The Crusaders rebuilt Lod in the twelfth century C.E. and named it Georgiopolis after St. George who was said to have been born there. The Crusader church of St. George still stands. Today Lod is an industrial city and the site of

Ben-Gurion International Airport. (See also BABYLONIAN EXILE; BEN-GURION AIRPORT; CRUSADES; HISTORY; ROME.)

LOD AIRPORT   see BEN-GURION AIRPORT

LOESS   Fertile yellow-brown soil. Areas of loess in the Negev Desert are now being farmed as water for irrigation is brought south through the National Water Carrier. (See also IRRIGATION; NATIONAL WATER CARRIER; NEGEV.)

LOEWE, HEINRICH (1869-1951) Zionist and scholar who founded the Society of the Lovers of Hebrew, in Berlin, in his native Germany, before settling in Palestine in 1933. Loewe was librarian of the Tel Aviv library and wrote several books on Zionism and on Jewish folklore. (See also ZIONISM.)

LOHAME HAGETTAOT   Kibbutz near Acre in upper Galilee. The name means Ghetto Fighters. Founded in 1949 by veterans of the Jewish resistance in Europe during World War II. The kibbutz's Yitzak Katznelson Museum contains exhibits of the Nazi massacre of the Jews. (See also GALILEE; KIBBUTZ.)

LOHAME HERUT ISRAEL   see STERN GROUP

LOT'S WIFE   Part of a mountain near the Dead Sea. It is pointed out to tourists as "the pillar of salt" that Lot's wife turned into when she looked back at the destruction of Sodom (Genesis 19:23). (See also DEAD SEA; SODOM; TOURISM.)

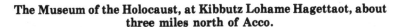

The Museum of the Holocaust, at Kibbutz Lohame Hagettaot, about three miles north of Acco.

LOURIE, ARTHUR (1903-)   South African lawyer who was a member of Israel's delegation to the United Nations and later served as ambassador to Great Britain. (See also UNITED NATIONS.)

LOWDERMILK, WALTER CLAY (1888-1974)   American soil expert who studied the soil of Palestine in 1939 and developed a plan for using river and underground water for irrigation. After Israel became a state, Lowdermilk spent a year as an adviser to the government on soil use and protection. He also served for three years as professor of soil conservation at the Haifa Technion. (See also IRRIGATION; TECHNION.)

LUAH ERETZ ISRAEL   Hebrew almanac containing information on the geography, people, and culture of Palestine. It was published in Jerusalem from 1896 to 1915 by Abraham Luncz. (See also LUNCZ, ABRAHAM MOSES.)

LUBETKIN-ZUCKERMAN, TZIVYA (1914-)   Underground leader who organized Jewish resistance to the Nazis in Poland during World War II. She was a leader of the uprising in the Warsaw Ghetto and was known as the Mother of the Ghetto. After escaping to Palestine in 1945, she became a member of the executive committee of the World Zionist Organization. (See also WORLD ZIONIST ORGANIZATION.)

LUNCZ, ABRAHAM MOSES (1854-1918)   Lithuanian-born scholar who settled in Palestine in 1869. Luncz published the first Hebrew guidebook to Jerusalem and the Hebrew almanac *Luah Eretz Israel*. He also edited a collection of 13 books of essays about Palestine. After becoming blind, he worked for the Jerusalem School for the Blind. (See also LUAH ERETZ ISRAEL.)

LUPINE   A flower with blue petals shaped like hands. Lupines bloom in Galilee in the spring. (See also GALILEE.)

LURIA, ISAAC BEN SOLOMON (also called ARI) (1534-1572) A Jerusalem-born scholar and Kabbalist who lived most of his life in Safed. Luria was known for the goodness and simplicity of his life. His teaching that God and creation are one has influenced Jewish thought for centuries. (See also KABBALAH; ARI.)

LURIE, ZVI (1906-1968)   Zionist who moved to Palestine from Poland in 1925 and became a founder and leader of Hakibbutz Haartzi (an organization of cooperative farming settlements). Lurie was a member of the executive committee of the Jewish Agency and one of the signers of the Israeli Declaration of Independence. (See also DECLARATION OF INDEPENDENCE; HAKIBBUTZ HAARTZI; JEWISH AGENCY; ZIONISM.)

LUZ, KADDISH (name changed from LUZINSKY) (1895-1972) Russian-born farming expert who settled in Palestine in 1920 and was a leader of the kibbutz movement. Luz was elected to the Israeli Knesset (legislature) and served as Minister of Agriculture. (See also AGRICULTURE; KIBBUTZ; KNESSET.)

LYDDA   see LOD

M

MAABAROT see IMMIGRANT CAMPS

MAALE HAHAMISHA Kibbutz founded in the hills near Jerusalem in 1938 and named for five of its founders who were murdered by Arabs while they were working the fields. (See also KIBBUTZ.)

MAALOT Town founded in 1957 in western upper Galilee. In May of 1974, Arab terrorists seized a school in Maalot and held 90 students hostage. Israeli soldiers attacked the school to free the hostages, but 21 students were killed in the raid. (See also GALILEE; TERRORISM.)

MAAPILIM see IMMIGRANTS, ILLEGAL

MAARIV Afternoon newspaper with the largest circulation in

Sholom Rosenfeld, editor
of *Maariv.*

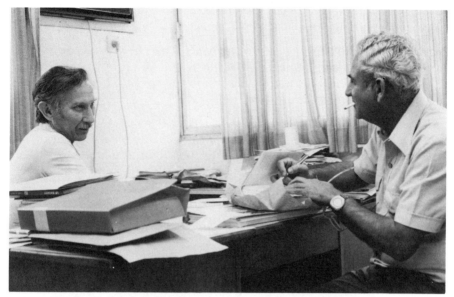

Naphtali Arbel (left), director of Maariv's Book Club, with author Hanokh Bartov, a popular Israeli writer.

Israel. It was founded in 1948 by Azriel Carlbach, who was its editor until his death. *Maariv* is not connected with any politcal party and is known for the independence of its reporting. Besides the news, *Maariv* runs columns on sports, literature, stamps, and features political cartoons. It also publishes a Friday night political and literary supplement, a weekly paper for children, and an almanac. (See also CARLBACH, AZRIEL.)

MAAYAN BARUKH Kibbutz founded in 1947 in the Huleh Valley by South Africans. (See also HULEH VALLEY; KIBBUTZ.)

MACCABEE Name given to Judah, the Jewish hero who led the revolt against the Syrians in 168 B.C.E. The Hasmoneans, the descendants of Judah's family who ruled Palestine for nearly a hundred years, are sometimes also called Maccabees. (See also HASMONEANS; JUDAH THE MACCABEE.)

MACCABI World organization of Jewish athletes founded in Berlin in 1895 and established in Palestine in 1912. Its headquarters are in Tel Aviv. Although Maccabi was the only sports organization in Palestine until 1926, today it is second in size to Hapoel (the labor sports federation). Maccabi has some 40,000 members in 110 clubs and is most active in soccer, basketball, and tennis. The World Maccabi Union is the organizer of the Maccabiah Games, an international sports festival held in Israel every four years. (See also BASKETBALL; HAPOEL; MACCABI HATZAIR; MACCABIA GAMES; SOCCER; TENNIS; SPORTS.)

MACCABI HATZAIR   The Young Maccabees. Sports organization of young people that is part of the World Maccabi Union. In 1978 Maccabi Hatzair had 7,000 members in Israel. (See also MACCABI; YOUTH MOVEMENTS.)

MACCABIA GAMES   Sometimes called the "Jewish Olympics," the Maccabia Games are held in the Ramat Gan sports stadium every four years in the year following the Olympic Games. The first Maccabia took place in Tel Aviv in 1932 and the second in 1935, but no games were held after that until 1950. The tenth Maccabia in 1977 drew 2,700 Jewish athletes from 34 countries to compete in 23 sports events. (See also MACCABI; OLYMPIC GAMES; SPORTS.)

MACDONALD, JAMES RAMSAY (1866-1937)   Prime Minister of Great Britain in 1924 and from 1929 to 1935. MacDonald visited Palestine in 1922 and wrote several articles praising its Jewish pioneers. However, as Prime Minister, his government favored the Arabs and issued the Passfield White Paper which declared that there was no more land in Palestine for Jewish settlement. (See also GREAT BRITAIN; PASSFIELD WHITE PAPER.)

MACHPELAH, CAVE OF (also called TOMB OF THE PATRIARCHS) Shrine near Hebron that is the burial place of Abraham, Isaac, Jacob, and their wives Sarah, Rebecca, and Leah. The Book of Genesis in the Bible tells how Abraham bought the cave for 400 shekels. The wall around the shrine is at least 2,000 years old and the Moslem mosque over the tombs was built on the foundations of a sixth century C.E. church. The cave itself has been sealed for nearly 1,000 years. Machpelah is holy to Jews, Moslems, and Christians alike, but Jews have only been able to visit it since the 1967 Six-Day War. (See also ABRAHAM; BIBLE; HEBRON; SHEKEL; SIX-DAY WAR.)

MAGDALA   Ancient city on the west shore of Lake Kinneret (Sea of Galilee) that was destroyed by the Romans during the 67 C.E. Jewish revolt. The modern town of Migdal stands near the ancient site. (See also HISTORY; MIGDAL; ROME.)

MAGEN DAVID (also called SHIELD OF DAVID and STAR OF DAVID) Six-pointed star made up of two triangles. The Magen David was probably first used as the symbol of the Jewish community in Prague in the 1500s. It appeared on the flag of the World Zionist Organization from 1897 on and is on the flag of the State of Israel. (See also FLAG; WORLD ZIONIST ORGANIZATION.)

MAGEN DAVID ADOM (English, RED SHIELD OF DAVID) Israeli first-aid and emergency medical organization similar to the Red Cross in other countries. Magen David Adom was founded in Palestine in 1930. Its function is to help the Army Medical Corps in wartime to provide first-aid and temporary housing in emergencies like floods or epidemics, and to operate blood banks. In the late 1970s it had 63 branches and four blood banks. (See also HEALTH.)

MAGIC CARPET see OPERATION MAGIC CARPET

MAGNES, JUDAH LEON (1877-1948) Rabbi who was secretary of the American Zionist Federation before he settled in Palestine in 1921. Rabbi Magnes was a founder of the Hebrew University in Jerusalem and was its first president. Afraid that the Zionist aim of a Jewish State in Palestine would lead to war, Magnes worked for a Joint Arab-Jewish nation. He was the founder of Berit Shalom, an organization devoted to creating a better relationship between Arabs and Jews. (See also BERIT SHALOM; HEBREW UNIVERSITY; ZIONISM.)

MAHAL Name given to the 3,000 to 4,000 volunteers from the United States, Europe, and South Africa who went to Palestine to fight for Israel during the 1948 War of Independence. About 200 of these volunteers were killed in action and many others stayed on to settle in Israel. (See also WAR OF INDEPENDENCE.)

MAHANOT HAOLIM Pioneer youth organization founded in 1927 by the students of Herzlia High School. The group established several kibbutzim. (See also HERZLIA HIGH SCHOOL; KIBBUTZ; YOUTH MOVEMENTS.)

MAIMON, ADA (name changed from FISHMAN) (1893-1973) Russian-born pioneer who settled in Palestine in 1912 and founded a school for girls in Safed. Ada Maimon was a leader in the struggle for women's rights and was a founder of Moetzet Hapoalot (Working Women's Council). She headed the Pioneer Women organization in Palestine, was a member of the executive committee of Histadrut (Israel's labor federation), and was elected to the Israeli Knesset (legislature). She wrote several books about working women in Palestine including *Women Build a Land*. Her brother was Rabbi Yehuda Maimon. (See also HISTADRUT; KNESSET; MAIMON, YEHUDA LEIB; MOETZET HAPOALOT; PIONEER WOMEN.)

MAIMON, YEHUDA LEIB (name changed from FISHMAN) (1872-1962) Russian-born rabbi and leader of Mizrahi (a religious Zionist organization). He went to Palestine in 1913, founded the Rabbi Kook Foundation to publish religious Hebrew books, and was on the executive committee of the Jewish Agency. Rabbi Maimon was a signer of the Israeli Declaration of Independence, was elected to the Knesset (legislature), and served as Minister of Religious Affairs and Minister of Social Welfare. He also wrote a number of Hebrew books on religion and Zionism. His sister was Ada Maimon. (See also DECLARATION OF INDEPENDENCE; JEWISH AGENCY; KNESSET; MAIMON, ADA; MIZRAHI; RABBI KOOK FOUNDATION.)

MAIMONIDES (full name, MOSES BEN MAIMON; also called RAMBAM) (1135-1204)   The most important Jewish scholar of the Middle Ages. Maimonides was born in Spain and lived in Egypt, where he became the personal doctor of Egypt's ruler Saladin. Maimonides' books influenced Jewish thought from his time up to the present day. In *The Luminary*, he showed the connection between Judaism and the best of human knowledge and ethics. In *Mishneh Torah*, he organized and clarified Jewish law. His great philosophical book, *The Guide of the Perplexed*, has been studied by Christians and Moslems as well as by Jews. Maimonides is buried in Tiberias in Israel, and his tomb can be visited there. (See also SALADIN; TIBERIAS.)

The entrance to the tomb of Moses Maimonides in the Tiberias cemetery. The inscription reads "From Moses [the great of the Bible] to Moses ben Maimon no one was as great as Moses ben Maimon [Maimonides]."

MAISEL-SHOHAT, HANNA (also spelled MEISEL-SCHOCHET) (1890-   )   Zionist and educator who left her native Russia to settle in Palestine in 1909 where she founded the first training farm for girls in the country. She also founded the Girls' Agricultural School of Nahalal and was its principal for almost 40 years. (See also AGRICULTURAL SCHOOLS; EDUCATION; NAHALAL.)

MAKHPELAH, CAVE OF   see MACHPELAH, CAVE OF

MAKI   Israel's Communist political party. The Palestine Communist Party (which later became Maki) was established in 1919. Before 1948, it was opposed to Zionism and to the founding of a Jewish State. Always a small party, in 1965 Maki split into the Arab-controlled Rakah (which became the New Communist List) and a Jewish section which became Moked. (See also POLITICAL PARTIES; RAKAH.)

MAKLEFF, MORDECHAI (1920-   )   Native Israeli soldier who fought with the British army's Jewish Brigade during World War II. Makleff led the Haganah (Jewish army) unit that captured Haifa during the 1948 War of Independence. In 1952 and 1953 he served as Chief-of-Staff of the Israel Defense Forces. After leaving the army, he became managing director of Israel Chemicals, the country's largest producer of inorganic chemicals. (See also DEFENSE FORCES; HAGANAH; JEWISH BRIGADE; WAR OF INDEPENDENCE.)

MALARIA   A serious disease spread by the bite of certain mosquitos. Malaria causes repeated attacks of chills and fever that last from six hours to four days. Until modern treatment and control of mosquitos, malaria was the prime cause of sickness and death in the world. Many early Jewish pioneers in Palestine died from malaria carried by the mosquitos that infested the swampy land of their settlements.

MALBEN   Part of the JDC (American Joint Distribution Committee) that cares for aged and handicapped immigrants in Israel. In the late 1970s Malben ran 12 homes and villages for 3,000 old people as well as four hospitals and a center for handicapped young people. (See also HEALTH; JDC.)

MALHA (also called ENAN)   Ancient site in upper Galilee where remains of Stone Age men have been found. Archaeologists have uncovered human bones, remains of houses, and round pits that were used as tombs. (See also ARCHAEOLOGY; GALILEE.)

MAMELUKES (also spelled MAMLUKS)   The line of sultans who ruled Egypt from 1250 to 1517 C.E. The Mamelukes drove the last of the Crusaders (European Christian knights) from Palestine in 1291 and occupied the country until the Turkish conquest of 1517. (See also CRUSADES; HISTORY; TURKEY.)

MAMRE Place near Hebron that is said to be the site of the Oak of Mamre mentioned in the Book of Genesis. An ancient oak tree still growing there is known as Abraham's Oak. (See also ABRAHAM; BIBLE; HEBRON.)

MANAHAT Site near Jerusalem where archaeologists have uncovered large stones thought to be one of the High Places of ancient Jewish worship. (See also ARCHAEOLOGY; HIGH PLACE.)

MANARA Kibbutz founded in 1943. It came under heavy Arab attack during the 1948 War of Independence. (See also KIBBUTZ; WAR OF INDEPENDENCE.)

MANASSEH Oldest son of Joseph. When the Israelites conquered Canaan in the thirteenth century B.C.E., the land of the tribe of Joseph was divided between his two sons—Manasseh and Ephraim. The tribe of Manasseh received land in the Jezreel Valley and in what is now Jordan. (See also CANAAN; EPHRAIM; JOSEPH; JEZREEL VALLEY; TWELVE TRIBES.)

MANASSEH King of Judah who ruled 692-638 B.C.E. Manasseh was influenced by the Assyrians to bring the worship of pagan idols back to Judah. He is known as one of the worst kings of Judah although the country was prosperous under his rule. (See also ASSYRIA; JUDAH, KINGDOM OF.)

MANDATE The Mandate system was created after World War I by the charter of the League of Nations. It transferred control of the former colonies of the defeated nations (Germany and Turkey) to members of the victorious Allies (United States, England, France). These colonies were now to be governed as "a sacred trust of civilization" and prepared for independence.

In 1922 Great Britain was given the Mandate to govern Palestine (which had belonged to Turkey). The terms of the Mandate recognized "the historic connection of the Jewish people with Palestine" and gave Britain the responsibility for governing the country in a way that would lead to the establishment of a Jewish national home. The Mandate also called for encouraging Jewish immigration and settlement in Palestine.

Britain did not live up to the terms of the Mandate. Arab pressure—including the riots of 1929 and 1936—and other political considerations gradually made British policy in Palestine more and more anti-Zionist. It was not until 1948, after Britain finally stopped trying to govern Palestine and referred the problem to the United Nations, that a Jewish nation was established. (See also ARAB RIOTS; GREAT BRITAIN; LEAGUE OF NATIONS; UNITED NATIONS; ZIONISM.)

MANDELBAUM GATE The 1948 War of Independence ended

with Jerusalem split in two. The New City was part of Israel, the Old City was in Jordan's hands, and a wall separated them. The Mandelbaum Gate was the only place to pass through the wall. Non-Jews could show their papers and go through the Mandelbaum Gate to the Old City, but the Jordanians did not allow Jews through. No Jew could visit the Old City until Jerusalem was united again in the 1967 Six-Day War. (See also JERUSALEM; JORDAN; SIX-DAY WAR; WAR OF INDEPENDENCE.)

MANN AUDITORIUM Main concert hall of Tel Aviv. The 3,000-seat Mann Auditorium is the home of the Israel Philharmonic Orchestra. Visiting orchestras and musicians also perform at the auditorium. It is one of the sites of the summer Israel Festival of music and drama. (See also ISRAEL FESTIVAL; ISRAEL PHILHARMONIC ORCHESTRA; TEL AVIV.)

MANUAL OF DISCIPLINE see DEAD SEA SCROLLS

MANUFACTURERS' ASSOCIATION OF ISRAEL Organization founded in 1923. The Manufacturers' Association tries to improve efficiency in industry, arranges exhibits of Israeli products, and sometimes represents management in dealings with labor unions. (See also INDUSTRY.)

MAPAI A Socialist Zionist political party formed in 1930. Until its merger with other parties in 1968, Mapai was the Israeli workers' party: its policies stressed the needs of labor, including good wages, absorption of immigrants into the working force, an economy that mixed socialism with free enterprise, and a willingness to sign peace treaties with the Arab nations. Mapai has been the strongest political party in Israel. In each election it won more seats in the Knesset (legislature) than any other party, and it supplied all of the country's Prime Ministers until Menachem Begin. It was the party of David Ben-Gurion, Levi Eshkol, and Golda Meir. In 1968 Mapai joined with Ahdut Ha-avoda and other small labor parties to form the Israel Labor Party. (See also AHDUT HA-AVODA; ISRAEL LABOR PARTY; KNESSET; POLITICAL PARTIES; PRIME MINISTER; SOCIALISM.)

MAPAM United Workers' Party. A Socialist Zionist political party whose policies are to the left of the more moderate Mapai Party. Mapam was founded in 1948 and drew much of its support from the kibbutzim. It began as a strong party—electing 19 of the 120 members of the first Knesset (legislature)—but gradually became less popular. In 1969 Mapam formed a voting bloc with the Israel Labor Party. (See also ISRAEL LABOR PARTY; KIBBUTZ; KNESSET; MAPAI; POLITICAL PARTIES.)

MARCUS, DAVID (1902-1948) American lawyer and soldier

who went to Palestine in 1948 as an adviser to the Haganah (Jewish underground army) and fought in the Israeli army during the War of Independence. Marcus was made commander of the Jerusalem area and helped lift the siege of the city. He was killed in action near Jerusalem and was awarded the Israeli Medal of Independence after his death. (See also HAGANAH; WAR OF INDEPENDENCE.)

MARRIAGE   There is no civil (state) marriage or divorce in Israel. Each person wishing to marry must belong to a religious community—Jewish, Moslem, Christian, or Druze—and the courts of each religion control the marriages of its members. All Jews, whether they are observant or not, must be married according to talmudic law. The rabbinical courts interpret the law and their decisions are legally binding. People of different religions may not marry in Israel. However, marriages that have taken place in other countries are legal in Israel. Therefore, couples who cannot marry according to religious law in Israel, or who do not wish to do so, travel to another country to get married and then return to Israel to live. Many mixed marriages take place in Cyprus, the nearest friendly country to Israel. (See also COURTS, RELIGIOUS; CYPRUS; TALMUD.)

MASADA (also spelled M'TZADA)   Fortress on a 1,700-foot-high flat mountain top near the west shore of the Dead Sea. Alexander Jannaeus built the first fortress at Masada in the second century B.C.E. and King Herod rebuilt it in the first century B.C.E. with two palaces and an elaborate water supply system.

When the Jews of Palestine revolted against Roman rule in 66 C.E., the Zealots (a group that believed that only God ruled the Jewish people) under Eleazar Ben Jair captured the fortress from the Romans. In 73 C.E., 10,000 Roman soldiers laid siege to Masada. The 960 men, women, and children held out for seven months, and then comitted suicide rather than surrender to the Romans. The bravery of the Zealots has made Masada the symbol of Jewish courage. Young Israelis take trips to the ancient fortress to promise, "Masada shall not fall again!"

In 1963-1965 archaeologists, led by Yigael Yadin, uncovered the remains of Masada. Today visitors can take a cable car partway up to the fortress and after climbing the rest of the way can see the camps of the Roman armies, the living quarters of the Zealots, Herod's palaces and water supply system, and the oldest synagogue in the world. (See also ALEXANDER JANNAEUS; ARCHAE-OLOGY; ELEAZAR BEN JAIR; HEROD I; HISTORY; MASADA MEDAL; ROME; YADIN, YIGAEL; ZEALOTS.)

MASADA MEDAL   Medal issued by the Israeli government to honor the courage of the Jewish people. On one side the words in English and Hebrew read, "Masada shall not fall again." The other side says, "We shall remain free men." (See also MASADA.)

MATTATHIAS (died 167 B.C.E.) First leader of the 167 B.C.E. Jewish revolt against Syrian rule and ancestor of the Hasmoneans (line of Jewish rulers of Palestine). When Mattathias died early in the revolt, the leadership was taken up by his son Judah the Maccabee. (See also HASMONEANS; HISTORY; JUDAH THE MACCABEE; SELEUCIDS; SYRIA.)

MATZLIAH Village near Ramla founded in 1950 by members of the Karaite religion from Egypt. (See also KARAITES; RAMLA.)

MATZO (also spelled MATZAH) (the plural is MATZOT or MATZOS) Unleavened bread eaten during the Passover holiday. When matzot are baked, great care is taken not to let the dough rise. Eating matzot during Passover reminds Jews that Pharaoh drove them from Egypt in such a hurry that they could not prepare ordinary leavened bread. (See also EXODUS; PASSOVER; SEDER.)

MAYER, LEO ARI (1895-1959) Expert on Oriental art and archaeology who was born and educated in Austria. He settled in Palestine in 1921 and taught at the Hebrew University in Jerusalem. (See also HEBREW UNIVERSITY.)

MAZAR, BENJAMIN (also spelled MAISLER) (1906-) Archaeologist who left Russia to live in Palestine in 1926 and took part in archaeological digs at Bet Shearim, Ein Gedi, as well as in the Old City of Jerusalem. Mazar taught at the Hebrew University in Jerusalem and was the university's president for eight years. He has written a history of Palestine and many books on archaeology. (See also ARCHAEOLOGY; HEBREW UNIVERSITY.)

MEA SHEARIM Neighborhood in the northern part of Jerusalem whose narrow streets are filled with little synagogues, ritual baths *(mikvaot)*, and schools. The people of Mea Shearim are Orthodox Jews who speak Yiddish and keep the customs of Eastern Europe of years ago. Many are members of Natore Karta, a group that does not recognize the State of Israel. (See also JERUSALEM; NATORE KARTA; TORAH.)

MEDITERRANEAN SEA Large sea—2,330 miles long—lying between Europe and Africa. It is connected to the Atlantic Ocean by the Strait of Gibraltar and to the Red Sea by the Suez Canal. Israel's western border runs along the east shore of the Mediterranean Sea and her major ports are on the Mediterranean. (See also GEOGRAPHY; PORTS.)

MEGGED, AHARON (1920-) Writer who was born in Poland

A typical street in the Mea Shearim section of Jerusalem.

and taken to Palestine at the age of six. Megged was a columnist for the newspaper *Davar*. He has written more than twenty novels and plays, many of them about kibbutz life or Jewish mysticism. Only a few of his books have been translated into English. The best known of these is *Living On The Dead*. Megged won the Bialik Prize in 1974. He is married to Eda Zoritte, who is also a writer. (See also BIALIK PRIZE; DAVAR; KIBBUTZ; ZORITTE, EDA.)

Aharon Megged

MEGGIDO Ancient city in the Jezreel Valley that is one of Israel's most important archaeological sites. Excavation has uncovered 20 different cities—each built on top of an older one— that go back about 5,000 years. Among the remains are Canaanite temples built long before the Israelites invaded Canaan, a 300-foot tunnel cut through solid rock to a spring on the plain below the city, and stables from the time that King Solomon used Meggido as a base for his chariot troops. Meggido was the battleground of so many wars that the New Testament says it is the site of Armageddon, where the forces of good and evil fought. A museum has been erected at the ruins of Meggido, and a modern farming village by the same name is located nearby. (See also ARCHAEOLOGY; CANAAN; HISTORY; JEZREEL VALLEY; SOLOMON.)

MEHTA, ZUBIN (1936-   )   Orchestra conductor who was born in India, studied music in Vienna, Austria, and lives in the United States. Mehta has conducted concerts throughout the world. He is the director of the New York Philharmonic Orchestra and the musical adviser to the Israel Philharmonic Orchestra. In 1972 he toured North and South America with the Israel Philharmonic. (See also ISRAEL PHILHARMONIC ORCHESTRA; MUSIC.)

MEIR, GOLDA (1898-1978)   First woman Prime Minister of Israel. She was born Golda Mabovitch in Kiev, Russia, and was brought to the United States by her parents at the age of eight. She soon learned English and was such a good student that she finished both high school and teacher training by age 18. Becoming a Zionist and a Socialist in her teens, Golda Mabovitch agreed to marry Morris Meyerson (who later changed his name to Meir) only if he would live in an agricultural village in Palestine. In 1921 they moved to a settlement in the Jezreel Valley.

Golda Meir soon became active in Palestine's labor and political movements. She was secretary of the Moetzet Hapoalot (Working Women's Council), head of the political department of Histadrut (federation of labor), and acting head of the political department of the Jewish Agency. When Israel became a state in 1948, Golda Meir was one of the signers of the Declaration of Independence and was elected to the Knesset as a Mapai Party member. Prime Minister Ben-Gurion asked her to be Minister of Labor, a post she held for seven years before being appointed Foreign Minister, a position she held for ten more years.

In 1969 Golda Meir became Prime Minister of Israel and formed a government that represented a number of different political views. Israel grew economically under her strong leadership; new programs were started to close the gap between the rich and the poor. Mrs. Meir was reelected Prime Minister in 1973, but retired in 1974 after a commission questioned her judgment about the conduct of the 1973 Yom Kippur War. Her story is told in her book, *My Life*. (See also BEN-GURION, DAVID; CABINET; DECLARATION OF INDEPENDENCE; HISTADRUT; JEWISH AGENCY; JEZREEL VALLEY; KNESSET; MAPAI; MOETZET HAPOALOT; PRIME MINISTER; SIX-DAY WAR; YOM KIPPUR WAR; ZIONISM.)

MEIR, YAAKOV (1856-1939)   Rabbi who was active in the community affairs of his native Jerusalem. His appointment as Chief Rabbi of Jerusalem in 1906 was canceled because of his Zionist activities, but in 1921 he was chosen Sephardic Chief Rabbi of Palestine. Rabbi Meir was known for his educational and charitable work and for his efforts to reestablish Hebrew as a spoken language. (See also CHIEF RABBINATE; HEBREW; SEPHARDIM; ZIONISM.)

On November 10, 1969 President Zalman Shazar appointed Golda
Meir to form a labor government. She became Israel's first woman
Prime Minister.

MEIROVICZ, MENASHE (1860-1949)   Russian agricultural expert who went to Palestine in 1884 as a member of BILU (a
pioneer group). Meirovicz settled in Rishon LeZion and experimented with raising grapes for the manufacture of wine. He later
became the director of Palestine's Winegrower's Association, a
job he held for 30 years. (See also BILU; RISHON LE-ZION; WINE.)

MEKOROT WATER COMPANY Public company founded in 1937 to supply Palestine with water for industry, irrigation, and private use. Mekorot searches for new sources of water and builds and operates the pipelines that carry water throughout the country. Its largest project was the building of the National Water Carrier to bring water from the north of Israel to the dry south. In 1964 Mekorot became the National Water Authority. (See also IRRIGATION; NATIONAL WATER CARRIER; TAHAL; WATER.)

MELTZER, SHIMON (1909-   ) Hebrew poet who left his native Austria for Palestine in 1924. His poems are influenced by Jewish folklore and Hassidic legends. Besides writing poetry, Meltzer has translated a number of Yiddish writers into Hebrew.

MEMORIALS Memorials for the war dead have been erected in all parts of Israel. Many of these memorials are exceptionally beautiful works of art.

MENACHEM King of Israel who ruled 744-735 B.C.E. Menachem killed Shallum, his rival for the throne, and put to death the people of the city of Tiphsah who would not accept him as king. When the Assyrians advanced on Israel, Menachem was forced to pay them large amounts of money and goods. (See also ASSYRIA; ISRAEL, KINGDOM OF.)

MENAHEMIYA Agricultural village founded in 1902. It was the first Jewish settlement in the Jordan Valley. (See also JORDAN VALLEY.)

MENORAH (the plural is MENOROT) Seven-branched candle holder. The menorah has been the symbol of Judaism from earliest times. Carvings and drawings of menorot have been found in synagogue decorations dating back to the first century C.E. In modern times the menorah was used as a symbol by several Jewish organizations, including the Jewish Legion of World War I. In 1949 the official seal of the State of Israel was designed. It features a menorah between two olive branches. A large menorah stands at the entrance of the Knesset building in Jerusalem.

The name "menorah" is also used for the eight-branched candelabra that is lit during the Hanukkah holiday. (See also HANUKKAH; JEWISH LEGION; MAGEN DAVID.)

MERCY GATE see GOLDEN GATE

MERHAVYA Two agricultural villages located next to each other in the Jezreel Valley. The first settlement at Merhavya was founded in 1911 on land bought by the Jewish National Fund. It was a Hashomer (Jewish "watchmen") camp that later became an experimental workers' cooperative which failed. The present

A memorial to Israel's war dead inside the national military
cemetery on Mount Herzl, in Jerusalem.

A memorial to Israel's war dead in the town Kiryat Tivon, near Haifa.

The seven-branched menorah at the entrance to the Knesset is the most popular symbol in Israel, after the Star of David.

villages were settled in 1922 and 1929 by immigrants from Eastern Europe. (See also HASHOMER; JEWISH NATIONAL FUND; JEZREEL VALLEY.)

MERIDOR, YAAKOV (1913-)   Russian-born soldier and politician who entered Palestine in 1932 as an illegal immigrant and joined the Irgun (a Jewish underground fighting unit). Meridor was commander of the Irgun for a short while, before turning the post over to Menachem Begin in 1943. After Israel became a state in 1948, Meridor helped bring the Irgun into the Israel Defense Forces and was elected to the Israeli Knesset (legislature) as a Herut Party member. (See also BEGIN, MENACHEM; DEFENSE FORCES; HERUT; IMMIGRANTS, ILLEGAL; IRGUN; KNESSET.)

MERON   Ancient town at the foot of Mount Meron in upper Galilee. Meron was a Canaanite city before its conquest by the Israelites around the thirteenth century B.C.E. It became an important Jewish settlement and was fortified by Josephus (the Jewish historian) during the 66-73 revolt against Rome. Rabbi Simeon Ben Yohai lived and taught at Meron in the second century C.E. and every year on Lag B'Omer thousands of Israelis travel to his tomb to celebrate the holiday by singing and dancing around bonfires. The ruins of a second century C.E. synagogue remain on the ancient site of Meron and a modern farming village of the same name is nearby. (See also CANAAN; GALILEE; JOSEPHUS FLAVIUS; LAG B'OMER; ROME; SIMEON BEN YOHAI.)

MESHEK POALOT (English, WOMEN WORKERS' FARM)   A training farm for girls. A number of these farms were established in Palestine soon after World War I. (See also AGRICULTURAL SCHOOLS.)

MESOPOTAMIA   The name means "land between the rivers" and in ancient times referred to the valley between the Tigris and Euphrates rivers in what is now Iraq. Mesopotamia was the birthplace of the world's earliest civilizations. The Sumerians established their city-states in southern Mesopotamia before 4000 B.C.E. The Babylonians took control of Mesopotamia in 1900 B.C.E. and were followed in turn by the Hittites, Assyrians, Chaldeans, and Persians. (See also ASSYRIA; BABYLON; FERTILE CRESCENT; PERSIA.)

MESSIAH   The name comes from the Hebrew word *mashiah*, meaning "anointed one." It refers to the expected savior of the Jews. Some of the prophets predicted a time when God's kingdom would be established on earth, and that the Messiah would appear at that point to bring peace and harmony to mankind.

The idea of the Messiah captured the imagination of the Jews.

Over the centuries many false Messiahs appeared. The most famous of these was Bar Kokhba, the leader of the 132-135 C.E. Jewish revolt against the Roman rule of Palestine. Even Rabbi Akiva (the most respected scholar of his time) believed that Bar Kokhba was the Messiah. Among the many other false Messiahs was Shabbetai Tzevi, who lived in Turkey in the 1600s. He had many followers in Palestine. (See also AKIVA BEN JOSEPH; BAR KOKHBA; JESUS; SIMEON; SHABBETAI TZEVI.)

METAPELET A woman who takes care of children on a kibbutz. Kibbutz children spend a few hours with their parents each afternoon. The rest of the time they live in a separate children's house with a group of children of their own age under the care of a *metapelet*. Until the children are old enough for school, their *metapelet* has complete charge of them. She—not the children's mothers—decides what they should eat, wear, etc. Later, she works together with the child's teacher. No *metapelet* is allowed to have her own child in her group. (See also KIBBUTZ.)

METMAN-KOHEN, YEHUDA LEIB (1869-1939) Educator who left Russia in 1904 to settle in Palestine, founded Herzlia High School, and taught there for 30 years. Metman-Kohen was also a founder of Ramat Gan where he set up the town's first elementary and high schools. (See also EDUCATION; HERZLIA HIGH SCHOOL; RAMAT GAN.)

METRIC SYSTEM System of measurement used in Israel and in almost all countries of the world, except the United States. The metric system is a decimal system, meaning that it works in multiples of ten. The basic measure of length is the meter, which is a little longer than a yard. A centimeter is 1/100 of a meter. A kilometer equals 1,000 meters, and is the measure used for road distances. The basic measure of weight is the gram. A kilogram (1,000 grams) is 2.2 pounds. The basic liquid measurement is the liter, which is a little more than a quart. (See also DUNAM; KILOGRAM; KILOMETER; LITER.)

METULLA Northernmost settlement in Israel, located in the hills of Galilee near the Lebanon border. Metulla was founded in 1896 with help from Baron Edmond de Rothschild. Today it is a farming village and a summer resort. (See also GALILEE; LEBANON; ROTHSCHILD, EDMOND DE.)

MIFAL HAPAYIS see ISRAEL LOTTERY

MIGDAL (also called MAGDALA) Farming village next to Lake Kinneret named for the nearby ancient site of Migdal. The village was founded by Russian Zionists in 1910 and part of its land was taken over for farming by British Jews in 1924. Today bananas, dates, and other tropical fruits are grown in Migdal. (See also LAKE KINNERET; MAGDALA.)

MIKVEH ISRAEL   Agricultural school founded near what is now Tel Aviv by Charles Netter in 1870, before there were any Jewish agricultural settlements in Palestine. Its purpose was to attract Jews to work the land. Mikveh Israel was the first agricultural school in Palestine and the only one for over 50 years. It has trained thousands of Jews in farming methods and has encouraged a great deal of agricultural research. In 1956 Mikveh Israel became a government school. Today it is a research center with botanical gardens and an agricultural museum as well as a school. (See also AGRICULTURAL RESEARCH; AGRICULTURAL SCHOOLS; NETTER, CHARLES.)

MILITARY CEMETERY   see MOUNT HERZL

MINERALS   Most of the minerals produced in Israel come from the Negev Desert or are extracted from the waters of the Dead Sea. Copper is the only metal found in sufficient amounts to be used commercially. It is mined at Timna near the site of King Solomon's ancient copper mines. Rich deposits of phosphates— used in making fertilizers for agriculture—are found in the rocks of the Negev. Clay and sand from the Negev are used in the manufacture of glass, pottery, and other ceramics. The Dead Sea Works refine the potash and bromine found in the waters of the Dead Sea and market them for use in agriculture and industry. (See also COPPER; DEAD SEA; DEAD SEA WORKS; KING SOLOMON'S MINES; NEGEV; OIL; PHOSPHATES; POTASH.)

MINTZ, BINYAMIN   (1903-1961)   Politician and writer who helped found Poale Agudat Israel (a religious labor organization) in his native Poland before settling in Palestine in 1925. Mintz was a member of the Israeli Knesset (legislature) and served as Deputy Speaker and as Minister of Posts. (See also KNESSET; POALE AGUDAT ISRAEL.)

MISHMAR   Hebrew word meaning "watch." It is part of a number of place-names in Israel.

MISHMAR HA-EMEK   Kibbutz founded in the Jezreel Valley in 1926 by immigrants from Poland. Mishmar Ha-Emek was attacked by Arabs in the riots of 1929 and 1936. In 1948, it fought off an Arab army during the War of Independence. (See also ARAB RIOTS; JEZREEL VALLEY; KIBBUTZ; WAR OF INDEPENDENCE.)

MISHMAR HAYARDEN   Village in upper Galilee founded in 1890 with help from Baron Edmond de Rothschild. Mishmar

Hayarden was destroyed by the Syrians during the 1948 War of Independence. After the war, two new settlements were built on its land, and a monument was raised to honor those who had died defending the village. (See also ROTHSCHILD, EDMOND DE; WAR OF INDEPENDENCE.)

MISHNA The first part of the Talmud. The Mishna is made up of the teachings of Jewish scholars and sages. These teachings were gathered together in 220 C.E. by Judah the Prince and his co-editor, Nathan. About 150 years later the Mishna was recorded in its present form along with the Gemara (a commentary on the Mishna). (See also ORAL LAW; TALMUD.)

MITLA PASS Place in the Sinai peninsula about 40 miles from the southern end of the Suez Canal. Israeli paratroopers were dropped there (well behind the Egyptian lines) at the beginning of the 1956 Sinai War. (See also SINAI; SINAI WAR; SUEZ CANAL.)

MITZ The Hebrew word for juice. The name of a citrus drink that is as popular in Israel as cola is in the United States. (See also GAZOZ STANDS.)

MIZRAHI World religious Zionist organization founded in 1901. Its aim was to establish a Jewish nation in Palestine in accordance with the Torah (religious law). Mizrahi is the largest of the religious movements in Israel. It has a moderate Orthodox point of view that tries to interpret religious law in the light of modern conditions.

As a community organization, Mizrahi has built a network of religious schools that includes kindergartens, elementary, vocational, and high schools, as well as Bar-Ilan University. It has established more than 72 agricultural settlements and has helped build synagogues and religious youth centers throughout Israel.

In 1956 the Mizrahi political party joined with Hapoel Hamizrahi (its labor organization) to form the National Religious Party, which has won about 10% of the seats in the Israeli Knesset (legislature) in every election since that year. (See also BAR-ILAN UNIVERSITY; EDUCATION; KNESSET; MIZRAHI WOMEN; NATIONAL RELIGIOUS PARTY; POLITICAL PARTIES; TORAH; ZIONISM.)

MIZRAHI WOMEN Organization of Orthodox Zionist women that is part of the Mizrahi World Organization. The Mizrahi Women's Organization of America was founded in 1925 by Batya (Bessie) Gotsfeld. It has established a number of child-care centers, schools, and community centers in Israel. These include vocational high schools for girls in Jerusalem and Tel Aviv, the Haifa Community Center, and the Kefar Batya children's village. (See also EDUCATION; MIZRAHI; YOUTH VILLAGES.)

MOAB   Ancient country in what is now Jordan. The Moabites were a Semitic people who spoke a language much like biblical Hebrew. King David conquered Moab in about 950 B.C.E. It remained subject to the kingdom of Israel until it revolted against Jehoram, king of Israel, 100 years later. Moab was again conquered by the Jews during the rule of the Hasmoneans (a line of rulers, 150-63 B.C.E.). (See also DAVID; HASMONEANS; ISRAEL, KINGDOM OF; JEHORAM.)

MODIIN   (also spelled MODIIM)   Ancient town located between Jerusalem and Tel Aviv where the 167 B.C.E. revolt of the Maccabees against the Syrian rule of Palestine began. Tombs cut in the rocks near Modiin are said to be the graves of the Maccabees. Each year at Hanukkah relay runners carry a burning torch from Jerusalem to the tombs. A frontier farming settlement was established at Modiin by members of Nahal (a military pioneer organization) in 1964. (See also HANUKKAH; MACCABEES; NAHAL.)

MOETZET HAPOALOT (English, WORKING WOMEN'S COUNCIL) (also called NAAMAT)   Council elected by female members of Histadrut (federation of labor) to protect the rights and fulfill the needs of the working women of Israel. Moetzet Hapoalot helps women get better jobs, provides women with agricultural and vocational training, and runs day-care centers, camps, and clubs for children. (See also HISTADRUT.)

MOHAMMED (also spelled MUHAMMAD) (about 570-632 C.E.) Arab prophet and founder of Islam. The followers of the Islamic religion (called Moslems) believe that Allah is the only God and that Mohammed is His prophet.

   Mohammed was born in Mecca in Arabia. He was a shepherd and then a merchant. At the age of 40 he had a vision which commanded him to preach. His teachings that Allah is the one God and that man will be judged by God are contained in the *Koran*, the Moslem holy book. Mohammed was persecuted and in 622 A.D. fled from Mecca to Medina where he founded a religious state, built the first mosque, and began the observance of the holy month of Ramadan. Moslems see this flight (called the *hegira*) as the beginning of their religion, and they date their calendar from it. (See also CALENDAR, MOSLEM; MOSLEMS, ISRAELI; RAMADAN.)

MOHAMMED, BIRTHDAY OF   Holiday celebrated by the Moslems of Israel as a day of feasting to mark the birth of the prophet of their religion. (See also HOLIDAYS; MOHAMMED; MOSLEMS.)

MOHAREM, FIRST OF   The first day of the Moslem new year.

The day is observed by Israel's Moslems with special prayer services at noon. (See also CALENDAR, INTERNATIONAL; CALENDAR, MOSLEM.)

MOKADY, MOSHE (1920-) Austrian-born artist who studied in Paris before settling in Palestine in 1932. Mokady's abstract paintings have been shown throughout the world. He has also painted stage sets for Habimah and other Israeli theaters. (See also HABIMAH.)

MOKED see MAKI

MONASTERY OF THE CROSS Greek Orthodox monastery near Jerusalem built on the place where it is believed that the wood for Christ's cross was cut.

MONEY see ISRAELI POUND

MONTEFIORE, SIR MOSES M. (1784-1885) English philanthropist who earned a great deal of money and retired at age 40. He devoted his life to helping his fellow Jews and gave large amounts of money to help individuals and Jews the world over. He visited Palestine seven times, the last time when he was 90 years old. In 1857 he provided the funds to build the famous section of Jerusalem called Yemin Moshe, which was named after him (Moshe is Hebrew for Moses).

The famous windmill in Jerusalem built in 1857 with funds provided by Sir Moses (Moshe) Montefiore, the English philanthropist. Three years later the first row of houses was built near the windmill. This section of Jerusalem is called Yemin Moshe.

MONTFORT (also called STARKENBERG) Crusader castle built in the early 1200s C.E. on a high hill northwest of Acre. The castle was the headquarters of the Teutonic (German) Knights until it was conquered by the Mamelukes in 1271. Although ruined by time and an earthquake, the remains of Montfort are still impressive. (See also CRUSADES; MAMELUKES.)

MOREH, PLAIN OF Ancient Israelite holy place in Samaria. Moreh is the place where God promised Abraham the land of Canaan. (See also ABRAHAM; SAMARIA.)

MOSAD Israel's secret service bureau, the equivalent of the American Central Intelligence Agency (CIA).

MOSAD BIALIK see BIALIK FOUNDATION

MOSAD HARAV KOOK see RABBI KOOK FOUNDATION

MOSAIC OF THE BIRDS see ARMENIAN MOSAIC

MOSAICS Picture or design made up of small pieces of glass, stone, or tile fitted together to form a pattern. Mosaics were often used in Byzantine architecture. The most complete ancient mosaic floor in Israel was found in a sixth century C.E. synagogue at Bet Alpha. (See also BET ALPHA; BYZANTINE EMPIRE.)

MOSENSOHN, YIGAL (1920-   ) Author who has written stories, novels, and plays for adults as well as a popular series of children's stories called *Hasamba*.

MOSES (fourteenth to thirteenth centuries B.C.E.) Liberator and lawgiver of the Jewish people. Moses was born in Egypt while the Israelites were enslaved there. The Pharoah of Egypt ordered all Israelite male babies killed, so Moses' mother hid him in a basket on the bank of the Nile River. There, he was found and brought up by the Pharoah's daughter. As a young man, Moses killed an Egyptian he found beating a Jewish slave. He was forced to flee and became a shepherd. As he watched his flocks, God appeared to him and told him to return to Egypt and lead the Jews out of slavery.

At first the Pharoah refused to let the Jews go, but after ten plagues were visited upon Egypt, he agreed. Then he changed his mind and sent an army after them. Moses led the Israelites safely across the Red Sea (which scholars think was really the Reed Sea in northwestern Sinai), but the Egyptian army pursuing them was drowned. The event is celebrated each year during the Passover holiday.

A bas relief from the menorah at the entrance to the Knesset depicts the arms of Moses being supported as the Israelites engage the Amalekites in battle.

When the Israelites came to Mount Sinai, Moses went to the top of the mountain, where God gave him the Ten Commandments. These became the foundation upon which all Jewish law would be based. Moses remained the Israelites' leader during the 40 years of wandering through the desert. Just before the Israelites entered the land of Canaan (Palestine), Moses died. The biblical books of Exodus, Leviticus, Numbers, and Deuteronomy describe the life of Moses, the laws that he taught, and the history of the Jews under his leadership. (See also BIBLE; EGYPT; JABEL MUSA; PASSOVER; TEN COMMANDMENTS.)

MOSES BEN MAIMON   see MAIMONIDES

MOSES BEN NAHMAN   see NAHMANIDES

MOSES, SIEGFRIED (1887-   )   German lawyer and businessman who settled in Palestine in 1937 and became Israel's first State Comptroller (overseer of government finances). Moses was also a founder of the Progressive political party. (See also PROGRESSIVE PARTY; STATE COMPTROLLER.)

MOSHAV (the plural is MOSHAVIM)   A demi-cooperative farming village. There are two kinds of moshavim. A family in a *moshav ovedim* (usually just called a moshav) holds the lease to its own farmland and the family lives together in a house that it owns. However, the farmers of the moshav cooperate in buying tools, and they usually own heavy equipment, like tractors or milking machines, in common. They also sell their crops as a group. Buildings like cultural centers are owned by the community. The general assembly of the moshav—elected by all the members—must approve all new members or transfers of farms.

The *moshav shitufi* is halfway between a moshav ovedim and a kibbutz. Land is leased and houses are owned in common (as on a kibbutz), but each family lives in a separate house and brings up its own children (as on a moshav). Profits from the sale of crops or from manufactured goods are usually divided among the families in the form of monthly money allowances. This differs from the kibbutz method where food and clothing is supplied to its members, rather than money.

Today more Israelis live on moshavim than in kibbutzim. In 1978 about 135,000 people (4% of Israel's population) lived and worked on 350 moshavim and 28 moshavim shitufiyim. (See also KIBBUTZ; LAND OWNERSHIP.)

MOSHAV OVEDIM   see MOSHAV

MOSHAV SHITUFI   see MOSHAV

MOSHAVA (the plural is MOSHAVOT)   The kind of farming village founded in Palestine in the late 1800s. Farmers leased their own land, bought their own tools, and sold their own crops. There are very few moshavot in Israel today. Many of the original moshavot have become towns, and later farming villages were organized as cooperative moshavim or kibbutzim. (See also MOSHAV; KIBBUTZ.)

MOSLEMS, ISRAELI Most of Israel's Arab population is Moslem, although there is a fairly large group of Christian Arabs. Moslem religious services are held regularly in about 90 mosques throughout the country. The most important mosques are El Aqsa and the Dome of the Rock, in Jerusalem, and El Jazzar, in Acre. Each Friday (the Moslem Sabbath) prayers from some of these mosques are broadcast over Israeli radio. The more than 200 Moslem clergy are paid by the state, as are the members of the Sharia (Moslem religious courts that rule on matters such as marriage and divorce). Moslems, like all religious groups in Israel, have their holy days and days of rest protected by law. (See also BROADCASTING; COURTS, RELIGIOUS; DOME OF THE ROCK; EL AQSA MOSQUE; HOLIDAYS; MOHAMMED; RELIGION.)

MOSLEM QUARTER Northeastern section of the Old City of Jerusalem. Herod's Gate leads into the Moslem Quarter. (See also HEROD'S GATE; JERUSALEM.)

MOSSINSOHN, BEN-ZION (1878-1942) Educator who was born in Russia and studied in Switzerland before he settled in Palestine in 1907. Mossinsohn was the principal of Herzlia High School for more than 25 years, and built it into Palestine's outstanding Hebrew high school. (See also HERZLIA HIGH SCHOOL.)

MOTZA (also spelled MOZA) Biblical town near Jerusalem that became a Roman army camp in the first century C.E. In 1933 a modern farming village was founded near the ancient site. (See also ROME.)

MOUNT CANAAN The 3,250-foot-high mountain near Safed in upper Galilee. Mount Canaan is a popular summer resort. (See also GALILEE.)

MOUNT CARMEL A mountain range between the Mediterranean Sea and the Haifa Plain that reaches a height of 1,790 feet. The city of Haifa is built part-way up the mountain slopes. The confrontation between prophet Elijah and the priest of Baal took place on Mount Carmel. The cave where Elijah hid from King Ahab was also in that mountain. The remains of Stone Age men have been found in other Carmel caves. (See also CARMEL CAVES; CAVE OF ELIJAH; ELIJAH; HAIFA.)

MOUNT GERIZIM A 2,900-foot-high mountain in Samaria. Mount Gerizim is sacred to the Samaritans, an ancient religious

The fenced in area is sacred to the Samaritans. Located on the top of Mount Gerizim, it is believed to be the site of Isaac's sacrifice. Jews believe the actual site to be on the Temple Mount.

The Samaritans believe that the Temple of Solomon was once built on this rocky surface atop Mount Gerizim, on the outskirts of Nablus (the biblical Shechem).

sect that still has about 500 members living in Israel. (See also SAMARIA; SAMARITANS.)

MOUNT GILBOA   Part of the Samarian mountains in northern Israel that rises to 1,700 feet above sea level. Mount Gilboa is the place where King Saul and his three sons were killed in a battle against the Philistines. (See also PHILISTINES; SAMARIA; SAUL.)

MOUNT HERZL   Hill west of Jerusalem where Theodor Herzl, the father of modern Zionism, is buried. It is the site of the Herzl Museum and Archives, which contain Zionist documents and a photograph of Herzl's study in Vienna. A military cemetery is on the north slope of Mount Herzl. (See also HERZL, THEODOR; ZIONISM.)

MOUNT MORIAH   Hill in the southeast corner of the Old City of Jerusalem. It was here that God tested Abraham by commanding him to kill his son Isaac. The Temple of Solomon was built on the spot fourteen generations later. Mount Moriah is now the site of the Dome of the Rock, a Moslem mosque. (See also ABRAHAM; DOME OF THE ROCK; TEMPLE.)

MOUNT OF BEATITUDES   Mountain northwest of Lake Kinneret that is holy to Christians as the scene of Christ's Sermon on the Mount. A church marks the place where the sermon was preached.

MOUNT OF OLIVES (also called OLIVET; Hebrew name, HAR HAMISHHA)   Hill in East Jerusalem. It was a Jewish place of worship during King David's reign (tenth century B.C.E.), and some of the tombs in the Jewish cemetery on the slope of the mountain date back almost that far. The Mount of Olives is holy to Christians as the place where Christ ascended to heaven. Among the Christian churches on the Mount are Dominus Flavit—said to be built on the site where Christ wept for Jerusalem—and the onion-domed Mary Magdalene Church. The Garden of Gethsemane, where Christ was arrested, is at the foot of the Mount of Olives. (See also JERUSALEM.)

MOUNT SCOPUS   Mountain in northeast Jerusalem that is the site of the original buildings of the Hebrew University and the Hadassah hospital. These buildings could not be used from 1948 to 1967 because Mount Scopus was in a United Nations supervised neutral zone between Israel and Jordan. After the 1967 Six-Day War, Mount Scopus became part of a united Jerusalem, under the control of Israel. (See also HADASSAH; HEBREW UNIVERSITY; JERUSALEM; UNITED NATIONS.)

MOUNT SINAI   see JABEL MUSA

MOUNT TABOR   Mountain in lower Galilee, about five miles

Entrance to the national military cemetery located on the northern
slope of Mount Herzl, in Jerusalem.

A typical gravesite in the well-kept national military cemetery on
Mount Herzl, in Jerusalem.

A familiar sight on the Mount of Olives is the Russian Church of Magdalene, built in honor of Czar Alexander III. It is easily recognizable by its onion shaped spires.

The Jewish cemetery at the base of the Mount of Olives (foreground) was destroyed and desecrated while in the hands of the Jordanians between 1948 and 1967.

Tombstones from Jewish graves on the Mount of Olives cemetery
were used by Jordanians as a walkway leading to a lavatory.
Tombstones were also used to build the walls of the Arab Legion
barracks on the Jericho road.

from Nazareth. Mount Tabor, where Deborah and Barak gathered the Israelite armies to fight the Canaanites, is holy to Christians as the site of Christ's Transfiguration. The modern Church of the Transfiguration was built on the remains of a sixth century C.E. Byzantine church. (See also DEBORAH; GALILEE.)

MOUNT ZION Hill just outside the south wall of the Old City of Jerusalem. Mount Zion is one of the hills on which King David built his capital at Jerusalem, and many people believe that he is buried there. The Dormition Monastery and the Cenacle (room of Christ's Last Supper) are also on Mount Zion. (See also DAVID; DORMITION MONASTERY; JERUSALEM.)

MUGHRABINS, GATE OF   see GATE OF THE MUGHRABINS

MUNICH MASSACRE In September of 1972, during the twentieth Olympic Games in Munich, Germany, Arab terrorists of the Black September group invaded the Israeli dormitory. The terrorists killed two athletes and took other athletes and coaches hostage. Nine of the hostages were killed two days later. Israel withdrew from the Olympics and the whole country mourned the dead. (See also OLYMPIC GAMES; TERRORISM.)

MURABAAT Site of four caves near the Dead Sea in Jordan that were the headquarters of a Jewish military commander during the 132-135 C.E. Bar Kokhba revolt against Rome. In 1952 archaeologists found ancient manuscripts in the cave, including letters to and from Bar Kokhba. (See also ARCHAEOLOGY; BAR KOKHBA, SIMEON; HISTORY; ROME.)

MUSEUM OF THE DIASPORA   see JEWISH DIASPORA MUSEUM

MUSIC Israelis are music lovers. Concerts are crowded and many people listen to classical and popular music on the radio. The Israel Philharmonic Orchestra, founded in 1936, is world famous. It gives about 180 concerts a year—performing in the Mann Auditorium in Tel Aviv, touring Israel, and making trips to other countries. Other important musical companies are the Israel Chamber Orchestra and the Israel National Opera. There are also orchestras in Haifa, Ramat Gan, and in a number of smaller cities, towns, and kibbutzim. The Jerusalem Symphony Orchestra, which plays on Israeli radio, often performs music written by Israeli composers. Every summer the Israel Festival presents concerts by native and foreign musicians, and the Ein Gev Music Festival is held each year during the Passover week.

Israeli orchestras give special concerts for school children. Children are taught music in most Israeli elementary schools and there are about 130 school orchestras and 400 school choirs in the country. The leading music schools for older students are the

Rubin Academies of Music, in Jerusalem and in Tel Aviv. Two colleges train music teachers. (See also DANCE; EDUCATION; EIN GEV; ISRAEL CHAMBER ORCHESTRA; ISRAEL FESTIVAL; ISRAEL NATIONAL OPERA; ISRAEL PHILHARMONIC ORCHESTRA; KOL ISRAEL; THEATER.)

MYSTICISM   see KABBALAH

N

NAAMAT   see MOETZET HAPOALOT

NABATEANS   A pagan Semitic people who had a kingdom in the Near East between the fourth century B.C.E. and the first century C.E. They built a chain of trade posts across the Negev and grew food crops in the desert by using every available drop of water. Modern Israeli scientists are studying the ancient Nabatean irrigation system to learn more about farming the Negev. (See also ADVAT; IRRIGATION; NEGEV.)

NABLUS (also called SHECHEM)   Shechem was an ancient Canaanite town near Mount Gerizim in Samaria. In 72 C.E. the Romans built a town there called Neapolis, from which comes the modern name of Nablus. Although today Nablus is mainly populated by Moslems, the city is also the home of most of Israel's Samaritans (a small religious sect). The Samaritans celebrate their holy days on nearby Mount Gerizim. (See also MOUNT GERIZIM; SAMARIA; SAMARITANS.)

NADAB   King of Israel 913-911 B.C.E.   Nadab was killed by his rival, Baasha, who then took the throne. (See also BAASHA; ISRAEL, KINGDOM OF.)

NAHAL   Pioneer Fighting Youth. As part of their national military service, young people can volunteer for Nahal. After a few months of army training, they live and work in a desert or frontier village and learn to farm while still in the army. Sometimes they establish new settlements (also called a Nahal). These settlements are usually at dangerous border points. The young settlers act as both soldiers and as farmers. There are several Nahal settlements in the Golan Heights. (See also DEFENSE FORCES; GOLAN HEIGHTS; NATIONAL SERVICE.)

NAHALAL   First moshav in Palestine. It was founded in 1921 by a group of settlers from the kibbutz Degania. Nahalal was built in a swampy area of the Jezreel Valley, which was drained by the settlers. The village was laid out in a circle around a group of communal buildings—a town plan that was later used as a model for other settlements. An agricultural training farm was also

The approach to Nablus (the biblical Shechem), on the West bank of Israel. The Old City and bazaar are below. The new city is set in the hills.

established at Nahalal. (See also AGRICULTURAL SCHOOLS; DE-GANIA; JEZREEL VALLEY; MOSHAV.)

NAHARIYA A resort town on Israel's Mediterranean coast. Founded as an agricultural village by immigrants from Germany in 1934, archaeologists have found a number of Bronze Age remains nearby, including a High Place of worship. (See also ARCHAEOLOGY; BRONZE AGE; HIGH PLACE.)

NAHLAT YEHUDA Farming village in central Israel founded by Russian immigrants in 1914. Hanna Maisel-Shohat established a girls' training farm there in 1922. For all practical purposes Nahlat Yehuda has become part of the city of Rishon Le Zion, although it is still governed by its own local council. (See also MAISEL-SHOHAT, HANNA; RISHON LE ZION.)

NAHMANIDES (also called MOSES BEN NAHMAN and RAMBAN) (1194-1270 C.E.) Spanish rabbi who was one of the leading Jewish scholars of the Middle Ages. He is best known for his Bible commentary, which tries to show the deeper meaning of the Bible's laws and stories. When Nahmanides was forced to leave Spain, he went to Palestine, where he became the leader of the Jewish community in the city of Acre. In 1267 he made his way to Jerusalem, where he established his synagogue in the present Jewish Quarter. (See also ACRE; BIBLE.)

NAMIR, MORDECAI (name changed from NEMIROVSKY) (1897-) Russian-born politician who settled in Palestine in 1924. He was active in the Histadrut (federation of labor) and the Haganah (Jewish underground army). After Israel became a state, Namir was its Minister to the Soviet Union, served in the Knesset (legislature), and was later elected Mayor of Tel Aviv. (See also HAGANAH; HISTADRUT; KNESSET; TEL AVIV.)

NAPHTALI Sixth son of Jacob. His descendants, the tribe of Naphtali, received the land in the mountains and along the sea coast of Galilee when the Israelites conquered Canaan in the thirteenth century B.C.E. (See also CANAAN; GALILEE; TWELVE TRIBES.)

NAPHTALI, PERETZ (FRITZ) (1888-1961) Economist who was active in the Socialist Party and the Zionist movement in his native Germany before he settled in Palestine in 1933. Naphtali taught economics at the Haifa Technion and was later elected to the Israeli Knesset (legislature). He also served as Minister of Agriculture and Minister of State. (See also KNESSET; SOCIALISM; TECHNION; ZIONISM.)

NARDI, NAHUM (1901-) Russian-born composer who settled in Palestine in 1923 and wrote many songs based on Sephardic folk music. (See also SEPHARDIM.)

NARKISS, UZI (1925-) Soldier born and educated in Jerusalem. Narkiss joined the Palmah (striking force of the Jewish underground army) while still in his teens. He was an officer in the 1948 War of Independence and the 1956 Sinai War, and he commanded the troops that reunited Jerusalem in the 1967 Six-Day War. (See also PALMAH; SINAI WAR; SIX-DAY WAR; WAR OF INDEPENDENCE.)

NASI Hebrew word meaning "prince." Nasi was the title given to the President of the Sanhedrin (ancient Jewish court) and the religious and political leader of the Jewish people. (See also SANHEDRIN.)

NASSER, GAMAL ABDUL (1918-1970) President of Egypt from 1956 to 1970. Nasser tried to unite the Arab countries of the Middle East into a strong union and was the organizer of the short-lived United Arab Republic of Egypt, Syria, and Yemen. He was the spokesman for the anti-Israel feelings of the Arabs and the leader of many political moves against Israel. In 1967, his closing of the Straits of Tiran to Israeli shipping and his demand for the removal of the United Nations peacekeeping force from the Israeli-Egyptian border resulted in the Six-Day War. It was only after Nasser's death, in 1970, and the election of Anwar Sadat as Egypt's President that peace between Egypt and Israel became possible. (See also EGYPT; SADAT, ANWAR; SIX-DAY WAR.)

NATIONAL AND UNIVERSITY LIBRARY The National Library of Israel is located at the Hebrew University in Jerusalem. The library was started with a collection of Hebrew books sent to Jerusalem by Joseph Chazonovitz in 1895. Today it owns two million books, more than 7,000 manuscripts, and a large collection of rare Hebrew books printed before 1500. The library publishes a magazine about books called *Kiryat Sepher*. (See also CHAZONOVITZ, JOSEPH; HEBREW UNIVERSITY; KIRYAT SEPHER.)

NATIONAL COUNCIL see VAAD LEUMI

NATIONAL INSURANCE The Israeli National Insurance Act of 1954 set up a social insurance organization much like the American Social Security system. Israeli workers pay a small percent of their wages into the National Insurance Fund. The fund provides money for old-age pensions, support for widows and dependent children, payment for treatment of injuries received at work, maternity benefits, and monthly family allowances for children under the age of 18. (See also SOCIAL SERVICES.)

NATIONAL PARKS The Israeli National Parks Authority builds and takes care of parks in scenic or historic areas of Israel. A number of important archaeological sites are preserved in national parks. Among these are Masada, Megiddo, Caesarea, and Bet Shean. (See also ARCHAEOLOGY.)

NATIONAL RELIGIOUS PARTY Political party formed in 1956 by the union of Mizrahi and Hapoel Hamizrahi. The National Religious Party is more moderate in its views than Agudat Israel, Israel's other religious political party. (See also MIZRAHI; POLITICAL PARTIES.)

NATIONAL SERVICE Starting at age 18, all Jewish young men, and most young women, are drafted into the Defense Forces. Arabs are not drafted, but some volunteer. Men serve as soldiers for 30 months, and after leaving the armed forces remain in the Reserves until they are 55 years old. The Reserves train for several weeks each year and can be called up immediately in time of war.

Unmarried women are required to serve in the armed forces for 20 months. Orthodox religious women need not serve. Although women receive the same sort of training as men, they do not fight. They work as clerks or drivers and some women spend their military service as teachers of immigrants from backward countries. Women only remain in the Reserves until they marry.

Women as well as men serve in Israel's defense forces. Here, women soldiers are preparing their rifles before going out to the firing range.

The main purpose of military service is defense of the country, but it also trains young immigrants for their new lives in Israel. The armed forces gives courses in Hebrew, teaches its immigrant soldiers to read and write if necessary, and trains them for jobs. (See also CONSCRIPTION; DEFENSE FORCES.)

NATIONAL WATER CARRIER   Since 95% of all the water in Israel is in lakes and rivers in northern Israel, it is important to bring water for irrigation to the dry south. Walter Lowdermilk drew up an overall water plan for Palestine in 1939, but the erection of the National Water Carrier was not begun until 1953. It was completed in 1964. The National Water Carrier is a system of canals, tunnels, pumping stations, and large underground water pipes that carry water from Lake Kinneret (Sea of Galilee) in the north to the Negev in the south. Along the way it picks up underground water from Galilee and provides water for the farms of the southern Coastal Plain and the city of Tel Aviv. (See also COASTAL PLAIN; IRRIGATION; LAKE KINNERET; LOWDERMILK, WALTER; MEKOROT WATER COMPANY; NEGEV; TAHAL; WATER.)

NATORE KARTA (also spelled NETUREI KARTA)   An extremely religious group of several hundred Jews who live in the Mea Shearim section of Jerusalem. Natore Karta believes that only the Messiah can establish a Jewish State, and it therefore opposes the State of Israel, which was created by mortal man. Its members refuse to pay taxes, and they mourn and fast on Israeli Independence Day. (See also MEA SHEARIM; MESSIAH.)

NAVI, ELIAHU (1920-   )   Mayor of Beersheba. Navi was born in Iraq and educated in Israel. He served in the Israeli army and was a Justice of the Peace in the Negev before he was elected Mayor in 1963. (See also BEERSHEBA.)

NAVON, ITZHAK (1921-   )   Fifth President of Israel. A native Israeli, Navon studied at the Hebrew University and became a teacher. Later, he served in Israel's embassies in Argentina and Uruguay in South America and then became a member of the Israeli Knesset (legislature). He was also a director of the government Ministry of Education and Culture. In 1978, Navon was elected for a five-year term as Israel's President. (See also HEBREW UNIVERSITY; KNESSET; PRESIDENT.)

NAZARETH   Town in Galilee that was first settled around 2000 B.C.E. but is best known as the home of Jesus Christ. The first Christian church was built in Nazareth by the Roman emperor Constantine in the 300s C.E., and the Crusaders rebuilt the town and its churches in the 1200s. Today the people of Nazareth are mainly Christian Arabs. Thousands of other Christians come

ברוכים הבאים
לנצרת

الناصرة ترحب بزائريها

WELCOME
TO NAZARETH

Nazareth, predominantly Christian city located in the Galilee, is famous for its Church of the Annunciation, one of the most hallowed sites in Christendom.

from all over the world to visit the town each year. Among Nazareth's more than 20 churches is the Church of the Annunciation where the Angel Gabriel appeared to the Virgin Mary. Also found in Nazareth is an old synagogue where Jesus is said to have worshipped. (See also CHRISTIANS; CONSTANTINE; CRUSADES; GALILEE; JESUS; ROME.)

NAZIS (full name, NATIONAL SOCIALISTS) Political party that took control of Germany in 1933. When Nazi leader Adolph Hitler became dictator of Germany, all other political parties were outlawed. People who opposed the Nazis were put in concentration camps, where they were tortured and killed.

Under the Nazis, Jews were no longer considered German citizens. Their jobs, businesses, homes, and possessions were taken from them. Synagogues were burned and Jewish children were forbidden to go to school. Jews were beaten in the streets and rounded up and sent to concentration camps.

In 1939 Germany invaded Poland, starting World War II. By 1942 the German armies had occupied France, Belgium, the Netherlands, Denmark, Austria, Czechoslovakia, Hungary, Poland, Rumania, Greece, Bulgaria, and much of Russia. Wherever the Nazis went, they oppressed the people. Their treatment of the Jews of the occupied countries was particularly horrible. Jews were forced to wear a yellow Star of David. Then they were rounded up and shipped to concentration camps, where they were gassed to death and their bodies burned in ovens. This murder of six million Jewish men, women, and children is often called the Holocaust. (See also HITLER, ADOLPH; HOLOCAUST; MAGEN DAVID.)

NEBUCHADNEZZAR   King of Babylon who ruled 605 to 562 B.C.E. and conquered all the land from the Euphrates River to the border of Egypt, including the kingdom of Judah. When Judah revolted, Nebuchadnezzar replaced Judah's King Jehoiachin with Zedekiah. When Zedekiah revolted a few years later in 586 B.C.E., Nebuchadnezzar captured Jerusalem, destroyed the Temple, and sent the Jews into exile. (See also BABYLON; BABYLONIAN EXILE; EUPHRATES RIVER; HISTORY; JEHOIACHIN; JUDAH, KINGDOM OF; TEMPLE; ZEDEKIAH.)

NEGBA   Kibbutz founded on the southern Coastal Plain in 1939. During the 1948 War of Independence, the defenders of Negba helped stop the Arab armies' drive toward the north of Israel. The village was destroyed in the fighting, but was rebuilt soon after. (See also COASTAL PLAIN; KIBBUTZ; WAR OF INDEPENDENCE.)

NEGEV   The dry southern part of Israel. Since the Negev takes up nearly two-thirds of the country's area, great efforts are being made to develop it for settlement, agriculture, and industry.

The northern Negev is a rolling plain of loess soil that only needs irrigation to become fertile. Water brought down through

The Negev is generally dry, sandy desert, but some areas are beautiful, like this oasis in Ein Gedi, in the Judean Desert near the western shore of the Dead Sea (facing page). (Below) Wild camels roam the Negev in the vicinity of the Dead Sea.

the National Water Carrier has turned the northern Negev into heavily settled farmland. Beersheba, at the southeastern edge of the fertile area, is a fast-growing city.

Below Beersheba is the central Negev, where some of the land can be farmed, and below that is the southern Negev, with its landscape of mountains, rocks, and sand. The Araba is a deep valley stretching one hundred miles through the Negev from the Dead Sea to the Gulf of Eilat.

Most of Israel's minerals are found in the southern Negev. Phosphates are mined from the rock, and oil and natural gas are pumped out of underground deposits. Roads, railroad lines, and pipelines have recently been built through the southern Negev to connect the port of Eilat with Beersheba and cities further north. (See also ARABA; BEERSHEBA; EILAT; GEOGRAPHY; IRRIGATION; LOESS; MINERALS; NATIONAL WATER CARRIER; OIL; WATER.)

NEHEMIAH (fifth century B.C.E.)   Jewish governor of Judah who rebuilt Jerusalem after the Jews returned from the Babylonian Exile. Nehemiah joined Ezra in leading the Jews back to the observance of their religious laws. His work is described in the Book of Nehemiah which follows the Book of Ezra in the Bible. (See also BIBLE; BABYLONIAN EXILE; EZRA.)

NES AMMIM   Moshav (partly cooperative village) in Galilee, a

Pastor Simon Schoon, spiritual leader of the Christian Kibbutz Nes Ammim, which is located about three miles north of Acco.

few miles north of Acre. Nes Ammim was founded in 1964 by Christians who believe in improving relations between Christians and Jews by living and working in Israel. In 1980 the village had about a hundred settlers from Holland, Germany, Switzerland, and the United States. Nes Ammim grows roses for export in the biggest flower-producing hot houses in Israel. (See also CHRISTIANS; FLOWERS; GALILEE; MOSHAV.)

NES TZIYONA (also spelled NESS ZIYONA)   Town located about ten miles south of Tel Aviv. Nes Tziyona was founded in 1883 by a group of BILU pioneers from Russia who drained the swamps and planted citrus trees. Today the town has a number of factories as well as large citrus plantations. (See also BILU; CITRUS FRUIT.)

NETANYA (also spelled NATANYA and NETHANYAH)   City founded in 1929 on the Mediterranean coast halfway between Haifa and Tel Aviv. It was named for Nathan Straus, the American businessman who donated the money to establish its citrus groves. Today Netanya is a city of about 80,000 people and is the center of Israel's diamond industry. It is also a popular beach resort for foreign tourists and Israelis alike. (See also DIAMONDS; STRAUS, NATHAN; TOURISM.)

NETTER, CHARLES (1826-1882)   French businessman who was active in helping European Jews, particularly those fleeing the pogroms (massacres) in Russia. In 1870 Netter founded Mikveh Israel, the first agricultural school in Palestine. (See also MIKVEH ISRAEL.)

NETZER SERINI   Kibbutz founded in 1948 by survivors of the Nazi concentration camps in Europe. (See also KIBBUTZ.)

NEW COMMUNIST LIST   see RAKAH

NEW GATE (Hebrew, SHAAR HEHADASH)   One of the eight gates in the wall around the Old City of Jerusalem. The New Gate was built in 1889. Compared to the age of the other gates, it is "new." (See also JERUSALEM; WALLED CITIES.)

NEW YEAR FOR TREES (Hebrew, TU BI-SHEVAT)   Holiday that falls on the 15th of Shevat in the Jewish calendar (January or early February in the international calendar). In biblical times, Tu Bi-Shevat was the day Jewish farmers figured out how much of the fruit of their trees they owed as a religious contribution. In modern Israel, the New Year for Trees celebrates the return of the Jewish people to farming the land of Palestine. School children go on trips to plant small trees—particularly almond trees. The holiday is also called Arbor Day. (See also ALMOND; CALENDAR, INTERNATIONAL; CALENDAR, JEWISH; HOLIDAYS; REFORESTATION.)

NEWSPAPERS The first Hebrew newspaper in Palestine, *Havasselet,* was founded in 1863 and published weekly. In 1901 one of its writers, Eliezer Ben-Yehuda, established Palestine's first daily paper, *Ha-Or.* Today (1980) Israel has fourteen daily newspapers written in Hebrew and three Arabic dailies, as well as newspapers in ten other languages. The two leading Hebrew papers are *Davar,* which is the voice of the labor movement, and *Maariv,* an independent paper. *Omer* is a newspaper written in easy-to-read Hebrew for new immigrants. The best known of the foreign-language papers is the English-language *Jerusalem Post.* (See also BEN-YEHUDA, ELIEZER; DAVAR; JERUSALEM POST; MAARIV; OMER.)

NILI An acronym from the Hebrew biblical verse: "The strength [God] of Israel will not be denied." Jewish underground group in Palestine founded in 1915 (during World War I) to help the British capture the country from Turkey. Its leaders, Aaron Aaronson and Avshalom Feinberg, hoped to see a Jewish State established in Palestine after a British victory. NILI smuggled military information out of the country, brought in gold to pay for food for Palestine's starving Jews, and helped Jews escape being drafted into the Turkish army. In 1917 the Turks captured, tortured, jailed, or killed a number of NILI members, including Sarah Aaronson. (See also AARONSON, AARON; AARONSON, SARAH; FEINBERG, AVSHALOM; GREAT BRITAIN; HISTORY; TURKEY.)

NIR DAVID Kibbutz (cooperative farming village) founded in the Bet Shean Valley in 1936. Nir David was the first of Palestine's stockade and tower settlements. It was also among the first kibbutzim to raise fish in ponds. (See also BET SHEAN VALLEY; FISH PONDS; KIBBUTZ; STOCKADE AND TOWER.)

NIR ETZION Farming village on Mount Carmel. It was founded in 1950 by the survivors of Kefar Etzion, a village which was overrun by the Arabs during the 1948 War of Independence. (See also KEFAR ETZION; MOUNT CARMEL; WAR OF INDEPENDENCE.)

NIRIM Kibbutz founded in the western Negev in 1946. Nirim was destroyed by shells during the 1948 War of Independence, but the Jewish defenders fought off the attacking Arab army and survived. The village was rebuilt after the war. A sixth century C.E. mosaic synagogue floor found by farmers plowing a field near Nirim is now on display in the Israel Museum in Jerusalem. (See also ISRAEL MUSEUM; KIBBUTZ; MOSAICS; NEGEV; WAR OF INDEPENDENCE.)

NIR-RAFALKES, NAHUM YAAKOV (name changed from RAF-ALKES) (1884-1968) Lawyer who was a leader of the Poale Zion (a

Wall newspapers are common in Israel. They announce local events and urge action on a variety of issues.

Socialist Zionist organization) in his native Poland before he settled in Palestine in 1925. Nir-Rafalkes was a signer of the Israeli Declaration of Independence and served in the Knesset (legislature) for many years. (See also DECLARATION OF INDEPENDENCE; KNESSET; POALE ZION.)

NISSIM, YITZHAK RAHIMIM (1896-   ) Rabbi who was a religious leader of the Jews of his native Iraq before settling in Jerusalem in 1926. He was elected Sephardi Chief Rabbi of Israel in 1955, a post he held until 1972. (See also CHIEF RABBINATE.)

NOTRIM   Jewish police recruited by the British (who were then governing Palestine) for guard duty, during the 1936-1939 Arab riots. They protected the railroads and electric lines, defended Jewish settlements, and struck back at Arab terrorists. Although the Notrim were under the command of the British, most of them were also members of the Haganah (underground Jewish army), whose secret orders they followed. (See also ARAB RIOTS; HAGANAH.)

NOVOMEYSKY, MOSHE (1873-1961)   Russian-born chemist who settled in Palestine in 1920. In 1929 Novomeysky established the Palestine Potash Company (which later (1952) became the Dead Sea Works) to extract minerals from the waters of the Dead Sea. He was the director of the company until it was taken over by the Israeli government in 1952. (See also DEAD SEA WORKS.)

NUCLEAR ENERGY   Since Israel has no coal and little oil, there is great interest in atomic and nuclear energy research. An atomic reactor was built at Nahal Sorek in 1960 and a second reactor at Dimona in the Negev in 1964. Both of these reactors are for research rather than for producing energy. Research is conducted into the use of nuclear material in medicine and industry as well. Thus far (1980) the construction of nuclear plants to produce electricity has been too expensive, but a plant that can produce electricity while it desalinates (takes the salt from) sea water is to be built in the early 1980s in Ashdod. (See also DESALINIZATION; ELECTRICITY.)

NUROCK, MORDEKHAI (1884-1962)   Religious Zionist leader who was Chief Rabbi of Latvia and a member of the Latvian Parliament before settling in Palestine in 1947. Rabbi Nurock was elected to the Israeli Knesset (legislature) as a member of the Mizrahi political party and served until his death. In 1952 he was a candidate for President of Israel, but lost to Yitzhak Ben-Zvi. (See also BEN-ZVI, YITZHAK; KNESSET; MIZRAHI; PRESIDENT.)

O

OCCUPIED AREAS see ADMINISTERED AREAS

OFAKIM (also spelled OPHAKIM)   Town founded in 1955 in the northwest Negev. Ofakim was built as a market town and cultural center for the farms and farming villages around it. (See also DEVELOPMENT TOWNS; NEGEV.)

OIL   The Heletz oil fields south of Tel Aviv produce only a small part of the oil Israel needs to run its cars, heat its homes, and power its industries. Most of the crude oil that is made into gasoline, fuel oil, etc., at the Haifa and Ashdod oil refineries must be imported from other countries. Israel has a particular problem obtaining oil because most of the oil-producing countries of the Middle East are Israel's enemies. Until 1979 half of Israel's oil came from Iran, but after the revolution in Iran that supply of oil was cut off. From 1967 to 1979, Israel got oil from the Sinai oil

An Arab attendant at a Jerusalem service station. Paz is one of the larger distributors of petroleum in Israel.

fields which it captured in the Six-Day War. The 1979 Israel-Egypt Peace Treaty returned the Sinai fields to Egypt, but promised Israel the right to buy Sinai oil.(See also ASHDOD; HAIFA; HELETZ OIL FIELDS; ISRAEL-EGYPT PEACE TREATY; PERSIA; SINAI; SIX-DAY WAR.)

OLIM   Hebrew word meaning "immigrants." One immigrant is called an *oleh*. Israel is a land of olim. In the first twenty-five years of its existence, one and a half million immigrants poured into the country. (See also ALIYAH; IMMIGRANTS; YORDIM.)

OLIVES   Olive trees have been grown in Israel for their fruit and oil since biblical times. Many of the trees still growing are hundreds of years old. To mark Israel's tenth anniversary, a group of 80-year-old olive trees was transplanted to line the avenue leading into Jerusalem. (See also AGRICULTURE.)

OLIVES, MOUNT OF   see MOUNT OF OLIVES

OLSHAN, YITZHAK (1895-)   Lithuanian-born judge who went to Palestine as a student in 1912 and later became one of the founders of the Haganah (Jewish underground army). After working as a lawyer for many years, Olshan was appointed a judge of Israel's Supreme Court. In 1953 he was appointed Chief Justice and served for 12 years. (See also HAGANAH; JUDGES; SUPREME COURT.)

OLYMPIC GAMES   International games held every four years in a different country. In the summer, athletes come from all over the world to compete for medals in swimming, track and field events, gymnastics, and other sports. Separate winter games are held for skating, skiing, etc. The Olympics are patterned after ancient Greek games, and the first modern Olympics took place in Athens in 1896. Israel sent athletes to the games for the first time in 1952, when they were held in Helsinki, Finland. A great tragedy occurred at the 1972 Olympics in Munich, when eleven Israeli athletes were killed by Arab terrorists. (See also MUNICH MASSACRE; SPORTS.)

OMAR, MOSQUE OF   see DOME OF THE ROCK

OMER   Daily newspaper written in easy-to-read Hebrew for immigrants to Israel who are still learning the language. *Omer* was founded in 1951 by *Davar*, one of the country's leading newspapers. (See also DAVAR; NEWSPAPERS.)

OMER; OMER FESTIVAL   The first sheaf (bundle) of barley the farmers of ancient Israel harvested from their fields. The Omer was taken to the Temple in Jerusalem as a thanksgiving offering on the second day of Passover. Today many Israeli

Mrs. Natasha Sharansky, wife of Anatoly Sharansky who was imprisoned in Russia on April 20, 1977. Mrs. Sharansky, a new immigrant to Israel, protested all over the world to pressure Russia to allow her husband to join her in Israel.

A 2,000-year-old olive tree in front of Sarah Pearl's Hotel, in Safed.
James Michener wrote much of his book *The Sourfe* while staying
in this hotel.

kibbutzim hold an Omer festival with singing and dancing in the fields on the day before Passover.

Forty-nine days of the Omer are counted from the second day of Passover and a special prayer is said each day. The holiday of Shavuot is celebrated on the fiftieth day. (See also AGRICULTURE; HOLIDAYS; KIBBUTZ; LAG B'OMER; PASSOVER; SHAVUOT; TEMPLE.)

OMRI King of Israel who ruled 887-876 B.C.E. Omri was a general under King Elah until he took the throne by murdering the king. He was a strong ruler who conquered Moab, built the city of Samaria, and made Samaria the capital of Israel. The kingdom of Israel was known as the Land of Omri for more than a hundred years after his death. (See also ELAH; ISRAEL, KINGDOM OF; MOAB; SAMARIA.)

ONEG SHABBAT Gathering held late Saturday afternoon for discussions and lectures on Jewish culture. The Oneg Shabbat (which means "Sabbath delight") was introduced into Palestine in the 1920s by the poet Hayim Nahman Bialik. Each week Bialik would lead discussions on literature, language, or religions at the Herzlia High School auditorium in Tel Aviv. Afterward the audience would sing Jewish songs. The Oneg Shabbat lecture, followed by singing, is still popular in Israel. The name is also used to mean any social or cultural event or celebration during the Sabbath. (See also BIALIK, HAYIM NAHMAN; HERZLIA HIGH SCHOOL.)

OPERATION ALI BABA (also called OPERATION EZRA AND NEHEMIAH) Airlift that brought almost all of the 130,000 Jews of Iraq to Israel. Operation Ali Baba was begun by the Israeli government and the Jewish Agency in May 1950 and lasted until December 1951. At the peak of the airlift it was carrying a thousand Jews a day from Baghdad (Iraq's capital) to Israel. The immigrants were forced to leave everything they owned behind in Iraq. (See also ALIYAH; IMMIGRANTS; JEWISH AGENCY; ORIENTAL JEWS.)

OPERATION MAGIC CARPET Airlift that carried almost all of the 50,000 Jews of Yemen to Israel. The airlift, organized by the Israeli government and the Jewish Agency, was conducted from December 1948 to September 1950. The Yemenite Jews had been oppressed and forced to live a primitive lifestyle. Many of them had never even seen an automobile, yet they were not afraid to board the planes to Israel. The Bible told them, "They that wait upon the Lord . . . shall mount up with wings as eagles." (See also ALIYAH; BIBLE; IMMIGRANTS; JEWISH AGENCY; ORIENTAL JEWS.)

OR AKIVA Town founded on the Sharon Plain in 1951. It was

An airplane is loaded to capacity with Yemenite Jews flying to

named for Rabbi Akiva who was killed in nearby Caesarea in the second century C.E. (See also AKIVA BEN JOSEPH; SHARON PLAIN.)

ORAL LAW The Bible (the Torah) is called the Written Law. The Oral Law means the teachings that explained and interpreted the Written Law from about 450 B.C.E. to almost 500 C.E. These teachings were called Oral Law because for a long time it was forbidden to write them down; they had to be passed on by the spoken word. In the 300s C.E. the Oral Law was recorded in the Talmud. (See also BIBLE; TALMUD; TORAH.)

ORIENTAL JEWS The word "Oriental" is used to mean Jews who immigrated to Israel from the Middle East or North Africa. Most Oriental Jews came from Arab countries. Between 1949 and 1951 the entire Jewish populations of Yemen and Iraq were airlifted to Israel. By the late 1970s almost a quarter of Israel's population was composed of Jews, who had been born in Arab countries; another quarter were the Sabra (native-born) children of Oriental Jews.

Since most Oriental Jews came from poor or backward countries, they did not have the education or job skills of immigrants from Europe and America. Israel has worked hard to close the cultural and economic gap between its Oriental and European citizens. There are job training programs for Oriental Jews, who are often given preference in hiring for government jobs. Much government effort is devoted to the health and education of Oriental children. Families are encouraged to bring their children to the mother-and-child health-care centers and to enroll them in school early. Gradually, the gap between Oriental and European Jews is being narrowed. (See also ASHKENAZIM; EDUCATION; HEALTH; JEWS; OPERATION ALI BABA; OPERATION MAGIC CARPET; POPULATION; SEPHARDIM.)

OROT Farming village in central Israel founded in 1952 by immigrants from the United States.

ORT (initials of ORGANIZATION FOR REHABILITATION THROUGH TRAINING) Organization founded in Russia in 1880 to train Jews for jobs. Today ORT has schools and workshops in 30 countries throughout the world. ORT runs more than 70 vocational schools, factory schools, technical schools, colleges, and teachers' institutes in Israel. Among these are Tel Aviv's Syngalowsky Center—the largest technical school in the Middle East—and the new School of Engineering in Jerusalem. ORT trains about 30,000 students a year in Israel, about 40% of the country's job training for industry. (See also EDUCATION; SYNGALOWSKY CENTER.)

At the ORT school in Givatayim (part of greater Tel Aviv) pastry
making is one of the many trades taught.

The ORT school in Jerusalem, where electronics and computer
sciences are taught.

OT HASPORT see PHYSICAL FITNESS BADGE

OUZIEL, BEN ZION see UZIEL, BEN ZION

OZ, AMOS (1939-   )   Author who is considered one of Israel's

Amos Oz

most talented younger writers. Oz was born in Jerusalem and educated at the Hebrew University, where he later became author-in-residence. He has written collections of short stories, novels, and a children's book. Most of his work is set in Jerusalem, but he lives and works on a kibbutz. Oz's books have been translated into many languages, including English, French, and German. His novel *My Michael* has also been made into a film. (See also HEBREW UNIVERSITY; KIBBUTZ; LITERATURE.)

P-Q

PALESTINE   Area in the Middle East that includes the State of Israel. At different times in history the area was called the Land of Canaan, the Land of Israel, Palaestina (by the Romans), and Falastin (by the Turks). From 1918 to 1948 the name Palestine was used to describe the land governed by Great Britain under the League of Nations Mandate. (See also CANAAN; GEOGRAPHY; GREAT BRITAIN; HISTORY; ROME; TURKEY.)

PALESTINE CORNFLOWER   A purple flower that is a member of the thistle family. Palestine cornflowers grow in such numbers in Israel that they sometimes overrun whole fields. Degania, the first kibbutz in Palestine, took its name from the Hebrew word for the cornflowers that grew all around the settlement. (See also DEGANIA.)

PALESTINE   ECONOMIC   CORPORATION   Company founded in the United States in 1926 that invests money in banking, industry, and agriculture in Israel.

PALESTINE ELECTRIC COMPANY   Company founded by Pinhas Rutenberg in 1923 to produce electricity in Palestine. The Palestine Electric Company was taken over by the Israeli government in 1955, and its name was changed to the Israel Electric Company. (See also ELECTRICITY; RUTENBERG, PINHAS.)

PALESTINE FOUNDATION FUND see KEREN HAYESOD

PALESTINE   JEWISH   COLONIZATION   ASSOCIATION (PICA)   Organization that supervises the economic needs of the Palestinian farming villages originally funded by Baron Edmond de Rothschild. When the villages were first established, Baron de Rothschild oversaw them himself, but in 1900 the work was taken over by the Jewish Colonization Association (ICA) and in 1923 was transferred to PICA. PICA was dissolved in 1957. (See also JEWISH COLONIZATION ASSOCIATION; ROTHSCHILD, EDMOND DE.)

PALESTINE LAND DEVELOPMENT COMPANY see ISRAEL LAND DEVELOPMENT COMPANY

PALESTINE LIBERATION ORGANIZATION (P.L.O.) Organization of Palestinian Arab groups whose aim is to destroy Israel and to set up a Palestinian state in its place. The P.L.O. was formed during an Arab League conference in 1964, and the League treated it as the government-in-exile of Palestine. President Nasser of Egypt controlled the P.L.O. until 1969. Then Yasir Arafat—the head of the Al Fatah terrorist group—combined the two organizations and became chairman of the P.L.O.

In the early 1970s there were as many as a thousand small terrorist attacks a year on Israel's borders and border settlements. Many of these were carried out by the P.L.O. In 1974 the P.L.O. began to devote much of its time to political activity. Arafat appeared at the United Nations and won the General Assembly's support for Palestinian independence. Terrorist activity was stepped up again in 1977 when peace talks began between Egypt and Israel. Bombs went off in Jerusalem and in other Israeli cities. In March 1978, 37 Israeli civilians were killed and 87 more wounded in the Al Fatah attack on a bus near Tel Aviv.

As Israel and Egypt began discussing the problem of the Palestinian Arabs in 1979, the P.L.O. continued to claim to represent the Palestinian people. Israel and the United States have refused to deal with the P.L.O. until it recognizes Israel's right to exist. However, some European leaders feel that the organization is a power in the Middle East that cannot be ignored. (See also AL FATAH; ARAB LEAGUE; ARAFAT, YASIR; NASSER, GAMAL ABDUL; ISRAEL-EGYPT PEACE TREATY; PALESTINIANS; TERRORISM; UNITED NATIONS.)

PALESTINE OFFICE Organization set up by the World Zionist Organization in Jaffa in 1908 with Arthur Ruppin as director. The Palestine Office provided money for settlements, organized a Hebrew school system, and generally helped the Jews of Palestine. In 1918 its work was taken over by the Zionist Commission. (See also RUPPIN, ARTHUR; WORLD ZIONIST ORGANIZATION; ZIONIST COMMISSION.)

PALESTINE SYMPHONY ORCHESTRA see ISRAEL PHILHARMONIC ORCHESTRA

PALESTINIAN REFUGEES Arabs who fled their homes when Israel became a Jewish State in 1948. Many thousands of these refugees and their children settled in refugee camps in Jordan, Syria, and Lebanon. Most of the Arab *fedayeen* (terrorists) who attack Israel have been recruited from the refugee camps. The fate of the Palestinian refugees has been a serious political issue. (See also FEDAYEEN; PALESTINIANS; TERRORISM.)

A boy carries home a chicken along the drab road of a refugee camp in Jericho.

A common form of transportation in the Arab refugee camp in Jericho along the West Bank of Israel.

PALESTINIANS   Name used to refer to the Arabs living in the land occupied by Israel in the 1967 Six-Day War (administered areas) as well as to the Arab refugees living in Jordan, Syria, and Lebanon. There are about three million Palestinians who claim that the land of Israel belongs to them. They demand a Palestinian state and have backed up their demand with terrorist attacks on Israel.

The Israel-Egypt Peace Treaty took the first steps toward solving the problem of the Palestinians. Israel promised Palestinian self-rule in the West Bank and Gaza Strip (two of the administered areas) and a pull-out of Israeli troops from this area after self-rule is working. However, many difficult problems remained unsolved. These include the fate of the Palestinian refugees in Arab countries and the terrorist activities of the Palestine Liberation Organization and other Palestinian groups. (See also ADMINISTERED AREAS; ISRAEL-EGYPT PEACE TREATY; PALESTINE LIBERATION ORGANIZATION; PALESTINIAN REFUGEES; TERRORISM.)

PALM SUNDAY Holiday celebrated in Christian churches throughout Israel on the Sunday before Easter. One of the processions carries palm branches to St. Ann's Church in the Old City of Jerusalem. The holiday marks Christ's entry into Jerusalem. (See also CHRISTIANS; EASTER; HOLIDAYS.)

PALMAH (full name PELUGOT MAHATZ) The striking force of the Haganah (Jewish underground army), organized in 1941. Its name means "shock companies." Although Palmah was formed during World War II to help the British resist a possible German invasion of Palestine, after the war it fought to free Palestine from British rule. The Palmah was also active in smuggling "illegal" immigrants into the country.

This underground army was organized into 11 companies of young men and women who lived in agricultural villages and divided their time between farming and training. There was also a naval unit, called Palyam, which later became the core of the Israeli navy. During the 1948 War of Independence, the 5,000 members of Palmah were in the thick of the fighting and almost one-fifth of them were killed. After the war, Palmah was absorbed into the Israel Defense Forces. (See also DEFENSE FORCES; GREAT BRITAIN; HAGANAH; HISTORY; IMMIGRANTS, ILLEGAL; WAR OF INDEPENDENCE.)

PANN, ABEL (name changed from PFEFFERMAN) (1883-1963) Russian-born painter who studied in Paris before settling in Palestine in 1925 and becoming one of the first teachers at the Bezalel School of Arts and Crafts. Pann painted pictures of Bible stories and of Oriental Jews in Israel. (See also BEZALEL SCHOOL OF ARTS AND CRAFTS; ORIENTAL JEWS.)

PARDES HANNA Town founded on the Sharon Plain in 1929 by the Palestine Jewish Colonization Association. Its economy is based on growing and selling citrus fruit. The town has a religious high school and an agricultural high school. In 1969 the village of Karkur became part of Pardes Hanna. (See also CITRUS FRUIT; KARKUR; PALESTINE JEWISH COLONIZATION ASSOCIATION; SHARON PLAIN.)

PARLIAMENT   A group of representatives of the people who make the laws in a democratic country. Another word for "parliament" is "legislature." In Israel the legislature is sometimes referred to as the Parliament, but is more often called the Knesset. (See also DEMOCRACY; GOVERNMENT; KNESSET.)

PARTITION   The word means "division" or "separation." The idea of the partition of Palestine into separate Jewish and Arab states had been suggested as early as 1902 by the Zionist Theodor Herzl. However, it was not seriously considered until 1937 when the Peel Commission (appointed by the ruling British to study possible changes in the government of Palestine) suggested dividing Palestine into independent Jewish and Arab states with an area remaining under British rule. The World Zionist Organization then rejected the idea.

In 1947 the United Nations partition plan drew the borders for the Jewish State of Israel and for a new Arab State in Palestine. The neighboring Arab nations refused to accept the plan and invaded Israel. At the end of the fighting, Israel's borders were different from those proposed by the United Nations plan and the land that had been meant for a new Arab State was occupied by Jordan and Egypt. (See also EGYPT; GREAT BRITAIN; HERZL, THEODOR; JORDAN; PALESTINE; PEEL COMMISSION; UNITED NATIONS; WAR OF INDEPENDENCE; WORLD ZIONIST ORGANIZATION.)

PARTOS, ODON (1919-   )   Composer and musician who was born in Hungary and settled in Tel Aviv in 1938. Partos became the lead violist in the Israel Philharmonic Orchestra and the director of the Israel Academy of Music. He composed music that combined Near Eastern melodies with Western musical techniques. In 1954 he won the Israel Prize for his musical fantasy *En Gev*. (See also ISRAEL PHILHARMONIC ORCHESTRA; ISRAEL PRIZE; MUSIC.)

PASSFIELD WHITE PAPER   Statement of British policy in Palestine issued by Lord Passfield, the British Colonial Secretary, in 1930. (At that time Great Britain ruled Palestine under the Mandate.) It took a different position from the 1917 Balfour Declaration which had favored a Jewish national home in Palestine. The Passfield White Paper said that Jewish settlement in Palestine was one of the causes of the Arab riots of 1929 and suggested that Jewish immigration and settlement be controlled or even temporarily stopped. (See also ARAB RIOTS; BALFOUR DECLARATION; GREAT BRITAIN; HISTORY; MANDATE.)

PASSOVER Jewish holiday celebrated for seven days in Israel and eight days in the rest of the world. Passover marks the anniversary of the Exodus of the Jews from slavery in Egypt in biblical times. Families begin the holiday with a *Seder* (holiday feast) on the first night of Passover. The *Haggadah* (story of the Exodus) is read at the *Seder*. *Matzot* (flat cakes of unleavened bread) are eaten instead of ordinary bread at the *Seder* and during the entire holiday. Services are held at the Western Wall and in synagogues throughout Israel.

Passover begins on the fifteenth of Nisan on the Jewish calendar (March or April on the international calendar). It comes at the end of the rainy season and at the beginning of the grain harvest in Israel. In ancient times, Jewish farmers brought the first bundle of barley harvested (called the *Omer*) to the Temple in Jerusalem as a thanksgiving offering on the second day of Passover. Today Israeli Jews and Jews from all over the world visit Jerusalem during Passover if they can.

In biblical times a lamb was sacrificed and eaten on Passover. Today in Israel the Samaritans (a small religious sect) hold a Passover ceremony on Mount Gerizim with a sacrifice of the Paschal lamb, exactly as it is described in the Bible. (See also BIBLE; CALENDAR, INTERNATIONAL; CALENDAR, JEWISH; EXODUS; HAGGADAH; HOLIDAYS; MATZO; MOUNT GERIZIM; SAMARITANS; SEDER; TEMPLE; WESTERN WALL.)

PATRIA French ship in which 1,800 "illegal" Jewish immigrants traveling to Palestine from Austria, Germany, and Czechoslovakia were held in Haifa harbor in 1940. The British (who then governed Palestine) planned to send the immigrants to camps on the British colony of Mauritius in the Indian Ocean. It has been reported that the Haganah (Jewish underground army) planted explosives to stop the ship from sailing. The *Patria* blew up and almost 250 immigrants died. (See also GREAT BRITAIN; HAGANAH; IMMIGRANTS, ILLEGAL.)

PATRIARCHS Name given to the three biblical fathers of the Jewish people—Abraham, Isaac, and Jacob. (See also ABRAHAM; JACOB.)

PEACE TREATY see ISRAEL-EGYPT PEACE TREATY

PEARLMAN, MOSHE (1911-) British-born writer who reported on the Arab riots of 1936 in Palestine. He settled there in 1948, and later became the director of the Israel Broadcasting Service. He is the author of nonfiction books about Israel. (See also ARAB RIOTS; BROADCASTING; KOL ISRAEL.)

PEEL COMMISSION Group of officials headed by Viscount

Peel who were sent to Palestine by the British government (which then ruled Palestine) to investigate the causes of the Arab riots of 1936 and to make suggestions for the future government of Palestine. The Peel Commission decided that the differences between the Jews and Arabs were so deep that the best solution would be to partition (divide) Palestine. It proposed an independent Jewish State in the north and along the Mediterranean coast, an independent Arab State in the south, and an area including Jerusalem to remain in British hands. (See also ARAB RIOTS; GREAT BRITAIN; PARTITION.)

PEKAH King of Israel who ruled 735-730 B.C.E. Pekah killed King Pekahiah and took the throne. He then invaded the neighboring Jewish kingdom of Judah. When King Ahaz of Judah asked Assyria for help, Assyria invaded Israel and occupied Galilee. (See also AHAZ; ASSYRIA; GALILEE; ISRAEL, KINGDOM OF; JUDAH, KINGDOM OF; PEKAHIAH.)

PEKAHIAH King of Israel who ruled for only one year (736-735 B.C.E.) before he was murdered by Pekah. (See also ISRAEL, KINGDOM OF; PEKAH.)

PEKIIN Village in upper Galilee. Pekiin is said to be the place where Rabbi Simeon Ben Yohai hid from the Romans in a cave for 13 years. Although Jews have lived in the village from biblical times, most of the inhabitants today are Druze (a Moslem religious sect) and Arabs. A restored synagogue from the 300s C.E. can be seen at Pekiin. (See also DRUZE; GALILEE; SIMEON BEN YOHAI.)

PELI, ALEXANDER Publisher who settled in Israel in 1925. He was the editor and publisher of *Hayom* (a Jerusalem daily newspaper) and is now chairman of the board of the Alexander Peli Publishing Company.

PELUGOT MAHATZ see PALMAH

PEOPLE OF THE COVENANT Another name for the Jewish people. (See also COVENANT.)

PERES, SHIMON (1923-) Polish-born politician who was brought to Palestine at the age of 11. He joined the Haganah (Jewish underground army) and was head of Israel's navy during the 1948 War of Independence. After Israel became a state, Peres was elected to the Knesset (legislature) and served as Minister of Defense. In 1977 he became the leader of the Israel Labor Party and was the Labor candidate for Prime Minister in the election that year. For the first time in nearly 30 years, the Likud Party received more votes than the Labor Party, and Menachem Begin, rather than Shimon Peres, became Prime Minister of Israel. (See also BEGIN, MENACHEM; HAGANAH; ISRAEL LABOR PARTY; KNESSET; LIKUD; PRIME MINISTER; WAR OF INDEPENDENCE.)

PERLMAN, ITZHAK (1945-   )   Native Israeli violinist who studied music in Tel Aviv and New York. Perlman gave his first concert at the age of ten. He has played with all the important American orchestras and has given concerts throughout the world.

PERSIA (now called IRAN)   Ancient Persia was a Middle Eastern nation on the Plateau of Iran east of the Tigris-Euphrates Valley. In the sixth century B.C.E. the Persians built an empire that stretched 3,000 miles from the border of Greece to India and lasted for about 300 years. In 538 B.C.E., under Cyrus the Great, Persia conquered the Babylonian Empire and occupied both Palestine and Mesopotamia (where Palestine's Jews had been sent into exile). It was Cyrus who let the Jews return to Palestine.

Persia was conquered by Alexander the Great in 330 B.C.E., rose again in the 200s C.E., and was conquered by the Arabs in the 600s C.E. Later it was ruled by the Mongols, and still later by the Turks.

In 1935 Persia's name was changed to Iran. Modern Iran stretches from Turkey and Iraq on the west to Afghanistan and Pakistan on the east. It has an area of 636,300 square miles, a population of 34,800,000, and is rich in oil.

Although Iran is a Moslem nation, it did not share the Arab hatred of Israel. Until 1979 Israel bought half of its oil from Iran. But after the 1979 Iranian revolution, the country's attitude toward Israel changed. Iran refused to sell Israel oil, and its government supported the aims of the Palestine Liberation Organization (a group dedicated to destroying Israel). (See also BABYLON; BABYLONIAN EXILE; CYRUS I; HISTORY; MESOPOTAMIA; OIL; PALESTINE LIBERATION ORGANIZATION.)

PERSITZ, SHOSHANA (1893-1969)   Publisher and educator who founded the Omanut publishing company in her native Russia before moving the company to Tel Aviv in 1925 and continuing to print Hebrew books for adults and young people. Shoshana Persitz also served in the Israeli Knesset (legislature) and headed Tel Aviv's Department of Education. In 1968 she received the Israel Prize for her work in education. (See also EDUCATION; ISRAEL PRIZE; KNESSET.)

PETAH TIKVA   City a few miles east of Tel Aviv. Petah Tikva was the first modern Jewish agricultural settlement in Palestine and was known as the "Mother of the Pioneer Villages." A group of Orthodox Jews from Jerusalem tried to establish a village at

Petah Tikva in 1878, but were unsuccessful because of the swampy land, malaria, and raiding Arabs. In 1882 young immigrants from Russia, helped by Baron Edmond de Rothschild, tried again. They planted vineyards of wine grapes and groves of citrus trees. The village grew and later became the center of the Jewish workers' movement in Palestine. Today Petah Tikva is a city of about 100,000 people. Besides its citrus fruit industry, it has textile mills, metalworks, and other factories. A monument to Baron Rothschild stands on the main street. (See also CITRUS FRUIT; MALARIA; ROTHSCHILD, EDMOND DE; WINE; ZIONISM.)

PHARISEES Jewish religious and political party active in Palestine from 135 B.C.E. to 135 C.E. The aim of the Pharisees was to make the Torah the way of life of the Jewish people. They therefore opposed many of the policies of the Hasmonean rulers John Hyrcanus and Alexdander Jannaeus. The Pharisees succeeded in making the synagogue an important Jewish institution, and they organized a system of religious education for children. The Pharisees themselves lived according to a strict set of religious laws. (See also ALEXANDER JANNAEUS; HASMONEANS; HISTORY; HYRCANUS, JOHN.)

PHILIP (died 34 C.E.) One of the three sons of Herod the Great. Philip inherited a small part of his father's kingdom and ruled it well. (See also HEROD I.)

PHILISTINES Ancient people who established the five city-states of Ashdod, Ashkelon, Ekron, Gath, and Gaza in Palestine in the twelfth century B.C.E. The Philistines were warriors who often fought the Israelites during biblical times. King Saul was killed in a battle against the Philistines in the eleventh century B.C.E., but his successor, King David, subdued them and conquered much of their land. (See also DAVID; HISTORY; SAUL.)

PHOSPHATES Minerals used in making fertilizers for agriculture. Phosphates are an important natural resource of the Negev. They are mined in several places in the Negev, including the large Oron field, and are refined at the Oron Phosphate Works for sale throughout Israel and export to the rest of the world. (See also FOREIGN TRADE; MINERALS; NEGEV.)

PHYSICAL EDUCATION Israeli children receive two hours of physical education instruction a week in school. High school students take an extra two hours a week of physical training to prepare them for their national military service. Students can take part in a number of sports programs through the schools including track-and-field, basketball, and swimming. Schools also hold monthly tests for the Physical Fitness Badge. Many physical education teachers are trained at the Wingate Institute near Tel Aviv. (See also EDUCATION; NATIONAL SERVICE; PHYSICAL FITNESS BADGE; WINGATE INSTITUTE.)

PHYSICAL FITNESS BADGE (Hebrew, OT HASPORT)   Badge awarded to Israeli young people if they pass tests in gymnastics and track-and-field events. The physical fitness tests were introduced in 1939 and are given in the schools every month. About 150,000 youngsters from the sixth grade up take the tests every year. (See also PHYSICAL EDUCATION.)

PICA   see PALESTINE JEWISH COLONIZATION ASSOCIATION

PINCUS, ARYE ABRAHAM (1912-1973)   Lawyer who practiced in South Africa before settling in Israel in 1948. Pincus was the director of El Al (Israel's national airline), and later served as chairman of the executive committee of the Jewish Agency. (See also EL AL; JEWISH AGENCY.)

PINES, JEHIEL MICHAL (1842-1912)   Polish-born writer and Zionist pioneer who settled in Jerusalem in 1878 and was one of the leaders of the movement to establish Hebrew as the spoken language of Palestine. (See also HEBREW; ZIONISM.)

PINKERFELD, ANDA (pen names, ANDA and AMIR) (1902-   )   Hebrew poet who was born in Austria and settled in Palestine in 1923. She spent several years in Germany after World War II, working with Jewish survivors of the Nazi oppression. Besides poetry, Anda has written Hebrew books for children that are popular in Israel. She won the Israel Prize in 1978. (See also ISRAEL PRIZE; NAZIS.)

PIONEER WOMEN   Women's Labor Zionist organization founded in the United States in 1925. It has about 100,000 members in 12 countries. The Pioneer Women work with Moetzet Hapoalot (its sister organization in Israel) to provide education and social services for Israeli women and children, to help new settlers, and to secure equal rights for women. It runs 500 day-care centers for children, 3 high schools and 15 vocational high schools, and 35 community centers in Israel. The organization makes special efforts to reach poor and uneducated women—Arab and Druze as well as Jewish—and to give them homemaking and job skills. (See also EDUCATION; MOETZET HAPOALOT.)

PITA   A small flat circular bread, popular in Israel and Arab countries. It is cut open to form a pocket, and is stuffed with different kinds of fillings, making a thick sandwich.

PITTSBURGH PROGRAM   Program for building a Jewish

National Home in Palestine issued by the World Zionist Organization at their Pittsburgh convention in 1918. It called for political equality for all men and women in Palestine, the acceptance of Hebrew as the language of the country, and the development of agriculture and industry in Palestine. (See also WORLD ZIONIST ORGANIZATION.)

PLAIN OF MOREH   see MOREH, PLAIN OF

PLUMBER, HERBERT CHARLES ONSLOW (1857-1932) British soldier who was High Commissioner for Palestine from 1925 to 1928. Plumber reduced the British security forces in Palestine, a move that encouraged the violence of the Arabs in the riots of 1929. (See also ARAB RIOTS; HIGH COMMISSIONER.)

POALE AGUDAT ISRAEL   Religious labor movement founded in Poland in 1922 as the workers' organization of Agudat Israel. Poale Agudat Israel trained many of its members to settle in Palestine and live there according to the Torah (Jewish religious law). It established several kibbutzim (cooperative farming villages) in Palestine. As a political party in Israel, Poale Agudat Israel has joined with Agudat Israel to form the Torah Religious Front. (See also AGUDAT ISRAEL; KIBBUTZ; POLITICAL PARTIES; TORAH; ZIONISM.)

POALE ZION   Socialist Zionist organization. Poale Zion groups, founded in the early 1900s in Russia, Austria-Hungary, the United States, and Palestine, were formed into a world organization in 1907. Poale Zion believed that Jewish settlement in Palestine must be based on Socialism and the needs of the working people. Over the years there were splits within the organization over political issues, but it succeeded in establishing a number of cooperative farming settlements and cooperative industries in Israel. It was also active in building the Histadrut (federation of labor). (See also HISTADRUT; SOCIALISM; ZIONISM.)

POGROM   Russian word meaning the organized murder of helpless people. The word "pogrom" usually refers to the attacks on Jews in Russia and the Eastern European countries between 1881 and 1921. The pogroms of the 1880s and 1890s helped bring about the birth and growth of the Zionist movement. Many young men and women left Russia to settle in Palestine during those years. (See also ALIYAH; ZIONISM.)

POLICE   The Israel Police is a nationwide organization with headquarters in Jerusalem. It is commanded by an Inspector-General who is responsible to the Minister of Police in the government Cabinet. The country is divided into three police districts, which are again divided into stations and posts. This is different from the American system where the police are directly controlled by city or local governments.

Besides the usual police jobs of enforcing the law, preventing crime, and catching criminals, the Israel Police also patrol the country's borders. The special Border Police guard the frontiers between Israel and the neighboring Arab states against terrorist attacks.

In the late 1970s there were about 14,000 police in Israel. About 1,300 were Arabs and Druze (a Moslem people); 1,500 were women. Some of the women were serving in the police as part of their national military service. There were also 850 local police in the administered areas of the Sinai, West Bank, Golan Heights, and Gaza Strip. When Israel took over these areas after the 1967 Six-Day War, it retrained many of the local Arab police to continue in their jobs. (See also ADMINISTERED AREAS; ARABS; CABINET; DRUZE; NATIONAL SERVICE; SIX-DAY WAR.)

POLITICAL PARTIES Unlike most democracies which have only a few political parties, Israel has *many* political parties. Elections to the Knesset (legislature) are by proportional representation. Each party presents a candidate "list" to the voters. Voters vote for the party list, rather than a particular candidate. Each party gets the same percentage of seats in the Knesset as it received in the popular vote. The party then sends representatives to represent it in the Knesset. Those at the top of the list are selected first. Since 1948 more than 20 different political parties have received enough votes to elect members of the Knesset. No party has ever received a majority of the 120 seats. Therefore, the government is always formed by a coalition of parties, with the head of the leading party as Prime Minister. His Cabinet is chosen from all parties in the coalition.

It would be impossible to govern a country with 10 or 20 parties, many at odds with each other, pulling different ways. In practice, parties with the same goals have formed political unions or temporary political blocs. There are three major political blocs—Labor, Likud, and Religious. The Labor bloc is made up of Mapam and the Israel Labor Party (which includes members of Mapai, Ahdut Ha-avoda, and Arab and Druze). For years the Labor alliance was the strongest political force in Israel and it headed every government until the 1977 election. The Likud is a union of Herut and the Liberal Party (formerly the Progressives). Likud is less Socialistic than the Labor bloc and more aggressive in foreign relations. In 1977 Likud won control of the government from Labor. The religious parties (including the National Religious Party and Agudat Israel) are the smallest bloc, but they have a good deal of influence on the government.

(See also AGUDAT ISRAEL; AHDUT HA-AVODA; CABINET; CITIZENS' RIGHTS MOVEMENT; GAHAL; GENERAL ZIONISTS; GOVERNMENT; ISRAEL LABOR PARTY; KNESSET; LIBERAL PARTY; LIKUD; MAKI; MAPAI; MAPAM; MIZRAHI; NATIONAL RELIGIOUS PARTY; PRIME MINISTER; PROGRESSIVE PARTY; PROPORTIONAL REPRESENTATION; RAFI; RAKAH; SOCIALISM; VOTING.)

POLYANTHUS NARCISSUS A white flower with a yellow center that grows on the Sharon Plain and on Mount Carmel. Many people believe that this narcissus is the Rose of Sharon mentioned in the Bible. (See also SHARON PLAIN.)

POMEGRANATE Pomegranate trees have been grown in Israel since biblical times. The tree is small with bright green leaves and the fruit looks like a thick-skinned apple. Pomegranates are filled with small seeds surrounded by a red juicy pulp. (See also AGRICULTURE.)

POMPEY (also called POMPEIUS GNAEUS) (106-48 B.C.E.) Roman general who conquered Spain, North Africa, Syria, and Palestine. While Pompey was in Syria in 64 B.C.E., he was asked by Hyrcanus II and Aristobulus II to decide who should be king of Judea. Pompey sided with Hyrcanus, invaded Judea, and captured Jerusalem. Although Pompey put Hyracanus on the throne, he made Judea a province of Rome. This marked the end of the independent Jewish State established by Judah the Maccabee a hundred years earlier. (See also ARISTOBULUS II; HISTORY; HYRCANUS II; JUDEA; JUDAH THE MACCABEE; ROME.)

PONEVEZ YESHIVA Religious college for the study of the Torah (Jewish religious law) in Bene Berak. The Ponevez Yeshiva, once located in Europe, is now a center of religious scholarship in Israel. (See also BENE BERAK; TORAH.)

POOL OF SILOAM see SILOAM

POPULAR FRONT FOR THE LIBERATION OF PALESTINE (P.F.L.P.) Arab Palestinian commando organization dedicated to destroying Israel. The P.F.L.P. was responsible for a number of airplane hijackings, including the 1970 hijacking in Amman, Jordan. It has refused to join the Palestine Liberation Organization (P.L.O.), which it considers too moderate. (See also FEDAYEEN; PALESTINE LIBERATION ORGANIZATION.)

POPULATION In 1977 the population of Israel was 3,550,000: 355,000 lived in Jerusalem, 354,000 in Tel Aviv, and 227,000 in Haifa. About 85% of Israel's people live in cities or towns and about 9% in some form of cooperative farming village. Israel's population is about 85% Jewish and 15% Arab and Druze (a

Five brothers from a family of Moroccan Jews, and triplets from a Jerusalem Ashkenazi family help fight the population battle. The Jewish population growth of Israel has not kept pace with the expanding Arab families.

Moslem people). Of the Jews, half are Sabras (native-born Israelis), slightly more than one-quarter are immigrants from Europe and America, and a little less than one-quarter are immigrants from Asia and Africa. Among the Arabs, about 80% are Moslem and 20% Christian. Moslems make up approximately 11% of the total population, Christians about 2%, and Druze about 1%. (See also ARABS; ASHKENAZIM; CHRISTIANS; DRUZE; HAIFA; JERUSALEM; JEWS, ISRAELI; MOSLEMS, ISRAELI; ORIENTAL JEWS; SABRA; SEPHARDIM; TEL AVIV.)

PORTS   Israel has three major ports—Haifa, Ashdod, and Eilat. Haifa, on the Mediterranean Sea, is the country's oldest and largest port. It handles more than half of all the goods shipped into and out of Israel. The port of Ashdod, also on the Mediterranean, was completed in 1965. When it was opened, the old ports at Tel Aviv and Jaffa were closed. By 1978 Ashdod was handling two-thirds as much cargo as Haifa.

Eilat is the smallest of Israel's ports. Situated on the Gulf of Eilat, it leads to the Red Sea and the Indian Ocean and is mainly used for trade with Africa and Asia. All three ports are regulated by the Israel Port Authority which was created in 1961 and is responsible to the Minister of Transport in the government Cabinet. (See also ASHDOD; CABINET; EILAT; HAIFA; MEDITERRANEAN SEA; RED SEA; SHIPPING.)

PORUSH, MENACHEM (1916-   )   Jerusalem-born rabbi who has served as Vice-Mayor of Jerusalem and as a member of the Israeli Knesset (legislature). Rabbi Porush is the founder of a number of day nurseries and homes for children, including the well-known Children's Town. (See also JERUSALEM; KNESSET.)

POTASH (chemical name, POTASSIUM CHLORIDE)   Mineral used in industry and in making fertilizers for industry. The Dead Sea Works at Sodom extracts potash from the water of the Dead Sea, which consists of about 1% potash. Part of the process of extracting the potash requires the use of solar energy to evaporate the water. Almost one million metric tons of potash are produced a year and much of it is exported to other countries. (See also DEAD SEA; DEAD SEA WORKS; FOREIGN TRADE; MINERALS; METRIC SYSTEM; SOLAR ENERGY.)

POUND   see ISRAELI POUND

PREMIER   see PRIME MINISTER

PRESIDENT   The President is the official head of Israel, but the real leader of the country is the Prime Minister. The office of President is mainly honorary—more like that of the Queen of England than like the President of the United States. Israel's

President greets foreign diplomats, signs laws and treaties passed by the Knesset (legislature), appoints judges, and appoints the State Comptroller. After an election, the President calls on the leader of the victorious political party to form a new government.

The President is elected by the Knesset for a five-year term, and may be reelected for a second term. The person chosen is usually someone who is highly respected by the people of Israel. The first four Presidents were Chaim Weizmann, Isaac Ben-Zvi, Zalman Shazar, and Ephraim Katzir. The current President, Itzhak Navon, was elected in 1978. (See also BEN-ZVI, ISAAC; GOVERNMENT; KATZIR, EPHRAIM; KNESSET; NAVON, ITZHAK; PRIME MINISTER; SHAZAR, ZALMAN; WEIZMANN, CHAIM.)

PRESS   see NEWSPAPERS

PRIME MINISTER (also called PREMIER)   The Prime Minister of Israel is the country's chief executive. Unlike the United States in which the President and Congress are part of separate branches of government, Israel's Prime Minister is a member of the Knesset (legislature).

After an election the President (whose office is largely honorary) calls on the leader of the party that received the most votes in the election to form a new government. He or she chooses the Ministers of the Cabinet and becomes Prime Minister.

The Prime Minister chairs Cabinet meetings, coordinates the work of the different Ministries (government departments), and shapes general government policy. If the Prime Minister wishes, he or she may also serve as a Cabinet Minister. For example, David Ben-Gurion was Minister of Defense while he was Prime Minister.

The Prime Minister and the Cabinet are responsible to the Knesset. The Knesset can give them a vote of no-confidence at any time, and force them to resign.

Israel's first Prime Minister was David Ben-Gurion who served from 1948 to 1953 and again from 1955 to 1963. Moshe Sharrett was Prime Minister from 1953 to 1955, Levi Eshkol from 1963 to 1969, Golda Meir from 1969 to 1974, and Yitzhak Rabin from 1974 to 1977. Menachem Begin became Prime Minister in 1977. (See also BEGIN, MENACHEM; BEN-GURION, DAVID; CABINET; ESHKOL, LEVI; GOVERNMENT; KNESSET; MEIR, GOLDA; POLITICAL PARTIES; PRESIDENT; RABIN, YITZHAK; SHARRETT, MOSHE.)

PRIZES   The Israeli government and several Israeli cities award prizes for achievement in the arts or sciences. The best known is the Israel Prize, given each year by the Ministry of Education for excellence in literature, art, science, Jewish studies, etc. The Jerusalem Prize, the Bialik Prize (given by Tel Aviv), and the

Ussishkin Prize (given by Haifa) are all literary prizes awarded to outstanding writers and poets. The Jerusalem Prize is not restricted to Israelis or Jews. Neither is the Harvey Prize, a science award. (See also BIALIK PRIZE; ISRAEL PRIZE; JERUSALEM INTERNATIONAL BOOK FAIR.)

PROCURATOR   Name given to the Roman governors of Judea from 6 to 66 C.E. There were 14 different Procurators during that period. (See also JUDEA; ROME.)

PROGRESSIVE PARTY   Political party formed in 1948 by the union of three earlier parties. The Progressive Party stood for cooperation between social classes and less government control of the economy. In 1965 the Progressives joined with the General Zionists to form the Liberal Party. (See also GENERAL ZIONISTS; LIBERAL PARTY; POLITICAL PARTIES.)

PROMISED LAND   Name sometimes used to refer to Israel, or before 1948 to refer to Palestine. The name comes from the promise that God made to Abraham that this land would belong to him and his descendants (Genesis 12:7). (See also ABRAHAM; COVENANT; PALESTINE.)

PROPORTIONAL REPRESENTATION   A system of electing government officials in direct proportion to the number of votes their political party receives. Israeli citizens do not vote for individual candidates to the Knesset (legislature). Instead they vote for the national candidate "list" of a political party. The number of a party's candidates to be elected to the Knesset depends on the number of votes cast for its list. For example, a political party receiving one-third of the total votes cast in an election would get one-third of the Knesset's 120 seats. The top 40 names (one-third of 120) on that party's candidate list would become members of the Knesset. (See also GOVERNMENT; KNESSET; POLITICAL PARTIES; VOTING.)

PUBLISHING   see BOOKS and NEWSPAPERS

PURIM   Jewish holiday that celebrates the triumph of Esther and Mordecai over Haman who, as Chief Minister of King Ahasueros, planned to kill all the Jews of Persia. The biblical Book of Esther, which tells the story, is read in the synagogues on Purim.

Purim is celebrated on the fourteenth of Adar on the Jewish calendar (in March on the international calendar). In Jerusalem the holiday is celebrated on the fifteenth of Adar, which is called Shushan Purim, after the ancient capital of Persia. The news of Haman's defeat reached the walled city of Shushan a day late.

Jerusalem, also being a walled city, celebrates on the day Shushan did.

Purim is a joyful holiday in Israel. Children dress up in costumes, make noises with *groggers* (rattles), and eat *hamantashen* (three-cornered fruit-filled cakes). A large carnival is held in Tel Aviv, and there are fireworks, folk dancing, and parties throughout the country. Gifts are sent to friends and relatives and charity is given to the needy. (See also BIBLE; CALENDAR, INTERNATIONAL; CALENDAR, JEWISH; ESTHER; HAMAN; HOLIDAYS; PERSIA; WALLED CITIES.)

QUMRAN (also spelled KUMRAN)   Site of the caves overlooking the northwestern shore of the Dead Sea where the 2,000-year-old Dead Sea Scrolls were found. Archaeologists have uncovered the remains of buildings close to where the Essenes (the religious sect that wrote the Scrolls) lived. (See also ARCHAEOLOGY; DEAD SEA SCROLLS; ESSENES.)

R

RAANANA Town a few miles north of Tel Aviv founded in 1921 by settlers from New York. Raanana's economy is based on growing citrus fruit. In 1949 the Mizrahi Women's Organization of America established a religious youth vil-LAGE KEFAR BATYA IN THE TOWN SEE ALSO CITRUS FRUIT; MIZRAHI WOMEN; YOUTH VILLAGES.)

RABBI KOOK FOUNDATION (Hebrew, MOSAD HARAV KOOK) Religious publishing company and research and cultural center in Jerusalem. It was founded in 1937 by the Mizrahi (a religious Zionist organization) and was named in honor of the Jewish scholar Rabbi Avraham Kook. (See also KOOK, AVRAHAM YITZHAK; MIZRAHI.)

RABIN, YITZHAK (1922-   )   Fifth Prime Minister of Israel.

Prime Minister Yitzhak Rabin (right) signing the Sinai accord on September 1, 1975. U.S. Secretary of State Henry Kissinger looks on.

343

Rabin was born in Jerusalem and grew up in Tel Aviv. His parents, Rosa Cohen and Nehemiah Rabin, were both active in the Palestine labor movement. At the age of 18, after graduating from agricultural school, Rabin joined the Palmah (the commando unit of the Jewish army) and fought in Syria on the Allied side during World War II. In 1945 he took part in an operation to free 200 "illegal" immigrants being held in a British detention camp (Britain then ruled Palestine), and he spent eight months in jail after he was caught. During the 1948 War of Independence, Rabin commanded the army brigade that helped end the siege of Jerusalem.

Rabin remained in the Israeli army, rose to the post of Chief-of-Staff, and commanded the army during the 1967 Six-Day War. He was elected to the Israeli Knesset (legislature) in 1974 and shortly thereafter succeeded Golda Meir as Prime Minister. During his term as Prime Minister, Rabin signed a temporary agreement with Egypt in which both sides pledged not to use force to resolve their differences. He also masterminded the commando raid on Entebbe, Uganda, that freed the hostages of a plane hijacking. After serving as Prime Minister for three years, Rabin was forced to resign when it was discovered that he had an illegal bank account in the United States. His resignation was one of the factors that caused his Labor Party to lose the next election in 1977. (See also EGYPT; GREAT BRITAIN; IMMIGRANTS, ILLEGAL; ISRAEL LABOR PARTY; KNESSET; MEIR, GOLDA; PALMAH; PRIME MINISTER; SIX-DAY WAR; WAR OF INDEPENDENCE.)

RABINOWICZ, MORDECAI   see BEN-AMMI

RABINOWITZ, ALEXANDER SUSSKIND (pen name, AZAR) (1854-1945)   Hebrew writer who was active in the Zionist movement in his native Russia before settling in Palestine in 1905. Rabinowitz was a founder of the Histadrut (federation of labor) and many of his stories and novels are about the labor movement. (See also HISTADRUT; ZIONISM.)

RABINOWITZ, YEHOSHUA (1911-)   Politician and labor leader who was active in the Hehalutz (young Zionist pioneer) movement in his native Poland before he settled in Israel in 1934. Rabinowitz helped set up the first supermarkets in Israel. He was a leader of the Israel Labor Party, was elected to the Knesset (legislature), and served as Minister of Finance and Minister of Housing. He was also Mayor of Tel Aviv for two terms. (See also HEHALUTZ; ISRAEL LABOR PARTY; KNESSET; TEL AVIV.)

RACHEL   One of the four biblical matriarchs (mothers) of the Jewish people. Rachel was the second wife of Jacob and the

A striking piece of sculpture on the grounds of Yad Vashem, in Jerusalem, symbolizing the verse in Jeremiah: "Rachel weeps for her children, she is beyond comfort."

mother of Joseph and Benjamin. Her burial place is in Beth-lehem.

RACHEL, TOMB OF   Domed limestone building at the north-ern entrance of Bethlehem that is said to be the burial place of the biblical matriarch Rachel. The tomb is a holy place which Jews could not visit between 1948 and 1967 because it was on Arab-occupied land. Today it is a popular tourist attraction. (See also BETHLEHEM; RACHEL; TOURISM.)

RADIO   see BROADCASTING and KOL ISRAEL

RAFI   Political party that split off from Mapai in 1965. In 1968 Rafi joined Mapai and Ahdut Ha-avoda to form the Israel Labor Party. (See also ISRAEL LABOR PARTY; MAPAI; POLITICAL PARTIES.)

RAKAH (also called NEW COMMUNIST LIST)   Political party for-med in 1965 by a split in Maki (the Israeli Communist Party). Rakah is a small party that supports Russian policies in the Middle East and usually elects about three of the 120-member Israeli Knesset (legislature). Its members are mainly Israeli Arabs. (See also ARABS; MAKI; KNESSET; POLITICAL PARTIES.)

RAMADAN   Holy month in the Moslem calendar. During Ramadan, Israeli Moslems—like Moslems in the rest of the world—fast from dawn to sunset and take their first meal of the day after dark. The month ends with the three-day holiday of Id el Fitr. (See also CALENDAR, MOSLEM; HOLIDAYS; MOSLEMS; MOHAM-MED; RELIGION.)

RAMAT   Hebrew word meaning "heights." It forms part of a number of place-names in Israel.

RAMAT GAN   One of the four largest cities in Israel, Ramat Gan had a population of 121,000 in 1978. It was founded in 1921 as a garden city near Tel Aviv by settlers who wanted to live in a country setting close to the city. Abraham Krinitzi, one of the original settlers, became its first Mayor. Ramat Gan grew rapidly and absorbed many new immigrants from 1948 to 1952. Today it is an important industrial city with the world's largest diamond exchange.

Ramat Gan (*gan* means "garden") has a number of lovely gardens and parks, including the 500-acre national park. Its sports stadium is the largest in Israel and is used for the Maccabia Games and other international sports contests. Bar-Ilan Univer-sity is among the city's more than 40 schools. (See also BAR-ILAN UNIVERSITY; DIAMONDS; KRINITZI, ABRAHAM; MACCABIA GAMES.)

RAMAT HAKOVESH   Kibbutz founded in 1932 about ten miles north of Tel Aviv. In 1943 the British army searched the village for weapons. (Great Britain was then ruling Palestine under the Mandate.) When the settlers resisted, one was killed and several wounded. This led to a general strike of Palestine's Jews. (See also GREAT BRITAIN; KIBBUTZ.)

RAMAT HASHARON   Town a few miles north of Tel Aviv founded in 1923 by middle class settlers. Ramat Hasharon absorbed many new immigrants in the first years after Israel became a state in 1948. Its economy is based on growing citrus fruit. (See also CITRUS FRUIT.)

RAMAT RAHEL   Kibbutz just south of Jerusalem founded in 1926. Ramat Rahel was destroyed during the Arab riots of 1929, rebuilt the next year, and again destroyed by the Egyptian army during the 1948 War of Independence. However, the brave Jewish defense of the settlement helped save Jerusalem, and the village was soon rebuilt once more.

The site of the biblical town of Beth Hakerem lies near modern Ramat Rahel. Archaeologists have uncovered a fortified palace from the seventh century B.C.E. as well as a Byzantine church from the 400s C.E. (See also ARAB RIOTS; ARCHAEOLOGY; KIBBUTZ; WAR OF INDEPENDENCE.)

RAMAT YOHANAN   Kibbutz in the Zebulun Valley founded in 1932 and named for South African Prime Minister Jan Smuts. (The Hebrew name for Jan (John) is Yohanan.) During the 1948 War of Independence the settlers of Ramat Yohanan fought off attacking Druze forces and contained the threat to nearby Haifa. (See also DRUZE; KIBBUTZ; WAR OF INDEPENDENCE; ZEBULUN VALLEY.)

RAMBAM   see MAIMONIDES

RAMBAN   see NAHMANIDES

RAMLA (also spelled RAMLE)   Town about 20 miles southeast of Tel Aviv. Ramla was built by the Caliph Suleiman in 716 C.E. and quickly became the largest city and the capital of Arab Palestine. It was captured by the Crusaders in the late eleventh century C.E. and later was occupied in turn by the Mamelukes and the Turks. Tourists to Ramla can still see the Great Mosque that was originally a twelfth-century Crusader church and the White Tower that was part of a fourteenth-century mosque.

Ramla has a population of over 35,000 (1978), most of whom came to Israel after it became a state in 1948. However, the town also has an Arab community and is the home of Israel's Karaites (a small religious sect). (See also ARABS; CRUSADES; HISTORY; KARAITES; MAMELUKES; TOURISM; TURKEY.)

RAPHAEL, GIDEON (also spelled RAFAEL) (1913-   )   Diplomat who was born and educated in Germany and settled on a kibbutz in Israel in 1934. Raphael was a member of the Israeli delegation to the United Nations for many years. He also served as Israel's ambassador to Belgium, Luxembourg, and to Great Britain. (See also GREAT BRITAIN; KIBBUTZ; UNITED NATIONS.)

RAVNITZKY, YEHOSHUA HANA (1854-1944)   Hebrew writer who founded and edited several small magazines in his native Russia before settling in Palestine in 1921. Ravnitzky was one of the founders of the Devir Publishing Company and was its director and editor for many years. (See also DEVIR.)

RAV-NOF, ZEEV (1926-   )   Polish-born filmmaker who settled in Israel in 1950. Rav-Nof has written, directed, or produced more than forty documentary films. His movies have been shown at a number of film festivals, including the Cannes festival.

RAZIEL, DAVID (1911-1941)   Soldier who was brought to Palestine from Russia in 1914 as a young child. Raziel was one of the early members of the Irgun (a Jewish underground fighting group) and became its leader in 1937. Although he had earlier served time in jail for activities against British rule in Palestine, during World War II he went to Iraq on a sabotage mission for the British. He was killed in an air raid while on the mission. (See also GREAT BRITAIN; IRGUN.)

RED SEA   The 1,450-mile-long sea between northeast Africa and Arabia. Ships leaving the Israeli port of Eilat sail down the Gulf of Eilat, through the Red Sea, and into the Indian Ocean to trade with the countries of Asia and Africa.

The Red Sea crossed by the Israelites during the biblical Exodus from Egypt was probably not the Red Sea at all, but the Reed Sea—a marshland near what is now the Suez Canal. (See also EILAT; EILAT, GULF OF; EXODUS; SUEZ CANAL.)

RED SHIELD OF DAVID   see MAGEN DAVID ADOM

REFORESTATION   The planting and care of forests. The forests that had covered much of Israel during biblical times were destroyed as a result of centuries of neglect. When Jewish immigrants began settling the swampy land of the Sharon Plain in the late 1800s, they planted eucalyptus trees to help drain the water from the swamps. By 1919 the Jewish National Fund had set up a program to reforest the land of Palestine. The Herzl Pine Forest, near Hulda, was planted to honor the Zionist leader Theodor Herzl. Later Jewish National Fund forests were also named in honor of important people or events. The work of reforestation continued after Israel became a state in 1948. Nearly 110,000,000 trees were planted in the next 30 years. Although large numbers of trees are usually planted at one time, it has also become the custom for a foreign visitor to Israel to plant a single tree. (See also EUCALYPTUS; HERZL FOREST; JERUSALEM PINE; JEWISH NATIONAL FUND; KENNEDY MEMORIAL AND PEACE FOREST; SHARON PLAIN.)

REFUGEE CAMPS　see IMMIGRANT CAMPS

REFUGEES, ARAB　see PALESTINIAN REFUGEES

REFUGEES, JEWISH　see IMMIGRANTS, ILLEGAL

REHAVIA　Residential section of Jerusalem. Rehavia's large homes and gardens make it a lovely place to live. Most of the streets of the area are named after outstanding Jews of the Middle Ages. (See also JERUSALEM.)

REHOBOAM　King of Judah who ruled 933-917 B.C.E. Rehoboam was the son of King Solomon. He succeeded his father as king, but could not keep the country together. The northern ten tribes broke away and formed the kingdom of Israel. Rehoboam was left governing two tribes that lived in the smaller southern part of the country, which became the kingdom of Judah. (See also DAVID; HISTORY; ISRAEL, KINGDOM OF; JUDAH, KINGDOM OF; SOLOMON.)

REHOVOT　Town about 15 miles south of Tel Aviv founded in 1890 by pioneers from Russia and Poland. Unlike many other early settlements that depended on funds from the outside, Rehovot was independent from the start. The village grew citrus trees and, as it became a town, added industries, including a citrus-packing plant. Chaim Weizmann, the first President of Israel, lived and died at Rehovot. Yad Weizmann, his memorial, draws visitors from all over the world. The Weizmann Institute of Science is also located at Rehovot, as is the agriculture department of the Hebrew University. (See also CITRUS FRUIT; HEBREW UNIVERSITY; WEIZMANN, CHAIM; WEIZMANN INSTITUTE OF SCIENCE.)

REIK, HAVIVA　(1914-1944)　Palestinian parachutist who joined Hashomer Hatzair (a Zionist youth movement) in Europe and reached Palestine in 1939. In 1944, during World War II, Haviva Reik volunteered to parachute into her native Slovakia and organize contact between the Allies and the Jewish partisans who were resisting the Nazi occupation of their country. She was caught by the Nazis in a raid on a resistance camp and was shot. (See also HASHOMER HATZAIR; HOLOCAUST; NAZIS.)

RELIGION　In the United States and many other countries,

there is a definite separation between religion and government. This is not true in Israel. There are religious political parties that elect members of the Knesset (legislature), and the government Cabinet has a Minister of Religious Affairs who sees to the needs of the country's religious communities. Each Israeli citizen is considered part of a religious community—either Jewish, Moslem, Christian, or Druze—and personal matters, such as marriage and divorce, are decided by the religious court of his or her community. Since Israel is about 85% Jewish, a number of Jewish religious laws are enforced by the laws of the state. For example, religious law prohibits Jews from riding on Saturday, so buses and trains are forbidden by law to run in most cities. (See also BAHAI; CABINET; CHIEF RABBINATE; CHRISTIANS; COURTS, RELIGIOUS; DRUZE; HOLIDAYS; KARAITES; JEWS; KNESSET; MOSLEMS; POLITICAL PARTIES; SAMARITANS.)

REMEMBRANCE DAY National holiday observed on the day preceding Israeli Independence Day (the fifth day of Iyyar on the Jewish calendar) to honor the men and women who died in defense of their country. The ceremonies begin at sundown the evening before the holiday with a parent of a dead soldier handing Israel's President a torch to light a memorial flame at the Western Wall. On Remembrance Day itself, flags are flown at half-mast and there are memorial services at military monuments and cemeteries. (See also HOLIDAYS; INDEPENDENCE DAY; WESTERN WALL.)

REMEZ, DAVID (name changed from DRABKIN) (1886-1951) Russian-born labor leader who settled in Palestine in 1911. Remez was one of the founders of the Histadrut (federation of labor) and was its Secretary-General for 13 years. He was chairman of Palestine's Vaad Leumi (National Council) for the last four years before Israel became a state, and then was elected to the Israeli Knesset (legislature) and served as Minister of Communications and Minister of Education and Culture. (See also HISTADRUT; KNESSET; VAAD LEUMI.)

REPARATIONS Payment by one nation to another nation for damage done to it in wartime. As early as 1945, the Zionist Organization said that Germany should pay reparations to Israel for the harm done to European Jews by the Nazis. After a long series of talks, in 1953, a treaty was signed in which the Federal Republic of Germany agreed to pay the State of Israel $715 million and to pay an additional $107 million to 23 organizations representing Jews outside of Israel. Much of the payment to Israel was in the form of machinery for agriculture and industry and ships for the merchant fleet. Although these reparations were of great help to the Israeli economy, many citizens objected to accepting "blood money" from the Germans. (See also WORLD ZIONIST ORGANIZATION.)

REPTILES   Among the poisonous snakes found in Israel are the Palestinian viper, the desert efa, and the black cobra. The most common non-poisonous snake is the black Syrian snake which can grow to a length of ten feet. Lizards, some of which grow three feet long, are found in the deserts and chameleons are common in the hills. (See also ANIMALS; BIRDS; INSECTS.)

REUBEN   In the Bible, the oldest son of Jacob and Leah. His descendants, the tribe of Reuben, received the land of Moab in what is now Jordan when the Israelites conquered Canaan in the thirteenth century B.C.E., but the land was soon recaptured by the Moabites. (See also CANAAN; MOAB; TWELVE TRIBES.)

REVISIONISTS   Zionist political party founded in 1925 by Vladimir Jabotinsky. The Revisionists believed in putting pressure on the British (who ruled Palestine under the Mandate) to support the establishment of a Jewish national home in Palestine. The Revisionists' active stand against the British brought them into conflict with the rest of the World Zionist Organization, whose policies were more moderate. In 1935 the Revisionists broke away from the World Zionist Organization to form the New Zionist Organization. Revisionists in the Haganah (Jewish underground army) formed the Irgun and the Stern Group—two military groups that were more aggressive in fighting the British than the Haganah had been. After Israel became a state in 1948, the Revisionists became the Herut political party. Their youth organization is Betar. (See also BETAR; GREAT BRITAIN; HAGANAH; HERUT; HISTORY; IRGUN; JABOTINSKY, VLADIMIR; STERN GROUP; WORLD ZIONIST ORGANIZATION; ZIONISM.)

REVIVIM   Kibbutz founded in the Negev in 1943. Revivim was an experimental settlement that used special methods for collecting storm waters to farm the dry Negev. The settlers fought off heavy Arab attacks during the 1948 War of Independence. (See also KIBBUTZ; NEGEV; WAR OF INDEPENDENCE; WATER.)

RICHARD I (also called RICHARD THE LIONHEARTED) (1157-1199 C.E.)   King of England who ruled 1189 to 1199 C.E. In 1191 (four years after the Egyptian sultan Saladin overran Palestine), Richard sailed from England with 8,000 men on a Crusade to take the Holy Land from the Moslems. Richard was a brilliant general. In spite of conflict with the Crusaders from other European countries, his army conquered the city of Acre and a good deal of land along the Mediterranean coast. However, he failed to conquer Jerusalem. (See also CRUSADES; HISTORY; JERUSALEM; SALADIN.)

RISHON LE ZION (also spelled RISHON LEZIYON and RISHON L'TZIYON)   City founded in 1882 a few miles south of what is now Tel Aviv, meaning "the first to return to Zion." Rishon Le Zion was the second modern Jewish village in Palestine and the first built by the BILU pioneer group. Money donated by Baron Edmond de Rothschild helped the settlers plant vineyards and build wine cellars. The village school was the first in Palestine to teach all subjects in Hebrew. *Hatikvah*, Israel's national anthem, was written at Rishon Le Zion and was sung for the first time in its dining hall. Today Rishon Le Zion is a city of about 65,000 people with many different types of industry. It still produces wine, and tourists can visit the original wine cellars. (See also BILU; HATIKVAH; HEBREW; ROTHSCHILD, EDMOND DE; WINE.)

ROAD OF COURAGE   Road built by Israeli soldiers to bring supplies to Jerusalem during the fierce fighting for that city in the 1948 War of Independence. The Road of Courage is now part of the modern highway connecting Jerusalem and Tel Aviv. (See also JERUSALEM; WAR OF INDEPENDENCE.)

ROBINSON'S ARCH   Arch coming out of the southern corner of the Western Wall in Jerusalem. In ancient times it was probably part of a staircase leading up to the Temple. Robinson's Arch is named for Edward Robinson, the American archaeologist. (See also TEMPLE; WESTERN WALL.)

ROCKEFELLER MUSEUM   Museum in Jerusalem. The Rockefeller Museum has an important collection of ancient objects found in the Holy Land. It also houses a library of archaeology and ancient history. The museum was built with the money given in 1927 by the American businessman John D. Rockefeller. (See also ARCHAEOLOGY; JERUSALEM.)

ROKAH, YISRAEL (1896-1959)   Native-born Israeli politician. After serving on Tel Aviv's City Council, Rokah became the city's Mayor in 1936. During the 16 years he held the office, Tel Aviv grew rapidly. Rokah was elected to the Israeli Knesset (legislature) while he was still Mayor of Tel Aviv, but resigned a few years later to serve as Minister of the Interior and later as Deputy Speaker of the Knesset. (See also KNESSET; TEL AVIV.)

ROM, JOSEF (1932-   )   Polish-born engineer who was brought to Israel as a young child. Rom is an expert on airplane design and heads the Department of Aeronautical Engineering at the Technion in Haifa. He is also a member of the Israeli Knesset (legislature). (See also KNESSET; TECHNION.)

ROME Today Rome is the capital city of Italy, but in ancient times it was a powerful empire. The city of Rome was founded in the eighth century B.C.E. It conquered the rest of the area now called Italy in the fourth and third centuries B.C.E. By the end of the first century B.C.E. the Roman Empire had conquered all the land around the Mediterranean Sea. Also, it controlled England, southern Europe from Spain to Greece, all of North Africa, and Turkey and Palestine in Asia. In spite of many wars and revolts of the conquered peoples, the Roman Empire remained strong for more than 400 years. During the 300s and 400s C.E., the Huns and the German tribes conquered small areas of the empire. Finally, in 476, both the western part of the empire and the city of Rome itself fell. The remaining eastern part (which included Palestine) became known as the Byzantine Empire.

Palestine (then called Judea) became part of the Roman Empire in 63 B.C.E. For a number of years Jewish kings remained on the throne of Judea and some of them—particularly King Herod—had some real power, but they always owed their power to Rome. Later, Palestine was directly ruled by Roman governors called Procurators. When Rome was destroyed, Palestine became part of the Byzantine Empire.

There were two major Jewish revolts against Roman rule in Palestine. The first began in 66 C.E., led to the destruction of the Temple in Jerusalem in the year 70, and ended with the fall of Masada in 73. The Bar Kokhba revolt of 132 to 135 C.E. was brutally put down by the Romans with a great loss of Jewish lives and the destruction of many Jewish towns. (See also BAR KOKHBA, SIMEON; BYZANTINE EMPIRE; HEROD I; HISTORY; JESUS; JUDEA; MASADA; MEDITERRANEAN SEA; POMPEY; PROCURATORS; TEMPLE.)

ROSEN, PINHAS FELIX (name changed from ROSENBLUTH) (1887-   ) Politician and legal expert who practiced law in his native Germany before settling in Palestine in 1931. Rosen was a founder and the president of the Progressive political party and was elected to the Israeli Knesset (legislature) in 1949. He served as Minister of Justice for many years and was largely responsible for organizing Israel's legal system and setting up a court system that was independent of the Knesset and the Cabinet. (See also CABINET; COURTS; KNESSET; PROGRESSIVE PARTY.)

ROSH Hebrew word meaning "head of" or "source of." It is used as part of many place-names in Israel.

ROSH HA'AYIN Town about ten miles east of Tel Aviv that began as an immigrant camp for Yemenite Jews in 1950. The new immigrants farmed the land or worked in nearby Petah Tikva. By 1979 Rosh Ha'ayin had grown to a town of 11,000 people. On an ancient site near the modern town, the remains of a Bronze Age settlement can be seen. (See also BRONZE AGE; IMMIGRANT CAMPS; PETAH TIKVA.)

ROSH HANIKRA Site on the Mediterranean coast near the Israel-Lebanon border where the sea has carved caves and grottoes into the limestone cliffs. A cable car carries tourists down the cliffs to explore the grottoes. The kibbutz of Kefar Rosh Hanikra is nearby. (See also KIBBUTZ; TOURISM.)

ROSH HASHANAH Holiday marking the start of the Jewish New Year and the beginning of the Ten Days of Repentance that end with Yom Kippur (Day of Atonement). In Israel, as in Jewish communities in the rest of the world, the blowing of the *shofar* (ram's horn) on Rosh Hashanah calls Jews to think about their actions of the past year and to work to improve themselves. Rosh Hashanah is celebrated on the first two days of Tishri on the Jewish calendar (September or October on the international calendar). Originally, it was a one-day holiday. (See also CALENDAR, INTERNATIONAL; CALENDAR, JEWISH; HOLIDAYS; RELIGION; YOM KIPPUR.)

ROSH PINA One of the first modern Jewish agricultural settlements in Palestine and the first to be established in the Galilee. Rosh Pina was founded in 1878 by Jews from nearby Safed, but malaria, failure of their crops, and Arab raids forced the settlers out. In 1882 a new group of BILU pioneers from Rumania tried to rebuild the settlement. Baron Edmond de Rothschild helped them financially. But the new settlers had a difficult time making it succeed. Growing crops in the rocky soil was a terrible problem. Finally, they succeeded and Rosh Pina survived. After Israel became a state, in 1948, the settlement absorbed many new immigrants. (See also BILU; GALILEE; MALARIA; ROTHSCHILD, EDMOND DE.)

ROTENSTREICH, NATAN (1914-) Austrian-born educator and philosopher who settled in Palestine in 1932 and studied at the Hebrew University in Jerusalem. Rotenstreich taught philosophy at the Hebrew University and later became its rector. He wrote several books on modern Jewish thought and won the Israel Prize for humanities in 1963. (See also HEBREW UNIVERSITY; ISRAEL PRIZE.)

ROTHSCHILD, EDMOND DE (1845-1934) French banker and Zionist who supported many new agricultural settlements in Palestine, including Rishon Le Zion, Petah Tikva, and Zikhron Yaakov. He donated the money to keep the settlements going and sent experts to help the settlers plant new crops. Although the settlers appreciated Baron Rothschild's help and probably could not have survived without it, they did not always get along with the experts he sent.

During his lifetime Baron Rothschild bought 125,000 acres of land in Palestine, helped found and support more than 30 settlements, started the wine industry in Palestine, helped establish the Palestine Electric Corporation, and contributed money to run the Jewish schools in Palestine. He visited Palestine five times and each visit was a great event for the country's Jews.

In 1899 Baron Rothschild turned over the running of his settlements in Palestine to the Jewish Colonization Association (ICA)—founded earlier by Baron Maurice de Hirsch—and gave ICA a large amount of money to carry on the work. In 1924 he established the Palestine Jewish Colonization Association (PICA) to replace ICA and named his son James president. (See also ELECTRICITY; HIRSCH, MAURICE DE; JEWISH COLONIZATION ASSOCIATION; PALESTINE; PETAH TIKVA; RISHON LE ZION; WINE; ZIKHRON YAAKOV; ZIONISM.)

ROVINA, HANNAH (1892-) Actress who was one of the founders of the Habimah theater company in her native Russia and went to Palestine with the company in 1928. Hannah Rovina was Habimah's leading actress and is best known for her role in the play *The Dybbuk*. (See also HABIMAH.)

RUBIN, REUVEN (1893-1974) Rumanian-born painter who studied at the Bezalel School of Arts and Crafts in Jerusalem, traveled and studied in Europe, and then returned to settle in Palestine in 1922. Rubin's oil paintings and watercolors of Israel's people and landscapes (scenery) have been shown all over the world. He is also known for his woodcuts and sculptures. (See also BEZALEL SCHOOL OF ARTS AND CRAFTS.)

RUPPIN, ARTHUR (1876-1943) German-born Zionist who settled in Palestine in 1908. He became the director of the World Zionist Organization's Palestine office. He helped establish the Palestine Land Development Company (later called the Israel Land Development Company) and bought land for a number of Jewish settlements in Palestine. Ruppin was one of the founders of the Berit Shalom movement—which worked for a joint Arab-Jewish State in Palestine—but resigned after the Arab riots of 1926. He served on the executive committee of the Zionist Organization and taught sociology at the Hebrew University in Jerusalem. (See also ARAB RIOTS; BERIT SHALOM; HEBREW UNIVERSITY; ISRAEL LAND DEVELOPMENT COMPANY; PALESTINE OFFICE; WORLD ZIONIST ORGANIZATION.)

The fields of Kefar Ruppin, in the Galilee. One of the first kibbutzim, it was named in honor of Arthur Ruppin and is the showplace of Israel's kibbutzim (facing page). At Kibbutz Kefar Ruppin, aside from many field crops that are grown, a prosperous dairy farm is operated (above).

RUTENBERG, PINHAS (1879-1942)   Russian engineer who settled in Palestine in 1919. Rutenberg founded the Palestine Electric Company (later called the Israel Electric Company) in 1923 and was its head for nearly 20 years. He also helped establish the port of Tel Aviv (now closed), served on the executive committee of the Zionist Organization, and was chairman of Palestine's Vaad Leumi (National Council). (See also ELECTRICITY; VAAD LEUMI; WORLD ZIONIST ORGANIZATION.)

S

SAAD Kibbutz founded in 1946 in the northern Negev by immigrants from Central Europe. From 1948 to 1967, when the nearby Gaza Strip was in Arab hands, Saad was considered an important security site. (See also GAZA STRIP; KIBBUTZ; NEGEV.)

SABBATH Weekly day of rest and worship. Israeli law gives each religious group the right to celebrate its own Sabbath. Since most Israelis are Jews, most of the country observes the Sabbath from sundown Friday to sundown Saturday. Offices, factories, stores, schools, and theaters are closed and most buses stop running. Families gather for festive meals and people attend synagogue services. Many people attend an *Oneg Shabbat*, a Saturday afternoon program of talk and songs. (See also HOLIDAYS; JEWS, ISRAELI; ONEG SHABBAT; RELIGION.)

SABIN, ALBERT (1906-) American doctor and scientist who has done much work in preventing infectious diseases. Dr. Sabin is best known for his vaccine against polio. In the early 1970s he served as president of the Weizmann Institute of Science in Rehovot. (See also WEIZMANN INSTITUTE OF SCIENCE.)

SABRA The fruit of a cactus plant that grows in the deserts of Israel. It has a thick skin with sharp thorns covering the sweet juicy fruit inside. Sabra is also the name given to native Israelis, who are supposed to be like the cactus fruit: tough on the outside, but softhearted.

SADAT, ANWAR (full name MUHAMMAD ANWAR AL-SADAT) (1918-) President of the Arab Republic of Egypt. Sadat graduated from military college and was a colonel in the Egyptian army. In 1959 he became Speaker of Egypt's National Assembly, and in 1964 became Vice-President under President Gamal Abdul Nasser. When Nasser died in 1970, Sadat succeeded him as President.

Sadat planned and was responsible for the 1973 Yom Kippur War against Israel. However, in 1975 he signed a temporary agreement with Israel in which the two countries promised not to use force to solve their differences. In November 1977 Sadat surprised the world by announcing that he would go to Jeru-

The cactus called *sabra* or *tzabra* in Hebrew, has become symbolic of the pioneer Israelis who were, like the cactus, firm and prickly on the exterior but soft and sweet on the inside.

Students at an ORT school, all born in Israel (sabras), enjoying a session of folksongs between classes.

President Anwar Sadat of Egypt (right) engages in conversation with Prime Minister Menachem Begin at their first meeting in Ismailia, Egypt, on December 25, 1977.

salem in search of peace. He met with Prime Minister Begin in Jerusalem, addressed the Israeli Knesset (legislature), and invited Begin to Egypt. In September 1978, at President Jimmy Carter's invitation, Sadat and Begin met at Camp David in the United States to discuss a peace treaty between their two countries. On March 26, 1979 Sadat and Begin signed the Israel-Egypt Peace Treaty, the first such treaty between Israel and an Arab nation.

Anwar Sadat and Menachem Begin shared the 1978 Nobel Peace Prize for their efforts towards peace in the Middle East. (See also BEGIN, MENACHEM; CAMP DAVID SUMMIT; EGYPT; ISRAEL-EGYPT PEACE TREATY; NASSER, GAMAL ABDUL; YOM KIPPUR WAR.)

SADEH, YITZHAK (name changed from LANDSBERG) (1890-1952) Soldier and writer who was one of the founders of the Hehalutz pioneering movement in Russia before he settled in Palestine in 1920. Sadeh was active in the Haganah (Jewish underground army) and was the founder and commander of Palmah (Haganah's striking force). In his later years, he wrote stories and plays as well as a regular column for the newspaper *Al Hamishmar*. (See also AL HAMISHMAR; HAGANAH; HEHALUTZ; PALMAH.)

SAFED (also spelled TZ'FAT and ZEFAT)   Ancient town built on a mountain top in eastern upper Galilee. Safed was fortified by the Jewish general Josephus in the first century C.E. It was a Crusader stronghold in the 1100s and 1200s C.E. before it was captured by the Mamelukes. In the 1500s, about 10,000 of the Jews forced out of Spain and Portugal settled in Safed and the city became an important center of Jewish scholarship and mysticism. It boasted 18 yeshivot (religious colleges) and 21 synagogues. A number of these old synagogues, rebuilt after the earthquakes of the 1800s, are still in use.

Today Safed still has a religious community, but it is also a popular summer resort. Visitors enjoy the artists' colony, art galleries, and interesting shops. September is "artists' month" in Safed, during which art exhibitions, a film festival, and a carnival are held. (See also ARTISTS' COLONY; CRUSADES; GALILEE; HISTORY; JOSEPHUS; MAMELUKES; PURIM.)

SAILING   Because Israel has a warm climate and is close to the sea, sailing has become a popular Israeli sport. Israel competes in international sailing races and has won several first prizes. (See also SPORTS.)

SALADIN (1138-1193 C.E.)   Sultan of Egypt who led his army in battles against the Crusaders (European Christian knights) for control of Palestine in the 1100s C.E. In 1187 Saladin crushed the Crusader army at the battle of Hittin, overran Palestine, and captured Jerusalem. However, in 1191 Richard the Lionhearted of England arrived in Palestine and recaptured Acre and much of the land along the Mediterranean coast. Saladin died two years later; the Crusaders remained in Palestine for another hundred years. (See also CRUSADES; RICHARD I.)

SALKIND, ALEXANDER (1866-1931)   Doctor who was active in the Zionist movement in his native Russia before settling in Palestine in 1921 and becoming the director of the Hadassah Hospital in Jerusalem. (See also HADASSAH; HEALTH; JERUSALEM; ZIONISM.)

SALOME ALEXANDRA   Ruler of Judah 76-67 B.C.E. She became queen after the death of her husband, Alexander Jannaeus. Salome Alexandra made peace with the Pharisees (a religious political group that had opposed her husband) and gave them a voice in the internal affairs of the country. (See also ALEXANDER JANNAEUS; JUDAH, KINGDOM OF; PHARISEES.)

SALOMON, KAREL (1897-   )   German musician and composer who settled in Palestine in 1933. Salomon was music director of the Israel Broadcasting Service for 27 years. He was a singer, played several musical instruments, and composed symphonies, chamber music, an opera, and a children's opera. (See also BROADCASTING; KOL ISRAEL; MUSIC.)

SAMARIA   Mountainous area between the Jezreel Valley on the north, the Jordan River on the east, and the Judean Hills on the south. Samaria is the northern part of the West Bank, which was occupied by Jordan from 1948 to 1967 and has since been one of the administered areas governed by Israel.

The ancient city of Samaria was founded around 880 B.C.E. by King Omri, who made it the capital of his kingdom of Israel. The city was destroyed by the Assyrians in 721 B.C.E. and was rebuilt and renamed Sebaste by Herod the Great in 25 B.C.E. Archaeologists have uncovered palaces from the periods of King Omri and King Ahab of Israel, and also buildings and a street of columns erected by Herod, plus a Roman theater of a later date. The twelfth century C.E. Crusader church still standing near the ancient ruins is said to be the burial place of John the Baptist. (See also ADMINISTERED AREAS; AHAB; ARCHAEOLOGY; ASSYRIA; CRUSADES; GEOGRAPHY; HEROD I; HISTORY; ISRAEL, KINGDOM OF; JOHN THE BAPTIST; OMRI; ROME; WEST BANK.)

SAMARITANS   A small Jewish religious sect. About 250 Samaritans live in Holon near Tel Aviv, and another 250 live in their holy city of Nablus. Samaritan children attend Israeli schools, but receive their religious education from the elders of their synagogue. The Pentateuch (the first five Books of the Old

Samaritans assemble on top of Mount Gerizim to celebrate the Shavuot holiday. They assemble here, dressed as above, to celebrate Passover and Sukkot as well.

Testament) is the complete Samaritan Bible. Their religion does not accept later interpretations or Oral Law. The Samaritans celebrate seven religious holidays a year. Their Passover celebration is held on Mount Gerizim and a lamb is sacrificed exactly as described in the Bible. (See also BIBLE; EDUCATION; MOUNT GERIZIM; NABLUS; PASSOVER.)

SAMPTER, JESSIE ETHEL (1883-1938) New York-born writer who was active in Hadassah (Women's Zionist Organization of America) before she settled in Palestine in 1919. Jessie Sampter wrote most of her poems and books in English, but in her later years she also wrote Hebrew poetry. (See also HADASSAH.)

SAMUEL (eleventh century B.C.E.) A prophet and the last of the Hebrew Judges in the Bible. He was dedicated to the service of God by his mother while still a very young child. Through his efforts a Jewish kingdom was established. After the Philistines crushed the Israelites, Samuel tried to bring them back to Jewish worship, which they had forsaken. When the Israelites insisted that they be ruled by a king, Samuel chose Saul. Later, Samuel anointed David to succeed Saul as king. The stories of Samuel, Saul, and David are told in the two Books of Samuel in the Bible. (See also BIBLE; DAVID; JUDGES; PHILISTINES; SAUL.)

SAMUEL, HERBERT LOUIS (1870-1963)   First British High Commissioner for Palestine. During his years of service, from 1920 to 1925, he organized the British government of Palestine, and improved the roads, sanitation facilities, and the educational system of the country. Although he was Jewish himself, Samuel promised the Arabs that Jewish needs would not be put ahead of Arab interests in Palestine. (See also GREAT BRITAIN; HIGH COMMISSIONER.)

SAN REMO CONFERENCE   Meeting held in San Remo, Italy, in 1920 to deal with the problems that were left unsettled when the Versailles Treaty that ended World War I was signed. At the conference, the representatives of Great Britain, France, Italy, and the other Allies decided the fate of the former colonies of Germany and Turkey. Palestine (which had belonged to Turkey) was to be governed by Great Britain under the League of Nations Mandate. (See also GREAT BRITAIN; LEAGUE OF NATIONS; MANDATE; TURKEY.)

SANHEDRIN (also spelled SYNEDRIUM)   A group of 71 Jewish scholars that served both as a Supreme Court and as a legislature in ancient Palestine. Its leader was called Nasi (Prince). The Sanhedrin existed from about the second century B.C.E. to the fourth century C.E. and many of its early members were Pharisees (a religious political party). Scholars are divided on how much political power the Sanhedrin had, but they agreed that it had full authority over religious matters. It set the calendar, regulated the activity of the priests, and ruled on questions of religious law. (See also NASI; PHARISEES.)

SANHEDRIN, TOMBS OF   A three-storied burial cave carved out of rock in northern Jerusalem. The cave is the burial place of first and second century C.E. judges of the Sanhedrin (Supreme Court). (See also JERUSALEM; SANHEDRIN.)

SAPIR, JOSEPH (also spelled SAPHIR) (1902-1972)   Native Israeli politician who was also an expert on growing citrus fruit. Sapir was Mayor of Petah Tikva for 11 years before being elected to the Israeli Knesset (legislature) and served as Minister of Communications and Minister of Commerce and Industry. He favored free enterprise and opposed Socialism. (See also CITRUS FRUIT; KNESSET; PETAH TIKVA; SOCIALISM.)

SAPIR, PINHAS (name changed from KOSLOWSKY) (1906-1975)

Politician and labor leader who left Poland in 1930 to settle in Palestine. Sapir was elected to the Israeli Knesset (legislature) and served as Minister of Finance and Minister of Commerce and Industry. He was also Secretary-General of the Israel Labor Party. (See also ISRAEL LABOR PARTY; KNESSET.)

SARAFAND   Village ten miles southeast of Tel Aviv. A British army camp at Sarafand captured by the Haganah (Jewish underground army) in 1948 is now used by the Israel Defense Forces. (See also DEFENSE FORCES; GREAT BRITAIN; HAGANAH.)

SASA   Kibbutz (cooperative farming village) founded in eastern upper Galilee in 1949 by settlers from the United States. Sasa is 2,850 feet above sea level, which makes it the highest settlement in Israel. (See also GALILEE; KIBBUTZ.)

SASSON, ELIYAHU HAI (1902-   )   Syrian-born journalist and politician who settled in Palestine in 1927. Sasson was an expert on Arab affairs and headed the Arab department of the Jewish Agency. He was Israel's Minister to Turkey and Ambassador to Italy before being elected to the Knesset (legislature). He also served as Minister of Police. (See also JEWISH AGENCY; KNESSET.)

SAUL (eleventh century B.C.E.)   First king of Israel. In the eleventh century B.C.E., when the Israelites wanted to be ruled by a king, the prophet Samuel chose Saul as the first king of Israel. Saul was a brave warrior. His victories over the Philistines and other Canaanite tribes laid the foundation for the powerful Jewish kingdom which was later ruled by David and Solomon. Later, Samuel was not pleased with Saul's conduct as king, and he anointed David to succeed Saul. Saul was angered and drove David out of the country. But after Saul and his three sons were killed in a battle with the Philistines on Mount Gilboa, David became king of Israel. The story of Saul is told in the Book of Samuel in the Bible. (See also BIBLE; CANAAN; DAVID; MOUNT GILBOA; PHILISTINES; SAMUEL.)

SAVYON   Garden suburb east of Tel Aviv founded in 1954 by settlers from South Africa. Savyon has become one of the most elegant neighborhoods in Israel. (See also TEL AVIV.)

SCARLET ANEMONE   A bright red flower. Scarlet anemones are among the most striking flowers growing in Israel, especially when they cover a whole field or hillside. In addition to the scarlet flowers, white and purple anemones grow on the Sharon Plain. (See also SHARON PLAIN.)

SCHAPIRO, ABRAHAM (1870-1965)   Pioneer who was brought to Palestine from Russia at the age of ten. Schapiro settled at

Petah Tikva, was the head of the settlement's "watchmen," and became known throughout the country for his bravery in fighting Arab raiders. (See also HASHOMER; PETAH TIKVA.)

SCHATZ, BORIS (1866-1932)   Lithuanian-born artist who was court sculptor of Bulgaria. In 1906, he migrated to Jerusalem, where he established the Bezalel School of Arts and Crafts. Schatz's aim was to create a Jewish art by combining the traditions and crafts of the Jews of Eastern Europe with those of the Middle East. He was an exciting teacher who inspired many young artists in Palestine. Both his son, Bezalel, and his daughter, Zaharah, became painters. (See also ART; BEZALEL SCHOOL OF ARTS AND CRAFTS.)

SCHOCKEN, GERSHOM GUSTAV (1912-   )   German-born publisher who settled in Palestine in 1933. Gershom Schocken became the publisher and editor of *Haaretz* (the newspaper bought by his father Shlomo Schocken) and the director of the Schocken Publishing Company in Israel. He was also chairman of the Ittim Israel news agency and served in the Israeli Knesset (legislature) for four years. (See also HAARETZ; KNESSET; SCHOCKEN, SHLOMO SALMAN.)

SCHOCKEN, SHLOMO SALMAN (1877-1959)   German publisher who published Hebrew as well as German books. He moved to Palestine in 1933, and later moved to the United States. He established branches of the Schocken Publishing companies in Palestine and the United States. His son, Gershom Schocken, took over the Israeli company. Shlomo Schocken was also a collector of rare Jewish books. The books he gathered are now part of the library of the Schocken Institute for Jewish Research in Jerusalem. (See also SCHOCKEN, GERSHOM GUSTAV.)

SCHOFFMANN, GERSHON (1880-1972)   Hebrew writer who edited several small magazines in Austria before settling in Palestine in 1938 where he wrote novels and short sketches.

SCHOLEM, GERSHOM GERHARD (1897-   )   German-born scholar who settled in Palestine in 1923. Scholem taught Jewish mysticism at the Hebrew University in Jerusalem, was vice-president of the Israel Academy of Sciences and Humanities, and won the Israel Prize for Jewish studies in 1958. (See also HEBREW UNIVERSITY; ISRAEL ACADEMY OF SCIENCE AND HUMANITIES; ISRAEL PRIZE.)

SCHREIBER, HAIM (1926-   )   Polish-born film and television producer who settled in Israel in 1950. Schreiber has produced more than one hundred documentary films.

SCHWABE, MOSHE DAVID (1889-1956)   German-born scholar

who settled in Palestine, taught ancient Greek culture at the Hebrew University in Jerusalem, and was the university's rector for two years. (See also HEBREW UNIVERSITY.)

SCHWARTZ, JOSEPH (1804-1865)   Rabbi who left his native Bavaria in 1833 to settle in Jerusalem. He wrote *A Descriptive Geography of Palestine.*

SCOUTING   Scouting developed in Palestine shortly after World War I. By 1979 there were 39,000 scouts in Israel. Of this number, 27,000 were members of the Hebrew Boy and Girl Scouts, 8,000 were members of the Arab Scouts Schooling Association, and about 1,000 each members of the Moslem Scouts, Orthodox Scouts, Catholic Scouts, and Druze Scouts. These six scouting organizations all belong to the Israel Boy and Girl Scouts Federation (founded in 1953), but each group has special rules designed to suit its own members. One of the primary aims of scouting in Israel is to build understanding between different religious and cultural groups.

Israeli scouts—like scouts all over the world—have a program of service and physical activities. They collect money for charity, plant trees, and go hiking and camping. In addition, many Israeli Senior Scouts become pioneers and help establish new villages.

Scouts are divided into three age groups: Cubs or Brownies, ages 8 to 10; Scouts or Guides, ages 11 to 14; and Seniors, ages 15 to 19. Girls and boys are separated in the two younger groups, but not in the Seniors. The Seniors also have a special group for Sea Scouting. Every four years a Jamboree (large camping gathering) is held for scouts of all ages from all over Israel. (See also YOUTH MOVEMENTS.)

SDE BOKER (also spelled SEDEH BOKER)   Kibbutz founded in 1952 in the Negev about 25 miles south of Beersheba. David Ben-Gurion (Israel's first Prime Minister) made Sde Boker his home. (See also BEN-GURION, DAVID; KIBBUTZ; NEGEV.)

SEA OF GALILEE   see LAKE KINNERET

SEDER   Feast held on the first night of the Passover holiday. A Seder is usually a family celebration, but there are also community Seders. Outside of Israel, there is also a Seder on the second night of Passover. The Haggadah—the book containing the story of the Exodus of the Jews from slavery in Egypt—is read at the Seder. Four cups of wine are drunk and matzot (flat cakes of unleavened bread) are eaten. (See also EXODUS; HAGGADAH; MATZO; PASSOVER.)

SEDOT YAM   Kibbutz founded in 1940 on the Mediterranean

The small house in the background was built by Ben-Gurion. He settled here, on Kibbutz (Sdeh) Boker in the Negev, after temporarily retiring from public office in 1953.

coast about 25 miles south of Haifa. Sedot Yam's cultural center is named for Hanna Szenes, a member of the kibbutz who was killed while carrying out a secret mission in occupied Europe during World War II. There is a fishery research station at the village as well as a camping ground for visitors who come to swim at the beach. (See also KIBBUTZ; SZENES, HANNA.)

SEJERA see ILANIYAH

SELEUCIDS A line of kings that ruled most of the Middle East from 312 to 65 B.C.E. The policies of the Seleucid king Antiochus IV in governing the Jews of Palestine led to the 168 B.C.E. Maccabee (Hasmonean) revolt. (See also HASMONEANS; HISTORY; MACCABEE.)

SELF-LABOR Many of the first Jewish agricultural settlements in Palestine were run on the principle of self-labor. The early pioneers believed that a people earns the right to its country by working the soil with its own hands. Aharon David Gordon was the leading proponent of the idea of self-labor. (See also GORDON, AHARON DAVID.)

SELTZER, DOV (1932-) Composer who was born in Rumania and was educated in Israel and the United States. Seltzer is interested in folk music and has taught music in several kibbutzim. He has writen symphonies as well as background music for Bible readings, plays, and films. (See also KIBBUTZ.)

SEMER, HANNA (1928-) Journalist who was born in Czechoslovakia and settled in Israel in 1950. Hanna Semer wrote for *Davar*, a daily newspaper, and became its chief editor in 1970. She has also been a radio and television commentator. (See also DAVAR.)

SEMITIC LANGUAGES A group of related languages spoken today by about 57 million people of the world. Modern Semitic languages include Hebrew, Arabic, and Abyssinian. Most of the peoples of the ancient Middle East spoke Semitic languages. The most widely used was Aramaic. (See also ARABIC; ARAMAIC; HEBREW.)

SENESH, HANNAH see SZENES, HANNAH

SEPHARDIM Name given to the Jews of Spain in the Middle Ages. When they were driven out of Spain after 1492, the Sephardim went to North Africa, Greece, Turkey, and Syria. Their language was Ladino—medieval Spanish with some Hebrew words. The Sephardic religious traditions and synagogue services are different from those of the Ashkenazim (descendants of the Jews of medieval Germany).

A young Sephardi who has just become Bar Mitzvah at the Western
wall is instructed by a Sephardi rabbi.

Until 1882, most of the 24,000 Jews in Palestine were Sephardim. Then, waves of immigrants began to arrive from Europe and the population became mainly Ashkenazi. In the 1950s large numbers of Oriental Jews immigrated to Israel from North Africa and Arabia. Some of these Oriental Jews were Sephardim; most were not. Today Israel's population is about half Sephardic and Oriental and about half Ashkenazi. (See also ALIYAH; ASHKENAZIM; JEWS; ORIENTAL JEWS; POPULATION.)

SEPPHORIS (also spelled TZIPPORI)   Ancient city in lower Galilee built in the second or first century B.C.E. Sepphoris was the capital of Galilee and for a time was the home of the Sanhedrin (Jewish Supreme Court) and a center of Jewish learning. Archaeologists have uncovered a Roman theater and aqueduct and a Crusader fortress at Sepphoris. A modern village founded in 1949 stands near the ancient site. (See also ARCHAEOLOGY; CRUSADES; GALILEE; HISTORY; ROME; SANHEDRIN.)

SERENI, ENZO HAYIM (1905-1944)   Italian Zionist who settled in Palestine in 1926 and was one of the founders of the village of Givat Brenner. During World War II, Sereni organized a group of men and women to parachute into occupied Europe and help organize Jewish resistance to the Nazis. Sereni parachuted into Italy and was captured by the Germans and killed. (See also GIVAT BRENNER.)

SERLIN, YOSEPH (1906-1974)   Lawyer and politician who was active in the Zionist movement in Poland and Russia before he settled in Palestine in 1933. Serlin was one of the founders of the General Zionists political party. He was elected to the Israeli Knesset (legislature) in 1952, and served as its Deputy Speaker and as Minister of Health. (See also GENERAL ZIONISTS; KNESSET; ZIONISM.)

SETER, MORDEKAI (1916-   )   Composer who was born in Russia and brought to Palestine as a child. Seter taught at the Israel Academy of Music in Tel Aviv and has written music for the ballet.

SHAAR HAGOLAN   Kibbutz founded in the Jordan Valley in 1937 as a "stockade and tower" settlement. Shaar Hagolan was captured and destroyed by the Syrians during the 1948 War of Independence, but the Syrians retreated and the Jewish settlers soon rebuilt their village. Nearby is an ancient site dating back about 12,000 years to the time when people were first learning to farm the land. Pottery from the site is shown in a small museum in Shaar Hagolan. (See also KIBBUTZ; JORDAN VALLEY; STOCKADE AND TOWER; WAR OF INDEPENDENCE.)

SHABBAT see SABBATH

SHABBETAI TZEVI (also spelled SABBETAI ZEVI) (1626-1676) Scholar from Smyrna, Turkey who claimed to be the Messiah (the expected deliverer of the Jews). He attracted a large following in Palestine as well as in many countries of Europe. In 1666 he went to Constantinople, where he predicted that the Sultan of Turkey would give up the throne to him. However, when the Sultan threatened him with death, Shabbetai Tzevi stopped claiming to be the Messiah and became a Moslem. (See also MESSIAH.)

SHAHAM, NATAN (1925-) Native Israeli author who has written a number of stories and plays about life in Israel's agricultural settlements. Shaham is the son of writer Eliezer Steinmann. (See also STEINMANN, ELIEZER.)

SHALLUM King of Israel who killed Zechariah to take the throne. Shallum ruled for only five months in 742 B.C.E. before he in turn was killed by Menahem. (See also ISRAEL, KINGDOM OF; MENAHEM; ZECHARIAH.)

SHAMIR, MOSHE (1921-) Hebrew author who has written novels about life in the kibbutzim (cooperative farming settlements) of Israel. Shamir also wrote a historical novel and a play about Alexander Jannaeus, a first century B.C.E. king of Israel. (See also ALEXANDER JANNAEUS; KIBBUTZ.)

SHAMIR, YITZHAK (1915-) Polish-born politician who settled in Israel in 1935. Shamir was a leader of the Stern Group, a Jewish fighting organization that used terrorism to drive the British out of Palestine. The British arrested him twice, but he escaped both times. He was not very active in politics for many years after Israel became a state, although he worked for freedom for Soviet Jews. In 1970 he joined the Herut political party, and in 1977 was elected to the Israeli Knesset (legislature) and became Speaker of the Knesset. (See also GREAT BRITAIN; HERUT; KNESSET; STERN GROUP.)

SHAMMAI (first century B.C.E.) Scholar who was one of the two leading rabbis of Palestine during King Herod's rule. (The other was Hillel.) King Herod owed his power to Rome, and Roman influence was strong in the country. Shammai tried to keep the Jews a godly people free of Roman pagan religious practices. He enacted many strict rules in order to make Jews more loyal to their own religion. (See also HEROD I; HILLEL; ROME.)

SHAPIRA, MOSHE HAYIM (1920-1970) Russian-born politician who was one of the founders of the Mizrahi Pioneers (a religious Zionist youth organization) in Poland before settling in Palestine in 1925. Shapira was elected to the Israeli Knesset (legislature) and held several posts in the Cabinet, including that of Minister of Religious Affairs. (See also CABINET; KNESSET; MIZRAHI; ZIONISM.)

SHARABI, ISRAEL YESHAYAHU (also called YESHAYAHU, ISRA-EL) (1910-   )   Politician who was born in Yemen and settled in Palestine in 1929. Sharabi helped organize Operation Magic Carpet—the airlift that flew Yemen's Jews to Israel. He was elected to the Israeli Knesset (legislature) and served as its Speaker. Sharabi wrote several nonfiction books, including *From Yemen to Zion*. (See also KNESSET; OPERATION MAGIC CARPET.)

SHAREF, ZEEV (1906-   )   Politician who was active in the Poale Zion (Socialist Zionist) youth movement in his native Rumania before he settled in Palestine in 1925. Sharef held a number of positions in the Israeli government, including Civil Service Commissioner and chairman of the Port Authority. He was later elected to the Knesset (legislature) and served as Minister of Finance and Minister of Housing. (See also CIVIL SERVICE; KNESSET; POALE ZION; PORTS; ZIONISM.)

SHARETT, MOSHE (name changed from SHERTOK) (1894-1965) Second Prime Minister of Israel. Sharett was brought to Palestine from Russia by his parents at the age of 12. At first the family lived in an Arab village and young Moshe learned about Arab customs. He was one of the first students at the Herzlia High School in Tel Aviv, and after graduation he went to Turkey to study law. During World War I, he served in the Turkish army, where he was made an interpreter because he spoke six languages.

After the war Sharett became active in the Zionist movement. He headed the Jewish Agency's political department and served on the executive committee of the World Zionist Organization. During the Arab riots of 1936, he introduced the idea of establishing the *Notrim* (Jewish police). He also backed the Haganah and raised money to support it. In 1939 he fought against the British White Paper restricting Jewish immigration into Palestine and helped organize "illegal" immigration. He spoke before the United Nations Committee on Palestine and later represented Israel at the United Nations.

Sharett was one of the signers of the Israeli Declaration of Independence. He was elected to the Knesset (legislature) and served as Foreign Minister. When David Ben-Gurion resigned in 1953, Moshe Sharett became Prime Minister. He held the post until 1955, at which time Ben-Gurion was returned to office. Although Sharett remained in the Knesset until his death in 1965, he resigned from the Cabinet in 1956 after a disagreement with Ben-Gurion. (See also ARAB RIOTS; BEN-GURION, DAVID; CABINET; DECLARATION OF INDEPENDENCE; GREAT BRITAIN; HAGANAH; HERZLIA HIGH SCHOOL; IMMIGRANTS, ILLEGAL; JEWISH AGENCY; KNESSET; NOTRIM; PRIME MINISTER; TURKEY; UNITED NATIONS; WHITE PAPER; WORLD ZIONIST ORGANIZATION; ZIONISM.)

SHARON, ABRAHAM (name changed from SCHWADRON) (1878-1957)   Austrian-born journalist who settled in Jerusalem in 1926 and wrote for a number of different newspapers, first in German and then in Hebrew. Sharon collected Jewish autographs and portraits. His collection is now in the National and University Library in Jerusalem. (See also NATIONAL AND UNIVERSITY LIBRARY.)

SHARON, ARIEL (1928-   )   Native Israeli soldier. Sharon joined the Haganah (Jewish underground army) as a teenager. He fought in the 1948 War of Independence and was wounded in the battle for Latrun. Remaining in the Defense Forces, he rose to rank of Brigadier-General and became known for his bravery. During the 1967 Six-Day War, Sharon commanded the troops that broke through the Egyptian lines near the Mitla Pass. He was elected to the Israeli Knesset (legislature) in 1974 and served as Minister of Agriculture. (See also DEFENSE FORCES; HAGANAH; KNESSET; LATRUN; MITLA PASS; SIX-DAY WAR; WAR OF INDEPENDENCE.)

SHARON, ARYEH (1900-   )   Architect and town planner who left Austria for Palestine in 1920. Sharon planned housing projects in Tel Aviv and designed buildings for the Hebrew University in Jerusalem and the Weizmann Institute of Science in Rehovot. While he was the head of the Israeli government planning department, he designed a number of new settlements. (See also ARCHITECTURE; HEBREW UNIVERSITY; WEIZMANN INSTITUTE OF SCIENCE.)

SHARON PLAIN   The central part of Israel's Coastal Plain. The Sharon Plain is about 30 miles long and 10 miles wide. It runs north-south along the Mediterranean coast between Tel Aviv and Haifa. In biblical times, Sharon was fertile land partly covered with oak forests, but hundreds of years of neglect turned it into a swampy wasteland. The Jewish settlers who reclaimed the land in the 1900s drained the swamps and planted citrus trees. Today Sharon is one of the most fertile and heavily populated areas of Israel. Millions of dollars worth of citrus fruit is grown there each year along with other fruits and vegetables. The most important towns of the area are Netanya and Hadera. (See also

AGRICULTURE; CITRUS FRUIT; COASTAL PLAIN; GEOGRAPHY; HADERA; NETANYA.)

SHARUHEN (also called TELL EL-FARA) Ancient site about 15 miles south of Gaza. Archaeologists have found remains from the Bronze and Iron ages. Among these are several coffins shaped like human bodies. (See also ARCHAEOLOGY; BRONZE AGE; IRON AGE.)

SHASHLIK (also called SHISH KEBAB) Meat —usually lamb—cut into chunks, threaded on a skewer, and grilled over a fire. Shashlik is popular in Israel as well as in most other Middle Eastern countries.

SHAVEI ZION (also spelled SHAVE TZIYON) Village founded in 1938 on the Mediterranean coast about 15 miles north of Haifa. Shavei Zion is a beach resort as well as an agricultural village. It is the site of the oldest church in Israel. The church contains a beautiful mosaic floor. (See also MOSAICS.)

SHAVUOT (also called PENTECOST) Jewish holiday celebrated in Israel on the 6th of Sivan on the Jewish calendar and also on the 7th in the rest of the world. Shavuot (which comes in late May or early June on the international calendar) marks the end of the grain harvest and the picking of the first fruit. In ancient times a sheaf (bundle) of the first wheat or loaves of bread made from the first wheat were brought to the Temple in Jerusalem on Shavuot. Today some farming villages in Israel have revived the ancient custom and bring the first fruits of the season to Jerusalem. The biblical Book of Ruth is studied in the schools and is read in synagogues throughout Israel.

Shavuot also celebrates the giving of the Ten Commandments to Moses on Mount Sinai. (See also AGRICULTURE; BIBLE STUDY; CALENDAR, INTERNATIONAL; CALENDAR, JEWISH; HOLIDAYS; MOSES; TEMPLE; TEN COMMANDMENTS.)

SHAZAR, RACHEL KATZNELSON (1888-) Labor leader and writer who was born in Russia and settled in Palestine in 1912. Rachel Katznelson Shazar was a leader of the Jewish working women's struggle for equal rights. She was a founder of the Moetzet Hapoalot (Working Women's Council) and the founder and editor of *Devar Hapoalot*, its monthly magazine. She is the author of several books, and in 1958 won the Israel Prize for her literary and cultural work. Her husband was Zalman Shazar, the third President of Israel. (See also ISRAEL PRIZE; MOETZET HAPOALOT; SHAZAR, SHNEUR ZALMAN.)

SHAZAR, SHNEUR ZALMAN (name changed from REBASHOV) (1890-1974) Third President of Israel. Shazar was active in the Zionist movement in his native Russia and was a delegate to

Pope Paul VI, during his visit to Jerusalem in 1964, is escorted by President Shazar.

several Zionist conferences before he settled in Palestine in 1924. He served on the executive committee of the Histadrut (Palestine's federation of labor) and edited its newspaper, *Davar*. He was a member of Palestine's Vaad Leumi (National Council) and spoke for the Jews of Palestine at the United Nations. After Israel became a state in 1948, Shazar was elected to the Knesset (legislature) and served as Minister of Education and Culture. In 1963, he became President of Israel and served two five-year terms. Shazar also wrote several books. He was married to Rachel Katznelson Shazar. (See also DAVAR; HISTADRUT; KNESSET; PRESIDENT; SHAZAR, RACHEL KATZNELSON; UNITED NATIONS; VAAD LEUMI; WORLD ZIONIST ORGANIZATION; ZIONISM.)

SHECHEM see NABLUS

SHEDEROT (also spelled SEDEROT) Development town founded in the northern Negev in 1951. Shederot has a number of industries, and also serves as a market town for the farming villages in the area. (See also DEVELOPMENT TOWNS; NEGEV.)

SHEFARAM (also spelled SHEPHARAM) Town east of Haifa in lower Galilee. Shefaram was the home of the Sanhedrin (Jewish Supreme Court) for a short time in the second century C.E. Today its population is mainly Arab and Druze. (See also ARABS; DRUZE; GALILEE; SANHEDRIN.)

SHEFEYA (also spelled SHEPHEYA) Agricultural school on Mount Carmel. Shefeya was founded in 1892, became a school for orphans in 1904, was closed before World War I, and reopened in 1923. In the 1930s it was a Youth Aliyah (immigration) village for young Europeans and was adopted and supported by the Junior Hadassah of America. (See also AGRICULTURAL SCHOOLS; HADASSAH; MOUNT CARMEL; YOUTH ALIYAH; YOUTH VILLAGES.)

SHEKEL A measured amount of silver first mentioned in the Bible in the Book of Exodus. By the second century B.C.E. the shekel was a silver coin. It was the amount paid each year by each Jew for the support of the Temple in Jerusalem. The shekel idea was revived by the First Zionist Conference in 1897, when it was used as a way of raising money to support the Zionist movement. The Zionist shekel was *not* a coin, but a piece of printed paper for which one paid a half-dollar in the United States, one mark in Germany, half a ruble in Russia, etc. It was the main fundraising source for the World Zionist Organization before it created the Keren Hayesod (Palestine Foundation Fund) in 1920. (See also BIBLE; KEREN HAYESOD; TEMPLE; WORLD ZIONIST ORGANIZATION.)

SHEMER, NAOMI Native Israeli composer and songwriter. Her song *Jerusalem of Gold* became a kind of national anthem during the 1967 Six-Day War and the liberation of Jerusalem. (See also JERUSALEM; SIX-DAY WAR.)

SHENHAR, YITZHAK (name changed from SHENBERG) (1905-1957) Hebrew writer who emigrated from Russia to Palestine in 1924 and became an editor of the Schocken Publishing Company. Shenhar wrote novels about Jewish life in Eastern Europe and

Israel, and also translated foreign novels into Hebrew. (See also SCHOCKEN, GERSHOM GUSTAV.)

SHENKAR COLLEGE OF FASHION AND TEXTILES
School founded in Ramat Gan in 1970. Textiles are one of Israel's most important industries. The Shenkar College trains young people to enter this field. Its courses deal with the manufacture of textiles and business management as well as fashion and fabric design. (See also EDUCATION; RAMAT GAN; TEXTILES.)

SHERUT (the plural is SHERUTIM)   A cross between a taxi and a bus. A sherut is smaller than a bus. The fare is higher, but they are less crowded. It travels along the same route as the regular buses, and also makes trips between cities. The sherut makes trips between cities on Friday night and Saturday when most buses are not permitted, but only special sherutim can run inside cities on the Sabbath.

SHIELD OF DAVID   see MAGEN DAVID

SHILOAH   see SILOAM

SHILOH   Ancient site in the mountains 30 miles north of Jerusalem. The first town was built on the site 4,000 years ago. Shiloh was an important Israelite city from the twelfth to the tenth century B.C.E., before it was destroyed by the Philistines. Archaeologists have uncovered a large house and bath from the time that the Romans occupied the city in the first centuries C.E. (See also ARCHAEOLOGY; HISTORY; PHILISTINES; ROME.)

SHIMONI, DAVID (name changed from SHIMONOVITZ) (1886-1956)   Hebrew poet who left Russia for Palestine in 1920. Shimoni's poems describe the experiences and feelings of the Jewish pioneers in Palestine. Besides writing poems, such as *In the Woods of Hadera* and *The Movement,* Shimoni translated Russian novels into Hebrew. He was the chairman of the Israeli Authors Association and won the Israel Prize for literature in 1954. (See also ISRAEL PRIZE.)

SHIMONI, YAACOV (1915-   )   German-born diplomat who settled in Israel in 1936. Shimoni served as Israel's ambassador to Sweden and to Switzerland. He has written several books about the Arab states in the Middle East and about the Arabs of Palestine.

SHIN SHALOM (pen name of SHAPIRA, SHALOM) (1904-   )   Hebrew writer who was born in Poland and lived in Austria. He settled in Palestine in 1922. Shin Shalom has written religious poetry, a novel, stories, and plays, and has translated Shakespeare's poems into Hebrew.

SHIPPING   Before World War II there were only a few Jewish-owned ships carrying goods to and from Palestine's ports. In 1945 the Zim Israel Shipping Company was established by the Jewish Agency and the Histadrut (federation of labor). When Israel became a state in 1948, ships were needed to bring thousands of immigrants into the country. Over the next three years the merchant fleet grew from a single ship to 31 ships, but most were old or old-fashioned. The reparations received from Germany in the 1950s helped Israel build a large modern fleet of ships. By 1975 Israel had three major shipping companies (Zim, El Yam, and Maritime Fruit Carriers) with 120 ships carrying millions of tons of goods a year to and from Israeli Ports. (See also HISTADRUT; IMMIGRANTS; JEWISH AGENCY; PORTS; REPARATIONS.)

SHITREET, BEHOR SHALOM (also spelled SHITRIT, B'KHOR) (1895-1967)   Native Israeli policeman and politician. Shitreet was educated as a rabbi, but in 1919 he joined the Palestinian police force that had been set up by the British (who ruled Palestine under the Mandate). He later became the head of the Tel Aviv police. After Israel became a state, Shitreet was elected to the Knesset (legislature). He served in the Cabinet as Minister of Police for almost 20 years and helped organize the national police system of Israel. (See also CABINET; GREAT BRITAIN; KNESSET; POLICE.)

SHIVTA (also called SUBEITA)   Ancient city in the Negev about 35 miles south of Beersheba. Shivta was built in the second to first centuries B.C.E. by the Nabateans, an ancient people who cleverly used small amounts of water to grow crops in the desert. It was a city of about 5,000 people under Byzantine rule in the 300s to 600s C.E. Archaeologists have uncovered and restored ancient Shivta. Today, tourists can walk along the old streets and see the remains of hundreds of private houses, three churches, shops, and a public pool. (See also ARCHAEOLOGY; BYZANTINE EMPIRE; NABATEANS; NEGEV; TOURISM.)

SHLONSKY, ABRAHAM DAVID (1900-1973)   Hebrew poet who was born in Russia and settled in Palestine in 1921. His stormy modern poetry has been a model for many young Israeli poets. Besides writing poetry, Shlonsky wrote articles and children's books, translated foreign novels and plays into Hebrew, and edited several magazines. He was a member of the Hebrew Language Academy and created many new Hebrew words. His sister is composer Verdina Shlonsky. (See also HEBREW; HEBREW LANGUAGE ACADEMY; SHLONSKY, VERDINA.)

SHLONSKY, VERDINA (1905-   )   Composer who was born in Russia and taught music in Paris and Berlin before settling in

Palestine in 1931. Verdina Shlonsky wrote orchestral music, music for the Habimah theater company, and Hebrew songs for children and adults. Her brother was the poet Abraham Shlonsky. (See also HABIMAH; SHLONSKY, ABRAHAM DAVID.)

SHOFAR   see ROSH HASHANAH

SHOHAT, ISRAEL (1886-1961)   Russian-born pioneer who settled in Palestine in 1904. In 1909, Shohat founded Hashomer, the "watchmen" organization that defended Jewish farming settlements against Arab attacks. He later became a lawyer, was active in the Histadrut (federation of labor), and served on Palestine's Vaad Leumi (National Council). (See also HASHOMER; HISTADRUT; SHOHAT, MANYA WILBUSCHEWITZ; VAAD LEUMI.)

The beautiful horns on this ram in the Biblical Zoo in Jerusalem are the type of horns from which the *shofar* is made.

SHOHAT, MANYA WILBUSCHEWITZ (1880-1961)   Manya Wilbuschewitz took part in the revolutionary movement in her native Russia before settling in Palestine in 1904 and marrying Israel Shohat. She helped her husband organize Hashomer (Jewish "watchmen" organization) in 1909, and was later active in the Haganah (Jewish underground army), and planned ways of bringing "illegal" immigrants into Palestine. (See also HAGANAH; HASHOMER; IMMIGRANTS, ILLEGAL; SHOHAT, ISRAEL.)

SHOVAL   Kibbutz (cooperative farming village) founded in the northern Negev in 1946 by settlers from other parts of Palestine and from South Africa. (See also KIBBUTZ; NEGEV.)

SHRAGAI, SHLOMO (1899-)   Religious Zionist who settled in Palestine from Russia in 1924. Shragai was on the executive committees of the Jewish Agency and the World Zionist Organization and was a member of Palestine's Vaad Leumi (National Council). He was elected Mayor of Jerusalem in 1951, but had to retire after a year because of his health. (See also JERUSALEM; JEWISH AGENCY; VAAD LEUMI; WORLD ZIONIST ORGANIZATION.)

SHRINE OF THE BOOK   Part of the Israel Museum in Jerusalem. The Shrine of the Book was built to house the 2,000-year-old Dead Sea Scrolls. The roof of the building is shaped like the lid of one of the jars in which the Scrolls were found; the inside gives visitors the feeling of being in a cave. (See also DEAD SEA SCROLLS; ISRAEL MUSEUM.)

The Shrine of the Book in Jerusalem, with the Knesset showing in the background.

SHWARMA (also called GYROS)   Lamb roasted on a spit, sliced, and stuffed into a pocket of pita bread with tomato and pickle. Shwarma is sold at stands (kiosks) in Israeli cities. (See also PITA.)

SICARII   Group of Jews that opposed the Roman rule of Palestine in the first century C.E. The Sicarii carried daggers under their robes to murder Jews who favored Roman rule. Eleazer Ben Jair, the leader of the Jewish rebels who held out against the Romans at Masada in 73 C.E. was a member of the Sicarii. (See also ELEAZER BEN JAIR; MASADA; ROME.)

SIEFF, REBECCA MARKS (1890-1966) English Zionist who was a founder of WIZO (Women's International Zionist Organization). Along with her husband, Israel Moses Sieff, she established the Sieff Research Institute in Rehovot that later became part of the Weizmann Institute of Science. Rebecca Sieff was also active in Youth Aliyah (young people's immigration), which helped bring 1,000 children from Germany to Palestine. (See also WEIZMANN INSTITUTE OF SCIENCE; WIZO; YOUTH ALIYAH; ZIONISM.)

SILBERG, MOSHE (1900-) Judge who was born in Lithuania, studied law in Germany, and settled in Palestine in 1929. Silberg was a District Court Judge in Tel Aviv and was later appointed to the Israeli Supreme Court. He wrote several books on law and was a visiting law professor at the Hebrew University in Jerusalem. In 1969 he won the Israel Prize. (See also COURTS; HEBREW UNIVERSITY; ISRAEL PRIZE; SUPREME COURT.)

SILOAM (also called SHILOAH) Pool south of the walls of the Old City of Jerusalem that was the ancient source of water for the city. To protect the city's water supply, about 700 B.C.E., King Hezekiah of Judah had an underground tunnel built to connect the pool of Siloam to the spring of Gihon. Today tourists can still walk through the ancient tunnel to the pool. (See also GIHON; HEZEKIAH; JERUSALEM; JUDAH, KINGDOM OF; TOURISM.)

SIMA, MIRON (1902-) Russian-born artist who settled in Palestine in 1933 and painted landscapes and portraits.

SIMEON In the Bible, the second son of Jacob and Leah. One of the smaller of the biblical Twelve Tribes of Israel. (See also JACOB; TWELVE TRIBES.)

SIMEON BEN YOHAI (also spelled SHIMON BAR YOHAI) Second century C.E. Palestinian scholar and teacher, a pupil of Rabbi Akiva. Simeon Ben Yohai shared Akiva's opposition to Roman rule over Palestine and was forced to hide from the Romans in a cave for 13 years. Many religious Jews in Israel travel to Simeon's tomb in Meron on the holiday of Lag B'Omer, which is said to be the day of his death. (See also AKIVA BEN JOSEPH; LAG B'OMER; MERON; ROME.)

SIMHAT TORAH (also spelled SIMCHAT TORAH) Jewish holiday whose name means "Rejoicing of the Law." Simhat Torah is celebrated on the eighth day of Sukkot in Israel, which is the 22nd of Tishri in the Hebrew calendar (late September or early October). The holiday marks the end of the year-long reading of the Torah (Five Books of Moses), and the Torah scrolls are carried joyfully around the synagogue. Children receive gifts of raisins or candy. (See also BIBLE; CALENDAR, INTERNATIONAL; CALENDAR, JEWISH; HOLIDAYS; RELIGION; SUKKOT; TORAH.)

Children in an American city celebrating Simhat Torah with
Torahs written by scribes in Israel.

SIMON THE HASMONEAN (also called THASSI or TARSI) (died 135 B.C.E.)   Son of Mattathias and brother of Judah the Maccabee. After his father's and brother's deaths, Simon continued the fight for Jewish independence from Syrian rule in Palestine. In 142 B.C.E., Simon the Hasmonean was declared the High Priest and Commander-in-Chief of the independent Jewish State of Judea. This marked the beginning of about a hundred years of Hasmonean rule. (See also HASMONEANS; HISTORY; JUDAH THE MACCABEE; MATTATHIAS; SELEUCIDS; SYRIA.)

SIMON, ERNST AKIVA (1899-   )   German-born educator who settled in Palestine in 1928. Simon was an educational adviser to Youth Aliyah (young people's immigration) and later taught at the Hebrew University in Jerusalem. He was also active in Berit Shalom and Ihud—two organizations working for the creation of a joint Arab-Jewish State in Palestine. Simon wrote several books on education and won the Israel Prize for education in 1967. (See also BERIT SHALOM; EDUCATION; HEBREW UNIVERSITY; IHUD; ISRAEL PRIZE; YOUTH ALIYAH.)

SINAI   Peninsula that connects Africa and Asia. The Sinai peninsula is shaped like a triangle with the Mediterranean Sea to its north and the Gulf of Suez and the Gulf of Eilat running along its other two sides. It covers an area of about 23,000 square miles of desert and rocky mountains.

Sinai lies between Israel and Egypt. Israel captured it from Egypt during the Sinai War of 1956, returned it the following year, and occupied it again in the 1967 Six-Day War. From 1967 to 1979 Sinai was one of the four administered areas governed by Israel.

The 1979 Israel-Egypt Peace Treaty drew a line from El Arish on the Mediterranean coast to Ras Muhammad on Sinai's southern tip. Israel agreed to pull all its soldiers out of the land west of the line within nine months. It also agreed to remove its soldiers and settlements from the rest of the Sinai within three years and return the whole peninsula to Egypt. Egypt agreed to keep its soldiers out of most of Sinai and to let Israel buy oil from the Sinai oil fields. (See also ADMINISTERED AREAS; EGYPT; EL ARISH; ISRAEL-EGYPT PEACE TREATY; OIL; SINAI WAR; SIX-DAY WAR; SUEZ CANAL.)

SINAI, MOUNT   see JABEL MUSA

SINAI WAR   Israeli military operation against Egypt from October 29 to November 5, 1956. Israel felt threatened by the buildup of arms in Egypt, needed to stop the fedayeen (Arab terrorist) raids on Israeli settlements, and wanted to break the Egyptian blockade that prevented Israeli ships from using the Gulf of Eilat as a route to the Indian Ocean. Israel invaded Sinai and within a few days occupied the Gaza Strip and the entire Sinai peninsula, stopping just short of the Suez Canal. Pressure from the United Nations forced Israel to pull out of the occupied land shortly after the war. However, Israel had achieved its aims. A United Nations peacekeeping force stationed along the Egypt-Israel border stopped the fedayeen raids, and the Gulf of Eilat was opened to Israeli shipping. (See also DEFENSE FORCES; EGYPT; EILAT, GULF OF; FEDAYEEN; GAZA STRIP; HISTORY; SHIPPING; SINAI; SUEZ CANAL; UNITED NATIONS.)

SIPHRIYAT POALIM Israeli publishing company founded in 1940. In its first 35 years it published 1,800 different Hebrew books including the *Encyclopedia of Social Sciences.*

SIX-DAY WAR War between Israel and the Arab nations of Egypt, Syria, and Jordan that lasted from June 5 to June 10, 1967. Shortly before the war started, the Arab nations signed a military pact and declared that they would destroy Israel. Egypt closed the Gulf of Eilat to Israeli shipping. (The blockade of Israeli shipping in 1956 had led to the Sinai War.) Egypt's President Nasser asked the United Nations to remove its peacekeeping force from the Sinai and the Gaza Strip. He then moved 100,000 Egyptian troops into Sinai. Israel promptly called up its own forces.

Israeli soldiers joyfully make their way to the Wailing Wall after liberating the Old City from the Jordanian army. Jordan did not allow Jews access to the Wall since 1948.

After The Wall was liberated in June 1967, Israeli soldiers and civilians flocked to it to pray and meditate.

A few hours after war broke out on June 5, the Israeli air force destroyed most of the Arab war planes on the ground. Its army moved against Egypt and occupied the Gaza Strip and the Sinai. When Jordan attacked, Israel captured the West Bank and the Old City of Jerusalem, which had been in Jordanian hands since 1948. In fighting with Syria, Israel captured the Golan Heights— high land from which the Syrians had often shelled Israeli settlements.

As a result of the war, Jerusalem was reunited and the Gulf of Eilat was again opened to Israeli shipping. Israel also held on to the land it captured. This land (called the "administered areas" or the "occupied areas") is being governed by Israel until its fate is decided by peace treaties between Israel and the Arab nations. (See also ADMINISTERED AREAS; DEFENSE FORCES; EGYPT; EILAT, GULF OF; GAZA STRIP; GOLAN HEIGHTS; HISTORY; JERUSALEM; JORDAN; NASSER, GAMAL ABDUL; SINAI; SINAI WAR; SYRIA; UNITED NATIONS; WEST BANK.)

SLOUSCHZ, NAHUM (1872-1966) Zionist, writer, and archaeologist. Slouschz was active in the Zionist movement in his native Russia, taught Hebrew at the Sorbonne in Paris, and was a student of the ancient Jewish Community in North Africa. In 1919 he settled in Palestine, and was the first Jewish archaeologist to dig near Tiberias. He wrote a number of books on archaeology and history, and also translated French novels into Hebrew. (See also ARCHAEOLOGY; TIBERIAS; ZIONISM.)

SMILANSKY, MOSHE (1874-1953) Hebrew writer and farmer who migrated to Palestine from Russia in 1890. Smilansky grew citrus fruit at Rehovot where he was a leader of the settlement. He founded the Palestine Farmers Association and served as the association's president for many years. He also wrote many stories and articles, and is remembered for his stories about Arab life, which were published under the pen name of Khawaja Musa. (See also CITRUS FRUIT; REHOVOT.)

SMILANSKY, YIZHAR see YIZHAR, S.

SMOLI, ELIEZER (1901-) Russian-born educator and writer who settled in Israel in 1920. Smoli has written more than fifteen books for children. He won the Bialik Prize for his books in 1935 and the Israel Prize in 1956. (See also ISRAEL PRIZE.)

SNEH, MOSHE (name changed from KNEINBAUM) (1909-) Politician who trained as a doctor and was active in the Zionist movement in his native Poland before settling in Palestine in 1940. Sneh joined the Haganah (Jewish underground army), became its leader, organized resistance to British rule, and directed "illegal" Jewish immigration into Palestine. He was later elected to the Israeli Knesset (legislature), first serving as a member of the Mapam Party and then as a Communist (Maki) Party leader. (See also BIALIK PRIZE; HAGANAH; IMMIGRANTS, ILLEGAL; KNESSET; MAKI; MAPAM; ZIONISM.)

SOCCER (called FOOTBALL in Israel)   Soccer is Israel's most popular game. More than 300 soccer teams belong to the Israel Football (Soccer) Association, which was founded in 1928. There is a National League of teams, two First Leagues, and a number of Second and Third leagues, as well as special Youth Leagues. The National League games draw large crowds, particularly for the cup finals held in May and June. (See also SPORTS.)

SOCIALISM   Many of Palestine's early Jewish pioneers were Socialists. They believed that the equipment used to produce food, clothing, housing, and all the needs of a community should be owned and operated by the people of the community, for the good of the whole community. They founded settlements in which the settlers leased the land in common and shared the work and profits. Today Israel's kibbutzim and moshavim (partly-cooperative farming villages) are still run according to Socialist ideas.

In a Socialist nation, the government owns and operates the factories, mines, railroads, etc. A Socialist nation can be a democracy or a dictatorship. Israel is a partly-Socialist democracy. Some factories or industries are owned by the government, some by the Histadrut (federation of labor), and some by individual owners or corporations. (See also DEMOCRACY; ECONOMY; HISTADRUT; INDUSTRY; KIBBUTZ; MOSHAV.)

SOCIAL SERVICES   The government, the Histadrut (federation of labor), and a number of voluntary organizations all provide social services to help Israelis who are sick, poor, old, or in special need. The government National Insurance system pays old age pensions, unemployment benefits, and family allowances. Kupat Holim (Histadrut's health insurance fund) and other labor funds and voluntary organizations provide medical, dental, and hospital care.

Israel has had the special problem of providing for large numbers of immigrants, many of whom have had no money or job skills. The government has worked closely with the Jewish Agency and the Keren Hayesod (Palestine Foundation Fund) to help these immigrants and to train them for new lives.

The government Ministry of Social Welfare runs 180 welfare offices throughout Israel to help the needy (1979). The government supports families who cannot earn enough money to support themselves, as well as old people not covered by the National Insurance system. It cares for orphans and for children whose families cannot take care of them. It also provides day-care centers and educational help for children of poor families, and runs special government programs for the blind and handicapped. (See also EDUCATION; HEALTH; HISTADRUT; IMMIGRANTS; JEWISH AGENCY; KEREN HAYESOD; KUPAT HOLIM; NATIONAL INSURANCE.)

SODOM (also spelled SDOM)   The lowest spot on earth. Sodom lies 1,286 feet below sea level on the southern tip of the Dead Sea. The city of Sodom, the Bible says, was destroyed by fire from heaven because of its wickedness (Genesis 19:24). Modern Sodom was the site of the Palestine Potash Company, which was founded in 1934 to extract minerals from the waters of the Dead Sea. The potash works were cut off by Arab forces during the 1948 War of Independence and reopened as the Dead Sea Works in 1953. (See also DEAD SEA; DEAD SEA WORKS; POTASH; WAR OF INDEPENDENCE.)

SOKOLOW, NAHUM (1860-1936)   Hebrew writer and Zionist leader. Sokolow edited several Hebrew language magazines in his native Poland and wrote a number of books, including the *History of Zionism.* In 1917 he joined Chaim Weizmann in persuading the British government to issue the Balfour Declaration favoring a Jewish national home in Palestine. Sokolow was on the executive committee of the World Zionist Organization and became its president in 1931. He was also active in the Jewish Agency, served as president of the Keren Hayesod (Palestine Foundation Fund), and visited Palestine several times. Twenty years after his death, Sokolow's remains were moved from London to Mount Herzl in Israel. (See also BALFOUR DECLARATION; JEWISH AGENCY; KEREN HAYESOD; MOUNT HERZL; WEIZMANN, CHAIM; WORLD ZIONIST ORGANIZATION; ZIONISM.)

SOLAR ENERGY   Because Israel is bathed in large amounts of sunshine, it is one of the world pioneers in using the sun for energy. In 1979 about one-fifth of all Israeli homes had simple rooftop panels collecting sunlight to heat the household's water. Research is now going on to find ways to use sun power for heating and cooling houses, and providing them with electricity. A solar collector developed in 1977 by Gershon Grossman of the Haifa Technion (along with Frank Kreith of the University of Colorado in the United States) points the way to the practical use of solar energy for the heating and cooling of homes in the near future. (See also TECHNION.)

SOLOMON (tenth century B.C.E.)   King of Israel who ruled from about 960 to 920 B.C.E. Solomon was the son of King David and Bathsheba. When David was near death, Bathsheba persuaded him to name Solomon his successor. The 40 years of Solomon's rule of Israel were quite peaceful and prosperous. He strengthened the kingdom built by David, signed treaties with Egypt and Tyre, expanded the country's trade, and became known for his wisdom.

Solomon was a great builder. He built the Temple and a splendid royal palace in Jerusalem, and made that city the center of his kingdom. He also built a port at Ezion Geber (now called Eilat) and fortified a number of cities—including Megiddo and Hazor—as bases for his chariot troops. However, all this building forced high taxes on the people and led to the breakup of his kingdom after his death. The story of Solomon's life and rule are told in the biblical First Book of Kings. (See also BATHSHEBA; BIBLE; DAVID; EZION GEBER; HISTORY; JERUSALEM; KING SOLOMON'S MINES; REHOBOAM; TEMPLE.)

SOSKIN, SELIG EUGEN (1873-1959) Russian-born agricultural expert who first went to Palestine in 1896 and then traveled and worked in a number of countries before settling there permanently. Soskin was one of the founders of the agricultural settlement of Nahariya. He introduced chemical farming into Palestine and wrote several books on agriculture. (See also AGRICULTURE; NAHARIYA.)

SPECIAL NIGHT SQUADS Military groups organized in 1938 by Orde Wingate, a British army officer, during a period of Arab riots in Palestine. The Special Night Squads were made up of British soldiers and members of the Haganah (Jewish underground army). They guarded the settlements, oil pipelines, and electric lines of the Jezreel Valley and lower Galilee against Arab raids, set ambushes for Arab terrorists, and attacked terrorist bases. The squads did their work well, but in 1939 the British removed Wingate from command of the squads and disbanded them. (See also GREAT BRITAIN; HAGANAH; WINGATE; CHARLES ORDE.)

SPORTS The Jewish pioneers who settled in Palestine in the late 1800s believed in building healthy bodies as well as educating minds. By 1900, Jewish schools had physical education classes and some organized sports for their students. In 1908 the first Sports Festival was held in Rehovot where young people from different villages competed in track-and-field events, wrestling, and horseback riding.

Today many different sports—including soccer, basketball, tennis, swimming, and sailing—are popular in Israel. Children

A major sports event in Israel is the annual Torch Relay from Modiin to Jerusalem to commemorate the Chanukah epic.

בית הספר למאמנים ומדריכים
ע"ש נט הולמן
THE NAT HOLMAN SCHOOL
FOR COACHES AND INSTRUCTORS

בית ספר
לפיסיותרפיה
SCHOOL OF
PHYSIOTHERAPY

The Nat Holman School for coaches and instructors is part of the Wingate Institute for Sports.

and adults alike enjoy marching; over 20,000 people, from age 14 up, turn out each year to make the three-day march to Jerusalem. There are several national sports organizations, including Hapoel (the workers' sports organization) and the Israel Sports Federation. Israeli teams compete at the international Olympic Games, and every four years Jewish athletes come to Israel from all over the world to take part in the Maccabia Games. (See also ACADEMIC SPORTS ORGANIZATION; BASKETBALL; BOXING; HAPOEL; ISRAEL SPORTS FEDERATION; MACCABEE; MACCABIA GAMES; OLYMPIC GAMES; PHYSICAL EDUCATION; PHYSICAL FITNESS BADGE; SAILING; SOCCER; SWIMMING; TENNIS; VOLLEYBALL; WINGATE INSTITUTE; WRESTLING.)

SPRINZAK, YOSEPH (1885-1959)   Labor leader and politician who helped establish a young Zionist organization in his native Russia before he settled in Palestine in 1908. Sprinzak was one of the founders of the Histadrut (federation of labor) and of the Mapai political party. When Israel became a state in 1948, Sprinzak was elected to the Knesset (legislature) and was made its Speaker—a post he held for the rest of his life. (See also HISTADRUT; KNESSET; MAPAI; ZIONISM.)

ST. ANNE'S CHURCH   One of the oldest churches in Jerusalem. It was built in 1100 C.E. by the wife of Baldwin I (Crusader ruler of Jerusalem) on the site of the Virgin Mary's parents' home. (See also BALDWIN I; JERUSALEM.)

ST. STEPHEN'S GATE see LION'S GATE.

STAMPFER, JOSHUA (1852-1908) Pioneer who fled from Hungary at the age of 17 and made his way to Palestine. Stampfer was a founder of Petah Tikva, the first modern Jewish farming settlement in Palestine. He traveled to Europe and helped persuade Baron Edmond de Rothschild to give money to support the settlement. (See also PETAH TIKVA; ROTHSCHILD, EDMOND DE.)

STAMPS From 1920 to 1948, the British (who ruled Palestine under the Mandate) issued stamps imprinted with the word "Palestine" in English, Hebrew, and Arabic. Many of these stamps had pictures of famous landmarks, such as the Dome of the Rock and Rachel's Tomb. When the British pulled out of Palestine in 1948, the temporary Jewish government hastily printed a set of nine new stamps. Since the name of the new country had not yet been decided, the new stamps said "Hebrew Post" instead of "Israel." These stamps have become quite valuable.

Commemorative stamps were issued in Israel in 1976 to celebrate the American Revolution of 1776.

Today stamps of the State of Israel are collected by people all over the world as well as by the country's own stamp collectors. New issues are put out on Independence Day and Rosh Hashanah (the Jewish New Year) and to mark important events or honor important people. (See also GREAT BRITAIN.)

STAR OF DAVID   see MAGEN DAVID

STARER, ROBERT (1924-   )   Native Israeli composer who has written songs as well as orchestral music.

STARKENBERG   see MONTFORT

STATE COMPTROLLER   The State Comptroller of Israel oversees all money spent by the government. He examines the financial accounts of all government Ministries (departments) as well as those of the local governments and the civil service. He also checks into the affairs of companies that the government owns or has a share in. He checks to see that they all operate legally and as efficiently as possible. An Annual Report of his findings is published each year, and any changes he suggests are taken up by the Knesset (legislature).

The State Comptroller is appointed for a five-year term by the President of Israel after he is recommended by the Knesset, to which he is responsible. A staff of about 400 examiners helps him in his work. The first Comptroller was Siegfried Moses, who served for ten years. (See also CIVIL SERVICE; GOVERNMENT; KNESSET; LOCAL GOVERNMENT; MOSES, SIEGFRIED; PRESIDENT.)

STATIONS OF THE CROSS   The fourteen stops that Jesus made as he was led to his execution by the Romans. A special event occurred at each of the Stations of the Cross. At the first Station, Jesus was condemned to death; at the last, he was laid in a sepulchre (tomb). Nine of the Stations lie along the Via Dolorosa, a street in the Old City of Jerusalem. The last five Stations are within the compound of the Church of the Holy Sepulchre. (See also HOLY SEPULCHRE; JERUSALEM; VIA DOLOROSA.)

STEIMATZKY, ERI (1942-   )   Native Israeli publisher. He is the managing director of the Steimatzky Agency, a publishing company founded by his father, Ezekiel Steimatzky. Today the company has 30 stores throughout Israel and plans to open stores in Egypt soon. (See also STEIMATZKY, EZEKIEL.)

STEIMATZKY, EZEKIEL (1900-   )   Lithuanian-born Zionist who settled in Palestine in 1925 and founded a publishing company called the Steimatzky Agency. He has published guides to Israel, textbooks, children's books, and books by many of Israel's leading politicians. (See also STEIMATZKY, ERI.)

STEINBERG, YAAKOV (1887-1947)   Russian born writer who

The Sixth Station of the Cross along the Via Dolorosa. According to
Christian tradition, as Jesus was carrying the cross on the way to
his crucifixion by the Romans his face was perspiring and Veronica
stepped forward to wipe his brow.

Ezekiel Steimatsky, founder of the Steimatsky Agency, confers with
an American publisher at the 1979 International Book Fair.

settled in Palestine in 1914 and wrote in both Hebrew and Yiddish. Steinberg's stories and poems were sad, often telling of the suffering of Eastern European Jewry.

STEINHARDT, JAKOB (1887-1968)   Artist who moved to Palestine from Poland in 1933 and later became the director of the Bezalel School of Arts and Crafts. He is known for his colorful paintings of the countryside of Palestine and his woodcuts of biblical subjects. (See also BEZALEL SCHOOL OF ARTS AND CRAFTS.)

STEINMANN, ELIEZER (1892-1970)   Hebrew writer who was already known in his native Russia before he settled in Palestine in 1924. Steinmann wrote a number of novels, was often published in the newspaper *Davar,* and translated Russian novels into Hebrew. His son is writer Natan Shaham. (See also DAVAR; SHAHAM, NATAN.)

STERN, ABRAHAM (also known as YAIR) (1907-1942)   Polish-born soldier who went to Palestine as a young man, joined the Haganah (Jewish underground army), and helped defend Jerusalem during the Arab riots of 1929. Finding the Haganah policy (of defense without revenge) too mild, Stern helped found the Irgun, a more aggressive military group. He left the Irgun in 1940 and formed the Stern Group, which bombed British military posts and assassinated British soldiers and officials. Stern was shot by the British police in 1942. (See also ARAB RIOTS; GREAT BRITAIN; HAGANAH; IRGUN; STERN GROUP.)

STERN GROUP (also called LEHI or LOHAME HERUT ISRAEL) Jewish fighting group formed by Abraham Stern in 1940. The Stern Group split off from the Irgun (an aggressive Jewish military organization) because Irgun joined the Haganah (Jewish underground army). The Stern group wanted to fight British rule in Palestine even while Great Britain was at war with Germany (World War II); the Haganah did not agree. Abraham Stern was killed in 1942, but the group continued its terror tactics against the British. Its members assassinated British Deputy Minister Moyne and were probably responsible for the 1948 murder of Count Bernadotte, the United Nations peacemaker. (See also BERNADOTTE, FOLKE; GREAT BRITAIN; HAGANAH; HISTORY; IRGUN; STERN, ABRAHAM.)

STOCKADE AND TOWER SETTLEMENT (the Hebrew name is HOMA U-MIGDAL)   A fortified Jewish farming settlement. Built with four hollow wooden walls filled with gravel (the stockade), forming a closed square around a watchtower topped with a searchlight. Cabins for settlers were built inside the walls. A whole settlement was put up in a single day with the help of hundreds of people from nearby villages. These settlements protected pioneers against Arab raids, and work on the fields could be carried out. Stockade and tower settlements were built in Palestine from 1936 to 1945.

STRAUS, NATHAN (1848-1931) American businessman and Zionist. Straus was born in Germany and brought to the United States as a young child. He became a prosperous businessman. When he was the head of Macy's department store in New York, he supplied milk to the poor children of the city. Straus and his wife, Lina Gutherz Straus, visited Palestine several times. On their 1913 visit, they brought two nurses with them and started the Hadassah Health Institute. During his lifetime, Nathan Straus donated over $12,000,000 to build health centers and other projects in Palestine. The city of Netanya is named in his honor. (See also HADASSAH; HEALTH; NETANYA; ZIONISM.)

STRUCK, HERMANN (1876-1944) Artist and Zionist who helped found the Mizrahi (religious Zionist) organization in his native Germany before settling in Palestine in 1922. Struck is known for his etchings of important Jews of his day, including one of his friend, Zionist leader Theodor Herzl. His book *The Art of Etching* is still studied by art students. (See also HERZL, THEODOR; MIZRAHI; ZIONISM.)

STRUMA Ship that sailed from Rumania in 1941 carrying 769 Jewish "illegal" immigrants to Palestine. The *Struma* was an old leaky boat, not fit to be at sea. When the ship tried to dock in Istanbul, the Turks would not let it dock unless the British (who governed Palestine) agreed to allow the immigrants to go on to Palestine. The British refused. The *Struma* sank in the Black Sea and all its passengers drowned. (See also IMMIGRANTS, ILLEGAL.)

SUBEITA see SHIVTA

SUEZ CANAL The 100-mile long canal that connects the southeast corner of the Mediterranean Sea to the Red Sea and lets European ships sail into the Indian Ocean without going all the way around Africa. The Suez Canal was built between 1859 and 1869. Although it is on Egyptian land, the British government controlled the company that owned the canal until the Egyptian government took control in 1956. Israeli forces stopped just short of the Suez Canal in the 1956 Sinai War, but camped along its east bank after the 1967 Six-Day War. The canal was then closed to all shipping. Egypt recaptured it in the 1973 Yom Kippur War, and it was opened again in 1975. Egypt had never allowed Israeli ships to use the Suez Canal, but this was changed by the 1979 Israel-Egypt Peace Treaty. In April 1979 the first Israeli ship passed through the canal. (See also EGYPT; ISRAEL-EGYPT PEACE TREATY; MEDITERRANEAN SEA; RED SEA; SINAI WAR; SIX-DAY WAR; YOM KIPPUR WAR.)

SUKENIK, ELIEZER LIPA (1889-1953)   Polish-born archaeologist who settled in Palestine in 1912, taught at the Hebrew University in Jerusalem, and became the director of the university's Museum of Jewish Antiquities. Sukenik helped uncover the Third Wall of the ancient city of Jerusalem, headed archaeological digs at Bet Alpha and in Samaria, and published several books of his findings.

In 1947, an Arab dealer showed Sukenik some pieces of leather with ancient writing on them. Sukenik realized how important they were. He went on a dangerous mission to Bethlehem (which was then in Arab hands) and bought three of the 2,000-year-old Dead Sea Scrolls for the Hebrew University. Several years later Sukenik's son, Yigael Yadin, was able to add four more scrolls to the collection, now kept in the Israel Museum. (See also ARCHAEOLOGY; BET ALPHA; DEAD SEA SCROLLS; HEBREW UNIVERSITY; ISRAEL MUSEUM; YADIN, YIGAEL.)

SUKKOT (also spelled SUKOT and SUCCOTH)   Jewish holiday that commemorates the wandering of the Jews in the desert after the Exodus from Egypt. Sukkot begins on the fifteenth of Tishri on the Jewish calendar (October on the international calendar). It is also a harvest festival. Jewish families celebrate Sukkot by building a *sukkah*. A *sukkah* is a little hut or booth whose open roof is covered with leaves. Fruits and vegetables are hung in the *sukkah* and the family eats in it for the seven days of the holiday. Sukkot is also celebrated by carrying the four species of plants (palm, citron, willow, and myrtle) around the synagogue.

In Israel, the holiday of Simhat Torah (Rejoicing of the Law) is celebrated after the seventh day of Sukkot. (See also CALENDAR, INTERNATIONAL; CALENDAR, JEWISH; EXODUS; HOLIDAYS; SIMHAT TORAH.)

SUPREME COURT   Israel's highest court. It is made up of ten judges and meets in Jerusalem. The Supreme Court rules on appeals from the lower District Courts. It also meets as the High Court of Justice and hears citizen cases against the central government, local governments, or public agencies. Unlike the United States Supreme Court, the Israeli Supreme Court cannot cancel laws passed by the Israeli Knesset (legislature). (See also COURTS; GOVERNMENT; KNESSET; JUDGES.)

SWIMMING   Israel's warm weather and its closeness to the sea make swimming popular with adults and children alike. Most Israeli children learn to swim at an early age. Each year many

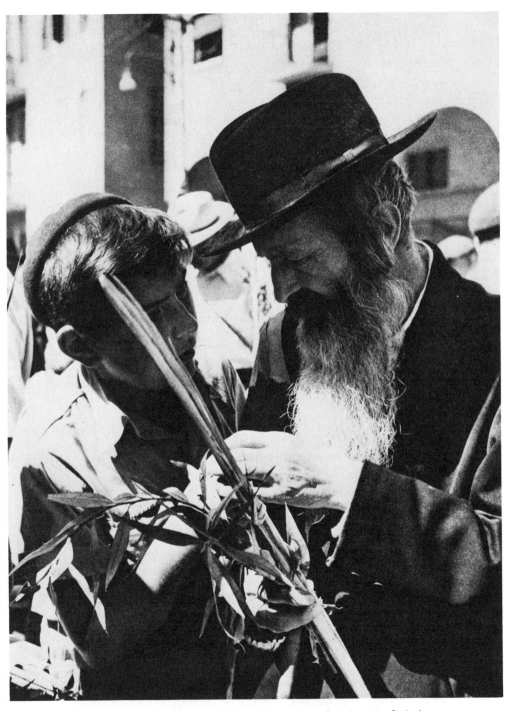

Selecting the very finest *etrog* (citron) and *lulav* (palm) is a longstanding tradition in Israel and all over the world.

thousands of swimmers turn out for the annual two-and-a-half mile swim across Lake Kinneret (Sea of Galilee). There are more than 300 swimming pools in Israel's inland kibbutzim. (See also KIBBUTZ; SPORTS.)

SYNGALOWSKI CENTER   Technical school in Tel Aviv built with money from Women's American ORT (Organization for Rehabilitation Through Training). It is the largest and most modern technical school in the Middle East. About 1,200 young people and 400 adults study electronics, mechanics, computer skills, etc., at the Syngalowki Center each year. (See also EDUCATION; ORT.)

SYRIA (officially called SYRIAN ARAB REPUBLIC)   Middle Eastern nation that lies northeast of Israel and borders the Jewish State along the Golan Heights. Syria has an area of 71,500 square miles and a population of 7,860,000 people (1977). About 86% of the population is Moslem and most of the rest is Christian. Arabic is the official language, although Turkish and Armenian are also spoken. The capital is Damascus.

Syria was called Aram in biblical times. King David of Israel conquered much of Aram in the tenth century B.C.E. There were frequent wars between Syria and the Jewish nations of Israel and Judah until the Assyrians conquered Syria in 720 B.C.E. From that time on, Syria—like the other countries of the area, including Israel—was ruled in turn by the Assyrians, Persians, Greeks, and Romans.

In 1920, after World War I, France received the League of Nations Mandate to govern Syria. Syria became an independent state in 1944. In 1958 it joined Egypt to form the United Arab Republic, but broke away again in 1961.

Israel and Syria have been at war three times since Israel became a state. Syrian forces were among the Arab armies that invaded Israel in the 1948 War of Independence, but their attacks on the Jezreel Valley and Galilee were beaten back. The fighting of the 1967 Six-Day War ended with Syria losing the Golan Heights to Israel, and Syria's attempt to recapture the heights in the 1973 Yom Kippur War failed. (See also ARAMEANS; ASSYRIA; DAVID; EGYPT; GALILEE; GOLAN HEIGHTS; HISTORY; ISRAEL, KINGDOM OF; JEZREEL VALLEY; JUDAH, KINGDOM OF; LEAGUE OF NATIONS; MANDATE; SIX-DAY WAR; WAR OF INDEPENDENCE; YOM KIPPUR WAR.)

SZENES, HANNAH (also spelled SENESH) (1921-1944)   Poet and heroine. At the age of 18, against her widowed mother's wishes, Hannah Szenes left Hungary and immigrated to Palestine. Shortly afterward, the Nazis occupied Hungary. Wanting to go back to her native country to help other young people come to

Palestine, she joined the British army and was trained as one of the Jewish parachutists who were to drop into Europe to organize Jewish resistance to the Nazis. She parachuted into Italy, but was captured before she could reach Hungary. Hannah Szenes was shot in 1944 at the age of 23. Her best known poem, *Blessed Is the Match*, was written shortly before her death. (See also HOLOCAUST; NAZIS.)

SZOLD, HENRIETTA (1860-1945) Writer, educator, Zionist leader, and founder of Hadassah. Henrietta Szold was born and educated in Baltimore in the United States, began teaching at the age of 17, and was writing articles for Jewish magazines before she was 19.

An ardent Zionist, she visited Palestine in 1909 and saw the terrible health conditions in the country. In 1912 she organized Hadassah (the Women's Zionist Organization of America) to begin to deal with Palestine's health problems. Hadassah has since grown into an organization of 360,000 women supporting hospitals, clinics, and schools throughout Israel.

Henrietta Szold

In 1920 Henrietta Szold settled in Palestine. She was the first woman to serve on the executive committee of the World Zionist Organization and was also elected to Palestine's Vaad Leumi (National Council). When the Nazis rose to power in Germany, she became a leader of Youth Aliyah—a movement started by Recha Freier to bring children and young people out of Germany (and later from all of Europe) and settle them in Palestine.

The village of Kefar Szold is named in honor of Henrietta Szold, as are schools, hospitals, and city streets throughout Israel. (See also FREIER, RECHA; HADASSAH; HEALTH; KEFAR SZOLD; NAZIS; VAAD LEUMI; YOUTH ALIYAH; WORLD ZIONIST ORGANIZATION; ZION-ISM.)

SZOLD INSTITUTE   Research section of the Jewish Agency. The Szold Institute is named in honor of Henrietta Szold and grew out of the Child and Youth Welfare Institute, which she founded in 1941. Today the institute studies all kinds of human behavior, although it still has a special interest in young people. (See also JEWISH AGENCY; SZOLD, HENRIETTA.)

T

TAANAKH Ancient Canaanite city in the Jezreel Valley that later became part of King Solomon's Jewish kingdom. Only a few stones remain of the ancient town. Since 1956, 15,000 acres of land in the Taanakh area have been developed with new villages and farms. (See also CANAAN; JEZREEL VALLEY; SOLOMON.)

TABGHA (also called HEPTAPEGON) Ancient town on the north shore of Lake Kinneret (Sea of Galilee). The Church of the Multiplication of the Loaves and Fishes stands on the place where Christians believe Jesus fed hundreds of people with five loaves of bread and two fishes. The church has mosaic floors from the 600s C.E. which picture local plants and animals. (See also LAKE KINNERET; MOSAICS.)

TABOR, MOUNT see MOUNT TABOR

TAHAL The Israeli government water planning corporation. Tahal was established by the government in 1952 to plan projects that would use the country's scarce water in the best possible way. Tahal plans irrigation systems, sewerage systems, city water supplies, flood control, and pollution control projects. Its largest undertaking was the National Water Carrier which brings water from the north of Israel to irrigate the dry south. Although Tahal planned and operates the National Water Carrier, the actual construction of the project was done by Mekorot, a construction organization. (See also DAN REGION PROJECT; IRRIGATION; MEKOROT; NATIONAL WATER CARRIER; WATER.)

TAHINA Paste made from sesame seeds. Tahina is used as a sauce on food in Middle Eastern countries, including Israel.

TAL, ISRAEL (1924-) Native Israeli soldier. Tal fought with the Jewish Brigade during World War II, joined the Haganah (Jewish underground army), and trained units of the Palmah (Haganah's striking force). He fought in the 1948 War of Independence and commanded troops in the 1956 Sinai War and the 1967 Six-Day War. He rose to the rank of Major-General and served as Deputy Chief-of-Staff before he retired from the Israel Defense Forces. (See also DEFENSE FORCES; HAGANAH; JEWISH

BRIGADE; PALMAH; SINAI WAR; SIX-DAY WAR; WAR OF INDEPEN-
DENCE.)

TAL, JOSEPH (name changed from GRUNTHAL) (1910-)
German-born composer who settled in Palestine in 1934. Tal was
the founder of the Institute for Electronic Music and wrote a
number of pieces of electronic music along with symphonies,
operas, and music for piano and violin.

TAL SHAHAR Village founded in the Judean Hills in 1948. It
was named to honor the American, Henry Morgenthau, Jr., for
his work with the United Jewish Appeal. The Hebrew name Tal
Shahar is a translation of Morgenthau, a German name meaning
morning dew. (See also JUDEAN HILLS; UNITED JEWISH APPEAL.)

TALMUD The word means "teaching" in Hebrew and refers to
the many books that interpret the Bible, particularly the Torah
(first five books of the Bible). The Talmud is made up of the
records of the discussions of scholars in the yeshivot (religious
schools) of Palestine and Babylon during the five centuries
ending in 500 C.E. There is a Babylonian Talmud and a Palestinian Talmud. The Babylonian Talmud is considered more
important because the greatest Jewish scholars lived in Babylon
at that time.

All Jewish religious law is based on the Talmud. In Israel,
where religion is not kept separate from government as it is in the
United States, many of the laws of the country also come from the
Talmud. (See also BABYLON; BIBLE; RELIGION; TORAH; YESHIVA.)

TAMARISK Low tree native to the deserts of Israel. The tamarisk has long thin branches with small narrow leaves and
clusters of very tiny flowers.

TAMMUZ, BENJAMIN (1919-) Hebrew writer who was born
in Russia and educated in Israel and France. Tammuz has
written a number of novels, of which *Golden Sands* is the best
known. He has also written short stories and articles, and is
editor of the literary supplement of the newspaper *Haaretz*. (See
also HAARETZ.)

TANNA (the plural is TANNAIM) Teachers of Judaism from
about 20 to 200 C.E. One of the last Tannaim was Judah Hanasi,
who edited the Mishna (the first part of the Talmud). The
teachings and legal opinions of the Tannaim were recorded in
the Mishna. (See also JUDAH HANASI; MISHNA; TALMUD.)

TARTAKOWER, ARYE (1897-) Austrian-born sociologist
who lived in Poland and the United States before settling in
Palestine in 1946. Tartakower taught sociology at the Hebrew
University in Jerusalem, was head of the Israeli section of the

World Jewish Congress, and wrote books about the Jewish labor movement. (See also HEBREW UNIVERSITY; WORLD JEWISH CONGRESS.)

TECHNION (also called ISRAEL INSTITUTE OF TECHNOLOGY) Israel's leading university of engineering and technical science. The Technion was founded in Haifa in 1912, but did not open for classes until 1924. At first the school gave courses only in engineering, but in the 1950s architecture, mathematics, and natural sciences were added to the program of studies. The Technion now trains over 10,000 students a year in its technical high school, colleges, and graduate schools at its Haifa campus. Another 11,000 students are taking courses given by the Technion in other parts of the country. About 70% of all of Israel's engineers and applied scientists have received their training at the Technion.

A good deal of research in the fields of engineering, mathematics, industry, and defense is carried out at the Technion. Important research had been done on the desalinization (removing salt) of water and in the design of airplanes and farm machinery. (See also DESALINIZATION; EDUCATION; HAIFA.)

TEL (also spelled TELL) Hebrew and Arabic word for "hill" or "mound." The word is usually used to mean a hill formed by soil covering the remains of an ancient settlement. "Tel" is sometimes part of place-names in Israel, as in "Tel Aviv."

TEL AVIV Israel's largest city. It has a population of almost 375,000, with another 400,000 people living in its suburbs (called the Dan Region). Tel Aviv is the arts, entertainment, business, and industrial center of Israel. It contains the headquarters of Israel's banks, insurance companies, newspapers, etc., and has theaters, concert halls, art galleries, cafes, and nightclubs.

Tel Aviv (whose name means "Hill of Spring") was founded in 1909 on the sand dunes north of Jaffa. During World War I (1914-1918) the Turks (who ruled Palestine) forced the Jews of Tel Aviv to leave the country, but they returned after the British conquered Palestine. Tel Aviv grew rapidly as it absorbed new immigrants, and by 1948 it had a population of 220,000. It was the scene of bitter fighting during the War of Independence. Israel was declared a state in Tel Aviv on May 14, 1948, and the city served as the country's capital for two years. In 1949 Tel Aviv was joined to neighboring Jaffa to form the twin city of Tel Aviv-Jaffa.

Visitors and citizens alike enjoy swimming at Tel Aviv's beaches (the city is on the Mediterranean Sea), sitting in outdoor cafes along Dizengoff Street (named for the first Mayor), wandering through the art galleries in the narrow streets of Old Jaffa, or going to the theater. The Habimah National Theater has its

Many street signs in Tel Aviv are electrified. This one not only names the streets intersected, but also advertises baby carriages.

home in Tel Aviv, and the Israel Philharmonic Orchestra plays at the Mann Auditorium. There are several museums including the Haaretz Museum (Museum of the Land), the Tel Aviv Museum, the Alphabet Museum, and the Haganah Museum (Beit Eliahu). (See also DAN REGION PROJECT; DIZENGOFF, MEIR; GREAT BRITAIN; HAARETZ MUSEUM; HABIMAH; ISRAEL PHILHARMONIC ORCHESTRA; JAFFA; JEWISH DIASPORA MUSEUM; TEL AVIV MUSEUM; TEL AVIV UNIVERSITY; TURKEY; WAR OF INDEPENDENCE.)

TEL AVIV MUSEUM   Museum founded in 1926 that shows paintings and sculpture by Israeli artists. A more modern building was built in 1971. The museum includes the Dizengoff House (given to the city by its first Mayor) where concerts are held every Saturday evening in the winter. (See also DIZENGOFF, MEIR; TEL AVIV.)

TEL AVIV UNIVERSITY   University founded by the City of Tel Aviv in 1956 by joining two schools established earlier. It moved to its campus in Ramat Aviv in 1963. Tel Aviv University has about 11,000 students studying under 1,900 teachers in its schools of science, humanities, law, business, social work, education, medicine, and engineering. Research in 40 different fields is being carried out at the university, including the study of the environment. The university uses the largest computer system in

An aerial view of Tel Aviv (1980) as seen from the Shalom Tower.
The Mediterranean Sea is in the background.

Tel Aviv University

the country for its research projects. (See also EDUCATION; TEL AVIV.)

TEL DAN see DAN

TEL HAI Settlement founded in upper Galilee in 1918. Tel Hai was attacked by Arabs in 1920 and several of its defenders, including Joseph Trumpeldor, were killed. Their tomb, topped by a large stone lion of Judah, has become a national shrine. Young people travel from all over Israel to visit the tomb on the anniversary of Trumpeldor's death. Tel Hai is now part of the village of Kefar Giladi. (See also GALILEE; KEFAR GILADI; TRUMPELDOR, JOSEPH.)

TELL EL-FARA see SHARUHEN

TEL MOND Farming settlement founded about 20 miles north of Tel Aviv in 1929. Tel Mond has since grown to a village of over 3,000 people.

TEL YOSEPH Kibbutz founded in the Jezreel Valley in 1921 and named in honor of the soldier Joseph Trumpeldor. The life of Trumpeldor and the kibbutz movement are featured in a museum at Tel Yoseph. (See also JEZREEL VALLEY; KIBBUTZ; TRUMPELDOR, JOSEPH.)

TELEVISION Television was not available in Israel until 1965, and regular television broadcasts did not start until 1969. Today, Israel has a single television network which broadcasts programs about seven hours a day. Most of the programs are in Hebrew and a few are in Arabic. Important programs have Hebrew and Arabic subtitles so they can be enjoyed by all people. (See also ARABIC; BROADCASTING; HEBREW.)

TEMPLE   The center of Jewish worship for a thousand years. The First Temple was built on Mount Moriah in Jerusalem by King Solomon in the tenth century B.C.E. Its entrance hall led to the shrine where the people worshipped and where sacrifices were brought. An inner room, the Holy of Holies, contained the Ark of the Covenant. Every Jew paid a tax of half a shekel a year for the Temple's upkeep.

The First Temple was destroyed in 586 B.C.E. when the Babylonians conquered Palestine and sent the Jews into exile. The Jews were allowed to return in 538 B.C.E. They then built the Second Temple, which was completed in 515 B.C.E. Over the next 500

A model of the Temple in Jerusalem. The Temple was first built by King Solomon.

The facade of the Second Temple, erected by Herod.

years the Temple was repaired and enlarged, and in the late first century B.C.E. King Herod built a larger and more elaborate building around the old Temple. This was the building that the Romans destroyed in 70 C.E. as part of their punishment of the Jews for the 66-70 revolt.

Today, the Dome of the Rock, which is a Moslem mosque, stands on Mount Moriah. All that remains standing of the Temple is the Western Wall, which was once part of the outer wall of Herod's Temple. However, archaeologists have dug near the Western Wall and found many objects from the times of the First and Second Temples. (See also ARCHAEOLOGY; ARK OF THE COVENANT; BABYLONIAN EXILE; DOME OF THE ROCK; HEROD I; HISTORY; JERUSALEM; JESUS; MOUNT MORIAH; ROME; SHEKEL; SOLOMON; WESTERN WALL.)

TEMPLE SCROLL   One of the ancient Dead Sea Scrolls. The

Of the many gates leading to the Temple Mount, this gate, the Gate
of Chains (Bab El Silsileh in Arabic), adjacent to the Western Wall,
is probably the most beautiful.

Temple Scroll was discovered in 1967 and describes Jerusalem and the Temple as they were about 2,000 years ago. (See also DEAD SEA SCROLLS; TEMPLE.)

TEMPLE MOUNT   see MOUNT MORIAH

TEN COMMANDMENTS (also called DECALOGUE) The ten laws given by God to Moses on Mount Sinai. The Ten Commandments are the foundation of Jewish religious law. They are found in the Bible in the Book of Exodus, Chapter 20. (See also BIBLE; JABEL MUSA; MOSES.)

TENNIS   Israel has a warm sunny climate where tennis can be played outdoors most of the year. However, there are not yet enough courts to accommodate the growing number of players. Most tennis is played in clubs, and about 40 tennis clubs belong to the Israel Tennis Association which was founded in 1949. Israel sends players to compete in the world tennis Davis Cup games, but the Israelis have never won the Davis Cup. (See also SPORTS.)

TENUAT HAMOSHAVIM   Organization of *moshave ovedim* (a type of cooperative farming villages) founded in 1925. The organization began with eight moshavim. In 1979 it had about 250 member villages in which 90,000 people lived and worked. (See also MOSHAV.)

TERRORISM   Threats or violence used by a group to force a government or a people to grant their demands. Arab groups like Al Fatah and the Palestine Liberation Organization have used terrorism in their struggle to destroy Israel. They have attacked Israeli towns, set off bombs in Israeli cities, and hijacked airplanes. Arab terrorists (called *fedayeen*) usually attack innocent civilians. In April of 1974 they killed 18 people in the town of Kiryat Shemona. That May they held 90 students hostage in Maalot. In March of 1978 terrorists seized a bus near Tel Aviv and killed 37 civilians and wounded 82 others.

Not all Arab terrorist attacks have been carried out in Israel. At the 1972 Olympic Games in Munich, Germany, terrorists invaded the Israeli athletes' rooms and 11 athletes were killed. In 1976 an airplane flying from Tel Aviv to Paris was hijacked and its passengers held hostage at Entebbe Airport in Uganda. A daring raid by Israeli soldiers freed the hostages.

Israel has tried to stop terrorist attacks on its civilians by bombing and raiding the terrorist bases in Lebanon. After the 1978 attack on the bus near Tel Aviv, Israeli forces moved across the border and occupied most of southern Lebanon. They held the Lebanese land for about a week until a United Nations

Signs warning passersby to be aware of mine fields can be seen all along the borders of Israel. They have helped reduce the number of terrorist casualties.

One of several bunkers at Kefar Ruppin into which members are evacuated when an attack is threatened.

גבול לפניך - אין מעבר
DEFENSE DE PASSER!
TERRITOIRE ENNEMI
خطر! الحدود امامك
ممنوع المرور
BORDER! NO PASSAGE!

Since it achieved statehood in 1949, Israel has been careful to make its borders secure. Above is an early posted sign.

peacekeeping force took their place. (See also AL FATAH; ARAFAT, YASIR; ENTEBBE RAID; FEDAYEEN; KIRYAT SHEMONA; LEBANON; MAALOT; PALESTINE LIBERATION ORGANIZATION; UNITED NATIONS.)

TEXTILES Israel's textile industry—which manufactures fabric and finished clothing—was started in the 1950s in part to provide work for many of the large number of new immigrants who had poured into the country. By the late 1970s the textile industry accounted for about 10% of all products manufactured in Israel. Three-quarters of the clothing produced is used by the Israelis themselves; the balance is exported to foreign countries. (See also FOREIGN TRADE; IMMIGRANTS; INDUSTRY.)

THEATER The theater is very popular in Israel. The average Israeli buys more theater tickets each year than citizens of any other country in the world. The three main theater companies are Habimah, Cameri, and the Haifa Municipal Theater. About two-thirds of the tickets bought are for performances in these theaters.

Habimah, founded in 1917, is Israel's national theater. Cameri (also called the Tel Aviv Municipal Theater) is smaller than Habimah and is popular with young sabras (native Israelis). The Haifa Municipal Theater, founded in 1961 and supported by the city of Haifa, is the newest of the three. There are also a number of small theater groups in Jerusalem, Tel Aviv, Beersheba, and other cities. In addition to the Hebrew-speaking companies, there are groups performing in English or Arabic. There are also

The Cameri Theater in Jerusalem is housed in one of the unique architectural structures of Israel.

several children's theaters which give shows for elementary school children.

Tel Aviv is the theater center of Israel. Habimah and Cameri have their theaters in the city. However, both the large and the smaller theater companies make frequent tours of the country. They bring live shows to other cities and towns, farming communities, and army bases. Many of the small towns and kibbutzim also have their own amateur theater groups that put on shows for themselves and their friends and neighbors. (See also BATZAL YAROK; CAMERI; DANCE; HABIMAH; HAIFA MUNICIPAL THEATER; KIBBUTZ; MUSIC; TEL AVIV.)

THON, YAAKOV (1880-1950)   Austrian-born lawyer and Zionist who settled in Palestine in 1907. During his career, Thon was the director of the Palestine Land Development Corporation, president of Palestine's Vaad Leumi (National Council), and a member of the executive committee of the Jewish Agency. He was one of the founders of Tel Aviv and helped buy land for Jewish settlement in the Jezreel Valley. (See also JEWISH AGENCY; JEZREEL VALLEY; PALESTINE LAND DEVELOPMENT CORPORATION; TEL AVIV; VAAD LEUMI; ZIONISM.)

TIBERIAS (also called TVERYA)   One of the holy cities of Israel,

The old and the new in Tiberias, on the western shore of Lake Kinneret (Sea of Galilee). In the foreground is an ancient fortress dating back to crusader days and used today as a museum. In the background is a recently built hotel: The Plaza.

Tiberias lies 690 feet below sea level on the western shore of Lake Kinneret (also called Lake Tiberias and Sea of Galilee). The city was built about 20 C.E. by Herod Antipas (son of Herod the Great) and named for the Roman emperor Tiberius. It became the home of the Sanhedrin (Jewish Supreme Court) in the 200s C.E. and remained the center of Jewish learning until the Arabs conquered it in the 600s. Many Jewish scholars, including Rabbi Akiva and Maimonides (Rambam), are buried there. Tiberias was conquered by the Crusaders in 1099 and fell to the Moslem sultan Saladin in 1187. Jews returned to Tiberias in the 1500s.

Today Tiberias is a winter resort with a population of about 25,000. Visitors come to enjoy the warm winter climate, go boating and swimming in the lake, bathe in the hot springs that are said to cure arthritis and skin diseases, and visit the historic tombs. (See also AKIVA BEN JOSEPH; ANTIPAS; CRUSADES; HEROD I; HISTORY; LAKE KINNERET; SALADIN; SANHEDRIN; TIBERIUS.)

TIBERIUS (full name: TIBERIUS CLAUDIUS NERO) (42 B.C.E.-37 C.E.) Emperor of Rome from 14 to 37 C.E. During his rule, Palestine (which was then part of the Roman Empire) was harshly governed, and Jesus Christ was crucified. (See also ROME.)

TICHO, ABRAHAM ALBERT (1883-1960) Doctor who specialized in treating eye diseases. Born and trained in Austria, Ticho went to Palestine in 1912 to head an eye clinic. He was active in the Hadassah (a women's Zionist organization) drive to wipe out trachoma (a serious eye disease) in Palestine. During his lifetime, he performed about 40,000 eye operations — many of them free of charge for poor Jews and Arabs. He was married to Anna Ticho, an artist. (See also HADASSAH; TICHO, ANNA.)

TICHO, ANNA (1894-   ) Austrian-born artist who studied in Vienna before settling in Palestine in 1912. Anna Ticho is known for her drawings of Jerusalem and her pictures of new immigrants to Israel. Her husband, Abraham Ticho, was an eye doctor. (See also TICHO, ABRAHAM ALBERT.)

TIGRIS RIVER One of the two rivers that border the Tigris-Euphrates Valley, an area that is now Iraq. The fertile land between the Tigris and the Euphrates rivers was called Mesopotamia in ancient times and gave rise to the world's earliest civilization. (See also FERTILE CRESCENT; MESOPOTAMIA.)

TISHA B'AV Hebrew words meaning "ninth of Av" (also spelled Ab). Jewish religious fast day commemorating the destruction of the First Temple by the Babylonians in 586 B.C.E., and the destruction of the Second Temple by the Romans in 70 C.E. Tisha

B'Av Falls on the 9th day of Av on the Jewish calendar, usually during July. (See also CALENDAR, INTERNATIONAL; CALENDAR, JEWISH; HISTORY; HOLIDAYS; TEMPLE.)

TITUS (full name FLAVIUS SABINUS VESPASIANUS TITUS) (40-81 C.E.)   Emperor of Rome who ruled 79-81 C.E. During the Jewish revolt against the Roman rule of Palestine, Titus took command of the Roman armies in Palestine from his father, Emperor Vespasian. After a five-month siege of Jerusalem, Titus destroyed the city and the Temple. (See also HISTORY; JERUSALEM; ROME; TEMPLE; VESPASIAN.)

TNUVA   see HISTADRUT

TOLKOWSKY, SAMUEL (1886-1965)   Dutch farming expert who settled in Palestine in 1911 and introduced new methods for growing and selling citrus fruit. Tolkowsky was the secretary of the Palestine Citrus Marketing Board, helped found the Zim Shipping Company, and served as Israel's Minister to Switzerland. (See also CITRUS FRUIT; SHIPPING.)

TOMB OF RACHEL   see RACHEL, TOMB OF

TOMB OF THE PATRIARCHS   see MACHPELAH, CAVE OF

TOMB OF THE VIRGIN MARY   Site in eastern Jerusalem where tradition says the Virgin Mary is buried. Visitors walk down a flight of 47 steps to the underground church containing the tomb. The first church on the site was built in the fifth century C.E. The present church dates from the twelfth century. (See also JERUSALEM.)

TOMBS OF THE KINGS   Large tomb in northern Jerusalem with a staircase and a court carved out of rock and six burial rooms. The Tomb of the Kings is really the tomb of Queen Helena, who went to Jerusalem from Iraq in the first centruy C.E. and became a Jew. (See also JERUSALEM.)

TOPOL, CHAIM (stage name, TOPOL) (1935-   )   Israeli actor who became known in his native country by acting with the Haifa Municipal Theater. Topol starred in a number of Israeli films and became world famous when he played Tevyo in the film *Fiddler on the Roof.*

TORAH   The first of the three sections of the Hebrew Bible. The Torah is made up of five books: Genesis, Exodus, Leviticus, Numbers, and Deuteronomy. Other names for the Torah are the Five Books of Moses, the Written Law, and the Pentateuch (a Greek work meaning "five books"). Jewish tradition says that the Torah was revealed to Moses when he received the Ten

In Jaffa, scribes write and correct Torah scrolls. The pen used is a quill. Since the destruction of the Jewish communities of Europe during World War II, new Torahs have been written by scribes in Israel.

Commandments on Mount Sinai. The word "Torah" is often used to refer to the whole body of Jewish learning. (See also BIBLE; MOSES; TEN COMMANDMENTS.)

TOURISM Holy places of three religions—Jewish, Christian, and Moslem—attract tourists to Israel from all over the world. (In 1978, about 1,176,000 tourists visited Israel.) There are also many biblical and historic sites to visit. While many tourists go to celebrate religious holidays in the Holy Land, others want to enjoy the warm climate in winter.

Tourism is an important industry in Israel. It brings more foreign money into the country than any other industry except the export of citrus fruit. The government Ministry of Tourism (established in 1964) encourages the development of tourist attractions and helps in the financing of hotels and other tourist services. Tourist offices are located in major cities throughout the free world. (See also BIBLE; CLIMATE; HISTORY; HOLIDAYS.)

TOWER OF DAVID The only one remaining of the many

The Tower of David

towers and citadels (fortresses) that topped the wall surrounding ancient Jerusalem. The Tower of David was built by King Herod in the first century B.C.E. and was left standing when the Romans destroyed Jerusalem in 70 C.E. It is located next to the Jaffa Gate. Today tourists can enjoy a sound-and-light show there, describing the history of the tower. (See also HEROD I; JERUSALEM; ROME; TOURISM; WALLED CITIES.)

TRANSFIGURATION, FEAST OF THE   Christian holiday that marks the appearance of Moses and Elijah before Jesus on Mount Tabor. It is celebrated on August 6th with a special ceremony in the Church of the Transfiguration on Mount Tabor and services in Catholic and Anglican churches throughout Israel. (See also CHRISTIANS; HOLIDAYS; MOUNT TABOR.)

TRANSJORDAN   see JORDAN

TRUMAN, HARRY S (1884-1972)   Thirty-third President of the United States. Truman served as a senator before he was elected Vice-President in 1944. He became President upon President Franklin Roosevelt's death, in 1945. After the end of World War II, President Truman asked the American Congress to allow Jewish refugees to enter the United States. He also spoke in favor

President Harry Truman (left) receives a Torah Scroll from President Chaim Weizmann in 1949.

of letting 100,000 Jewish refugees enter Palestine. He originally supported the partition (division) of Palestine and favored having the United Nations handle the Palestine situation. He recognized the new State of Israel as soon as it was established in 1948. (See also IMMIGRANTS, ILLEGAL; PARTITION; UNITED NATIONS.)

TRUMPELDOR, JOSEPH (1880-1920)   Soldier and leader of the Hehalutz (pioneer) movement. Trumpeldor was born in Russia, lost his left arm fighting in the Russo-Japanese War, and became the first Jewish officer in the Russian army. He went to Palestine in 1912 and tried to establish a cooperative farming settlement at Migdal, but failed. When the Turks (who ruled Palestine) exiled him from the country during World War I, Trumpeldor (along with Vladimir Jabotinsky) worked to form the Jewish Legion as part of the British army. They then went to Russia and organized Hehalutz pioneer groups of Jews to settle in Palestine. Returning to Palestine, Trumpeldor took charge of the Jewish defense against Arab raids on settlements in Galilee. He was killed at Tel Hai. His last words were, "It is good to die for our country."

Joseph Trumpeldor became a symbol of Jewish courage and an inspiration to young Zionists. Today young Israelis still visit his tomb at Tel Hai on the anniversary of his death. (See also GALILEE; HEHALUTZ; JABOTINSKY, VLADIMIR; JEWISH LEGION; TEL HAI; TURKEY; ZIONISM.)

TSCHERNICHOWSKY, SAUL (1875-1943) Hebrew poet. Tschernichowsky was born in Russia, trained as a doctor in Germany, and settled in Palestine in 1931. He began writing poetry at an early age and became one of the best-known Hebrew poets of modern times. Like Hayim Bialik (who wrote his poetry during the same years), Tschernichowsky experimented with new forms and subjects for Hebrew poetry that became an inspiration to young poets. Many of his poems were about the pioneers who were building a new nation in Palestine. Others dealt with the beauty and power of nature. He also wrote children's poems and stories, translated ancient Greek plays into Hebrew, and edited a Hebrew medical dictionary. The Tel Aviv center of the Hebrew Writers' Association has an exhibit featuring his life and work. (See also BIALIK, HAYIM NAHMAN; TEL AVIV.)

TSUR, JACOB (also spelled TZUR) (1906-   )   Russian-born diplomat who settled in Palestine in 1921. Tsur served as the Israeli Minister to several South American countries and was later Ambassador to France.

TU BI-SHEVAT   see NEW YEAR FOR TREES

TUMARKIN, YIGAL (1933-   ) Native Israeli painter and sculptor. Tumarkin's sculptures are usually made of scrap metal and other old and odd objects.

TUR-SINAI, NAPTHALI HERZ (name changed from TORCZYNER, HARRY) (1886-1973)   Austrian-born scholar and language expert. Tur-Sinai taught in Austria and Switzerland before moving to Palestine in 1933. He became a professor at the Hebrew University in Jerusalem, was the president of the Hebrew Language Academy, wrote several books on language, and edited the last volumes of Eliezer Ben Yehuda's huge Hebrew dictionary. In 1956, Tur-Sinai won the Israel Prize for Jewish studies. (See also BEN YEHUDA, ELIEZER; HEBREW LANGUAGE ACADEMY; HEBREW UNIVERSITY; ISRAEL PRIZE.)

TURKEY   Country between the eastern end of the Mediterranean Sea and the Black Sea. Turkey has an area of 301,380 square miles, of which 9,120 square miles lie in Europe and the rest in

Asia. Its capital is Ankara and its largest city is Istanbul (formerly called Constantinople). Turkey's 41,125,000 people (1977) are Moslems, 90% of whom speak Turkish.

The Suljuk Turks became a power in the Middle East in the 1000s C.E. (these were the Turks that fought the Crusaders in Palestine) and paved the way for the rise of the Ottoman Turkish Empire. The Ottoman Turks conquered the Balkans in Eastern Europe in the 1300s and were responsible for the collapse of the Byzantine Empire in 1453, when they captured Constantinople. In 1516 Turkey occupied Palestine and held the country for 400 years.

When Jewish pioneers immigrated to Palestine in the late 1800s and early 1900s, the Turkish Empire was falling apart. The settlers had to deal with corrupt and cruel Turkish governors. During World War I, the Turks exiled many of Palestine's Jews for fear of their helping the Allies. An underground Jewish group called NILI worked with the British to free Palestine from Turkish rule. At the end of World War I, Turkey lost control of Palestine and the Mandate to govern the country was given to England. (See also ALIYAH; BYZANTINE EMPIRE; GREAT BRITAIN; HISTORY; MEDITERRANEAN SEA; NILI.)

TVERYA see TIBERIAS

TWELVE TRIBES In biblical times the Israelites were divided into twelve tribes or groups. Each tribe was made up of the descendants of one of the twelve sons of Jacob. The sons of Jacob were: Reuben, Simeon, Levi, Judah, Zebulun, Issachar, Dan, Gad, Asher, Naphtali, Joseph, and Benjamin. Levi's descendants became priests; they did not form a tribe. The descendants of Joseph formed the tribes of Ephraim and Manasseh, named for Joseph's two sons. Therefore, the Twelve Tribes were: Reuben, Simeon, Judah, Zebulun, Issachar, Dan, Gad, Asher, Naphtali, Manasseh and Ephraim, and Benjamin.

When the Israelites conquered Canaan in the thirteenth century B.C.E., the conquered land was divided among the Twelve Tribes. In the tenth centrury B.C.E., after the death of King Solomon, the united Jewish kingdom split into two parts. The tribes of Judah, Simeon, and most of Benjamin joined the southern kingdom of Judah and the other tribes became the northern kingdom of Israel. (See also ASHER; BENJAMIN; CANAAN; DAN; EPHRAIM; GAD; HISTORY; ISRAEL, KINGDOM OF; ISSACHAR; JACOB; JOSEPH; JUDAH, KINGDOM OF; MANASSEH; NAPHTALI; REUBEN; SIMEON; SOLOMON; ZEBULUN.)

TZEMA, SHELOMO (1886-1974) Polish-born writer and farming expert who lived in Palestine for several years before settling there permanently in 1921. Tzema's short stories describe life in Israel.

TZIPPORI   see SEPPHORIS

U-V

ULPAN (the plural is ULPANIM) School for the teaching of Hebrew to adults. An ulpan uses special fast methods to teach the Hebrew language, and was established to help newcomers to Israel to learn the language quickly. Ulpanim also give immigrants a background in Israeli citizenship and practices.

The first ulpan was established in Jerusalem in 1949. In 1975 there were about 70 ulpanim in Israel. There are three kinds of ulpanim: residential, kibbutz, and day student. Immigrants live at residential ulpanim for five months. At the end of that time, they are able to speak enough Hebrew for everyday life. Students also live at kibbutz ulpanim. For six months they study four hours a day and work four hours a day to pay for their upkeep. There are also ulpanim for day students who attend classes in the afternoons or evenings, 12 to 16 hours a week, for four months. (See also EDUCATION; HEBREW; IMMIGRANTS; KIBBUTZ.)

UNITED JEWISH APPEAL (UJA) Fund-raising organization founded in the United States in 1939. The billions of dollars raised by the UJA has permitted the Jewish Agency to settle over one million immigrants in Israel, to reclaim land, to establish new settlements, and to build houses and schools. (See also IMMIGRANTS; JEWISH AGENCY; KEREN HAYESOD.)

UNITED NATIONS (UN) Organization of the nations of the world founded in 1945, with headquarters in New York City. Its aims are to keep peace in the world, to build friendly relations between countries, and to encourage member nations to cooperate in solving the world problems of hunger, disease, human rights, etc.

The two political bodies of the United Nations are the Security Council and the General Assembly. The Security Council is made up of five permanent members (United States, Soviet Union, Great Britain, France, and China) and ten temporary members. Its main job is to keep the peace. The Security Council has the power to send a UN force, consisting of soldiers of member nations, to stop war and restore peace in an area. But all the members of the Council must first agree when such a force is sent.

In 1948 Albert Einstein (right) served as UJA Honorary Chairman. Here, he meets with Chairman William Rosenwald and two young refugees.

The General Assembly is made up of all the member nations (149 countries in 1978). Each nation has one vote. Although the General Assembly can discuss almost any matter brought before it and make recommendations, it has no power to enforce its decisions.

In 1947 Great Britain (which was then still governing Palestine under the Mandate) brought the Palestine question before the United Nations. The UN Special Committee on Palestine recommended the partition (dividing) of Palestine into separate Jewish and Arab states, with Jerusalem becoming an international city. The partition plan was approved by the General Assembly and the date for the birth of the new nation of Israel was set for May 14, 1948.

The United Nations peace symbol adorns the entrance to the UN in New York. Its theme is from Isaiah Chapter 2: "And they shall beat their swords into plowshares."

The United Nations did nothing when the Arab countries invaded the new Jewish State and the War of Independence began. However, the UN peacekeeper, Ralph Bunche, helped bring the Arabs and Jews together to sign the armistice agreements that ended the war in 1949.

When the Sinai War broke out in 1956, the Israeli army advanced to the Suez Canal. Pressure from the United States and other countries persuaded Israel to pull its troops out of Sinai. A UN peacekeeping force was then stationed in Sinai and the Gaza Strip. Egypt's demand that the UN troops leave in 1967 led to the Six-Day War.

Israel has been a member of the United Nations since 1949. The problems between the Jewish State and its Arab neighbors have been discussed many times in the Security Council and in the General Assembly. In the 1970s the one-nation, one-vote policy of the General Assembly let the numerous Arab nations push several anti-Israel votes through the Assembly. Despite this, Israel continues to work within the United Nations and is active in a number of UN special agencies that deal with problems of law, labor, refugees, scientific developments, etc. Abba Eban was Israel's first ambassador to the United Nations. The current (1980) ambassador is Yehuda Blum. (See also BUNCHE, RALPH; EBAN, ABBA; EGYPT; GAZA STRIP; GREAT BRITAIN; BLUM, YEHUDA; HISTORY; JERUSALEM; MANDATE; PARTITION; SINAI; SINAI WAR; SIX-DAY WAR; SUEZ CANAL; WAR OF INDEPENDENCE.)

UNKNOWN SOLDIER MEMORIAL   Monument in Jerusalem to Israel's war dead. It is a column of Jerusalem stone engraved with the single word *yizacher* (Hebrew for "will be remembered"). (See also JERUSALEM.)

UNTERMANN, ISSAR YEHUDA (1886-1976)   Religious scholar who was a rabbi in his native Russia and in England before settling in Palestine in 1947 and becoming Chief Rabbi of Tel Aviv. Rabbi Untermann was active in the Mizrahi (a religious Zionist organization), the Keren Hayesod (Palestine Foundation Fund), and the Jewish Agency. He served as Ashkenazi Chief Rabbi of Israel from 1964 to 1972. (See also ASHKENAZIM; CHIEF RABBINATE; JEWISH AGENCY; KEREN HAYESOD; MIZRAHI.)

URBACH, EPHRAIM ELIMELECH (1912-   )   Polish-born religious scholar who settled in Palestine in 1938 and taught at the Hebrew University in Jerusalem. (See also HEBREW UNIVERSITY.)

URIEL   Village about 20 miles south of Tel Aviv founded in 1951 by Malben (a health organization). Blind people are taught to lead useful lives at Uriel. (See also MALBEN.)

USHA   Kibbutz founded on an ancient site near Haifa in 1937. Ancient Usha had a famous yeshiva (religious school) in the first century C.E., and was for a time the home of the Sanhedrin (Jewish Supreme Court). (See also KIBBUTZ; SANHEDRIN.)

USSISHKIN, MENAHEM MENDEL (1863-1941)   Russian Zionist leader who helped found BILU, a group of young Russian

Jews who wanted to settle in Palestine. Ussishkin was an early supporter of Theodor Herzl (the father of modern Zionism), but later disagreed with some of Herzl's policies. He visited Palestine several times before settling there in 1919. He became chairman of the Jewish National Fund and made land purchases in the Jezreel, Hefer, and Zebulun valleys. (See also BILU; HEFER VALLEY; HERZL, THEODOR; JEWISH NATIONAL FUND; JEZREEL VALLEY; ZEBULUN VALLEY; ZIONISM.)

UZI Automatic submachine gun used by Israeli soldiers. The Uzi is a nine-millimeter gun with an automatic safety feature. It is fired from the shoulder or the hip.

UZIEL, BEN ZION MEIR HAY (also spelled OUZIEL) (1880-1954) Religious scholar born and educated in Jerusalem. Rabbi Uziel served as Chief Rabbi of Jaffa and Tel Aviv before he was chosen Sephardi Chief Rabbi of Israel in 1939. He founded the Mizrahi (a religious Zionist organization) in Palestine, served in Palestine's Vaad Leumi (National Council), and wrote on religious subjects. (See also CHIEF RABBINATE; MIZRAHI; SEPHARDIM; VAAD LEUMI.)

UZZIAH (also called AZARIAH) King of Judah who ruled about 780-740 B.C.E. At the age of 16, he inherited the throne from his father, Amaziah. Uzziah was a successful general, and the kingdom of Judah was powerful and prosperous under his rule. He rebuilt the walls of Jerusalem and the port of Eilat. When Uzziah fell sick with leprosy, his son, Jotham, ruled the country. (See also AMAZIAH; EILAT; JOTHAM; JUDAH, KINGDOM OF.)

VAAD LEUMI (English, NATIONAL COUNCIL) The executive committee of the Asefat Hanivharim (meaning "assembly of the chosen ones"), the elected body representing Palestine's Jews during the British Mandate (1920-1948). The Vaad Leumi was elected by the Asefat Hanivharim, and its 23 to 42 members represented all the political views of the larger group. The Vaad Leumi (like the Asefat Hanivharim) had little power, but it served as a place for the leading Jews of Palestine to discuss the country's problems and to try to deal with them. (See also ASEFAT HANIVHARIM.)

VIA DOLOROSA Narrow winding street in the Old City of Jerusalem that leads to the Church of the Holy Sepulchre. Its name means "path of sorrow." The Via Dolorosa was the path along which Jesus carried the cross on his way to the Crucifixion on Golgotha. The stops he made along the route are called the Stations of the Cross. Nine of the fourteen Stations are on the Via Dolorosa. (See also GOLGOTHA; HOLY SEPULCHRE; JERUSALEM; JESUS; STATIONS OF THE CROSS.)

VIRGIN MARY, TOMB OF   see TOMB OF THE VIRGIN MARY

VITKIN, YOSEPH (1876-1912) (also spelled WITKIN)   Pioneer who left Russia for Palestine in the 1890s. Vitkin inspired other Russian Jews to settle in Palestine during the Second Aliyah (wave of immigration) in the early 1900s. The village of Kefar Vitkin is named in his honor. (See also ALIYAH; KEFAR VITKIN.)

VOLCANI, YITZHAK   see ELAZARI-VOLCANI, YITZAK

VOLCANI INSTITUTE OF AGRICULTURAL RESEARCH The Volcani Institute was named for its first director, farming expert Yitzak Elazari-Volcani. It was founded by the World Zionist Organization as an agricultural experiment station in Tel Aviv, was moved to Rehovot in 1927, and was taken over by the Israeli government in 1951. The Institute works to improve farming methods and land and water use in Israel. It has three large experimental farms—including one in the Negev Desert—and also helps local communities run a number of smaller research farms. Its staff of about 1,200 people includes 300 research scientists. It publishes *Ketavim,* a magazine of its findings. (See also AGRICULTURAL RESEARCH; ELAZARI-VOLCANI, YITZHAK; NEGEV; WORLD ZIONIST ORGANIZATION.)

VOLLEYBALL   A very popular game in Israel's kibbutzim, volleyball is beginning to be played in the cities as well. The Israeli volleyball team has competed in the European Cup games. (See also SPORTS.)

VOTING   All Israeli citizens have the right to vote. Unlike citizens of the United States, Israelis do not vote directly for the individual candidates of their choice. Instead, they vote for the candidate "list" of a political party. The number of candidates each party sends to the Knesset (legislature) depends on the number of votes the list receives. The top name on the list that receives the majority of votes becomes Prime Minister. (See also CITIZENSHIP; GOVERNMENT; KNESSET; POLITICAL PARTIES; PRIME MINISTER.)

The famous street that runs through the Christian Quarter of the Old City of Jerusalem. The Stations of the Cross are situated along this street, which carries a Latin name meaning "the street of sorrow."

W

WADI An Arabic word meaning "the bed of a stream, or a river, in a desert area." A wadi is dry except immediately after a rainfall, when it may suddenly flood and wash away everything in its path. Wadis are common in the Negev. (See also NEGEV.)

WADI HEVER Archaeological site west of the Dead Sea. The Cave of Letters, containing letters and objects from the 132-135 C.E. Bar Kokhba revolt against Roman rule in Palestine was discovered at Wadi Hever. (See also ARCHAEOLOGY; BAR KOKHBA, SIMEON; CAVE OF LETTERS.)

WAHRHAFTIG, ZORACH (1906-) Lawyer and politician who was active in the Mizrahi (a religious Zionist organization) in his native Poland before settling in Palestine in 1947. Wahrhaftig was elected to the Israeli Knesset (legislature) and

Aerial view of the Old City of Jerusalem showing the wall that surrounds the entire area. The golden dome of the Dome of the Rock Mosque can be seen above.

served as Minister of Religious Affairs. (See also KNESSET; MIZRAHI.)

WAILING WALL   see WESTERN WALL

WALLED CITIES   Ancient cities were built with high strong walls around them for protection against enemy attacks in time of war. A city wall was usually made by building two walls of brick or stone, one inside the other, and then filling the center with earth. The finished wall would be thick enough for a path along the top on which soldiers could patrol. Towers were often built on the wall for extra protection.

Jerusalem was a walled city, and the remains of the ancient wall can still be seen. The Tower of David—one of the fortresses on the wall—is still standing. (See also JERUSALEM; TOWER OF DAVID.)

WAR OF INDEPENDENCE   1947-1949 war between Israel and the Arab countries of Egypt, Jordan, Iraq, Syria, and Lebanon. The war began on November 29, 1947, when the Arabs refused to accept the United Nations decision to divide Palestine into Arab and Jewish states. Local Palestinian Arabs—with help from volunteers from the neighboring Arab countries—attacked Jewish settlements, blocked roads, and set off explosives in Jewish sections of cities. The Jewish defense groups—Haganah, Palmah, Irgun, and the Stern Group (Lehi)—fought back. The British (who were still supposed to be in charge) did nothing.

On May 14, 1948, Israel was declared a nation. The regular armies of the Arab nations immediately invaded the Jewish State. The Egyptian army drove north through the Sinai, Negev, and Gaza Strip to within 25 miles of Tel Aviv. The Iraqi drive east toward the Mediterranean Sea threatened to cut Israel in two while the Syrians invaded Galilee. Although the Jewish forces were badly outnumbered by the Arabs, they drove the invaders back on most fronts.

The War of Independence ended in 1949 with Ralph Bunche, the United Nations peacemaker, arranging an armistice between Israel and the Arab nations. Israel lost 6,000 men and women in the war. Its borders were set at the lines where the armies had stopped fighting and half of Jerusalem remained in Arab hands. The question of Israel's borders remained a problem for many years after the war as did the question of the Palestinian Arabs who had fled to neighboring countries. (See also BUNCHE, RALPH; EGYPT; GALILEE; GAZA STRIP; GREAT BRITAIN; HAGANAH; HISTORY; IRGUN; JERUSALEM; JORDAN; LEBANON; MEDITERRANEAN SEA; NEGEV; PALESTINIAN REFUGEES; PALMAH; SINAI; STERN GROUP; SYRIA; TEL AVIV; UNITED NATIONS.)

WARBURG, FELIX (1871-1937)   German-born banker who set-tled in the United States in 1894 and became active in Jewish causes. For eighteen years Warburg was chairman of the JDC (American Jewish Joint Distribution Committee), an organiza-tion that helped Jewish victims of pogroms, wars, and other tragedies. Although he was not a Zionist, Warburg helped found the Palestine Economic Corporation, which supported Jewish settlement in Palestine. (See also JDC; PALESTINE ECONOMIC COR-PORATION; POGROM; ZIONIST.)

WARBURG, OTTO (1859-1938)   German Zionist and plant ex-pert. Warburg joined the Zionist movement at its beginning in 1897, and worked with Theodor Herzl (the father of modern Zionism). He was one of the founders of the Jewish National Fund, and also served as president of the World Zionist Organiza-tion from 1911 to 1920. In addition, he helped establish the Palestine Office in Jaffa and the Bezalel School of Arts and Crafts in Jerusalem. In 1922, Warburg went to Palestine, taught botany at the new Hebrew University in Jerusalem, and (along with Yitzak Elazari-Volcani) ran the experimental farm that later became the Volcani Institute for Agricultural Research. (See also AGRICULTURAL RESEARCH; BEZALEL SCHOOL OF ARTS AND CRAFTS; ELAZARI-VOLCANI, YITZAK; HEBREW UNIVERSITY; HERZL, THEODOR; JEWISH NATIONAL FUND; PALESTINE OFFICE; WORLD ZIONIST OR-GANIZATION; ZIONISM.)

WATER   Finding enough water to meet the agricultural, indus-trial, and the personal needs of its people is one of Israel's major problems. The southern half of the country is largely desert, with little or no rainfall. Even in the north, where there is usually enough water, rain only falls in the winter, and many crops must be irrigated during the summer growing season.

   In 1956 the Israeli government adopted a master plan for using every drop of water that could be found. Today, 95% of all water available from rain, dew, streams, rivers, and lakes is put to good use. The National Water Carrier (planned by Tahal, the govern-ment planning agency, and built by Mekorot, the construction company) brings water to the dry south from the Jordan River and Lake Kinneret in the north. In addition, new ways of tapping the water deep underground are being tested, desalinization plants to remove the salt out of sea water are being built, and some waste water from cities is being cleaned and reused for agriculture. (See also AGRICULTURE; CLIMATE; DAN REGION PRO-JECT; DESALINIZATION; GEOGRAPHY; IRRIGATION; JORDAN RIVER; LAKE KINNERET; MEKOROT; NATIONAL WATER CARRIER; TAHAL.)

WEINSHALL, ABRAHAM (1893-1968)   Russian-born lawyer

This reconstructed Roman viaduct, typical of those built by the Romans, is situated on Kibbutz Lohame Hagettaot, about three miles north of Acco.

who settled in Palestine in 1920. As an expert on land laws, Weinshall helped buy land for Jewish settlement. He was a member of Palestine's Vaad Leumi (National Council) and later became president of the Israeli Bar Association. (See also VAAD LEUMI.)

WEISGAL, MEYER WOLF (1894-   )   Zionist who was born in Poland and lived in the United States for many years. Weisgal organized the American office of the Jewish Agency and was one of the founders of the Weizmann Institute of Science. In 1949 he moved to Israel and became president of the Weizmann Institute. (See also JEWISH AGENCY; WEIZMANN INSTITUTE OF SCIENCE; ZIONISM.)

WEIZMANN, CHAIM (1874-1952)   First President of Israel. Chaim Weizmann was born in Russia and studied chemistry in Germany. He became a Zionist at an early age and attended the first Zionist conference at Basle, Switzerland, where he met Theodor Herzl. While Herzl tried to establish a Jewish State through negotiations with the governments of important countries, Weizmann believed that a Jewish State had to be based on the support of the Jews of the world.

In 1904 Weizmann moved to England, taught chemistry at Manchester University, and became the leader of the English Zionist movement. He was largely responsible for convincing the British government to issue the 1917 Balfour Declaration favor-

Yad Chaim Weizmann, the burial place of Chaim Weizmann, first President of the State of Israel.

ing the establishment of a Jewish national home in Palestine.

Weizmann was elected president of the World Zionist Organization in 1920. As the Zionist leader, he stressed the importance of Jewish immigration to Palestine and spent much time raising money to buy land and establish settlements. He also believed that Great Britain would not betray the Zionist cause. Other Zionists—particularly the Revisionists—opposed his attitude of patience with the policies of the British in Palestine.

The White Paper of 1939 limiting Jewish immigration into Palestine destroyed Weizmann's faith in the British. He fought the White Paper and, after World War II, argued for an independent Jewish State before the United Nations Special Committee on Palestine. In 1948 Chaim Weizmann was honored for a lifetime of work for the Zionist movement by being elected Israel's first President.

Besides his political work, Weizmann was a scientist who made important discoveries in the field of chemistry. He was also one of the founders of the Hebrew University and of the research center that later became the Weizmann Institute of Science. His burial place in Rehovot has become a national shrine. (See also BALFOUR DECLARATION; BASLE CONFERENCE; GREAT BRITAIN; HEBREW UNIVERSITY; HERZL, THEODOR; HISTORY; PRESIDENT; REVISIONIST; UNITED NATIONS; WEIZMANN INSTITUTE OF SCIENCE; WHITE PAPER; WORLD ZIONIST ORGANIZATION; ZIONISM.)

WEIZMAN, EZER (1924-) Native Israeli soldier and politician. Ezer Weizman was a pilot in the British Royal Air Force during World War II. He became one of the first pilots in the new Israeli Air Force in 1948, flew in the first air attack on Egyptian forces in the War of Independence, and rose to the post of commander. He was largely responsible for the excellent training of Israeli pilots. Weizman became Chief-of-Operations of the Israeli Defense Forces and played an important part in his country's victory in the 1967 Six-Day War. Upon leaving the army, he joined the government Cabinet as Minister of Transport and later Minister of Defense. He is the nephew of Chaim Weizmann, Israel's first President. (See also CABINET; DEFENSE FORCES; SIX-DAY WAR; WAR OF INDEPENDENCE; WEIZMANN, CHAIM.)

WEIZMANN INSTITUTE OF SCIENCE Scientific research center and school of higher education in the natural sciences. The Weizmann Institute was opened in Rehovot in 1949. It was named in honor of Chaim Weizmann (who was both a scientist and Israel's first President) and took over the work of the Sieff Research Institute where Weizmann had done his research.

Approximately 2,100 people work and study at the Weizmann Institute, including 600 graduate students and 500 scientists carrying out research in 19 different fields. Among the research projects being conducted are study of the cells of the human body that may someday help find a cure for cancer, the study of earthquakes, nuclear research, and studies in the desalinization (removal of salt) of sea water. The Yeda Research Development Company applies many of the Weizmann Institute's research findings to practical use in industry. (See also DESALINIZATION; NUCLEAR ENERGY; REHOVOT; WEIZMANN, CHAIM.)

WEIZMANN, VERA CHATZMAN (1882-1966)   Born in Russia, Vera Chatzman trained as a doctor in Switzerland, where she met Chaim Weizmann (later Israel's first President) and soon married him. Vera Weizmann became active in the Zionist movement, was a founder of WIZO (Women's International Zionist Organization), and worked with Youth Aliyah to bring young people from Europe to Palestine. (See also WEIZMANN, CHAIM; WIZO; YOUTH ALIYAH; ZIONISM.)

WEST BANK (also called SAMARIA and JUDEA)   Land mass on the

A small West Bank Arab businessman in Bethlehem tries to sell his home-grown melons to a fellow Arab.

Arabs in Israel dress in a variety of styles and are involved in many types of businesses and occupations. Above is a small businessman in Nablus; below an Arab in Bethlehem.

western side of the Jordan River that was part of Palestine under the British Mandate, was occupied by Jordan during the 1948 War of Independence, and was captured by Israel in the 1967 Six-Day War. The West Bank is one of the four administered areas governed by Israel since 1967. By the terms of the 1979 Israel-Egypt Peace Treaty, the Palestinian Arabs of the West Bank will be given self-rule by 1980. However, the treaty left the final fate of the West Bank and of the Israeli settlements in the area to be worked out in the future. (See also ADMINISTERED AREAS; EGYPT; ISRAEL-EGYPT PEACE TREATY; JORDAN RIVER; MANDATE; PALESTINIANS; SAMARIA; SIX-DAY WAR; WAR OF INDEPENDENCE.)

WESTERN WALL (also called WAILING WALL)   The holiest shrine of the Jewish religion. The Western Wall was part of the outer wall that surrounded the Temple in Jerusalem in ancient times. It was built by King Herod in the first century B.C.E. and was all that remained when the Temple was destroyed by the Romans in 70 C.E.

Jews have made pilgrimages to pray at the Western Wall since the Temple was destroyed. However, there have been many periods in history when Jews were not permitted in Jerusalem or near the Wall. During the 1948 War of Independence, Jordan occupied the Old City of Jerusalem. For the next 19 years Jews

A view of the Wall from Wilson's Arch, on the northern side of the Western Wall.

Men praying at the Western Wall.

could not visit the Old City or the Western Wall in it. Then
Jerusalem was reunited in the 1967 Six-Day War. Two hundred
thousand Jews prayed at the Western Wall the first day it was in
Israeli hands.

Women at the Western Wall crowd into the ladies' section, which is
separated from the men's section by an iron fence.

The wall showing most of its layers of huge stones. Eighteen to nine-
teen courses extend below ground level.

The old and the young are eager to say their morning prayers at the
Western Wall.

Despite the large crowds that assemble at The Wall each day, individuals are able to concentrate on their own prayers.

Regular visits to the Wall by every segment of the population is commonplace. Above are armed soldiers and men in wheelchairs.

Today Jews come from all over the world to pray at the Western Wall and to put slips of paper containing their prayers between the stones of the Wall. Special ceremonies are held at the Wall on Tisha B'Av, the Jewish fast day that marks the destruction of the Temple. The old houses near the Wall have been torn down and a large plaza has been built to hold the many visitors. (See also HEROD I; HISTORY; JERUSALEM; ROME; SIX-DAY WAR; TEMPLE; TISHA B'AV; WAR OF INDEPENDENCE.)

WHITE PAPER   Statement issued in 1939 by Great Britain (which then ruled Palestine under the Mandate). The White Paper declared that Palestine would become an independent state within ten years. But it also limited the immigration to Palestine to 75,000 over the next five years. The sale of land to Jews was also restricted.

Zionists attacked the White Paper. They felt that it betrayed Britain's promise in the 1917 Balfour Declaration to help establish a Jewish national home in Palestine and that it also went against the terms of the Mandate. In addition, there were hundreds of thousands of European Jews whose lives were threatened by the Nazis in Europe and who had no place to go but to Palestine. Zionist protests did no good. The White Paper remained British policy until Britain referred the Palestine question to the United Nations in 1947. (See also BALFOUR

DECLARATION; GREAT BRITAIN; HISTORY; MANDATE; UNITED NATIONS; ZIONISM.)

WIESEL, ELIE (1928-   )   Author who was born in Rumania, imprisoned in Auschwitz concentration camp during World War II, and went to the United States after the war. Wiesel has written many books about Jews, the Holocaust, and Israel. His novel *The Jews of Silence* is about Soviet Jewry, and *A Beggar in Jerusalem* takes place in Israel during the 1967 Six-Day War. Wiesel is on the board of governors of Tel Aviv University and Ben-Gurion University. (See also BEN-GURION UNIVERSITY; HOLOCAUST; SIX-DAY WAR; TEL AVIV UNIVERSITY.)

Elie Wiesel

WIESENTHAL, SIMON (1909-   )   Known as "The Nazi Hunter." Wiesenthal was born in Poland, spent World War II in several concentration camps and has since devoted his life to tracking down the Nazis responsible for the camps. His Jewish Documentation Center in Vienna, Austria, has provided evidence leading to the arrest of more than a thousand Nazi war criminals. Wiesenthal is the man who found Adolph Eichmann in Argentina and helped bring him to trial in Israel. He works closely with the Israeli police. (See also EICHMANN, ADOLPH; HOLOCAUST; NAZIS.)

WILBUSCHEWITZ, MANYA   see SHOHAT, MANYA WILBUSCHEWITZ

WILSON'S ARCH Arch at the left of the Western Wall in Jerusalem. In ancient times it was part of a bridge connecting the Temple with the upper part of the city. (The Western Wall was part of a wall around the Temple court.) Today Wilson's Arch is a place for prayer. (See also TEMPLE; WESTERN WALL.)

WINE Grapes for wine were grown in Palestine in biblical times. In the 1890s vineyards were again planted by the new Jewish settlers and wineries were built at Rishon Le Zion and Zikhron Yaakov. By the late 1970s there were 25 wineries in Israel, but the two oldest ones were still producing about 70% of the 14 million quarts of wine bottled in Israel each year. All wine made in Israel is kosher and most of it is drunk by the country's citizens. Half of the 3 million quarts of Israeli wine exported to foreign countries each year is bought by the United States. (See also FOREIGN TRADE; RISHON LE ZION; ZIKHRON YAAKOV.)

WINGATE, CHARLES ORDE (1903-1944) British soldier who was sent to Palestine during the Arab riots of 1936. Wingate, a religious Christian, soon became a Zionist as well. He organized and trained the Special Night Squads, groups of Haganah (Jewish underground army) members who defended settlements, roads, and railroads against Arab terrorists. While on leave in London in 1939, Wingate met with British officials and argued for the Jewish cause in Palestine. Soon after, he was ordered out of the country. During World War II, he wanted to organize an army of Palestinian Jews to fight alongside the British, but the British would not permit it. He was sent instead to India where he was later killed in an airplane crash.

The Special Night Squads organized by Wingate later became the Palmah, the striking force of the Haganah. A forest was planted in his honor on Mount Gilboa and the Wingate Institute of Physical Education was named for him (1953). (See also ARAB RIOTS; GREAT BRITAIN; HAGANAH; MOUNT GILBOA; PALMAH; SPECIAL NIGHT SQUADS; WINGATE INSTITUTE; ZIONISM.)

WINGATE INSTITUTE Physical education center opened in 1953 about 20 miles north of Tel Aviv. Israel's sports coaches and physical education teachers are trained at the Wingate Institute. It is also a training camp for the national football (soccer), tennis, swimming, and track-and-field teams. In addition, it runs a research center for sports medicine and publishes books on sports. The Institute is named in honor of Charles Orde Wingate, the British soldier who became a Zionist. (See also PHYSICAL EDUCATION; SPORTS; WINGATE, CHARLES ORDE.)

WISE, GEORGE S. (1906-   ) Businessman and educator who was born in Russian Poland and lived in the United States for

To the north of the Western Wall is an arched entrance to an underground hall that is a continuation of The Wall. Discovered by English archaeologist Sir Charles Wilson (1836-1905), it is used today as a place of worship.

The Wingate Institute

Exercises in physical education on the grounds of the Wingate
Institute.

many years. In 1963 Wise went to Palestine to become the president of Tel Aviv University. (See also TEL AVIV UNIVERSITY.)

WISE, STEPHEN SAMUEL (1874-1949)   American rabbi and Zionist leader. Rabbi Wise helped write the 1917 Balfour Declaration (declaring that Britain favored a Jewish state in Palestine) and argued for a Jewish state at the 1918 Versailles Peace Conference. He became president of the Zionist Organization of America and after helping found the American Jewish Congress became its president. Before World War II, Wise warned against the Nazi menace in Europe and worked to help its victims. (See also AMERICAN JEWISH CONGRESS; BALFOUR DECLARATION; NAZIS; ZIONISM.)

Rabbi Stephen S. Wise

WITKON, ALFRED (1910-   )   Judge who was born and educated in Germany and settled in Israel in 1934. He practiced law in Israel, served as president of the District Court in Jerusalem, and was appointed a judge of the Supreme Court. Witkon has also taught at Jerusalem's Hebrew University and Tel Aviv University and has published books and articles on law. (See also COURTS; HEBREW UNIVERSITY; JUDGES; SUPREME COURT; TEL AVIV UNIVERSITY.)

WIZO (initials of WOMEN'S INTERNATIONAL ZIONIST ORGANIZATION) Organization founded in London in 1920 by Rebecca Sieff and Vera Weizmann. Its aims were to train young women for life in Palestine, to help new immigrants, and to care for the children of Palestine. Today, WIZO has about 25,000 members in 55 countries and 90,000 in Israel. (In the United States the Women's Zionist Organization is Hadassah, not WIZO.) WIZO runs 140 day-care centers for children in Israel, as well as 55 youth centers, 13 agricultural and vocational schools, and 190 women's clubs. It also operates workshops, job training courses, legal advice centers, and libraries. (See also EDUCATION; HADASSAH; HEALTH; SIEFF, REBECCA MARKS; WEIZMANN, VERA CHATZMAN.)

WOLFFSOHN, DAVID (1856-1914)   Zionist leader who was born in Lithuania and lived most of his life in Germany. He worked closely with Theodor Herzl (the father of modern Zionism) and became the president of the World Zionist Organization when Herzl died. Wolffsohn helped found the Jewish Colonial Trust—the first bank of the Zionist Organization—and headed it until his death. (See also HERZL, THEODOR; JEWISH COLONIAL TRUST; WORLD ZIONIST ORGANIZATION; ZIONISM.)

WOMEN WORKERS' FARM   see MESHEK POALOT

WOMEN'S INTERNATIONAL ZIONIST ORGANIZATION see WIZO

WOMEN'S LEAGUE FOR ISRAEL   Organization founded in New York in 1928 to help young women immigrants in Palestine. By 1979 its centers in Jerusalem, Haifa, Tel Aviv, and Netanya had given homes or job training to 100,000 girls and women. The Netanya Vocational Training Center has special programs for blind and handicapped girls. (See also EDUCATION.)

WORKING WOMEN'S COUNCIL   see MOETZET HAPOALOT

WORLD HEBREW UNION   see BERIT IVRIT OLAMIT

WORLD JEWISH CONGRESS   Organization founded in 1936 in Geneva, Switzerland. Its aims are to protect the rights and interests of Jews throughout the world and to encourage Jewish cultural life. The World Jewish Congress is a central organization that works to bring together the efforts of Jewish community organizations from 65 countries, including Israel and the United States. It represents its member organizations at the United Nations and speaks for the needs of the Jews of the world. (See also UNITED NATIONS.)

WORLD ZIONIST ORGANIZATION (WZO) Organization founded in Basle, Switzerland, in 1897 by Theodor Herzl. The purpose of the Zionist Organization (as it was first called) was "to create for the Jewish people a home in Palestine, secured by public law."

Zionist congresses were held regularly to set policy for the World Zionist Organization. Delegates to each congress were elected. All the Jews who had bought a shekel (see SHEKEL), were allowed to cast one vote. Among the decisions made at the Zionist congresses were: founding the Jewish Colonial Trust in 1898, establishing the Jewish National Fund in 1901, deciding to build the Hebrew University in 1913, turning down the plan to partition (divide) Palestine in 1937, and dealing with problems of immigration to Israel in 1956.

In 1968 the Zionist congress adopted the new Jerusalem program. The aims of this program were to gather the Jewish people into Israel, to strengthen Israel, and to preserve Jewish identity through education. To bring about these aims WZO encourages immigration to Israel, trains teachers and provides books for Hebrew education and culture, and works with Zionist organizations in over 40 countries. (See also BASLE PROGRAM; EDUCATION; HEBREW UNIVERSITY; HERZL, THEODOR; IMMIGRANTS; JEWISH COLONIAL TRUST; JEWISH NATIONAL FUND; PARTITION; SHEKEL; ZIONISM.)

WRESTLING Russian athletes and coaches immigrating to Israel in the 1970s sparked interest in the sport of wrestling. By 1979 there were about 600 wrestlers organized into 18 clubs. (See also SPORTS.)

Y

YAARI, AVRAHAM (1899-1966) Scholar who was born in Austria, settled in Palestine in 1920, and worked in the National and University Library in Jerusalem. Yaari also wrote books on the history of Palestine. (See also NATIONAL AND UNIVERSITY LIBRARY.)

YAARI, MEIR (1897-) Politician who was a leader of Hashomer Hatzair (a Zionist youth organization) in his native Austria and in Palestine after he settled there in 1920. Yaari was active in the Mapam political party, served in the Israeli Knesset (legislature), and wrote several books on political theory. (See also HASHOMER HATZAIR; KNESSET; MAPAM.)

YAARI, YEHUDA (1900-) Hebrew writer who settled in Palestine from Austria in 1920 and wrote novels and stories about life in Eastern Europe.

YAD Hebrew word usually meaning "hand" that also means "monument" or "memorial." It is part of many place-names in Israel.

YAD HANNAH Kibbutz (cooperative farming village) founded by Hungarian immigrants in the Hefer Valley in 1950. Yad Hannah was named to honor the heroine Hannah Szenes. (See also HEFER VALLEY; KIBBUTZ; SZENES, HANNAH.)

YAD MORDECAI Kibbutz founded near the Gaza Strip in 1943 and named in honor of Mordecai Anilewicz, a fighter in the Warsaw Ghetto. A monument to Anilewicz stands in the village. Yad Mordecai was captured by the Egyptians during the 1948 War of Independence. After it was freed, months later, it was rebuilt. (See also ANILEWICZ, MORDECAI; GAZA STRIP; KIBBUTZ; WAR OF INDEPENDENCE.)

YAD VASHEM Heroes' and Martyrs' Authority founded by the Israeli Knesset (legislature) in 1953 as a memorial to "the members of the Jewish people who gave their lives, or rose and fought against the Nazi foe" during World War II (1939-1945). The Yad Vashem buildings on the Mount of Remembrance east of Jerusalem contain a synagogue, museum, library, photographic

Entrance to Yad Vashem, established as a memorial to the victims of the Holocaust. It is located on the southern shoulder of Mount Herzl.

The main road leading to the Commemoration Hall of the Holocaust is the Street of the Righteous, with its trees dedicated to the righteous people of all nations and religions who helped to save Jews during World War II.

A striking Hebrew sign in the Yad Vashem Commemoration Hall, which reads: "In this place we hope to see what can no longer be seen, to hear the voices that can no longer be heard, and to comprehend that which can never be comprehended."

The Yad Vashem Commemoration Hall, in which an eternal flame burns. The flame sheds its light on slabs of stone on which the names of all concentration camps that existed in Europe during World War II are engraved.

exhibits, a research center, and archives. Much of the evidence at the trial of the Nazi general Adolph Eichmann came from the Yad Vashem archives. In the Hall of Remembrance an eternal flame burns in the center of a large bare room. The flame is surrounded by the names of the Holocaust victims set in the mosaic floor. The Avenue of the Just, which leads to the memorial, honors the Christians who helped Jews during the Holocaust. President Jimmy Carter of the United States and President Anwar Sadat of Egypt are among the millions of people who have visited Yad Vashem. (See also ARCHIVES; AVENUE OF THE JUST; CARTER, JIMMY; EICHMANN, ADOLPH; HOLOCAUST; KNESSET; NAZIS; SADAT, ANWAR.)

YADIN, YIGAEL (1917-) Native Israeli soldier and archaeologist. Yadin was active in the Haganah (Jewish underground army) from an early age. During the 1948 War of Independence he was Chief of Operations of the Israel Defense Forces and was responsible for planning much of the strategy of the war. He rose to the post of Chief-of-Staff, but left the army in 1952 to become a professor of archaeology at the Hebrew University in Jerusalem.

Archaelogist Yigael Yadin (left) and James Biberkraut examine fragile pieces of an ancient papyrus scroll.

Yadin is Israel's best-known archaeologist. He organized and led the expedition that uncovered the Jewish fortress of Masada, discovered letters from the 132-135 C.E. Bar Kokhba revolt in a cave in the Judean Desert, and directed archaeological digs at Hazor and Megiddo. Yadin's archaeologist father, Eliezer Sukenik, had been the first to recognize the importance of the 2,000-year-old Dead Sea Scrolls. Yadin continued his father's study of the scrolls and wrote several books about them including *The Message of the Scrolls.* (See also ARCHAEOLOGY; BAR KOKHBA, SIMEON; CAVE OF LETTERS; DEAD SEA SCROLLS; DEFENSE FORCES; HAGANAH; HAZOR; MASADA; MEGIDDO; SUKENIK, ELIEZER LIPA; WAR OF INDEPENDENCE.)

YAFO   see JAFFA

YAGUR   One of Israel's largest kibbutzim. Founded near Haifa in 1922 by immigrants from Eastern Europe. The settlers had to drain the swamps in order to plant their crops. (See also KIBBUTZ.)

YANAIT, RACHEL see BEN-ZVI, RACHEL YANAIT

YARIV, AHARON (1920-   )   Soldier and politician who was born in Eastern Europe and came to Israel as a teenager. Yariv was a member of the Haganah (Jewish underground army) and later served in the Israel Defense Forces. He was the Director of Military Intelligence of the Defense Forces and rose to the rank of Brigadier-General. In 1974 he was elected to the Knesset (legislature) and served as Minister of Transport and Minister of Information. (See also DEFENSE FORCES; HAGANAH; KNESSET.)

YARKON RIVER   River about 20 miles long that flows into the Mediterranean Sea north of Tel Aviv. Water from the Yarkon River is carried south through the National Water Carrier to irrigate crops in the dry Negev. (See also GEOGRAPHY; IRRIGATION; NATIONAL WATER CARRIER; NEGEV.)

YARKONI, YAFFA   Native Israeli singer who has made records of many popular songs. She has performed in Israel, the United States, and many other countries of the world.

YARON, REUVEN (name changed from ROSENKRANZ) (1924-   ) Austrian-born lawyer. Yaron taught law at the Hebrew University in Jerusalem and at several universities in Great Britain and the United States. He wrote a number of books on law and served as director of the National and University Library in Jerusalem. (See also HEBREW UNIVERSITY; NATIONAL AND UNIVERSITY LIBRARY.)

YASSKY, HAYIM (1896-1948)   Doctor who studied medicine in his native Russia and in Switzerland before settling in Palestine in 1921. Yassky was a leader in the fight against trachoma (a serious eye disease) in Palestine and later became the director of the Hadassah medical organization. He was killed by Arabs in 1948 while bringing medical supplies to the Hadassah Hospital on Mount Scopus during the War of Independence. (See also HEALTH; HADASSAH; WAR OF INDEPENDENCE.)

YAVNEEL   see JABNEEL

YAVNEH   see JABNEH

YEDIOT AHARONOT   Israeli evening newspaper founded in 1939 by Azriel Carlebach. *Yediot Aharonot* became one of the country's largest daily papers. It is an independent paper, not connected to any political party. (See also CARLEBACH, AZRIEL; NEWSPAPERS.)

YEHOSHUA, AVRAHAM B. (1936-   )   Native Israeli writer who is known for his short stories. Yehoshua also wrote a play about the beginning of the 1967 Six-Day War. His first novel, *The Lover,* was translated from Hebrew into English and was also made into a film. (See also SIX-DAY WAR.)

A.B. Yehoshua

YEHUD   Town founded in 1948 on an ancient site southeast of Tel Aviv. It was settled by immigrants who came to Israel after it became a state. Many of the people of Yehud work in Tel Aviv. (See also TEL AVIV.)

YELLIN, DAVID (1864-1941)   Scholar who was born and educated in Jerusalem. Yellin was an early supporter of Hebrew as the spoken language of Palestine. He helped set up the organization that later became the Hebrew Language Academy and organized a network of Hebrew schools. Yellin served as head of the Vaad Leumi (Palestine's National Council) and as Deputy-Mayor of Jerusalem. He also taught at the Hebrew University in Jerusalem and published books on poetry and Bible studies, as well as a Hebrew dictionary. (See also HEBREW; HEBREW LANGUAGE ACADEMY; HEBREW UNIVERSITY; JERUSALEM; VAAD LEUMI.)

YEMENITE JEWS   see ORIENTAL JEWS

YEMIN MOSHE   see MONTEFIORE, SIR MOSES M.

YESHAYAHU, ISRAEL   see SHARABI, ISRAEL YESHAYAHU

YESHIVA (the plural is YESHIVAS or YESHIVOT)   School of Jewish religious studies. The teachers in a yeshiva are often rabbis, and the students are young men between the ages of 17 and 24 who are studying the Torah and Talmud. Many yeshivas have younger pupils as well; they are taught reading, arithmetic, social studies, etc., along with religious subjects.

Israeli parents can choose to send their children either to a state school or to a religious school. In 1979, 69% of elementary school students attended general state schools, 25% attended state religious schools, and 6% went to yeshivas run by Agudat Israel (an Orthodox religious movement). (See also AGUDAT ISRAEL; EDUCATION; TALMUD; TORAH.)

Most Orthodox students attend yeshivot where the educational program concentrates on the study of Bible and Talmud. Here, students are reviewing their lesson in Talmud.

YESHURUN SYNAGOGUE   The largest synagogue in Jerusalem. "Yeshurun" is a poetic name for Israel. (See also JERUSALEM.)

YESUD HAMAALA   Village founded in 1883 in the swampy Huleh Valley. Many of its early settlers fell sick with malaria. Yesud Hamaala was one of the villages supported by Baron

Edmond de Rothschild, but it grew slowly in spite of his help. (See also HULEH VALLEY; MALARIA; ROTHSCHILD, EDMOND DE.)

YEVIN, SHEMUEL (1886-)   Russian-born archaeologist who settled in Palestine before 1918 and took part in a number of digs on ancient sites. Yevin was the head of the Israel Department of Antiquities and the editor of the *Biblical Encyclopedia*. (See also ARCHAEOLOGY.)

YEZREEL VALLEY   see JEZREEL VALLEY

YISHUV   Hebrew word meaning "settlement." Yishuv is usually used to mean the Jewish community in Palestine before Israel became a nation.

YIZHAR, S. (name changed from SMILANSKY, YIZHAR) (1916-) First native Israeli writer to deal with the people and problems of the new land. The characters in Yizhar's Hebrew short stories are usually young people born in Palestine. His novel *Days of Ziklag* is about the 1948 War of Independence and the struggle to establish the State of Israel. Yizhar is one of Israel's most respected writers. He was awarded the Israel Prize for literature in 1959. (See also ISRAEL PRIZE; LITERATURE; WAR OF INDEPENDENCE.)

YOFFE, SHLOMO (1909-)   Polish-born composer who went to Israel in 1930. Yoffe wrote symphonies and choir music as well as music for different instruments.

YOM HA-ATZMAUT   see INDEPENDENCE DAY

YOM KIPPUR (English, DAY OF ATONEMENT)   Considered the holiest Jewish holiday of the year, Yom Kippur falls on the tenth of the Hebrew month Tishri (usually in September and occasionally in October on the international calendar). It closes the Ten Days of Repentance that begin with Rosh Hashanah (New Year). Jews throughout the world pray and fast for 24 hours, atoning for wrong actions of the past year and hoping to become better people in the coming year. The day of prayer and fasting ends with the blowing of the *shofar* (ram's horn) in the synagogue at sundown. In ancient Israel, there was a special Yom Kippur ceremony in the Holy of Holies in the Temple in Jerusalem. (See also CALENDAR, INTERNATIONAL; CALENDAR, JEWISH; HOLIDAYS; ROSH HASHANAH; TEMPLE.)

YOM KIPPUR WAR   War between Israel and the Arab nations of Egypt and Syria (with some troops from Iraq and Jordan) from October 6 to 23, 1973. The Egyptian and Syrian armies attacked Israel across the Suez Canal and through the Golan Heights on the Jewish High Holy Day of Yom Kippur. The Israelis were caught by surprise.

Golda Meir, Prime Minister of Israel, visits with troops on the Golan Heights after the Yom Kippur War. (Above) General Yitzhak Hofi (seated left) and Moshe Dayan (seated center) listen to her words of encouragement.

Youth in Israel is treasured highly. Here are happy youngsters in a nursery school on the Mount of Olives.

For the first two days, the Arabs—who outnumbered the Israelis 12 to 1—made rapid gains, but they were soon driven back to the borders established by the 1967 Six-Day War. When the Israelis began to advance onto Egyptian and Syrian land, the Soviet Union (who had supplied the Arabs with weapons) called for an end to the war in the United Nations Security Council. The United States (who had supplied Israel) backed the move. The Yom Kippur War ended two weeks after it had begun.

Although Israel won a military victory, it lost 2,500 men and had many more wounded. The Israeli people wanted to know why the Defense Forces had not been prepared for the surprise invasion. A commission was called to investigate. As a result of the commission's report, a number of army officers, including army Commander-in-Chief David Elazar, resigned. Prime Minister Golda Meir also resigned and was replaced by Yitzhak Rabin. (See also DEFENSE FORCES; EGYPT; ELAZAR, DAVID; GOLAN HEIGHTS; MEIR, GOLDA; PRIME MINISTER; RABIN, YITZHAK; SIX-DAY WAR; SUEZ CANAL; SYRIA; UNITED NATIONS; YOM KIPPUR.)

YORDIM (the singular is YORED) Hebrew word for Israelis who have left Israel to live in other countries. *Yordim* is the opposite of the Hebrew word *olim*, which means immigrants to Israel. In 1980, about 300,000 to 400,000 yordim were living in the United States. (See also OLIM.)

YOSEF, OVADIAH (1920-) Rabbi who was born in Iraq and was taken to Palestine as a child. Yosef was Chief Rabbi of Tel Aviv before being elected Sephardi Chief Rabbi of Israel in 1972. (See also CHIEF RABBINATE; SEPHARDIM.)

YOUNG MACCABEES see MACCABI HATZAIR

YOUTH ALIYAH Organization founded in Berlin in 1933 by Recha Freier to bring Jewish orphans out of Nazi Germany and settle them in Palestine. Under the leadership of Henrietta Szold, Youth Aliyah grew into an organization that had rescued 30,000 young people by the time Israel became a state in 1948. By the late 1970s Youth Aliyah had settled 140,000 young people from 80 countries in Israel and had educated them and trained them for jobs. Its work was (and is) supported by money raised by Hadassah and other Zionist women's groups and by the Jewish Agency.

Most of the boys and girls brought to Palestine in the 1930s were orphans whose families had been killed by the Nazis. They found new homes in youth villages and new families in the housemothers, teachers, and other children of the villages. When they grew up, many of the young people who had been trained in farming skills in the youth villages founded new agricultural settlements.

Generations apart, but lives in tune.

In the 1960s and 1970s most of the young immigrants to Israel came from Eastern Europe and North Africa. To meet their special needs, Youth Aliyah added more vocational training to the agricultural training given in youth villages and also opened a number of day schools. Youth Aliyah also teaches its wards the Israeli way of life and helps them with their personal problems. (See also AGRICULTURAL SCHOOLS; ALIYAH; FREIER, RECHA; HADAS-SAH; JEWISH AGENCY; NAZIS; SZOLD, HENRIETTA; YOUTH VILLAGES.)

YOUTH MOVEMENTS   One-third of all Israeli boys and girls between the ages of 11 and 18 belong to some kind of youth movement. Some of these groups, such as the Israel Boy and Girl Scout Federation, are part of larger international organizations. Others, such as Hanoar Haoved (Federation of Working and School Youth), only exist in Israel. There are pioneering groups that train young people to establish new settlements, kibbutz (cooperative farming village) organizations, religious organizations, and sports groups. Except for the Scouts, each Israeli youth movement is a branch of an adult organization. (See also BENE AKIVA; BETAR; GAHAL; HANOAR HAOVED; HANOAR HATZIYONI; HASHOMER HATZAIR; MACCABI; SCOUTING.)

YOUTH VILLAGES   Villages where young people live, study, and work. Most of the 50 youth villages in Israel are part of Youth Aliyah (the organization that settles young people in Israel) and many of the boys and girls who live in the villages have no other homes or families. Youth villages train most of their young people in farming skills—both in agricultural high schools and through performance of practical farm work in the village. Many of the graduates go on to establish new agricultural settlements. There are also special youth villages for troubled youngsters. (See also AGRICULTURAL SCHOOLS; EDUCATION; YOUTH ALIYAH.)

YUVAL, MOSHE (1913-   )   Diplomat who went to Israel from Eastern Europe in 1932. Yuval served as Israel's ambassador to Australia and to Peru and Bolivia.

Z

ZADOK, HAIM JOSEPH (1913-) Polish-born politician who settled in Israel in 1935 and joined the Haganah (Jewish underground army). Zadok was elected to the Israeli Knesset (legislature) and served as Minister of Justice and Minister of Commerce. (See also HAGANAH; KNESSET.)

ZAHAL Name for the unified Israel Defense Forces. Zahal includes the army, navy, and air force. The Minister of Defense is Zahal's Commander-in-Chief. (See also DEFENSE FORCES.)

ZARITSKY, YOSEPH (1891-) Russian-born artist who settled in Palestine in 1923. He became noted for the colorful landscapes he painted of Israel. Zaritsky later became an abstract painter interested in shapes and colors.

ZEALOTS Jewish group that fought against Roman rule in Palestine in the first century C.E. They believed that only God should rule the Jewish people. The Zealots were founded in 6 C.E. and were among the leaders of the 66-70 C.E. revolt against Rome. During the revolt, they seized Jerusalem from the more moderate Jewish forces after a bitter fight. The Zealots, led by Simon Bar Giora, Eleazar Ben Simon, and John of Gischala, then defended the city against Titus' Roman army. Although the Jews fought bravely, Titus finally conquered Jerusalem. He killed the defenders of the city and burned the Temple. Another group of Zealots, under Eleazar Ben Jair, fled to the fortress of Masada near the Dead Sea. They held out against a long Roman siege and then killed themselves rather than surrender. (See also BAR GIORA, SIMON; ELEAZAR BEN JAIR; ELEAZAR BEN SIMON; HISTORY; JERUSALEM; MASADA; ROME; TEMPLE; TITUS.)

ZEBULUN One of the Twelve Tribes of Israel. Its ancestor was Zebulun, the sixth son of Jacob. When the Israelites conquered the land of Canaan in the thirteenth century B.C.E., the tribe of Zebulun settled in the Jezreel Valley. (See also CANAAN; JACOB; JEZREEL VALLEY; TWELVE TRIBES.)

ZEBULUN VALLEY (also spelled ZEBULON) Northern part of Israel's Coastal Plain. The Zebulun Valley (also called Emek

On the top of Masada, in the southern part of Israel, the Zealots
held out against a three-year attack by the Romans, who finally
succeeded in reaching the mountain-top, only to find that the 960
Zealots had committed suicide rather than risk being captured.

Zebulun) runs for about 123 miles along the coast from Haifa to Acre. The area was swampy, infested with malaria-carrying mosquitoes, before it was bought by the Jewish National Fund in 1928. The swamps were drained and cleaned, and ponds were built for raising fish. Today the southern Zebulun Valley is the location of many of Haifa's factories. A number of agricultural villages have been built in the northern part of the valley. (See also COASTAL PLAIN; FISH PONDS; GEOGRAPHY.)

ZECHARIAH   King of Israel who ruled for six months in 744 B.C.E. before Shallum killed him and became king. (See also ISRAEL, KINGDOM OF; SHALLUM.)

ZEDEKIAH (name changed from MATTANIAH)   Last king of Judah who ruled 597-586 B.C.E. Zedekiah was appointed king by Nebuchadnezzar (the ruler of Babylon). Although Zedekiah promised friendship with Babylon, he joined Egypt in a revolt against Babylon in 586 B.C.E. The Babylonians invaded Judah, made it part of their empire, and sent the Jews into exile. Zedekiah was captured and he was blinded. (See also BABYLON; BABYLONIAN EXILE; HISTORY; JUDAH, KINGDOM OF; NEBUCHAD-NEZZAR.)

ZEIRA, MORDEKHAI (1905-1968)   Russian-born composer who settled in Palestine in 1932 and wrote many popular Israeli songs.

ZIKHRON YAAKOV   One of the earliest modern Jewish villages in Palestine, Zikhron Yaakov was founded on Mount Carmel in 1882 by settlers from Rumania. It was named for the father of Baron Edmond de Rothschild, who supported the village and helped set up its vineyards and winery. Baron Rothschild is buried at Zikhron Yaakov, and the wineries he started still produce much of Israel's wine.

During World War I, the village was the headquarters of NILI—a Jewish group, headed by Aaron Aaronson, that helped the British free Palestine from Turkish rule. Sarah Aaronson, who died rather than reveal NILI's secrets, is buried there.

Today visitors to Zikhron Yaakov can see the Rothschild and Aaronson graves, tour the wineries, swim at the lovely beach, or walk to the nearby Carmel Caves where remains of Stone Age people have been found. (See also AARONSON, AARON; AARONSON, SARAH; CARMEL CAVES; MOUNT CARMEL; NILI; ROTHSCHILD, EDMOND DE; WINE.)

ZIKLAG (also called TEL ZIKLAG)   Ancient city north of Beersheba where the Bible says David hid from Saul. Today Tel Ziklag is the tallest hill on Israel's Coastal Plain. There is a lookout post on top of the hill. (See also COASTAL PLAIN; DAVID; SAUL.)

ZIMRI   Soldier who killed King Elah and ruled Israel for seven days in 887 B.C.E. Zimri was killed by Omri, who then became king. (See also ELAH; ISRAEL, KINGDOM OF; OMRI.)

ZION (also spelled TZIYON)   Originally the name of a fortress in Jerusalem. The word Zion came to mean "Jerusalem" or "the Promised Land," and was identified with the Jewish people. (See also ZIONISM.)

ZION   Hebrew magazine published four times a year by the Israel Historic Society. It prints articles on Jewish history.

ZION GATE (Hebrew, SHAAR TZIYYON)   One of the eight gates in the wall around the Old City of Jerusalem. The Zion Gate still shows marks of the heavy fighting that took place there during the 1948 War of Independence. (See also JERUSALEM; WALLED CITIES; WAR OF INDEPENDENCE; HAIFA.)

ZION, MOUNT   see MOUNT ZION

ZIONISM   Movement for setting up a Jewish homeland in Palestine. Although Jews scattered throughout the world had prayed for centuries to return to Zion (another name for Palestine or the Land of Israel), the drive to build a Jewish nation in Palestine really began in the late 1800s. Discrimination against Jews in Western Europe and pogroms (killing of Jews) in Russia made many European Jews long for a land where they could be free and proud to be Jewish.

In the early 1880s, the Hibbat Zion (Love of Zion) movement in Russia encouraged young Jews to settle in Palestine. The first groups of BILU settlers founded the farming villages of Rishon Le Zion, Petah Tikva, and Zikhron Yaakov. Baron Edmond de Rothschild helped support these villages and others. By 1900 there were 17 new Jewish settlements in Palestine.

In 1897 Theodor Herzl (who became known as the father of modern Zionism) founded the Zionist Organization (later called the World Zionist Organization). He arranged the first Zionist congress which adopted the Basle Program calling for a home for the Jewish people in Palestine. Later Zionist congresses established the Jewish Colonial Trust and the Jewish National Fund to buy land in Palestine for Jewish settlement.

Herzl met with the rulers of Turkey (who governed Palestine) and with leaders of important European countries to get their support for a Jewish homeland. When Herzl died in 1904, the Zionist movement spent less time negotiating with governments, and started making practical moves towards establishing settlements in Palestine. Land was bought, and young pioneers from

Draped in the Israeli flag that graced the platforms of Zionist congresses for almost a century, a young girl joins the crowd in Rehovot Park to celebrate Independence Day on the fifth of Iyyar.

Europe cleared stones and drained swamps to build farming villages. Degania, the first kibbutz, was established in 1909 and the City of Tel Aviv was founded the same year. By 1914, when World War I broke out, there were about 85,000 Jews living in Palestine.

In 1917 Zionist leaders in Great Britain, led by Chaim Weizmann, convinced the British government to issue the Balfour Declaration favoring the establishment of a Jewish national home in Palestine. In 1920 Britain received the League of Nations Mandate to govern Palestine and more Jews immigrated into the country. The Jewish Agency was founded to encourage Jewish settlement and to work with the the British to establish a national home in Palestine.

Although the Zionists worked with some moderate Arab leaders, Arab riots broke out in Palestine in 1920, 1929, and 1936. The British blamed Jewish settlement for the riots in the 1930 Passfield White Paper, suggested the partition (dividing) of Palestine into separate Jewish and Arab states in the 1937 Peel Report, and limited Jewish immigration into Palestine in the 1939 White Paper. The Zionists fought each of these moves, but without success.

During World War II, Zionists continued to work in the United States. American Zionists tried unsuccessfully to get the American government to pressure Britain into opening Palestine to Jewish immigration. When the Palestine question was referred to the United Nations in 1947, Zionist leaders argued for the establishment of a Jewish State.

The Zionist movement continued its work even after Israel became a nation in 1948. Much of the money needed to settle a million and a half new immigrants in Israel was raised by Zionists throughout the world. The World Zionist Organization still encourages Jews to settle in Israel and works to keep Jewish culture alive in the rest of the world. (See also ALIYAH; ARAB RIOTS; BALFOUR DECLARATION; BASLE PROGRAM; BILU; DEGANIA; GREAT BRITAIN; HERZL, THEODOR; HIBBAT ZION; HISTORY; IMMIGRANTS; JEWISH AGENCY; JEWISH COLONIAL TRUST; JEWISH NATIONAL FUND; KIBBUTZ; MANDATE; PARTITION; PASSFIELD WHITE PAPER; PEEL COMMISSION; PETAH TIKVA; RISHON LE ZION; ROTHSCHILD, EDMOND DE; TEL AVIV; TURKEY; UNITED NATIONS; WEIZMANN, CHAIM; WHITE PAPER; WORLD ZIONIST ORGANIZATION; ZIKHRON YAAKOV; ZION.)

ZIONIST   A person who believes in the importance of Israel as a Jewish homeland. (See also ZIONISM.)

ZIONIST COMMISSION   Organization set up in 1918 to help the Jews of Palestine recover from World War I. The Zionist Commission took over the work of the old Palestine Office. The

Three of the most prominent Zionists in the 1920s were philanthropist Nathan Straus (left), U.S. Supreme Court Justice Louis D. Brandeis (center), and Rabbi Stephen S. Wise.

Commission helped new immigrants to Palestine, bought land for settlement, and planted forests. It supported the Hebrew school system and helped build the Hebrew University in Jerusalem. Its first chairman was Chaim Weizmann. (See also HEBREW UNIVERSITY; PALESTINE OFFICE; WEIZMANN, CHAIM.)

ZIONIST ORGANIZATION see WORLD ZIONIST ORGANIZATION

ZOHAR, MIRIAM Actress who was born in Eastern Europe, settled in Israel in 1949, and joined the Habimah Theater. She played many roles including the part of Hannah Szenes in a play about the World War II heroine. (See also HABIMAH; SZENES, HANNAH.)

ZORITTE, EDA (1926-   )   Native Israeli writer and painter. Eda Zoritte has published novels, plays, and stories, and has had several exhibits of her paintings. She is married to Aharon Megged, the writer. (See also MEGGED, AHARON.)